THE LAND THEY POSSESSED

THE LAND
THEY
POSSESSED

by

Mary Worthy Breneman

SOUTH DAKOTA COMMITTEE ON THE HUMANITIES
AND SOUTH DAKOTA LIBRARY ASSOCIATION
— Brookings, SD 1991 —

Second Printing, South Dakota Committee on the Humanities, 1991

Printed in the United States of America

Library of Congress catalog card number: 56-9617

South Dakota Committee on the Humanities
John W. Whalen, Executive Director
Box 7050, University Station
Brookings, SD 57007

To

Clement D. Breneman

and to the memory of

Joseph and Martha Worthy

NOTE TO THE READER

During Catherine of Russia's reign many Germans were lured to the Ukraine by her promises of freedom from conscription and taxes. The Germans kept to themselves, did not intermarry, and farmed the land. Several generations later, when conscription and taxation once more bled them white, they began the great migration to the Dakotas and other mid-western states. While the first settlers kept their language and their aloofness, their children became part of the great melting pot which is America.

Supplemental note to the 1984 edition

The Germans who were lured into Russia under Catherine the Great by her Manifesto of 1763 did not settle in the Ukraine. Rather they settled along the Volga River. Those who settled in the Ukraine came at the invitation of Alexander I, her grandson, who issued a Manifesto in 1804.—Karen Retzlaff

Introduction

I discovered *The Land They Possessed* as a "good read" while I was researching South Dakota women writers in the late seventies. I wanted to share my enthusiasm for this forgotten novel set in the north central wheat area of the state with as many readers as possible. The book, however, was out of print and unavailable until the Germans from Russia Heritage Society of North Dakota reissued it in a small printing in 1984, largely through the efforts of Karen Retzlaff. The South Dakota Committee on the Humanities enabled many more readers across the state to enjoy it by selecting it for the Centennial Reading Series in 1987, but the small edition was soon exhausted. Now, the South Dakota Committee on the Humanities has funded a second reprinting of the original to respond to the demand by readers who have been further encouraged by hearing the novel read on public radio.

I also became intensely curious about the author Mary Worthy Breneman. Who was she? How did she come to write such an absorbing tale of Anglo-American and German-Russian pioneers in the eighteen eighties and nineties? With the help of Leonore Schick of Eureka, South Dakota, I learned that "she" was, in fact, a mother-daughter combination (Mary Worthy Thurston and Muriel Breneman) and that the daughter resided in a retirement home in Washington, D.C. Letters led to a visit which led to friendship. Finally, in 1987 Muriel Breneman journeyed to South Dakota to attend the centennial celebration of Eureka, the scene of the last third of the novel. She was interviewed by the press and made a video tape for the Humanities Committee. At long last, this book and its living author, so long forgotten and ignored, have been rediscovered, to the delight of many readers.

The novel provides another chapter in the great American saga of settlement of the plains recounted by such storytellers as Willa Cather, Hamlin Garland, Ole Rølvaag, Bess Streeter Aldrich, Mari Sandoz, and Frederick Manfred. Like Cather in *O Pioneers!* and *My Ántonia*, the writers of this book explore both the meaning of the land to the inhabitants upon it and the cultural and ethnic differences that the homesteading enterprise made manifest. In this story, the conflict is between Anglo-American settlers and Germans from Russia who poured onto the plains in the late nineteenth century after Czar Nicolas I revoked their exemption from military service. Having maintained their cultural integrity in that alien land, they were quite prepared to cope with diversity as free homesteaders on the American prairie. Through sacrifice and hard work, they produced abundant crops and prospered, while Anglo-Americans failed to find the financial bonanza they expected from the Dakota boom and at the end of the novel move on to more promising dreams in Montana.

This theme finds concrete expression in the adventures of the Ward family who have come originally from England, moving ever farther west in search of the fortune John Ward expects to make. The reader views the action through the eyes of Michal Ward, the pioneer heroine who grows from girlhood to maturity and marriage in a prairie setting. Her experiences are the substance of the novel: her relationship with her father John Ward, who fancies horses and hunting dogs and runs a business in town while hired hands farm his land; her sympathy for her mother, the reluctant pioneer wife who longs for a settled community and cherishes her books, *pot pourri*, china, and gentility; her loyalty to her German-Russian friends Katie Keim and Karl Gross whose ethnic differences challenge the values of the Ward family. The land itself is an omnipresent reality throughout the book — beautiful to Michal, terrifying to Mavis, tantalizing to John, and promising to Karl.

Although its theme gives the novel substance and richness, this is not a "heavy" book. Readers will find it a "rattling good love story" as editor Cecil Scott of MacMillan Company did in 1956 when he accepted it for publication. Believable characters move through compelling dramatic scenes. Historical background is subtly interwoven in this action. Most notably, images of land and sky, wind and grass, birds and flowers fill its pages, powerfully evoking the sight, sound, smell, and feel of the northern prairie.

Mary Worthy Thurston wrote vividly about this country because she knew and loved it as a child. She drew on her own experience for the detail in the novel, and Michal's adventures are loosely based upon her own growing up years near Leola and Eureka, South Dakota. Her parents, Joseph and Martha Worthy, are models for John and Mavis Ward and some of the incidents are based on actual fact. Others, Muriel Breneman maintains, are purely fictional, especially Michal's marriage to Karl Gross. Mary Worthy attended Madison Normal School, became a teacher in Eureka, married a young man she had met at Madison, and moved first to Washington and then to Arizona. Joseph and Martha Worthy left Eureka in 1903 and ultimately settled on the Saskatchewan plains so that he could die on British soil.

Yet Mary never forgot the joy of her prairie childhood. Like other women writers (Laura Ingalls Wilder, Lucile Fargo, Frances Gilchrist Wood), she did not turn to this material until late in life — in the nineteen thirties. Stimulated by the publication of the fifty year history of Eureka in 1937 and by the popularity of other books about pioneer life on the prairie, she began writing descriptive passages and developed a loose outline for the story, but the book progressed very slowly. In 1942, her daughter Muriel Breneman became her co-author and together they finished the first draft in 1946. Breneman did two revisions and extensive cutting before it was published ten years later.

Although a long labor of love for the two women ("It was our love letter to the German-Russian people," claims Muriel Breneman), the book did not sell and disappeared for a quarter of a century. Perhaps South Dakota in the nineteen fifties was still too close to its past to wish to examine it. Possibly, readers in the German-Russian communities still remembered the anti-German sentiments during the World Wars, particularly virulent during World War I, and feared reawakening such feeling. In any case, thirty years after its publication, few South Dakotans knew of its existence.

However, the search for "roots," the cherishing of our ethnic diversity, and centennial preparation have changed all that. Much attention is now focused on the past. Readers have been eager to

ix

learn more about their heritage and to mine the rich field of local and regional writing. *The Land They Possessed* is certainly a welcome addition to that body of literature.

Readers who are interested in expanding their knowledge of this book, its writers, and its background can find more information in Ruth Ann Alexander, "Nature, Ethnics, and Land: The Making of a South Dakota Novel," *South Dakota History*, XVIII, 3, Fall, 1988, pp. 152-172; Elizabeth E. Williams, "An Author's Homecoming," *South Dakota Magazine*, September 1987, pp. 45-46; and a 30-minute video taped interview of Muriel Breneman by Ruth Ann Alexander, available from the Resource Center of the South Dakota Committee on the Humanities, Box 7050, University Station, Brookings, SD 57007.

The first task is to read and enjoy!

Ruth Ann Alexander
South Dakota State University
March 1989

Part One

THE HOMESTEAD
AND TREE CLAIM

I

Dakota Territory
1885-1887

The Wards were moving again. West, of course. Father always went west.

As they stood on the carriage block in front of the Ipswich Hotel and the stable hand brought around the team, nine-year-old Michal tried to be calm and grown up. When her tall blond father, the buckled reins looped over his left arm, helped Mother carefully into the front seat and tucked in the dust robe, Michal stifled an impulse to bounce into the back seat before Father turned and helped her. Then, lifting little dark-eyed, curly-headed Faith high above his head with an "Up you go," he deposited her in the back seat with Michal, climbed in beside Mother, gathered the lines carefully together, and nodded to the stable hand. The man jumped quickly to one side; the Hambletonians lunged forward.

They were off!

Leaving the hotel behind, they drove down a street of false-fronted buildings. Father pointed out among them his office with a long fenced-in shed behind it from which he sold farm machinery. They passed the railroad station, grain elevator, and section house, slowing for the crossing where the sign warned LOOK OUT FOR THE CARS. Then they were out on the dirt road with seventeen miles to go.

Michal loved moving. The rhythmic clip—clop, clip—clop of the spirited bays made a joyous echo of her mood. They left the town be-

3

hind and were on the prairie, the Dakota prairie at its best. Sunshine after deep winter snowfall and heavy spring rains had covered it all—broad sweep of plain, low hills rounded like Mother's breasts, and the valleys in between—with a bright carpet of grass. Meadow larks poured out their free bubbling song more blithely than ever before; pink feathery plumes of prairie smoke brightened the roadside, and orange and gold puccoons burned on the hills.

"Comfortable, Mavis?" asked Father in that low caressing voice he always used when he had been away from them a while.

"Quite comfortable, John," returned Mother contentedly.

"How long yet?" He had lowered his voice, but Michal's ears were keen.

"About two weeks."

"You'll feel right at home," said Father. "Hetty had things about settled when I left. She was sure leading that husband of hers a dog's life. Every five minutes it was, 'You, Gus Perkins! Find me that hammer,' or, 'Help me stretch this carpet!' " And Father smiled, his face alight with the joy of this new venture. Father liked moving as much as Michal.

"I'm glad we're out of Ordway," he went on. "I sure thought it would be the capital of Dakota Territory. Well, I wasn't the only one who gambled on the wrong town. Good thing Fred wanted to relinquish this Homestead and Tree Claim. I'm sure we'll do much better here. The railroad grade to Leola passes just east of our line; the steel will be laid any time now."

"Won't it be hard, selling farm machinery in Ipswich and running a farm, too?"

"Not with Gus on the place. I'll hire another man soon."

"What about Matt McGuire?"

"I had to let him go. He drank worse all the time; and when I caught him smoking in the haymow last week after all my warnings, I paid him off."

"What ailed him, John?"

"I don't know except that he seemed to be influenced by a worthless bunch in town. Every time he came home he'd be drunk as a lord. I hated to let him go. He was the best man I ever had with horses—when he was sober."

"How did he take it?"

"Not too well. He got nasty and blustered about getting me yet—"

4

"What?"

"Well, I lost my temper and threatened to kick him off the place."

"Where'd he go?"

"Haven't seen him since. Probably left the country."

Presently they turned off the main dirt road onto a newer one not yet worn down to the grass roots and rode through a silence broken only by the thin monotonous buzzing of a cloud of mosquitoes following the horses, the swish of tall grass hitting against the wheels, and the steady clip, clop—clip, clop of hoofs. Michal's head drooped and she dozed.

The buckboard had traveled the road a good two hours, and the girls were still asleep when, "Yonder is Herman Haar's place," said Father; and Michal, waking with a jerk, looked eagerly to where he pointed with the buggy whip. She could see no house, only a large barn, and to the left, against and built into a sidehill, a door with a window in its upper frame. The window was covered with a Turkey-red calico curtain which glared like a huge bleary eye. An awful place! No house at all, just a burrow.

Father was reining in his team and speaking eagerly to Mother. "Herman Haar's dugout. He was the first settler. Came out here about five years ago with nothing, and now," waving the whip in a great sweeping arc, "all this is his."

Michal leaned forward. "But how can people live in a place like that?"

"Lots of these German-Russians live in dugouts. It cost them plenty to come here from the Ukraine. Some have money, but many bring only their good seed wheat, sheepskin coats, and featherbeds. Haar built this barn last year, might build a house next. He owns all the fields you can see, and yonder he is breaking new land for flax."

From the left of the road to where, on a distant hill, a man was breaking sod with a bull team lay great fields, vast bright checkers of wheat alternating with blue-green checkers of oats. The air was heavy with the sweet smell of growing grain.

In the foreground not far from the road a large woman and several children were pulling yellow-flowered weeds from the field. "Mustard," explained Father. "It's blooming earlier than usual on account of the rains. These people all work all the time; that's why they succeed. Let's just drive up and speak to Mrs. Haar. After all, they're near neighbors."

"But, John, it's late and—" She broke off, her low voice pleading.

5

"It'll only take a few minutes, and we're nearly home now."

As Father turned from the main road to the tracks leading to the Haar place, the mustard pullers stopped their work and stared. Then the woman, after pulling down her ample outer skirt and admonishing the children, came toward them.

"Mrs. Haar, this is my *Frau*," said John Ward proudly, pointing to Mavis.

Mother smiled, extending her small white hand. Mrs. Haar, wiping hers hastily on her skirt and saying "*Ja!*" came closer, and Michal caught the pungent smell of wild mustard even before the woman engulfed Mavis's hand in her own, begrimed with dust and greenish stains.

Michal looked curiously over at the children. There were five, the three oldest being boys. When the tallest looked up furtively and wiped his nose on his shirt sleeve from elbow to cuff, she decided she'd have nothing to do with them.

As Father backed and turned the team, Michal felt disappointed. She wished she might have seen the dugout inside. She had never been in a cave, and she wondered if it would look like one.

On the prairie road again and heading north, "Are we nearly there?" asked Michal excitedly.

"Well, not quite, Mike," said Father. Then, turning to Mother: "This is a grand country, Mavis! If a Rooshan like Herman Haar can do all that, imagine what any man with capital and push can do. The boom's on now, and a fellow like myself can clean up."

Mother smiled but made no answer. Suddenly Michal wondered, Did Mother enjoy moving? She was so quiet today, she who usually talked as much as Father. Father really was a mover; he always wanted to go to towns where the railroad was just built or expected. She remembered vaguely the first two moves out from the east, but the third one to Ordway had been very exciting, particularly the "straddlebugs" —long boards put up like the skeleton of a wigwam—that marked boundaries, then the stakes that followed them after the final surveys were made. Everyone had been excited about Ordway, but when they had been disappointed—everyone had been sure it would be the capital —Father had moved out here to the Homestead and Tree Claim five months before with Hetty and Gus to put in crops and make the place homelike before they followed.

They passed a shallow pond rimmed with cattails and rushes where

6

blackbirds, red-splashed wings extended, balanced and sang their liquid o-ka-lee-ee, when Father pointed his whip toward a lone shack and tiny barn on the rise of prairie far to the left. "Oulette's," he explained briefly.

"What a desolate place for people with such an exotic name!" commented Mother.

"He's a French Canuck; she was raised in Paris and taught music in a girl's private school in Ottawa. I think you two will be congenial."

"And her husband?"

"He's no farmer—runs a store in Ipswich and usually makes it home only for Sundays. She gets pretty lonesome holding down the claim."

Then John Ward turned the team onto another road, saying buoyantly, "We'll just swing over for a glimpse of the Tree Claim."

"Oh, no! I'm so tired!"

"This takes us right by the midwife's place," argumentatively. "You'll be needing her any day now."

"Well—if I don't have to get out."

The widow Tannyhill's house was a frame shack battened with tarpaper and sodded halfway to the eaves. It had one door and a four-paned window, one filled with tin from which projected a stovepipe elbowing out and up well above the level of the low roof. An old black-and-white pointer came up, barked unconvincingly, and wagged his tail. Before the team had halted, the door opened, and a gaunt raw-boned woman, not too clean as to dress and rather wispy as to hair, came out, wiping floury hands on her gingham apron.

"Well, well, I declare! If it ain't John Ward—and this is the missus I presume, and this . . ." She cocked her head sidewise like an inquisitive fox terrier.

"Our daughters, Michal and Faith," said Father proudly.

The woman looked avidly at Michal. "What you got a boy's name for?"

"I didn't know it was," slowly.

"Well it is, if you know it or don't know it. But here I go a-gabbin', not even asking you to light and hitch."

"Another time, thank you," returned Mavis quietly.

While the women talked in low voices Michal, glancing through the open door, had a quick glimpse of a spotless interior, the stove black-leaded, the worn floor scrubbed creamy white with a strip of rag

7

carpet down the exact middle. As they left, Mrs. Tannyhill shrilled after them, "Send for me any time, day or night, Mis' Ward!"

But Michal had forgotten her. She would soon now see trees, feel their rough trunks, walk in the shade of their spreading branches. A bobolink from a tall milkweed flaunted his smart black-and-white suit and flung his banjo-like *plink, plink, plink,* after them.

Far away they saw a man mowing grass in the slough; the clatter of the mower came faintly to them as Father reined in the team at the top of the hill and looked back. "Here we are, Chicken."

Michal looked in every direction but saw only the swell and fall of prairie. "The trees! Where's the Tree Claim?"

"This is the Tree Claim; look down—not up—for these trees, Michal. Eighty acres of them. They grew last spring from seed, and in a few years will make a grove and windbreak." He pointed the tip of the buggy whip, and she saw plants no larger around and but little taller than slate pencils.

He thinks they're wonderful; I mustn't let him know how disappointed I am. "Can I have one?"

"Sure. Here's my jackknife. Take that willow—they grow fast—and plant it by the dam."

A few minutes later they were crossing a ravine. The road ahead where spring torrents of water had run was now silt mud, as shiny and slick as the black horsehair sofa. Over it myriads of butterflies—blue, white, yellow—floated and lit, closing and expanding their wings. Now, as the team approached them, they fluttered up like a cloud of delicate petals blown by a whirlwind. *The prairie is a lovely place,* thought Michal, looking back to see the bright cloud settle again. Then Father's voice "We're here!" brought her facing front.

At the top of the gently sloping hill they were now ascending she saw a huddle of buildings. Facing them in the foreground was a neat white frame house with an A roof—no dugout, thank goodness! The walls were sodded up to the windows for extra warmth and protection against wintry winds. The red outbuildings—privy, granary, barn, chicken house, and hog shed—were to the right and back of the dwelling.

Lucky Lady, Father's liver-and-white pointer, followed as Gus and Hetty came forward to meet them. John Ward drove up to the hitching block with a flourish and pulled in the lathering horses; they champed their bits and tossed their heads. Gus, grinning up at them, his teeth

8

white against the brick red of his face—went to the horses' heads while his employer helped the family down.

Inside, Hetty—a thin, angular woman—was brushing her mistress' dress with a whiskbroom. Faith, wide-eyed with curiosity, hopped restlessly from one foot to the other. Hetty, after one expert glance, said briskly, "Come here, Faith, and I'll unbutton you."

"I can unbutton my own panties now, thank you," she said with dignity before she bolted from the room.

"Michal, better wash up for supper," called Hetty, pouring water from a ponderous white pitcher bordered with pink roses into an equally ponderous matching washbowl.

She still sounds like a sheep bleating, thought Michal, glancing at the familiar fringed white linen splasher along the back of the commode on which in red cotton thread were outlined birds bathing and above them the motto *Go Thou and Do Likewise.*

The starched pillowshams had been carefully thrown back over the rod lest they be wrinkled, and Mavis—who had slipped into a Mother Hubbard wrapper—lay on the pillows resting. "My, that coffee smells good, Hetty," she remarked.

"Yes, Mis' Ward, and we'll eat now as soon as the dumplin's is done." She bustled out, Michal in her wake.

The table was set, the best silver on, spoons in the sandwich-glass spoonholder, the napkin rings gleaming in the light of the hanging lamp, its long glass prisms dangling from the milky white shade. How good to be with the home things again! thought Michal, looking through into the sitting room where the luster of well rubbed black walnut glowed richly under the soft low-turned light of the best lamp.

The sun was near setting before they finished the meal. John Ward pushed his chair back from the table impatiently. "I know you're dead tired, Mavis, but let's just take a look about the place."

"She has no business going out, tired as she is," scolded Hetty.

Ignoring her, Father pulled Mother to her feet, tucked her hand in the crook of his arm, and calling, "Come along, Chicken," to Michal, started them toward the door. Faith began to cry, and Hetty's bleat rose quickly in Gus's favorite song:

> " 'Down in a diving bell at the bottom
> of the sea,
> A dear little mermaid came
> a-courting me!' "

Slowly they ascended a knoll that gave a view of the homestead and stood looking silently down on the fields and buildings. The land now rested in the long leisurely prairie twilight. Michal's mood had changed. Her eyes solemn with interest, she looked out over the prairie where the hand of night was pressing. A nighthawk, flying high, uttered a piercing *crank* with rising inflection, then, swooping for mosquitoes just above their heads, with a deep *b-o-o-m!* it again flew aloft.

Father spoke eagerly. "Isn't this great, Mavis?"

"It's more than great; it's vast," she answered quietly.

The weird tremulous cry of a plover settling for the night came to them, rising and swelling, then falling and dying away in a hollow windlike whistle that seemed prolonged by a chill night breeze stirring in the grass. Michal trembled at the sound and her hand sought her mother's; but Mavis's hand was first and gripped hers so tightly that the girl barely restrained a cry of pain. Then she knew. Mother feared the prairie. All the way down to the house she held Mavis's hand and felt nearer to her now that she understood something no one else ever suspected.

At the door Mavis's hand gripped hers again, but differently, and she clutched Father, too. "John, you'd better send for the doctor."

"I thought you said two weeks!" bellowed Father. "Hetty! Gus!"

After Gus had gone, John Ward moved the trundle bed into the sitting room, awkwardly settled drowsy Faith, and thundered off to get Mrs. Tannyhill, first shooting a hard glance at Hetty, who was muttering loudly: "Poor little thing. But nobody listens to me. Oh, no—"

Mother was braiding her hair, while Hetty carried newspapers into the bedroom. Then the door was closed.

Michal intended to stay awake. But her legs ached, and she was glad to relax in her trundle bed beside Faith and enjoy the clean smell of fresh straw in the tick.

She lay in the faint moonlight, thinking of all that had happened that long day. Mrs. Tannyhill. The Tree Claim. But most of all Mother in the carriage, above great sprawling wheat fields, trying to talk with that other woman. That so-different woman with her sunburned face and eyes squinted from sun glare, and her big feet, in rough shoes, planted deep in the black earth.

And their hands. Hands moving as each tried to make the other understand. Mother's hand, slender and white as the crescent moon looking down through the window, one finger weighed down by her massive cameo ring. And over everything the greenish, pungent smell of mustard juice.

A coyote howled from the hills far away, and through the thin moonlight came the wavering wail of a distant plover—like Mother's fear....

II

All night Michal sensed confusion about her. Voices. A dim feeling that she had experienced this once before.

Little winds murmured through her dreams. Little lost winds afraid of the dark whimpered softly. Like the little Indian babies who had lived here long ago. Disturbing her, wailing thinly against a background of low voices and moans.

The soft whir of the striking clock on the mantel wakened her. The thin wailing wind still blew. She looked up at the steel engraving of the Garfield Family hanging over the sofa; the lambrequin trimmed with chenille balls; the clock, pendulum swinging busily; the mirror above the cottage organ gleaming softly. It seemed strange to be sleeping in the sitting room.

Faith stirred but did not rouse as Michal dressed, thinking, I'll plant my willow tree right now down by the dam. The door to the bedroom was still closed, but hushed voices sounded there. Carefully holding the small clump of earth and tree, she tiptoed out toward the dam.

Already the morning was bright with sunlight and bird song; and as she knelt on the muddy shore scooping, planting, and tamping, Michal sniffed delightedly the damp earth and the air, faintly sweet with the smell of growing grain.

There was Gus by the barn. Maybe he could tell her about Mother. But everything must be all right, for his voice was raised in song:

> " 'The J-huice runs down your chin
> And you lick it up ag'in—
> An' you spit it out ag'in—
> In Khan-an—zus!"

At sight of Michal he stopped abruptly, reaching back in his pocket for his plug. "Chaw, Michal?" he asked politely.

"No, thanks." As he detached with his thumbnail a red star from the plug she added, "But I'll take the star for my picture of heaven," and closed her hand tightly over the little red star. "Is Mother all right?"

"Yer maw's gonna be fine." As he went on into the barn he added, "Go look on that wide bank there along the middle-barn foundation."

Tense with excitement Michal crawled along the bank until she saw something white and two green shining lights. Lucky Lady and a bunch of puppies! One by one—and gently so as not to upset Lady—Michal held each, smelling the sweet puppy breath, choosing finally—for her own—the tan-eared one. Then Hetty was calling, and Michal tore herself away from the nest. At the hitching block Gus stood at the heads of a strange team. A man with a black satchel shook hands with John Ward, got into the rig, and took the Ipswich road.

In the large kitchen, Hetty, sleeves rolled up, hair done more tightly than ever, was scouring bone-handled steel knives with a damp cloth dipped in brick dust. "Help Faith dress," she snapped, "then come eat yer minute pudding and prunes."

Faith was sitting up, blinking soberly. "What's we doing out here?"

"Last night after you were asleep a lot of things happened." Michal's voice was grave. "Gus galloped off on War. Father went for Mrs. Tannyhill. When they moved our trundle bed out here you didn't even wake up."

"Is Mother sick?" Faith's mouth trembled.

"Of course not. She smiled at me." Then Michal whispered, "Can you keep a secret?"

Faith's eyes grew big. "Yes."

"I've got a puppy."

"What's its name?"

"Tan Ears." Michal looked dreamily out the window. "Little Tan Ears. Pretty soon I'll show him to you."

The door opened, and the Widow Tannyhill bustled out with a pillow in her arms. She had on a white calico dress sprigged with small black anchors and starched so stiffly it rustled as she walked.

Father came—grinning mysteriously—and beckoning, led the girls into the bedroom and to the bed where Mother lay, her black hair tightly braided, and all the rich color drained from her face. For an instant Michal saw a resemblance to the portrait of Uncle Gordon, the Highlander, who had fought in India; then Mavis smiled faintly, and the stern pale look was gone.

Michal stood awkwardly beside the bed, but Faith went over and laid her head down on the pillow for a moment as Father said: "Let Mother rest now. I've work outside, but you'd better come see what Mrs. Tannyhill has."

The widow, sitting before the open door of the warm cook stove, glanced up slantingly. "Well, we've got a real boy here now, so they won't have to name any more girls with a boy's name. Look."

Michal and Faith tiptoed cautiously to where they could see the squirming red thing on her lap. Fascinated, they stood in the heat streaming from the oven while the midwife chose from a saucer the largest of several plump soaked raisins, split it and flipped out the seeds with an expert, not too clean thumbnail, then carefully placed it on the baby's navel before swathing his little red middle tightly with a woolen band and pinning it securely in place with three safety pins.

"I guess your nose is all out of joint now!" This to Faith, who reached out and clutched Michal's hand.

Hetty came up and, looking over Mrs. Tannyhill's shoulder, crooned, "Ain't he little?"

"Where'd it come from?" demanded Faith.

Hetty spoke quickly. "The doctor brought him in his satchel."

Mrs. Tannyhill said, "Better get out now, girls."

"Why?"

"I'm going to change him, that's why."

"I watched Mother change Faith."

"That's different. She's a girl. Scat now!" The sisters went, Faith rubbing her nose. Once inside the dining room, she burst into a bellow.

Hetty appeared instantly at the door. "Sh-h-h-!" she hissed. "I'll bring your breakfast, but keep quiet."

"Who is that, Hetty?" asked Faith.

"Your baby brother."

"Oh."

Soon Mrs. Tannyhill came through the room, the baby now a woolly white cocoon in her arms. Without a glance or word for the girls she passed into Mother's room and closed the door with finality.

13

The morning dragged. Feeling strangely alone, the girls wandered disconsolately about, finally discovering a pigweed patch north of the house. For an hour they lay hidden in the cool, silvery-green growth watching cloud shadows and playing with some ducklings which, mothered by a fussy old hen, had wandered near.

One of them climbed into Faith's lap and picked at her teeth, thinking they were corn. Michal watched impatiently, feeling restless. The day was passing, and she wanted to be alone to explore and think. When Hetty banged the back door, Faith jumped up and hurried in.

Hastily Michal ran for the barn. Gus was sitting on a box outside the granary oiling a harness. The door was closed.

"Where's Father?" asked Michal without pausing.

Gus, absorbed in his work, pointed briefly over his shoulder, then called, "Hey, wait!" But she was on her way, for she had heard a whining and thought it might be her puppy.

At her entrance into the middle barn, John Ward threw a gunny sack over a large candy pail in the corner. "Father!" she panted, "Lucky Lady has puppies. I've already picked out mine."

"Oh, you have, have you?" Father's voice was silky. "I found her with her God-damned whelps! I'll not have a mongrel on the place and you know it."

"She's not a mongrel."

"No, but she got out on me."

Accustomed now to the cool half-darkness, Michal noticed that he stood in front of the pail, and that a ladder was set against the wall. She climbed it hurriedly and looked in the nest. Lucky Lady was gone, and all the puppies except little Tan Ears.

Michal turned. "Where are they?" she demanded.

"Lady's in the granary; the pups are gone."

"Gone where?" Coming down the ladder, the remaining pup clutched close to her, she looked at the pail and knew. Her eyes went bleak. "How dare you!"

"Don't speak to me like that!" thundered John Ward, advancing.

Straight as a willow whip she stood her ground. "It's my puppy." Her voice was metallic. "Everything's wrong! That cross old woman at the house, Faith whiny, Mother sick; and then I come to play with the pups, and they're gone." Great sobs shook her.

John Ward took out his handkerchief, and wiped the tears from her face. "There, there, pull yourself together," he said uneasily.

14

"Then I keep the puppy?" She looked up, smiling through her tears.

"No! There'll never be a mongrel on this place. I saved the one pup to nurse Lady so she won't get caked breasts; when it's weaned— it goes."

"But—"

"No. I'll get you a real puppy, soon. One we'll all be proud of." Breaking off he lowered his voice, "Hush! Here come the Rooshans."

Michal wiped the tears from her cheeks hurriedly, and gave the handkerchief back before Mrs. Haar and her oldest son reached them.

"*Guten Tag*," said Mrs. Haar heartily. She had a small covered lard pail in one hand and a flat parcel wrapped in a clean white cloth in the other.

John Ward nodded. Catching sight of Tan Ears, the boy exclaimed, "*Der Kleine Hund!*"

Father smiled. "Ya," he said jovially. "It's yours when it's older if you want it." Michal handed him the puppy reluctantly. The boy looked at his mother, who nodded.

"Put it back up there and come in a month or so." Then John Ward turned to Mrs. Haar, "How'd you know?"

She pointed toward the Ipswich road and said simply "*Doktor*."

"Ya." John Ward smiled. "A boy."

"So? Goot!"

"Michal, take Mrs. Haar up to the house. Tell your mother I'm going to Ipswich and I'll be back before supper." He patted her awkwardly on the shoulder before they started to the house, the immense woman talking volubly all the way in German—not one word of which the girl understood.

Michal tapped on Mother's door, with moon-faced Mrs. Haar, clutching the pail and parcel, close behind her. The guest took the proffered chair, exclaiming, "*Himmel! Bis jetzt im Bett?*"

Mavis smiled her greeting but shook her head helplessly at the question. While Mrs. Haar opened the pail of rich chicken noodle soup and the parcel of fresh light *Kaffeekuchen*, Michal gave Mother the message from Father.

After Mavis had drawn the covers carefully back from Baby Brother's face for her visitor's inspection, Hetty came in with gingerbread and a pot of strong coffee. Mrs. Haar leaned over her tray and ate heartily and took in her hot drink with loud slurps.

15

As she rose to leave she glanced admiringly about the comfortable room, a wistful look clouding for a moment the good-natured face. "*Sehr schön,*" she said simply, waving her hand in an all-inclusive gesture.

"Yes." But Mavis's eyes turned to the window for a moment—to the unbroken stretches of earth and sky.

Michal went out and sat in the shade of the house watching Mrs. Haar, her son beside her, plod down the road. The visit had diverted her mind from the awful happening of the morning, but now it flooded over her. She drew up her knees, folded her arms on them, then hid her face in their support as she lived it all again. She shuddered as she thought of the big wooden candy pail covered with damp sacking and oozing water slightly from between the staves; the emptiness of the nest when she had put her hand in and found little Tan Ears alone; and poor Lucky Lady in the granary, not knowing.

Restlessly she rose and wandered into the kitchen.

Hetty, muttering darkly to herself, glanced up as Michal burst out miserably, "What can I do?"

"Well, you can git out from under my feet for one thing," she said briskly, opening the oven door to stir the rice pudding and test the layer cake with a broom straw. "Let's see. Why don't you drink a big glass of milk, then take this piece of gingerbread," cutting a huge slice as she spoke, "and go find the Little People?"

"Where?"

"Most anywhere you look if you're quiet. There oughta be some in the cocklebells by now—you know, out in the west field."

Michal finished her milk, took her gingerbread, and hurried out the front way to avoid the Widow Tannyhill, who was washing up out back. She was glad to be alone in the field, for Father and Gus frowned on such excursions.

The wheat was high. It towered well above her head, and except in low spots was already changing from green to gold. The smell of it was changed, too. No longer faintly sweet, it now gave out a rich hot smell as warm breezes tousled the heads.

Michal yawned. It was hot. Grasshoppers whirred and rasped above her as she walked, but there seemed to be no corn cockles; nothing but tall wheat stalks, unrelieved by even a glimpse of the reddish-purple tubular bells. Gus had done a thorough job of cleaning out the "poison weeds," as he called them; but Michal knew that if she kept on she'd find one, for the Little People had to have a place to live. Hetty said so, and besides there was that song Mother had often sung to her —the one beginning:

> "Oh, where have you been, sweet sister fay?"
> "I've swung in a lily-bell all the long day."

She was tired and sweaty when she finally caught a hint of purple in the maze of wheat stalks ahead. At last. A fine cockle plant! Walking slowly toward it—the Little People must not be frightened—she sat down carefully, facing it. It was cooler close to the ground. Grasshoppers were still rasping, but far away crickets were beginning to chirp. She would just sit and rest; the Little People might be taking their naps, for the song said:

> "So I sang my own lullaby, sleeping at ease
> In the bell of a lily that swayed in the breeze."

The wheat heads swayed high above her, and from time to time the cocklebells bent. She fixed her eyes on the largest blossom and waited. The Little People were a long time coming. Perhaps they had heard her footsteps and were hiding in the hairy cup; in time they would be lulled by the quiet and peer out to see if she had gone.

The sun was no longer overhead. It was cooler, and multitudes of crickets were shrilling cheerfully—some of them close by. It seemed the Little People were not at home, or they might be dressing for their party.

> "I've jeweled my hair and I've spangled my wing,
> And I'm going to dance at the court of my king."

That was it! The king of the Little People was giving a dancing party, and they were now all jeweling their hair and spangling their wings. They would have fun, she knew, for:

> "The day is for pleasure, the night is for glee;
> Come brother, come sister, trip lightly with me."

She would wait until sunset; then they'd be going, and she might see not one but many. She need not hurry; the feel of the earth rested

17

her when she lay close to it. Besides, she had something worth waiting for. It would be something to see the Little People all spangled and jeweled.

A great peace stole over her. She felt pleasantly drowsy. A slanting ray of sunlight touched the largest bell and wavered as a little breeze swayed it. Then she saw something tinged with gold. A wing! Tiny, iridescent.

She had seen—Michal knew she had seen—a wing of one of the Little People. . . .

The bed was hard and lumpy, and Michal was cold. Then, as she sat up rubbing her eyes, she heard the swishing sound. Overhead the dark cup of sky pressed close to the earth, and black feathery clouds drifted across the few glittering stars. That swishing sound, then, was the wind stirring in the wheat.

The cocklebells had been in front of her. By turning and hurrying in the opposite direction, she'd soon come to the edge of the field and see the home lights.

But even though she walked and walked, the wheat seemed to have no ending. The swishing sound grew louder, and the dark night pressed closer. She must hurry.

Her feet were aching now from the rough earth, and she was thirsty. The smell of dust and ripening wheat was no longer pleasantly familiar but oppressive—smothering. The wind had risen, and now the grain hissed like something alive. She began to run, stumbling a little.

Then she tripped and almost fell over something that moved and slithered quietly away. Michal screamed and ran blindly through the dark, away from that terrible Thing—uttering soft cries like a little animal. Stumbling, falling, only to rise and run once more, until finally, in exhaustion, her heart thundering in her ears, she fell and could not rise again.

Then, far away, above the hissing all about her, she first heard it—faintly, like a voice in a dream, a voice calling, "Michal!"

She raised her head. Again—a little nearer this time—"Michal! Michal!"

She answered, her voice sounding small and reedy in the night.

"Michal!" It was Father, and he was coming closer.

Gathering her strength, she rose crying, "Father—Father!"

18

Then, through waving darkness, she saw faintly the dim light of a lantern. She stumbled toward it sobbing, pushing frantically at the wheat stalks. A moment later John Ward swung her to him.

In relief her sobs grew more violent, and she didn't notice the other one at first. A wriggling silky something under Father's other arm that was struggling toward her, lapping up her tears with a warm wet tongue. Then she was down on her knees in the wheat hugging a gangling puppy, and Father was holding the lantern up as he watched them, chuckling excitedly.

"Mine?" asked Michal dazedly.

"Of course, Chicken. Don't you remember I told you when you wanted that mongrel that I'd get you a real pup? Let's get back to the house so you can take a good look at him."

As they hurried homeward, Michal hugging her puppy, Father said: "Your mother doesn't know you've been lost. Don't mention it to her or Faith. It'll be our secret."

Hetty met them at the door. "Poor little darlin'!" she whispered. "It's all Hetty's fault. How do you like your dog?"

Michal smiled vaguely, following Father toward Mother's room as Hetty added, "I'll dish your food up right away."

"I've missed you today," began Mavis, then, "What on earth—" as she saw what Michal was holding.

"Irish setter male," beamed John Ward, "with a pedigree as long as your arm."

"He's beautiful. So that's why you went to town today." She smiled at him accusingly.

Father grinned sheepishly. "I've had my eye on that pup ever since he was whelped three months ago. There were seven in the litter, and McGinnis sold the rest and kept Rory for himself, but I talked him out of it. This little Irisher"—Father was well under way now, and his voice rose—"has fine stock back of him."

"John, John, calm yourself—we can hear you."

Father grinned again, then lowered his voice impressively. "When McGinnis makes out that six-generation pedigree for me next week, I can show you a three-way-cross of Elcho back of the dam," he finished reverently in exactly the same hushed tone a preacher in church speaks of the Father, the Son, and the Holy Ghost.

Mavis yawned daintily. "I've slept all afternoon, and I'm sleepy again. Put the dog in the kitchen on a blanket; I don't want my Brussels carpet spotted."

Later Father took little Rory out on the leash while Michal—clean and well fed—crept into bed. Faith sat up quickly, half awake; when she saw her sister she gave a drowsy smile and settled back on her pillow again, sound asleep almost at once.

As Father undressed in his and Mother's room before coming out to the cot in the dining room where he now slept, Michal heard him say, "Isn't Rory a fine pup, Mavis?"

"What did you pay for him, John?"

"Well, he asked $100 for him, but he finally came down to $75."

"With the baby and all, wasn't that quite a sum to spend on a pet?"

Father's voice rose in instant irritation. "Pet! My God, I'll make a field dog out of him. With those blood lines—"

"All right, John." Mother's voice was soothing. "I just asked."

When the lights were out and the house quiet, Michal still lay wide awake, listening. A pathetic little whine sounded softly from the kitchen. She stiffened. It came again.

Poor little lonely pup! He'd probably fuss all night and keep Mother awake. There was just one sensible thing to do if she could get past Father.

Stealthily she crept through the dining room, following a bright streak of moonlight to the kitchen door. Rory, wiggling rapturously, was waiting for her. With one deft motion Michal scooped him up, wheeled, and tiptoed noiselessly across the room. At the door she ventured one swift glance toward the cot. Father's eyes were closed, but he was smiling.

Rory cuddled at her feet as though he had slept there all his life. Michal sighed contentedly and settled down for sleep. Then she was swept back, returned to the awful loneliness of the grain field, the hissing, the dark wind in the wheat. She wished she might have told Mother about it. She would have understood.

The pup was inching his way up toward the head of the bed. Convulsively, Michal drew him beside her and under the covers, stroking the silky body nervously. Then, as the eager little wet tongue lapped her hand, she relaxed, thinking, Now that I have Rory, I'll never be alone on the prairie again.

20

III

There was a bountiful crop that first year. The wheat—except where in certain low places patches of it had "lodged"—fallen from its own rank growth—stood proudly tall, or swayed gently, exhaling the rich smell of ripeness as erratic breezes stirred through the fields.

The week before cutting, Father brought home a new self-binder that cut a six-foot swath. It had cost over $300, but—as Father pointed out—it was well worth it, for it did away with the old attachment on which two men stood to bind the grain by hand. With this machine Gus and one other man could handle the work.

A few days later he bought a span of fine young Percherons—dappled gray, perfectly matched. Riding them was Glen McGee, a pleasant-faced young man of eighteen, a fine hand with horses and helper for Gus.

When Mavis asked gravely, "What did they cost, John?" Father said, too loudly "Only $600. A small price when you consider that they're young and just what we need to haul grain with." For the railroad had not yet reached Leola, but the grade, weed-grown now and slightly weatherbeaten, was still a symbol of hope to the settlers.

Cutting began the first week in August. The days moved in a procession of bright sunrises, goldenrod spangling the hills, wild sunflowers bordering the roadsides, the bubbling *quip-ip-ip-ip, quip-ip-ip-ip* of the upland plover hurrying with quick wingbeats as he flew high above the farm.

Mother was always busy with Little Brother, and Hetty went about her kitchen grumbling incessantly about the new man's appetite.

Michal and Faith, Rory at their heels, followed the work from the first days of cutting until the shocks of grain were piled in stacks shaped like huge round beehives to wait the coming of the threshing machine sometime before snowfall.

One day Father came home early with the news that Uncle Fred was coming for a visit and that the family was to meet the train and spend the day as his guests in Ipswich. As Mother, cheeks flushed and dark eyes glinting gold, discussed with Hetty how they'd rearrange the bedroom situation, Michal began to count the days.

Uncle Frederick Gordon, Mother's brother. The fine-looking fastidious Uncle Fred with his pipe, tweedy suits, quiet charm, and mischievous dark eyes.

She hoped that this time there wouldn't be that thing—almost like words between them—that happened when Mother and he talked about certain subjects. Mostly about Aunt Phyllis who lived in Rochester with two white Persian cats while Uncle Fred practiced law in Denver City far away.

Michal knew that he had tried to teach Aunt Phyllis to love the West. That's why he'd taken the Homestead and Tree Claim as a retreat during hunting season. But she had hated the place and had hurried home; and Uncle Fred had turned it over to Father and moved to Denver City, where he already had a good practice.

Mother had said one night after the house was dark and still: "John, I'm so worried about Fred and Phyllis. Of course, I blame her more than I do him—a wife's place is with her husband; but if the separation goes on it could lead to divorce."

Father muttered impatiently something about foolish to worry, and Mother broke in: "He's my favorite brother, yet I don't understand him. Before they separated, Phyllis hinted to me that he might be"— she lowered her voice—"a freethinker!"

"Freethinking! Divorce! What'll you worry about next? Fred's a fine man, and he'll get to Heaven as fast as any of us. As for their marriage, if he and Phyllis are happier apart, that's their business, not ours."

The week before his arrival Michal, thinking of these things from the shelter of the pigweed patch, saw a woman walking with quick eager grace up from the ravine. She was wearing a black alpaca dress with a small bustle and tight fitting basque piped with cherry-red ribbon. Her black hat was trimmed with two red silk pompoms.

When Michal ran to meet her, the woman introduced herself as Louise Oulette. Her voice was low and soothing—like soft music, Michal thought, and her dress gave off a faint flower fragrance. The girl inhaled delightedly, wishing it were stronger, as she proudly ushered their guest into the house, happy to see the glow in Mother's eyes as they met.

Mrs. Oulette talked rapidly with many gestures; as the soft liquid

22

words poured from her lips they reminded Michal of the red-winged blackbirds ok-a-lee.

"It would not be so lonely if only I had my piano. Pierre may send for it next year if we build another room."

Soon Hetty brought in tea; and as Mavis poured, Mrs. Oulette leaned forward. "You feel lonely here, no?"

"It is strange and different," answered Mother slowly.

"Strange, yes; the wind whispers from the long grasses—you have heard it? I miss here the noises, the lights and laughter of the city; but" —she shrugged—"Pierre say this is a land to make us rich."

"John thinks that, too, so I try not to miss my old home and friends too much."

"But you have your children." She leaned closer to Mother; the smile was erased from her face, leaving it sad. "It is the wind. Always there are winds in the grass; never are they still; always they murmur sadly." Her voice now a whisper, she continued: "Could they be the voices of Indian women who long ago lived here? Or"—she shrugged— "you do not hear them, perhaps; you have always your children near."

"I don't mind the winds so much," said Mavis, "but I miss the trees. The land seems so big—so bare and empty. John tells me I should see it as it will be. He and Michal do. But I long for short distances and sheltering groves. However, let us speak of pleasant things." Her hand went out and covered Mrs. Oulette's in a rare gesture of sympathy.

Little Brother cried out, and when Mavis returned with him Mrs. Oulette held out her arms for the child. "Such a little," she crooned softly, studying the small face. "Went it hard with you?"

Mavis looked at Michal. "Hetty may need you now. Faith—"

"But Faith is with Gus."

"We have some fine fat cattails in our slough, Michal," Mrs. Oulette said softly. "I saw a little blond girl wading there on my way over. She visits Haar's. If your mother does not mind—"

"I don't mind in the least. Watch the sun and be home by supper-time."

As Rory rose from the shade of the house and capered delightedly ahead of her, Michal's spirits soared. After all, she and Mother had a new friend. Uncle Fred would be here soon. And she'd been wanting to go to the slough because she hoped to find empty nests and, if lucky, even a few young blackbirds from second matings, just learning to fly. Besides, she might glimpse the strange girl visiting the Haars. Probably

23

she'd be just like the Haar children, mused Michal, as she skirted the south side of the slough where cattails grew rank and tall.

First she waded in the bright shallow water, looking for tadpoles and snails, and keeping a cautious eye out for water snakes and salamanders. She could hear Rory rattling through the reeds ahead. He flushed a sandhill crane, and Michal watched it take off with loud cries and wing flappings.

Next she picked brown plush cattails with long stems, the way Mother liked them. It wasn't until she had a big bunch carefully placed on the bank that she missed Rory. The last time she'd heard him was when he'd flushed the crane.

With a small mounting panic she rushed out of the water and put on her shoes and stockings without even waiting for her feet to dry.

"Rory!"

She pushed through the rushes onto the open prairie. "Rory!" Then she heard him bark, and looked to the south. A girl was holding out her hand and speaking gently to the dog, who was smelling it suspiciously. Then he wagged his tail and looked back toward his mistress.

"He won't bite," said Michal, smiling in relief at the stranger. She was a round-faced girl Michal's age, very blond, with long thick braids and dressed neatly in a white calico dress dotted with blue stars.

"I know," said the girl. "I'm Katie Keim from"—she pointed vaguely—"over vest forty mile."

"I'm Michal Ward, and I live across the ravine in that white house." Michal pointed in turn. She had not expected to find this girl so poised. Besides, she wore a straw hat with a blue ribbon band, and an elastic under her chin. Michal was bareheaded.

"I know," said Katie gravely. "Mine Tante, Mrs. Haar, tell me about you."

"Let's sit down on those big stones and talk a while, shall we?"

"Ya."

"How did you happen to come here?" asked Michal.

"Mine Vater come to Leola for business, so ve come to be by mine Tante. Ve move from Yankton last mont'. I vent to English school a yahr in Yankton. It iss so I learnt to spik unt read."

"You're lucky. My mother will have to tutor me. Why are you down here by the slough? Where are the Haars?"

"Mine Unkle ist by Leola mit mine Vater. The rest"—she shrugged, indifferently—"dey work in the field."

"Oh. Why—" Michal paused. It was not polite to ask so many questions.

"You mean vy not I? Becos, mine Mutter and I—we do not vork on the land."

"Oh, I see," said Michal.

"Mine Vater and I, we cum forty miles in one day," said Katie proudly.

"Did you? Well, we're going to Ipswich next week—that's seventeen miles—to meet my uncle here from Denver City?"

"Vere is dot?" asked Katie, with interest.

"Well, it's in the Rocky Mountains somewhere—thousands and thousands of miles from here, I guess," she concluded lamely.

"So?" Katie paused, considered. "Vell, I have Unkle, Tante, and Cousinks, more far as that. In Russland, by Odessa—across."

"Across what?" demanded Michal.

"Across—you know—across the Meer. Big Water."

"But they don't come to see you like my Uncle Fred." Michal stared at the other suspiciously. This girl was carrying things a little too far.

Katie flushed. "In two yahr, maybe t'ree, they come," she said loftily. "Ve get letter last week—and picture." Impressively. "I show you. Come."

Michal, slightly crestfallen, followed her. Anyway, she'd have a look at the inside of the dugout. But when they reached the house, Katie said: "You vait out here. I bring." And she went in alone and closed the door. She was out again in an instant. "Here!" she cried triumphantly.

It was a family group. The father, a stocky blond man, was seated. Behind him stood two blond girls, both older than Michal. Beside the father sat a woman with keen eyes and a severe proud face.

A little apart from the rest was a boy, dark-haired, unlike the rest of the group. He stood there arrogantly, head high, and returned Michal's gaze boldly with eyes that seemed alive, until almost uncomfortably, she spoke, "This one—who is he?"

"Dot is Karl. The only poy."

"But he doesn't look like the others."

Katie came close and peered at the picture as though seeing it for the first time. "Dot is so."

"You say they are coming to this country?"

"Ya, two, maybe t'ree yahr."

25

"Oh," said Michal, still looking at the picture closely. "Where will they stay? Is it a town where you live?"

"No, but soon there will be a beeg town there. The train she comes not yet, but the grade iss already. It iss call End-of-Track, and mine Vater have land there, and so the Unkle Wilhelm will take land near us."

"Will they ever come over here to visit the Haars?"

Katie shrugged. "*Ich weiss nicht*. But she iss their *Tante* too, so dey come, I t'ink."

Michal returned the picture to Katie slowly. "Walk back to the slough with me Katie, and we'll talk."

"Vait. I put the picture away." Then as she came back the two girls went arm in arm, talking as though they had always known each other. For an hour they lingered, then Katie squinted up at the sun. "I tell *Tante* I cook *Nachtessen* today ven she iss come from the field. I must go." She spoke regretfully.

"Yes, I promised Mother I'd be home at supper too," said Michal. "How much longer will you be here?"

"I tink Vater goes home *morgen*."

"I hope you'll stay longer. If he doesn't go, will you come see me?" asked Michal eagerly.

"*Ja*, if he stay I come. Maybe you come to End-of-Track and see me, *nicht so?*"

"If we go there ever, I'll surely see you, Katie. Let's be friends always."

"You are my *Kamerad*." She shook Rory's paw. "Adieu, nice dog. You come to End-of-Track and see me too."

Then both girls stood up, and each went her way, turning at intervals to wave goodbye.

IV

These nights a giant orange-red harvest moon floated lazily over the prairie.

Mother had not been interested in her account of Katie. Michal had told her all about it, but Mother had seemed hardly to hear.

The day after the meeting she had returned to the slough to bring the cattails for Mother she had forgotten; but Katie had not joined her, nor had she come to call on Michal. She and her father had probably left that next morning, Michal decided. If only Mother had seen her! Nobody could help liking such a nice girl.

Now that cutting was done, Gus and Glen spent all their spare time digging a long deep pit north of the house. It was to have a wooden A-roof covered with earth, and would be lined with straw. The girls and Rory watched the progress of the new project from the staking of the site and the removal of the first grassy sod.

By the end of the first day they were well into the deep layer of black topsoil. Michal sniffed the rich earthy smells of sun-drenched moist loam and torn grass roots. She picked up a handful of it, squeezed it into a little ball, and inhaled it deeply from time to time: it gave her the same satisfaction she always felt when she caught the smell in spring of a gusty breeze blowing from newly turned furrows.

A few days before Uncle Fred was to arrive they were digging through yellow-clay subsoil shot through with thin lines and pockets of deep orange-red. This subsoil had a flat dead smell, but Michal longed to taste the bright ocherous earth.

After dinner, while the men were resting, she came quickly, climbed down the small ladder, and hunted until she found a large pocket that would yield her a mouthful. She put it tentatively to her tongue—it was not too bad; Lucky Lady barked; Michal started guiltily. Quickly scrambling up the ladder, she picked up Rory, muzzling his jaws with her hand, then ran for her pigweed patch, peering out from behind its shelter.

Up the hill from the ravine came the oldest Haar boy. For Tan Ears, of course. He was weaned now, and since Glen had come Lucky Lady had abandoned the place she and her surviving puppy had shared since the whelping and had become Glen's slave, following him by day and sleeping on a blanket beside his bed at night.

Michal watched Gus come out and point toward the barn. The boy went down and presently came back, followed cautiously by the mongrel. She had avoided the dog since the scene with Father, and as she looked at the gangling pup she felt again a surge of nausea at the memory of that awful candy pail. Then, as the boy started proudly toward home, Michal noticed that Tan Ears looked different. He did not

27

resemble a pointer or any other kind of dog she knew, and his hair was long and a faded dun.

Stroking Rory's shining red coat, she held him closer. He pulled his muzzle from her hand and licked her fingers carefully. She put him down, studied him critically, then turned to look again toward the road. Raising her head proudly, she said: "Why, he's nothing but a mongrel! He hasn't even got a pedigree," then spat contemptuously in the direction of the receding pair, not tobacco juice but a good thick reddish ochre imitation.

It was then that she saw the Hambletonians coming swiftly down the hill on the far side of the ravine. Something important must have happened for Father to come home so early and so fast. There was someone with him. Another man who waved as he saw Michal running. Uncle Fred!

By the time the high-steppers turned in at the home place, the whole family was gathered around the carriage block. Mavis was in her brother's arms. "More beautiful than ever," he murmured. "Three children, but your eyes as bright and cheeks as pink as when you were sixteen."

Mother flushed with pleasure. "Thank you, Fred. You've surprised us. I'm afraid we aren't dressed properly for—"

"Because he has to get back to Denver City a bit early, he came ahead without telegraphing," interrupted Father buoyantly, lifting out a gun case and several bags.

"But we'll still have a day in town," promised Fred, then turned back to where Michal stood waiting. When he faced her squarely, she saw before he gave her a bear hug the thing she remembered best—his serious brown eyes, so like Mother's, with the lift of brow entirely unlike hers.

Gravely he shook hands with Faith, who had forgotten him. "Now for a look at my namesake," studying Little Brother carefully. "A little crumpled yet, but with great possibilities, eh, Mavis? He's a Gordon, isn't he?" And he grinned at Father.

In the house he glanced quizzically at the girls. "Maybe we'd better see what we can find in this valise." As he opened it Faith drew in her breath sharply. He first brought out a long box and handed it to her. "Oh!" she exclaimed as she took up a large blond china doll, completely dressed. "That string of corals about her neck is for you, Faith." But

28

Faith refused to remove it, and going over to her little chair examined the doll and its clothes minutely.

"She's got panties!"

"You're a little old for a doll, Michal, but I brought you one anyway." Michal took from the box a doll exactly like Faith's except that it was brunette and instead of the chain it had pinned to its dress a small brooch of gold and coral intertwined.

"Thank you, Uncle Fred." And Michal returned to her chair thinking: I'm glad he gave me the doll. But the pin is a real grown-up present.

For Mavis there was a large cameo brooch. "I tried to duplicate your ring."

"They match beautifully." And Mother, flushing with pleasure, pinned it in place and went to look in the mirror.

"John, I almost kept this for myself." It was a revolver, and Father was pleased as they examined and discussed the present in the way of men.

"By the way, Mavis, Phyllis sent me this last year to give you. She never cared for it. It's an old potpourri jar—English china. She said to keep the recipe and renew it from time to time. Hetty can grind the flowers in the coffee mill."

Mother took the jar and held it carefully, as though it might crush like a petal. Then she looked up and smiled. "Phyllis cannot realize there are not roses enough in all Dakota Territory to make a potpourri," and to Michal the smile was as sad as tears.

Uncle Fred spoke hastily. "Listen to this recipe: 'Rose leaves dried in the shade at about four feet from the stove, one pound; cloves, caraway seeds and allspice, of each one ounce. Pound in a mortar or grind in a mill. Dried salt, a quarter of a pound. Mix all together and put the compound in little bags or store in an airtight jar.' "

"What'll women think up next!" snorted Father, examining his revolver.

Mavis took the jar to the mantel, placed it carefully beside the old clock, removed the covers, and stirred it with a spill until the whole room was pervaded with its fragrance. "This will be opened only on extra-special occasions," she said quietly.

And hours later, at bedtime, fragrance from the potpourri still filled the room.

Uncle Fred's visit was a round of hunting, and for a few days it seemed as though the old tension between him and Mother had been something imagined. Michal heard the men go out before daylight every morning to hunt upland birds and prairie chickens, for Father came home nights this week. Then they'd come in, laughing and joking, about the time the rest of the family was ready for breakfast.

Evenings they'd bring out their shotguns, and there were clicking of hammers and squinting into barrels, while Mavis sat quietly mending or rolling slender spills of newspaper for the blue vase on the clock shelf where they would be handy for lighting the lamps.

Then one day Uncle Fred took the whole family into Ipswich for dinner; on the way home conversational undercurrents made Michal uneasy, and she knew that nothing had changed.

It had been a lovely day. On the way in, Father had let the team out and they had got there in time to see the train come swimming out of the distance and glide slowly into the station—the mighty wheels revolving more and more slowly, the platform trembling with the vibrations of weight and power.

They had eaten a wonderful dinner at the hotel—thick steak, creamed onions, mashed potatoes, blancmange, and four-layer cocoanut cake. Then while Mother retired to a room to rest and nurse Little Brother, Uncle Fred had taken the girls into a grocery store where he ordered all the candy Faith wanted and a crate of oranges for Michal.

It seemed that there was nothing left to wish for, Michal thought drowsily, listening to the familiar *clip, clop—clip, clop* of the Hambletonians speeding them homeward.

It was almost sunset when they reached Haar's. Herman was out repairing a break in the cattle corral.

"I'd like to see him a minute, John, if you're not too tired, Mavis," said Uncle Fred.

"I'm not at all tired, Fred."

Herman Haar came up to the carriage and smiled broadly when he saw Uncle Fred.

"Hi, Herman—*wie geht's?*" exclaimed Fred Gordon, extending his hand.

"*Es geht sehr gut, aber langsam, Frederick,*" he returned as they shook hands heartily.

"Pretty good crops this year," said Father.

"Goot every yahr now for drei." He held up three fingers. "You stay long, Frederick?"

"No, till Wednesday. You speak good English, Herman."

Herman shrugged. "Not so goot," but he smiled delightedly, then turned to Michal. "Mine Frau, her sister's *Kind* like you."

"We're comrades," Michal said earnestly.

"Well, Herman, we must go. I'll see you again."

"Those are fine stacks," said Fred as they drove out of Haar's gate.

"The wheat was six feet tall this year, and there was a good stand," said John. "I bought that span of young Percherons for the hauling. Had to have 'em. Got 'em from Smith the big draft-horse breeder."

"You didn't really have to have them," interjected Mavis. "Herman Haar has managed without Percherons."

Michal could see Father's neck and ears turning red. "Haar works his family. I use horses. When I want any advice I'll just turn things over to you, and I'll run the damned house."

"Very well, John," stiffly.

"Percherons are fine for long hauls," said Uncle Fred cheerfully.

"They're the best," said John firmly. Restored to good humor he looked sidewise at Mother, who had lapsed into hurt silence.

Uncle Fred smiled down at her. "It's been doubly like coming home again, this year."

Mavis's face relaxed. "I wish I could feel at home here on the prairie as you and John do. The land so empty, and settled mostly by people like the Haars." Her voice trailed off bitterly.

"But can't you see, Mavis." Fred spoke eagerly. "Haars and their type are the strong ones—the ones who'll possess the land. In a generation they'll be well off, and their children good Americans."

Father flicked the whip impatiently. "I can't agree with you about the Rooshans, Fred. It'll take men with imagination and capital to develop the country."

Fred Gordon grinned. "Well, we've always disagreed on that score." He looked back and smiled at Michal. "Too bad your friend Katie doesn't live nearer."

"You'd love her, Uncle Fred! We just talked and talked. She showed me a picture of relatives who are coming here all the way from Russia and—"

John Ward interrupted. "It's all right to neighbor with Rooshans, Michal; but don't forget that they aren't of our class. Your mother and I agree on that."

"You're both snobs," Fred remarked amiably, but Michal caught

31

the tinge of bitterness, and for the first time she sensed—dimly—a bit of what made Mother and Uncle Fred so different.

The last afternoon Michal walked up from the ravine slowly, after a long stroll on the prairie. She wondered why the time always went so fast. By this time tomorrow, Uncle Fred would be gone, and she still hadn't had much visit with him. There were so many things she wanted to talk over with him before he left. But he and Father had wanted one last hunt, and probably she'd have no chance at all now.

The men had reached home—she could hear them in the kitchen cleaning their guns. The shade north of the kitchen was littered with prairie chicken and plover and grouse. Michal sat down beside them to rest. She stroked the smooth breast of a pinnated grouse, snowy white except for black arrow-point markings; the eyes were closed; it might be the very one Rory had flushed last week in the stubble. It had whirred suddenly from almost under their feet, and flown with a beat and a soar, then several beats and a soar, uttering its low, guttural chuck-uk-uk-uk-uk—ak; chuck-uk-uk-uk—ak.

She raised the wing of a plover to expose the lining. It was different from any she had seen before. Most plovers stood an instant after lighting, with both wings raised straight up, as though showing her proudly the beautiful pattern hidden when the wing was closed. This one was white with sharp dusky markings as delicately gorgeous as a butterfly wing. As she stroked the soft surface she noticed how limp the birds all lay, how lifeless, how very dead.

A qualm of nausea shook her. Walking to the kitchen bench beside the door for a drink of water, she heard Father speaking to Hetty. "I'm hanging these birds we just got, up on the north side of the kitchen in the shade. Don't let me catch you using any of them until they're decently tender."

Hetty sniffed. "Well, Mr. Ward, I've cooked game since I was knee high to a grasshopper, but you're the first person I ever knew who likes it tainted."

"Not tainted, just on the relaxed edge of it—just high," Father said earnestly. "Mr. Gordon likes game birds, and you sure know how to cook 'em. Have supper late. I have to go to town."

After Faith's nap, Mother, Michal, and Faith dressed up in honor of Uncle Fred. Mother had Hetty bring in four o'clock tea, and Michal tried again to make Mother realize about Katie. "She had the nicest

32

hat, Mother, with a wide brim and a blue-ribbon band, just the same shade as the blue stars in her dress. She looked so clean and pretty."

Mavis glanced at her and spoke, a slight impatience edging her usually placid voice. "Michal, I'm sure you're boring your uncle with all that talk about the strange child. After all, as Father and I told you the other day, we must remember that she is a German-Russian."

Michal's heart pounded, and she felt her face grow tight in her disappointment. Mother really wasn't trying to understand.

Then Uncle Fred was speaking in a flat tired voice. "Mavis, after all, you must remember that people are people."

"Well, of course, I presume she has an immortal soul to save," reflectively. "However, she is a foreigner, and as Michal will never see her again I fail to see why she should be so interested in her. 'Katie, Katie!' That's all I've heard since she came home that day. She even forgot the cattails she went to pick for me."

"Please excuse me, Mother," said Michal in a low voice. She left the tea table and went over to the bookcase and took down Hill's *Manual* with the pictures of penmanship, turning the pages at random to keep the tears from falling.

Uncle Fred now came over to the glass-fronted black walnut bookcase that topped the large writing desk, and took a book from the shelf. Michal could see that it was *The Life of John B. Gough*. He turned the pages quickly, then turned to his sister. "Still strong on the good works, Mavis, I see."

Michal saw her mother's back stiffen, and what Father called her Gordon look came into her face as she said severely, "Well, Fred, I'm doing my best, even though we live on the prairie, to bring up my family in the Christian faith."

"Then why are you trying to make a snob out of Michal?"

Michal could bear no more. There it was again out in the open, that old antagonism when Uncle Fred began teasing Mother about her books. The high wall was still there. Feeling very miserable, she put down her volume quickly and slipped out.

As she stepped out into the bustling peace of evening on the farm, Rory waked from his nap in the shade, licked her extended hand, and stretched his long gangling puppy body before rising. Michal heard Mother's voice—raised in argument.

"Almighty God who planned everything realized that we are born to different stations in this life. We can be kind to these German-Russians, but that doesn't mean that we must associate with them any more than we would with cattle."

"What you're telling me, Mavis, is that because Christ was born in a manger you would have denied him."

"Fred!" Mother's voice was shocked. "Christ was the Son of God. No true Christian denied Christ. That was different."

There was a pause, then Uncle Fred said gently: "I'm sorry, Mavis. We should never discuss the subject, you and I."

Michal stepped away from under the window guiltily, her heart still heavy. The northwest breeze brought her a faint reminder of freshly turned earth from the vegetable pit and from the kitchen stovepipe the mingled smoke from paper, corncobs, and fresh pine as Hetty started the kitchen fire for supper. From the north slough came the clank-clank of the cowbell as Daisy led the procession of cows to the home corral.

Michal ran to the granary, her steps impeded by noisy hens, cheeping chicks, and plaintive turkey poults in from hunting grasshoppers on the stubble; important quibbling ducks, their orange feet still wet with water from the dam. She laughed to see the bantam, Napoleon, fraternizing with the old turkey gobbler long enough to pick up his share of the wheat and corn Glen had scattered for them.

"What's funny?" asked Uncle Fred's voice beside her.

"Everything. Usually Nap is afraid of the gobbler, but just look at him now. I like to see them all eat—every night if I can."

He was quiet for a moment, then touched her cheek gently. "Do you know, Michal, I wish you were my daughter."

"But I am your goddaughter."

"You are, indeed." He paused. Then, "Did you know that I suggested your name?"

"But I thought Mother—"

"I chose it for one reason, and your mother liked and decided on it for another."

She was round-eyed with interest. "Mrs. Tannyhill told me it's a boy's name."

"Oh, no! Michal was the daughter of King Saul and became the wife of King David. She lived a colorful, very independent life. That's why I wanted her name for you."

"And Mother?"

"Well, Mavis liked it because it was unusual and a good scriptural name." He grinned.

"Uncle Fred"—Michal's voice was serious—"you'll be gone soon, and there are a few things I'd like to ask you. Will you come up with me to my pigweed patch?"

"I'd like to," he said gravely. They walked in silence to the little place back of the house, and Michal pointed him to a smooth boulder as she seated herself on a wooden box. I don't know how to start asking him, Michal thought as Uncle Fred took out his pipe, tapped it, filled and lighted it, and began calmly puffing.

A yellow-headed blackbird, probably from her willow tree down by the dam, gave voice, a raucous, choking cry. "Why doesn't Mother like me to be Katie's friend? She didn't even see her and yet she doesn't like her. Why?"

Uncle Fred puffed away a minute, took his pipestem out of his mouth, then said: "A lot of people have a prejudice against foreigners. It's a great pity."

"The way Mother acts about Katie, I can't ask her anything. But there's so much I don't understand. Katie and the Haars speak German, yet Father calls them Rooshans. Why do Mother and Father look down on them?"

"I'll try to explain, Michal. You've heard your folks brag about our ancestors who came to America in search of religious freedom. Probably those same ancestors of ours were looked down on by the people who had been there longer or who had been born here. But they worked hard, prospered, and became good Americans. Now the same thing is happening to the German-Russians."

"Why have they come to America?"

"For the land. This is the frontier. The land is free for those who'll live on it and work it. In Russia it wasn't. Something tremendous is taking place here in this country. I probably won't live to see it, but you will."

"What?"

"The melting pot. The German-Russians will intermarry and they'll become good Americans. They'll become part of the life stream of America just like us. We were all foreigners ourselves to this country originally. It's not the nationality but the individual that counts. I'm sure Katie is a fine girl, and you and she could teach each other

35

many things. On the other hand, you don't seem to care for the Haar children, even though they are her cousins. They don't interest you, but neither does Mrs. Tannyhill."

"That's true. Will it always be that some people won't like the German-Russians?"

"Probably not. You'll find as you live among them that some will like them and others will be indifferent."

"Like Father and Mother?"

"They're new here," said Uncle Fred tolerantly. "However, these people are thrifty and strong. In thirty years they will have conquered this prairie, and men like Herman Haar will be independent, well-to-do. Their children will go to the same schools you attend. They will be Americans."

"Then I'll play with those I like just as I do with people like ourselves," said Michal firmly, thinking of Katie.

"If you do that," he paused, then continued thoughtfully, "you'll really be living out one of the finest teachings of Christ."

They drifted into a comfortable silence, punctuated only by the shrill of crickets from the stubble field. Uncle Fred relit his pipe. 'Way off in the west the sun was setting behind a curtain of burning red and gold as live as a prairie fire. A smoke of haze settled slowly down over the earth, softening everything.

At first Michal thought she imagined it—far off—a faint mellow note, too beautiful to be real. Then it came again—nearer this time—that soft deep organ note.

Uncle Fred leaned forward and grasped her arm. "Listen!" he whispered.

Again and yet again, nearer with each repetition, it swelled and died away, but still softly, a deep organ note until it was above them. It was so high not even a whisper of the mighty white wings could reach them, but the deeptoned call like a magnificent trumpet, swelled triumphantly down to them from the sweeping solitudes of the upper air. Then gradually, as it had swelled, it diminished, coming faintly and more faintly until distance muted it to soft echoes that finally died away.

"What was it?" whispered Michal.

"A trumpeter swan."

"I've never heard one before."

36

"I did—once—in Wyoming." He spoke softly, almost as though to himself.

A last few embers in the west were fading, and the deepening haze was drifting over the prairie as they walked hand in hand to the house.

V

These days the winds blew high over the dying prairie. Now that harvest was over, Glen was hauling. For weeks he and Father had been leaving at five o'clock in the morning with the load so that John Ward could reach his office on time. Then, after the team had rested in the livery stable, Glen would hitch them up, fill the wagon box with coal, flour, a barrel of apples, and they would start on the long homeward drive when the office closed.

Michal loved to watch the dappled gray Percherons, necks proudly arched, moving steadily, gripping the ground firmly with their large hoofs.

"They're certainly proving their worth, Mavis." John often said to Mother, his gray eyes warm with pride.

"They are handsome, John."

And so the last days of November passed. The sky was overcast with leaden clouds, snow threatened, and the prairie was filled with the hoarse voices of honkers going south.

Now that the pigweed patch was dead, Michal loved to bundle up well and climb onto the shed roof and listen for the first faint notes of geese flying over. Sometimes they would be above the clouds but their cries would drift through to her, listening below. Sometimes V-shaped wedges of them would shoot low over the farm, strong and beautiful and wild, and always going south.

One day a northwest wind was blowing, and the sky seemed filled with bird cries. John Ward stalked into the house that evening in a rage.

"What do you think I saw that Rooshan, Haar, doing this morning, Mavis?" he asked grimly, holding his hands out to the heater.

"I'm sure I don't know," said Mother quietly, glancing tenderly down at Little Brother, who was nursing.

37

"Just as I drove through the ravine, he was driving off with six wild geese, legs tied together, flopping about in the bottom of the wagon box."

"How in the world did he catch them?" asked Michal curiously.

"Now that the ponds are freezing, some of them get their feathers frozen into the ice. So our sporting neighbor," went on Father bitterly, "goes out and catches them for his own private use. When I came past tonight, there they were in the barnyard with their wings clipped."

"But you shoot them," said Michal, somewhat bewildered.

"Of course I shoot them," snapped Father. "That's the point. They're not meant to be tamed. If he wants domesticated geese, let him get Embdens instead of—"

"But, John," interrupted Mavis gently, "isn't that a very practical thing for him to do? After all, it saves time and money."

"Damn it all, Mavis, what do you know about such things? This is a country of sportsmen, not peasants. When we want food or sport, we go hunting. We don't rob the skies for our barnyards!"

Michal went outside and slowly climbed the ladder onto the shed roof. Everything looked so dreary. She could see what Father meant, all right. It was awful to think of those great wild birds with their proud wings clipped, never to sweep over the prairie again.

Then above—the spear formation flying fast and high with the wind—a late flock moved steadily across the deepening sky, their wild joyous cries echoing to the earth. And in a moment Michal heard an answer as the earthbound captives in Haar's barnyard called out in hoarse frantic clamor—lost cries—as their fellows flew on with the wind.

These days the prairie was hidden under a soft snow blanket. Everything had changed. Mornings the lower windowpanes were frost-stippled with delicate, fantastic shrubs, and at dawn the scent of pine and corncob smoke filled the house.

One blissful day Gus drove Mavis and the children over to call on Mrs. Oulette. The slough had changed. Exotic blackbirds no longer swayed and preened from green rushes. Along the bank lemon-brown reeds pierced the snow, and a flock of horned larks hopped about on the pure white expanse where water had stood in summer. Most of all, Michal missed the familiar hiss of dry grass in the wheels.

Mrs. Oulette's little one-room house was bright and immaculately kept. The tea and sweet cakes were delicious, the frail china exquisite.

But when the woman, thinner and whiter than before, began to speak of the prairie, "Even the geese—always flying—are glad to leave this desolate land. But while they fly over it they cry—they clamor so piteously," Michal felt herself go tense, and wished the subject would change.

"The geese are gone now," returned Mavis soothingly.

Mrs. Oulette poured another cup of tea. Turning, she held it out to Mavis and her eyes softened and grew large as she said, "Pierre and I went to the opera last night."

Mavis's outstretched hand paused for just an instant before she took the cup, then returned quietly: "Thank you. I'm afraid I didn't hear what you just said."

"Will you not have cake?" Mrs. Oulette held out the plate, and the moment passed.

Michal thought of that strange moment many times as the winter days grew shorter and colder. The base burner was banked to last all night now, and the kitchen fire was kept up until bedtime. White rime was thick on the windows, darkening the house. Mornings, Michal and Faith stayed in bed until the floors were warm and the frost forests had melted from the tops of the windows.

Mother was always busy with Little Brother, who looked like a doll in his long ruffled white dresses. Faith was solemnly counting the days until Christmas. And Michal worked every day on her lessons, enjoying the cozy warmth of the house after her romps in the snow.

Even Hetty's spine-tingling stories of the lost ones heightened the excitement. Michal knew exactly how to get her started.

"Oh, Hetty," she'd sigh happily, "I'm so glad winter's here at last."

"Humph! You'll be singin' another tune come Feb'ary."

"Don't you like snow?"

"Like it!" intoned Hetty mournfully. "Like it, when I remember the ones who hev died and who will die?" She would narrow her eyes and lean toward Michal avidly. "Do you think that's wind you hear screechin' around the chimneys and rattlin' the winders on stormy nights? No! It ain't!"

"Then what is it?"

"I'll tell yuh what tiz." The lowered voice, the glance toward the bedroom. "It's the ghosts of poor souls that fruz, wandering over the snow all winter long. It's their voices we hear a-shriekin' and a-screamin'

39

when the wind howls in winter—cryin' out their dyin' agony." And she would nod impressively.

"Tell me how they died?"

"Well," with another glance bedroomward, "let me see. There wuz my uncle's cuzzin' . . ." And she would be off, usually winding up with the young lovers who froze to death in a haystack, while Michal shivered blissfully, over every "one dark night" and "And they wuz found —dead."

On the day before Christmas, at nap time, Michal was permitted to bundle up and watch Gus drive a small flock of sheep up a great drift which sloped gradually from ground to roof. Then he carefully pulled the cutter through the small imprints and joined Michal, a broad grin creasing his red face.

" 'Tain't many years you kin do this. Drifts ain't always so obligin'." He chuckled. "This'll give Miss Faith somethin' to wonder about."

The next day, after present opening and Hetty's huge delicious dinner, Father went over to Haar's to ask something about the spring's work; Faith was asleep; Little Brother, rosy and sweet, was propped up on the sofa behind a barricade of pillows, solemnly tearing bright paper; Michal, curled up in a chair before the hard-coal burner, had begun *Alice in Wonderland*. The only sounds were the turning of leaves in her book and the small noise made when at intervals a burning coal dropped from the fiery mass to the ash pan far beneath. And, once, a small sigh from Mavis, who, seated at the window, was looking out over the vast white prairie.

After Christmas the cold increased. As Hetty said, "When the days begin to lengthen, then the cold begins to strengthen."

As week followed monotonous week, the cold weather intensifying until the old homemade stone oven in the dining room was pressed into service during the daytime, and the men kept busy stuffing it with twisted hay and corncobs, Michal began to resent the frost, like a thick rim of white coral, always under the outside doors, the hinges covered with rime until they resembled tiny snowmen; but most of all the half-inch thickness of ice that in spite of the storm windows covered the lower panes even in the warmest rooms. Besides, now that Christmas was over and spring so far away, there was nothing to look forward to. Father, who was home most of the time, seemed restless and irritable.

40

To make matters worse, Michal ran out without her coat one morning to watch Gus unload strawy manure from a stoneboat, and caught a terrible cold. Mavis—eyes bright and color high—dosed her daughter with onion syrup, hot Jamaica ginger tea, and mustard plasters. As she sat by the bed tearing an old soft linen tablecloth into tiny squares—"The handkerchiefs won't begin to hold out," she said cheerfully—Michal felt that she hadn't seen Mother so lively and happy since they had moved here. As Hetty said, "A borned nurse."

In spite of the fires, the floors were always cold until Father grudgingly gave Gus permission to heap fresh strawy horse manure high on the window sills over the earth banking around the foundation, where it steamed in the sunshine during the middle of the day. At night Michal in her snug bed could hear the house creak in every joint from the cold.

The day she got up and dressed for the first time in over a week, the weather moderated. It was almost up to zero by noon and growing even warmer. The chores were done, dinner over, and John Ward—felt pacs changed for carpet slippers—sat in his big chair in high good humor—ready to begin reading *Encyclopaedia Britannica* Volume VI.

"Mavis," he began, looking at Mother, who sat in her rocker darning socks, "I still say that if you'd have given Michal here a good hot toddy every night and made her sweat, she'd have shaken off that infernal cold a damn' sight sooner."

"You know very well that none of that vile stuff will ever pass her lips with my consent." She glanced up from her darning, met Father's grin, and smiled back.

It was good that Father felt so gay; she had noticed during the cold weather that he had sometimes paced up and down the room restlessly, as though chafing at the routine and enforced confinement. Today he seemed content.

"Mother likes to take care of us when we're sick," observed Michal.

"Sure. She wanted to be a doctor, you know. Just imagine—a little thing like her a doctor!" He smiled indulgently.

"Did you really?"

"More than anything."

"Why didn't you, then?"

"My father wouldn't hear of it. 'Who,' he said, 'ever heard of a woman doctor?' About the only thing a girl can do is teach, and I didn't care for that." Her voice held an edge of bitterness.

"She got over that idea in a hurry when she met me." Father grinned at her.

Just then Little Brother woke, and Mavis rose to go to him. She smiled, and on her way to the bedroom came and leaned over the back of Father's chair and rested her slender hand for an instant on his shoulder in one of her rare caresses. Then she was gone, but Michal noticed she had not answered him. Thoughtfully she went back to her place and picked up her book.

"Why do you read the encyclopedia so much, Father?"

"Because it's not wasted time; when I went to school one of my copy books had a line, 'Read, reflect, and inwardly digest!' To do that you have to read something worth reading; anyway, it stuck by me."

Mavis came back with Little Brother and Faith, who at once ran to Father shouting, "Pitchers! Show me pitchers!"

But Father said irritably: "Go to your sister. She'll show you pictures."

Michal put down her book resignedly. "We'll make a picture of Heaven."

"Oh, my God!" muttered John Ward.

Michal got a box from her bookcase drawer, and the girls worked busily arranging red stars from Gus's plug tobacco on a piece of blue silesia Mother had bought for the purpose that lovely day in Ipswich.

Presently Michal looked up. "Why don't you read the Bible? Isn't it worth while?"

"Huh?" said John. "What'd you say?"

"I asked why you never read the Bible. Isn't it as worth while as the encyclopedia?"

"It's all right for women," growled Father, glancing at Mavis, who sat nursing little Fred. "Now, don't interrupt me again."

The room was so still for a time that coals falling from the grate into the ash pan made a loud clatter. Suddenly from the kitchen came a weird noise as Hetty, mixing down bread dough, burst into song:

" 'Then scatter (thump—thump) seeds of kindness (thump—thump)
For our reaping (thump—thump) by and by'" (thump—thump).

Father sprang to his feet, snapped the book shut and, exclaiming, "Why does that damn' woman have to howl her hymns all day!" put

42

the calf-bound volume in its place with restrained violence, then slammed the bookcase door.

"John! She heard you." Mavis's voice was tragic. A sudden silence from the kitchen bore out her words, and Mavis went on. "I do wish you'd learn to control your temper and refrain from profanity."

"Very well, Mavis. I know it's too much to try to concentrate around here," snapped Father. Rummaging about in the drawer of the writing desk, he fished out a Montgomery Ward catalogue and went back to his chair. As he turned the pages until he found what he wished, his face gradually grew cheerful, and the house, except for the loud silence from the kitchen, became quiet and relaxed, the girls whispering over their play, Mavis holding her child.

Mavis went quietly to the bedroom and put away the sleeping baby. When she returned and picked up her mending, Father spoke cheerfully. "I've decided to get a really A-number-one harness for the Hambletonians. I think Wentz'll sell me one for about $10 more than this outfit asks."

"What's wrong with the old one?"

"Shabby. No use driving a good team unless the harness is just as good. It's an insult to the team."

"What'll it cost?"

Father bounded out of his chair and, slamming down the catalogue, exploded, "God damn it all, I'm going to town to get a little peace!"

"John!" To Michal's surprise Mother's face turned pale, and tears filled her eyes. "We don't need anything from town; you know how I worry."

"Nonsense. It's a fine day. Look! The windows are clear of frost for the first time in weeks. There are perfect roads for the cutter; the Hambletonians'll whisk me into town and right back. Do you realize that we haven't had the mail for over three weeks? Besides"—he was joking now—"Michal here is out of horehound candy, Gus needs more plug tobacco, and I'm sure"—he raised his voice and opened the door to the dining room—"Hetty'll never speak to me again unless I bring her a package of licorice drops."

He left in a flurry of hoofbeats and jingling sleighbells as the Hambletonians, anxious for exercise and hampered not at all by the light cutter, skimmed lightly along the Ipswich road.

Michal stood on the horse block until Father turned and waved at her before he disappeared below the hills beyond the ravine. A warm gentle wind—almost a chinook—came from the southwest, and a soft blue haze blurred the horizon. As she turned to go in she wished Father had asked her to go with him.

The afternoon dragged. Mother, usually so placid, moved restlessly through the rooms, and kept looking anxiously out at the calm blue sky. Then at four o'clock she went in and sat by the window to watch the road. When Gus came into the sitting room with a scuttle of coal for the base burner and stooped to take out the ash pan, she asked, "Isn't it time for Mr. Ward to be getting back?"

He grinned. "Land sakes, it's seventeen miles each way, and you know he figgered on doin' a bit o' tradin'."

"But with good roads and the light cutter he should make fast time."

"Mebbe he's met McGinnis, an' if so they'll be talkin' pedigrees this very minute."

"I suppose so." But as he went out, Michal saw her turn again to the window and look toward the south.

At five Gus came in with the milk; and Mother, followed by Michal, went to the kitchen. Gus looked up quickly and spoke too heartily. "Well, the chores is done. I did 'em early so he wouldn't have to bother helpin'."

"Gus, is there trouble?"

"There, there, everything's all right."

"Don't you 'there, there' me!" she said sharply. "What's wrong?"

"Th' wind's changed."

"Well?"

"I don't quite like the look of it." He pointed to the west window.

Michal followed Mother. The whole day had suddenly faded. The sun hung pale and low, with bright burnished sundogs on either side. Over and about it all, like northern lights, streaked an eerie shimmering glow. A wind was blowing out of the northwest, driving dark, shaggy storm clouds toward them from the horizon. Even as they stood there frost whitened the windowpanes and sudden fantastic figures appeared —wavering seaweed and fan-shaped coral like pictures Michal had seen of the floor of the sea.

"I got everything snug for the night," Gus said awkwardly.

"Good." Michal knew from the tone of Mother's voice that she

44

didn't realize what he had said. Holding her daughter's hand tightly, she went to the front window and stood looking over the prairie, hoping, Michal knew, to see the Hambletonians sweep over the hills and down toward the ravine. But the road was empty.

The wind paused. A few snowflakes came down slowly, erratically, as though unwilling to touch the earth. Mother said, "I believe it won't hit after all," and started, smiling, for the kitchen.

Then the storm exploded. The wind seemed to hit the house from all directions at once; daylight was instantly blotted out by whirling clouds. The house strained and creaked; windows rattled; and Michal's ears ached as the hissing snowflakes—slivers of ice—driven with terrific force hit the panes. It brought back another experience—the dark night when, lost in the field, she had wakened to run, with the wind hissing through the wheat.

Hetty and Gus lit the lamps, and Hetty moved the set of three flatirons forward on the stove to heat.

"I thought the ironing was all done," Michal said.

"So 'tis," Hetty replied grimly. "This un is different."

Mavis came into the room. "Good! You have the irons on. We must have a light in every window tonight."

"We ain't got that many," began Hetty, but Gus interrupted.

"Here's my lantern, and there's another in the stormshed. That'll do it." And he reached for his from the nail behind the door and began polishing the chimney with crumpled paper.

Faith came in from the sitting room. She clutched Mother's skirts and clung there crying: "I want Father! I want candy."

"Hetty, dish up the girls' supper now; we'll all be busy tonight."

Michal couldn't eat. She felt sick with fear for Father somewhere out there, probably wandering about like the people in Hetty's stories. But he surely would get home some way. He wouldn't give up, and as she helped Faith undress she felt more hopeful. Father was so big and strong that no storm could beat him. He'll come walking in any time now, she thought.

As the storm continued her ears grew used to the noises, even the hissings. In the sitting room Mother, holding a warm flatiron with its cloth holder to protect her hands from the heat, had moved the center table—on which was the largest lamp in the house—back from the window and was busy ironing away the frost from the pane, then wiping it dry with a clean cloth. As she returned the table to its place she said:

45

"If there's even a little lull he'll see it. Michal, stay out in this room with me, but sit where you can see Faith if she goes near the lamp in the bedroom window. Give her a picture book or something so she'll be quiet. That'll help, because we've got to go over the windows every time enough frost collects to dim the lights."

"All right." Then, "The baby's awake," she reported. "Lying just as still and sucking his thumb."

"I forgot to feed him, poor child!"

"I'll do your winder for you while you nurse him," Hetty said, bustling in. "But ain't it dangerous for him—I mean, ain't you too upset and won't the milk just cruddle in his little stumick?"

"It'll be better for him now than later," Mavis whispered, half to herself.

Michal sat down in the little chair upholstered with Brussels carpeting and trimmed with ball fringe. She folded her hands and looked at Mother's face, so tense and white, bending over the child at her breast. Again a chill of fear passed over her. She wondered if they would find him after the storm in the ravine like the people Hetty had told about. She put her hands over her eyes to shut out the thought.

The wind lulled for an instant, dying away in a low weird cry. What had Hetty said? "It is not the wind you hear but the voices of the dead ones."

Mother called to Gus, who was doing the east window in the dining room. "Is it going down?" He came to the door, but shook his head, as—beginning with an eerie screech—an even louder blast replied for him.

Michal smiled. That was never Father—his ghost would never scream in fear. Hurrying in to the kitchen to Hetty she touched her arm. "If my father is out there—even if he died, he wouldn't come home wailing and screaming; my father wouldn't scream. He couldn't."

Hetty moved the lamp back close to the pane, put her iron back on the stove, and drew Michal awkwardly to her. "Listen, child," she said, her own eyes filling with tears, her voice unsteady, "you jest forgit all them stories I told you—jest forget 'em. Of course he wouldn't come like that. He'd come callin' strong and deep."

As time passed it was harder to keep the windows clear because of the increasing cold.

"If he's lost and going in circles, he'll see the lamps if there's any lull," said Mother, working feverishly on the south window, her large dark eyes staring out from a face drained of all color, and her hair—for the first time in Michal's memory—falling in disorder about her shoulders.

Gus brought in another scuttle of coal for the baseburner. Mavis looked at him dully. "Will this never end?"

"Seems to me the wind is letting up jest a little."

She shook her head. "It's as loud as ever. You're just trying to make me feel better."

Gus poured the coal with a clatter into the top of the stove. Then he adjusted the damper and drafts and was leaving the room when he stood still and lifted his hand. "Hark!"

There was nothing to hear. The storm was over. As suddenly as it had begun, it had passed.

"Thank God!" Mother said fervently, and went to the bedroom. Michal followed. She looked in. Mother was kneeling by her bed, praying. Realizing with a twinge of conscience that she hadn't done more than babble her regular nightly prayer for a long time, Michal shut her eyes and prayed: Oh, God, I know I've not paid much attention to you lately. Even though the storm's over, there's plenty to worry about yet. If you bring my father home to us, safe and unfrozen, I'll make it up to you. Amen.

Then she went to the kitchen; and as she entered, Hetty did a queer thing. She slumped into a chair and began crying aloud—hard tearing sobs that rasped her throat.

"Hetty! What ails you?"

"Oh, it's just too terrible!" she said through her sobs. "Mis' Ward looking so tired and drabbled, and that poor man out goodness knows where, an' to think that only this afternoon I was so mad at him."

Gus took her by the shoulders and shook her hard. "Stop that blattin', Het Perkins, and git supper good an' hot. I'm goin' down to meet him."

"What if it starts stormin' again?"

"It won't. It's gone fer good this time." Gus drew on his felt pacs, then his gum overshoes, and put on his storm coat and cap with earmuffs. Going to the cupboard he took the bottle Father used for hot toddy and put it in his pocket.

As he opened the door of the front stormshed, they heard him say, "Well, I swan!" Hastily throwing on shawls, the three crowded out behind him.

47

The night was already clear, and light from the stars shone on them. Then Michal saw that the whole house was surrounded by a perpendicular wall of drift about twelve feet from the building, higher than the roof. All they could see was the sky and the wall of snow encircling them. Then Gus, going back to the shed for the scoop shovel, began digging steps to the top of the drift. "Sposin' the crust breaks through with you!" cried Hetty.

"It's all right. This crust would hold a elephant." And they heard his footsteps disappear in the direction of the barn.

"I'm freezing," complained Michal, and Hetty remarked:

"It's mighty sharp. We'd best go in."

She looked at Mavis, who said, "Yes, it's cold without shelter." And her face was bleak.

The heat rushed to meet them as they opened the door. Mavis's hands were shaking as she extended them to the bulging mica-paned doors. "Our lamps did no good, after all." Her voice broke the silence.

"I was jest a-thinkin' that," replied Hetty. "I'll get some hot supper ready, now; none of us has et."

Mavis began drawing her shawl about her. "Let's go out again, Michal. I can't stand it—so still, and nothing I can do."

As they opened the door they heard the crisp thud of hoofs— War with Gus on his back galloping sure-footedly over the hard crust toward the ravine. Mavis reached for Michal's hand and gripped it tightly—as she had that first night when from the knoll they had heard the weird cry of the plover; and again, as then, Michal felt close to her mother as she wordlessly shared her fear.

They stood in silence, listening to War's hoofs, thudding more and more faintly but still steadily, surely, over the well packed drifts.

Michal looked up. The stars, like little silver bells, trembled against the deep sky. She could almost hear them tinkle—faintly to be sure, because they were so far away.

"Mother," she whispered, "I can almost hear the stars."

"Hush!" Mother dropped Michal's hand, clutched her arm tightly, and stood tense—listening. Suddenly she relaxed, let out her breath in a sigh. "It's Father," she breathed. "Thank God!"

They stood listening until the sound of bells came closer, and voices mingled in greeting. Then Mother said hurriedly: "Let's go in. I must comb my hair."

Michal lingered and listened once more to the clear sweet jingle

48

of approaching sleighbells, before she followed Mavis in and closed the door.

Mother was before the bureau glass, and Hetty was bustling about the kitchen. "Michal, you straighten the sitting room while Hetty sets the table. We want the house looking cozy when the men come in from the barn."

In a few minutes Father, with Gus close behind him, burst into the house. The pockets of his fur coat bulged with mail and small parcels. Mother walked into his arms and leaned her head for an instant against his coat.

"There, there, Mavis; there, there," he soothed, patting her back reassuringly.

She drew back as though embarrassed. "Where were you?"

"At Haar's," he said cheerfully. "There's a lot of mail." And he threw a big bundle tied with twine on the center table. "I'll go wash up —I seem to smell food. Here's your horehound candy, Chicken." He tossed her a small sack. "And by the way, Hetty"—he grinned at her as she stood in the doorway—"I didn't forget those licorice drops."

"Thank you, Mr. Ward." Primly.

"While I wash, set two extra places, and Gus, you draw up a couple of chairs. We'll all eat together so I can tell you about my trip. After I got the mail and a few things we needed," Father began, dishing portions of the boiled dinner, "I ran into McGinnis and we had a little talk; then I started home early to be sure and make it before dark."

"Where were you when you noticed the first signs?" asked Mavis.

"About five miles south of Haar's. I saw that the wind had changed, then that storm clouds were gathering in the northwest. I let the horses out. Mavis, I wish you could have seen those Hambletonians trot. Against the wind, too. Prettiest thing you ever saw!

"I sighted Haar's barn before the blizzard hit. As long as the wind was from the northwest, I was absolutely sure I could keep my bearings until I got there.

"Suddenly the wind let up; it began to snow a little. I thought, Good! Maybe I'll make it home after all. It had turned colder, so I pulled the buffalo robe higher and wound my woolen scarf up over my cap and around my neck good and tight. Just then it hit."

"What did it seem like, Father?" Michal asked eagerly.

"Well—one minute, even though I was facing a stiff wind, I was skimming along in the sunshine. The next, the wind and snow stung

49

me like a million whips. My nose and throat were filled with snow. I fought for breath."

"Could you see anything?" ask Hetty.

"Not a thing. Not even the horses. Not even my hand held close to my eyes. Ice formed on my lashes and froze them together. I pulled my scarf down over my face to protect it."

"How did the horses act?" This was Gus.

"After their first surprise when they reared, they went straight ahead—or so I hoped. I gave them their heads. It was the only thing I could do. I was lost. Everything depended on the team. I thought I was a goner sure, for I doubted if they could keep the road."

"It must'a' been just plain hell," Gus broke in impulsively, then flushing—"beggin' yer pardon, Mis' Ward."

"It wasn't heaven, that's a cinch! And the worst of it was, I knew I might pass only an arm's length from Haar's corral leading to the barn and never know it.

"The horses struggled on. My hands were numb, so I wrapped the lines around the whip socket and began beating my arms against my shoulders to keep up the circulation. I might be a gone goose, but I wasn't just going to sit still and freeze to death in a cutter.

"Then I thought I heard someone calling. I didn't dare stop the team, but I listened and heard it again—closer. Someone was yelling, 'Whoa, whoa!' The horses heard it, too, and slackened a bit. I pulled 'em up, and yelled back. The answer seemed to come just back and to the left of me. It was Haar's voice, of course.

"I got out of the cutter and, hanging tight to the reins, worked my way, talking to the team all the time, until I reached their heads. I couldn't see a thing for the icicles on my lashes, but I couldn't have seen anything anyway.

"Well, he kept calling and I called back until, leading the horses, I felt him. Then I led the horses with one hand and held fast to a rope about Haar's waist with the other. He reeled in the rope. I hung tight. The horses followed like humans. I believe they understood.

"When Haar reached the post I changed sides to keep the horses near the fence but away from the barbed wire. We went slowly along until the fence hit the barn near the big rolling door on the south side.

"We stopped there to get our breaths and give the team a little rest. Then suddenly there was a lull. The wind came only from one direction instead of from every point of the compass. Haar rolled open the door and we went in—cutter and all.

"That barn seemed the most peaceful place I ever struck. Maybe you don't know how glad I was to get in where I could pull the ice from my eyes and see again. Eight horses and twenty head of cattle make plenty of body heat, so it was warm. That's a good tight barn of Haar's and well built.

"As soon as we could talk I asked Haar how it all happened. Seems he saw me go by this afternoon and he knew I'd bring his mail and was keeping an eye out for me."

"Only this afternoon!" murmured Mavis. "It seems more like a week!"

"When the wind changed he was doing the night chores; he had that oldest boy of his take a rope from the barn to the dugout so they could always go back and forth safely. In the meantime he tied one end of a long picket rope about his waist and fastened the other to the corral post nearest the road.

"Just before the storm broke he saw me coming. He walked out to the end of the rope that almost reached to the road, and kept yelling 'Whoa!' He figured the team would keep to the road and that I'd hear him too."

"Did you go into the dugout?" Michal's voice was eager.

"No, Chicken. I didn't even unhitch the horses. Haar asked me in for hot soup, but I knew how Mother, here, would be worrying, and I wanted to pull out as soon as there was another lull and see if I couldn't eat supper with my own family. Lucky for me it worked out that way."

"God was watching over you, John," said Mavis piously.

"I was just damn' lucky," said Father, leaning back. "This is a dandy supper, Hetty. Could you spare me another cup of coffee?"

VI

Spring broke early over the prairie. In late February a chinook wind gently stirred the pulses of the earth; long icicles dripped from the eaves and water melted from under snowbanks and trickled down the ravine.

Every day Hetty would say: "This good weather can't last. It's too soon. Jest you wait—it'll storm plenty yet." But every day the gentle warm wind persisted, melting the snows until Oulette's slough was brimful and water rushed in torrents down the ravine.

Michal, lying safe in her bed at night, listening to the steady roar, shivered, remembering the troll that, according to Hetty, lived under the wet steppingstones crossing the ravine. Once a year, when the water ran highest, it would come out on moonless nights and dance wildly over the swirling flood; then before dawn it would go back to its hiding place to watch for children.

By the second week in March, the prairie, except on northern hill slopes, was bare of snow, and high above the quiet brown fields that waited patiently for their quickening, Michal saw the first long irregular line of wild geese going north, a dark rhythmic pattern of flight against the cool blue of the sky, silent except for the high clear call of their leader. She listened. Haar's geese heard it too, for a hoarse raucous clamor rose from the south, and Michal knew they were flapping their clipped wings in wild futile efforts to raise their heavy bodies and follow.

Haar was already plowing on the higher land. The leaf buds on Michal's little willow down by the dam were swelled almost to bursting.

It happened on a warm misty morning in mid-March. Michal woke early, before sunup, but Father and Mother were awake and talking.

Father said drowsily: "I notice the price of wheat is up; by the time Glen gets back he and Gus can handle spring's work and I'll finish the hauling."

"Won't that be hard on you?"

"Not too bad. I'll start early mornings, and that'll give the team a long rest while I'm at the office. Then I'll leave town in time to get home by dark."

"John, there's something—"

"Yes, Mavis?"

"Could I take Baby and go in with you some day to Wall's Studio? We have no picture of him yet, and he's getting so big and handsome now that I'd like photographs to send back to the families."

"Sure, Mavis. I don't want you riding in on a load of wheat, but as soon as hauling and spring's work are over it'll be fine." Father's feet hit the floor, and he looked at his watch. "By George—time to get up; almost six and no sun." Michal heard him walk to the window, then: "No wonder it's so dark—there's a mist; what do y' know! A mist in March!"

Breakfast over, Michal wandered into the sitting room and leaned her head against the south window. The mist had lifted from the prairie, but tattered shreds of it still hung over the ravine. She shivered a little and thought of the troll. Could that be his breath rising like gray veils from the water?

Then at Rory's bark she first saw him—a huge black shape looming out of the mist. She thought it was the troll; then he resolved himself into an immense black ox with spreading horns, moving slowly but steadily up the hill toward the place as though he belonged there.

Going straight to the cattle pen, he stopped and, looking over the bars toward the haystack, gave a long, mournful low.

Father, followed by Gus, came from the harness room. They opened the gate, and the animal went in to the haystack and began eating as though he could not get enough.

"Mother, may I go down to the barn? We have a black ox!" cried Michal. Hetty came in quickly from the kitchen, saying, "What's this I hear? Did you say black ox?"

"He just came. See him down in the pen?"

Hetty took one look. "May the good God help us!" she exclaimed, her lips paling.

Mavis came slowly from the bedroom. "You'd probably better not—" she began, when Hetty interrupted grimly.

"Let 'er go with me, Mis' Ward, I'll tell 'em plenty what about a black ox!"

Hetty, a gray shawl over her head, stalked out, and Michal was hard put to keep up with her. She strode down to the bars where the men were inspecting the new beast. Splashed and muddy, he was eating greedily. As he pulled hay from the stack, Michal noticed brass guards on the tips of his long horns, gleaming yellow in the pale sunlight.

"You ain't calculatin' to keep *that*, are you, Mr. Ward?" she began severely.

"No such luck, I'm afraid," answered her employer amiably. "You see, someone has lost him, and when we advertise the owner will claim him."

"Turn him loose, right away, Mr. Ward. A black ox is the worst kind of luck—I tell you if you keep him even one day it'll mean terrible luck!" The words rushed in a torrent from her lips.

"Nonsense. That's just a lot of superstitious rigmarole. Don't you believe it!"

"Mr. Ward"—she spoke desperately—"you don't know! A black ox means death!"

Father's face grew grim and his eyes like gray ice. "Woman," he said quietly, "go back to the house and attend to your own business; I'm still able to run mine."

Hetty turned without another word. As muttering to herself she splashed through the mud and marched to the kitchen, completely forgetting Michal, Gus said apologetically, "Women git foolish notions," and went to the barn.

"He feels right at home here," ventured Michal as the kitchen door slammed behind Hetty.

"Uh-huh," replied John Ward, taking Michal's hand absently in his own.

It was lovely, Michal thought, to be out in the cheerful sunny barnyard again without being muffled to the ears and smothered in heavy wraps. Streams of water ran through the yard, amber colored after it flowed out from under the manure pile that steamed in the sunshine. Ducks and chickens, liberated at last from the confines of winter houses, went contentedly about, shaking their plumage, flapping their wings, and hunting for tender grass shoots.

"I wish I owned him," Father said musingly. "I'll advertise, and perhaps the owner will sell him to me. He'd be good on the breaking plow with the white bull."

Even as he spoke, Michal noticed that the wind had changed. A small chill breeze came from the north; the sun paled and a few ragged flakes of snow zigzagged slowly earthward. She shivered.

Picking her way carefully back to the house, she heard a faint cry. Looking up into the pale blue sky, she heard it again—high, high, above her—the slender silver call of the first killdeer.

Cold weather succeeded, and for days the prairie was beaten by winds while the hoofs of horses rang loud and metallic on the bare frozen roads.

54

VII

Hetty never mentioned the black ox when John Ward was home, but Michal knew by her muttering that every household calamity was blamed on the creature.

By the time the first pasqueflowers were blooming on the sunny slopes of the little round hills across the ravine, Glen and Gus were well into spring's work, while Father was hauling the rest of last year's wheat.

The railroad grade into Leola—now crumbling a bit from erosion and untidy with dead tumbleweeds and thistles—was faintly green with new growth. There was still talk among farmers as to when the steel would be laid. Wheat prices were up, and John Ward decided to sell rather than hold over.

The girls could not get enough of spring sunlight. Rory trotted along with great dignity while they searched for early clumps of the vivid little purplish-pink windflowers huddled in their furry gray-green coats.

One morning Michal, with Rory, started out for the day with spoon and pail. Because Hetty was baking and Faith was making a gingerbread man, this would be a good chance to look for buttercups to plant in a dish for Mother.

Rory headed downhill and Michal followed slowly, looking carefully for the dark green leaves. There were none on this side, so she crossed the ravine east of where the troll lived—no point in taking too many chances—and saw some in the low damp earth beyond.

As she dug and lifted each plant into the pail, Michal thought: It's good to have Glen back. And Lucky Lady, too. Father had let him take the pointer home last fall, and having them here again added to the cheerful confusion of spring.

Even that fat little peddler yesterday had been exciting, in spite of that awful moment just before he left. Mother had bought a boot-shaped glass toothpick holder, needles, pins, and thread; Hetty chose buttons and red ruching, all the while commenting acidly on his scant supply of wares.

It was when Michal had taken him to the barn so that Glen could get some shoelaces that she saw how odd he was—how his queer green eyes kept sliding toward the wheat sacks that were left as he asked questions about last year's crop.

As they left the barn Michal noticed that even though it was cool in the spring sunshine, his face was greasy with sweat. He wiped his head with a dirty red handkerchief, shifted his case to his left hand, and suddenly gripped her upper arm with his fat fingers. "Did you know that you're a pretty little thing?" He had smiled, slanting those strange eyes down over her slim body.

Swift as a prairie bird, Michal slipped out of his grasp and skimmed toward the house. She had felt goosebumpy all over. It was rude not to answer people, so she didn't tell Mother.

Even as the image of that moment shadowed her thoughts, Michal glimpsed some sandhill cranes far up the ravine. This was luck. Gripping Rory's collar and cautioning him to silence, she edged up the hill and along it until they were above and close enough to see clearly the flock feeding quietly west of the Ipswich road.

It was nice to sit here behind a boulder and watch the soft grayish birds, all but one of them moving daintily as they hunted food. Michal had never seen any so close before, and she pressed Rory down—petting and soothing him—as she studied them carefully so she could tell Mother.

The one who stood apart seemed to give a signal, for they all stopped feeding and lifted their heads—listening. Then as Michal heard it too—the far-off rattle of wagons—the cranes ran and took off with cries of alarm. As they gathered momentum they began sailing around in great, ever widening circles—higher, higher—their loud calls —gar-oo-oo-oo, gar-oo-oo-oo—echoing down.

Then the rumble from the south grew louder, and Rory growled. Three wagons, traveling fast, rattled by on the road toward the house.

Michal, with a brief "Come, Rory," started running for home. As they crossed the ravine and ascended the gentle slope that led to the yard, she saw three more wagons pound in from the north on the Leola road and join the others in front of the granary.

Rory was growling deep, and Michal was puzzled as she saw men running from the granary with sacks of wheat and throwing them into the shallow wagon boxes. Probably Father had sent them out to help with the hauling, but it was queer he hadn't said anything about it before he and Gus had left that morning.

As she and Rory entered the yard, her heart lurched. The men were wearing masks—blue work handkerchiefs with two holes for eyes.

In panic she looked toward the house. Where was Mother? The house was quiet, the door closed, the windows empty.

Gripping Rory's collar tightly, Michal—face straight ahead, heart pounding—moved quickly across the yard toward the back door. Something was wrong. She must get into the house. Mother and Faith would be frightened. She must get into the house. She was halfway across the yard when Rory growled, and Michal turned to see a small plump masked figure moving toward her.

She screamed. The figure came on as though it could not hear. A voice shouted: "You, Asa, git over here! We're after wheat, not girls." Still without a sound—like a puppet—the little figure turned and went back, while the man who had yelled strode up to them. Rory growled again.

"You live here?" His voice was muffled.

She nodded.

"Take that dog, git into the house, and stay there."

Shaking, she pulled Rory and stumbled up the steps and in through the kitchen door.

Mavis, holding Faith's hand, and Hetty—eyes glittering—were standing in the center of the room.

"Thank God!" Mother's voice broke; she reached out convulsively and clutched Michal, who, still holding the dog, crowded up against Mavis and Faith.

"Keep quiet!" The order came harshly from the dining room. Michal saw a man, also masked, standing by the window; he held an ugly-looking gun.

It was quiet. The silence was broken only by the sounds of their breathing, and muted clock ticks from the sitting room, and the muffled curses and thuds from the yard.

The pounding of Michal's heart quieted as Faith's cold little hand crept into hers. She felt the same desperate stillness of a tiny wild rabbit they had cornered once down by a stone pile near the wheat field.

What about Little Brother? Michal wondered. She looked at Mother. Mavis was standing very straight, like a statue, never taking her eyes off the intruder in the dining room. Hetty was glaring, her eyes glittering, obviously holding herself back.

The man moved a little. Rory growled deep, then broke suddenly

57

and started for him. There was a curse, a thud, a heart-rending howl as the dog—kicked for the first time in his life—crouched in the doorway, growling, ready to plunge again. Michal grabbed his collar just as Hetty seized the long poker and, bleating shrilly, "I'll kill you fer that, you bastard!" pushed through the door and whacked furiously at the man. He ducked, grabbed the weapon, hurled it away, and shoved her roughly to the kitchen floor.

"Don't try nothin' again, you slut!" he warned savagely.

There was a loud whistle from the yard. The guard moved to the window swiftly, then strode into the kitchen.

"Don't move fer fifteen minutes," he ordered. "We'll shoot anybody we see." And Michal caught the strong smell of dust and sweat as he slammed out.

Hetty rose, swished over, bolted the door, and muttered darkly, "I'm goin' to' git Mr. Ward's gun and give those—" but Mavis interrupted sharply.

"We'll take no chances. Watch the girls while I get the baby!"

As she reentered the kitchen a moment later, there was a little color in her face. Baby Brother, rosy with sleep, had his head nestled as usual in her neck.

From outside came whistles and the sound of whips, then a great rumble as the wagons began to pull out. They crowded cautiously to the windows and peered into the yard. "Well, I'll be jiggered," muttered Hetty. "They's splittin'."

Sure enough, three of the wagons were headed south on the Ipswich road and three were going north toward Leola. Until they were almost out of sight Mavis would not permit a door to be opened. Finally she said: "All right. I believe it's safe to look for Glen now."

Hetty marched out first, followed by the others—Mother still carrying the drowsy baby. The granary was empty, the air thick with settling dust. Hetty sneezed, then warned: "Better let me look into Glen's room first. You girls git back."

She peered into the dimness, then shrieked. "They've kilt 'im Mis' Ward. They've kilt Glen! And Lucky Lady too!"

Without a word Mavis handed Little Brother to Michal and stepped in. The girls followed her unnoticed. At the sight Faith began to cry, and Michal was nearly sick right there. Lucky Lady lay very still just inside the door, her head a bloody pulp. Glen was on the bed, securely bound, his head, shoulders and the pillow covered with blood. But his eyes were open, and he managed a faint grin, saying, "It's about time you got here."

Mavis bent over him, then said quickly: "Hetty, take Faith and get hot water, clean rags, and a knife. Oh, yes, and that old white linen tablecloth, too. Hurry, please!"

"Did they get the wheat, Mrs. Ward?" Glen asked anxiously.

"All that was left. What happened to you?"

"I was busy with the harnesses when first thing I knew the yard was full o' wagons. I ran out, seen the men were masked, and started back so I could get my gun. But somebody must o' hit me over the head, because I come to about the time they was leaving."

Michal burst out, "Were you scared?"

"Didn't have time." He grinned.

Hetty bustled in, followed by Faith, importantly carrying rags. "Here they is, Mis' Ward. My, my." She clicked her tongue, and shook her head sadly, looking at Glen. "Is he gonna live?"

Mavis smiled. "Of course he'll live! Will you cut the rope, please? They surely did a good job."

Then as Hetty sawed away viciously, muttering, "I'd like t' git this knife into them thieves, specially one," Mavis went on cheerfully, "It's only a scalp wound."

Michal's arms were getting tired; but she watched curiously, still feeling a little sick, as Mother gently wiped away the blood, carefully avoiding the clotted wound itself, then bound soft white strips neatly around Glen's head.

"There. How do you feel?"

Glen sat up cautiously, flexing his shoulders and moving his head a little. "Just fine." Then, admiringly, "You're sure good at doctoring." He paused. "I'll take War and get right into town to tell Mr. Ward about what's happened. We want to catch 'em if we can. If you don't mind being alone, that is. Anybody that'll kill a dog is too low to live," he added bitterly.

"Are you strong enough to make the trip?"

"Not without a strong cup a coffee, he ain't," exclaimed Hetty officiously, starting for the house. "I'll bring it right down."

"And a sandwich too," he called. "I'll eat it on my way."

As he thundered off a few minutes later, Hetty, after shooting a sharp glance at Michal and Faith walking ahead, hissed to Mavis, "It's that black ox; that's what it is."

"Nonsense. Please don't talk that way. You know how Mr. Ward feels."

It seemed to Michal that the day would never end. All afternoon, as she moved impatiently from the top of the shed to the highest knoll beyond the ravine then back to the shed again, always watching the road, the soft air had been filled with the liquid trills and *o-ka-leee* of red-winged blackbirds from the slough. Now, with dusk settling over the prairie, the blackbirds were stilled; but the sweet wavering call of killdeer was punctuated by the hoarse abrupt cry of nighthawks far above. At last she saw swift-moving shapes beyond the ravine which meant that Father, Gus, and Glen were coming.

By the time the men had put away the horses, Hetty had supper all ready. Mavis said: "Set the table for all of us, Hetty. We'll eat together tonight."

The men washed up, then burst in—sweaty and tired.

"Are you all right?" asked Father, shooting a piercing glance at Mavis.

"Fine." Mother sighed. "I was so afraid the baby would wake up and cry when that man was in here. Did you catch them?"

"We caught Matt McGuire. Figured he was back of this as soon as Glen got to me with the news." Father spoke with great satisfaction as they all sat down. "Those who went south angled off on a crossroad, and we saw the wheel marks. About three miles from the main road we came to a slough and found Matt beside an empty wagon. He'd been shot through the leg."

"But why?"

"Don't know. He started to talk, then shut up when he saw me. Said, 'I'll see 'em get away before I'd lift a finger to help that—uh—Ward.' "

"But why was he shot?"

"Well, the axle of the wagon was broken; hit a big stone just out of sight under the water. They were in too much of a hurry to go around the slough. Matt probably got into an argument about it with some-body and got shot. So they left him. Don't know that I blame them. He's an ugly customer."

"You mean"—Mavis was incredulous—"that he hates you so much that he protected the men who deserted him?"

60

"Looks like it. Well, I spread the word and the sheriff has scouts out; but this thing was too well planned. I doubt if they'll be found."

Mother sighed. "Well, it's a bad loss. But we're all safe. Until Michal came in I was frantic."

"Where were you, Mike?"

"Watching some cranes down by the ravine." Then Michal told what she had seen, and finished, "You know, the only time I was really scared was when a man came toward me when I was coming through the yard." She paused thoughtfully. "He was about the same size as that peddler who was here yesterday."

John Ward hit the table with a closed brown fist. "That peddler! Spying out the wheat we had left so they'd know how many wagons to bring! I was a fool not to get it!"

"After all, John," interjected Mavis quietly, "even if it was the same man, peddlers are common in the country at this time of year. Why should you have suspected anything?"

"You know," said Hetty, "that man who watched us, Mis' Ward, was probably Matt."

"Maybe," doubtfully. "But masked the way he was, and his voice muffled, it'd be hard to say." Mavis glanced up. Then her dark eyes widened and her voice changed noticeably, "Look!" She was pointing toward the opposite wall where a large portrait of Father—Mother's favorite—was hanging.

In place of eyes two empty holes gaped emptily down on the table. Someone had punched them out.

"And we never seen that till now!" gasped Hetty.

"It's the only one I have." Mother's voice broke as she turned to Father.

"Matt was your guard, all right. Knows this country like the palm of his hand. That's why they *happened* to choose our place. Everything. Probably they split so they could come in by separate roads to some shipping point—maybe Ordway or even Aberdeen. They'll leave the country. But only Matt would hate me enough—and be stupid enough—to do a thing like that."

Gus looked up, mouth full, gulped some water, and spoke between bites. "I think you got it figured right, Mr. Ward. And if you have we'll never see that wheat again. Or the rest a that gang."

John Ward nodded.

Michal spoke up in the silence that followed. "Father, what's a bastard?"

There was a loud clatter as Hetty upset her coffeecup, dabbed violently at the mess, then, muttering vaguely, hastily left for the kitchen.

Father scowled. "What'd you say?"

"You mean bustard," Mavis interrupted smoothly.

"No, Mother," politely. "I'm sure she said bastard."

"Where'd you pick up that word?" John Ward asked curiously.

"Hetty said today, 'I'll kill you, you bastard!' "

Gus choked and coughed noisily into his handkerchief. But Father flung back his head and roared until Mavis interrupted reprovingly, "John!" then turning to Michal, "Hetty said bustard, daughter. It's a sort of bird."

This was too much for Father. He leaned back and laughed until tears streamed down his face.

Mother's cheeks were pink as prairie roses.

Glen and Gus went on eating without once raising their eyes from their plates.

Out in the kitchen Hetty was picking up dishes. She didn't come back to the table.

VIII

By June everything pointed to fine crops. At evening Mavis with Michal and Faith went to the edge of the west field and picked the buds of the wild prairie roses and put them in a glass bowl on the table. By morning the bright red blossoms would be opening, and all day the room would be sweet with their perfume.

The vegetable garden, too, was in good order. Hetty bragged, "If this weather keeps up we'll have a mess of new potaties an' green peas by the Fourth of July, jest like we used to back in Wisconsin."

Now with the haying season so well under way, whenever Michal heard the cheerful *click-click* of the mower she could tell by the distance and direction from whence it came where Gus was mowing—whether upland grass, the meadows along the ravine, or the tough wiry grass fringing the slough.

On this particular morning in June, Michal woke at dawn. Dressing quickly she slipped out. Dew drenched the grass. Spiderwebs stood out in delicate jeweled patterns; the gray-green arrowy leaves and dainty pinkish funnels of wild morning glories along the edge of the garden were spangled with crystal drops. Michal looked back; the sun was up now, and except where she had brushed the dew away the whole grass plot sparkled.

Just beside her were little mounds of fresh black earth. She had noticed them lately and wondered. Gus had said: "They's made by moles, Miss Mike, but not many's lucky enough to see the little critters."

This morning she might see one, for the earth was moving! She could actually see it tremble as the small animal tunneled along just under the surface. She was standing, tense, scarcely breathing for fear she might frighten it, when it appeared—a short, compact little creature, with a pointed muzzle, crouching there resting. The sun shone on its gray fur coat, as thick and soft as shimmering velvet. Impulsively, Michal reached out to touch it, and it was gone.

By eight o'clock the dew was gone. It would be a still hot day, decided Michal, going to the kitchen for a drink as Gus put his head in at the door. "Het, if you can send my dinner out to the field just this side the Oulette slough, I'll not take time to come in at noon. They's a lotta grass out and it'll be a good day for curin', so I wanta clean it up."

"Makin' hay while the sun shines, eh?"

"Haw, haw, haw!" he roared, throwing his head back. Then, wiping his eyes, he went on admiringly: "You allays could turn a mighty neat phrase, Het. That's one reason I took a shine to you."

"Aw, go on, you ol' coot!" But Hetty bridled and smiled. "Sure I'll bring it out to you. They ain't much to do here, and I ain't never seen that Oulette slough."

"May I go, too?" asked Michal. "I'll carry the basket."

"It'll be fine with me. Ask your maw."

They had dinner early, and Hetty stacked the dishes. She was to come back on the first load, but Michal had permission to stay and call on Mrs. Oulette.

Mother stood on the front steps to see them off. "Remember to tell her that when we go to Ipswich to have the photographs taken we'll call. Don't forget to sit near the window so you will see when the second load's ready. Be sure to come home on it."

"All right." And they started, Michal carrying the lunch basket and Hetty a large jug of cold water flavored with vinegar, ginger, and sugar—a prairie cocktail.

Oulette's yard was neat and clean, the bright blue bachelor's-buttons blooming, and the morning-glory vines already covering the lower half of the window. No one was in sight, and the place was so still that Michal hesitated before knocking.

There were quick steps inside before the door was opened cautiously. No recognition gleamed in the dark eyes staring at her intently. "Oh. You are bringing my piano," Louise Oulette said tremulously.

Michal shrank back and her heart began to pound. Then the blank look gradually faded. Mrs. Oulette opened the door wide. "Ah, it is you, little Michal," and as the girl hesitated she took her hand and pulled her gently inside.

"Gus is haying, and Mother said I might stay with you until the load is ready," she explained, seating herself near the window.

"I am very glad you are come; we will drink tea; also I have fresh cake—I baked this morning." And she bustled about the spotless room.

She filled the teakettle and put it forward on the shining black-leaded stove: then coming to set the table she picked up a litter of sheet music strewn over it. "I sometimes take it out to read and pretend I'm playing it again," she remarked, smiling apologetically as she stooped to put it on the lower shelf of her bookcase.

Michal looked through the shining window. Glen was just bringing the hayrake. In spite of the cheerful table with its white cloth and dainty china and the morning-glory vines twining up the white cords, the room somehow seemed lonely. Maybe Mrs. Oulette could explain about death. But no, it might make her more sad.

"You are troubled today, Michal," her hostess said gently. "Wait. I know something to make you glad." She brought from the top of her book shelves a large spiraled shell. Placing the delicate yellow-pink lip to Michal's ear, she whispered excitedly, "Listen! Hear the song of the sea?"

Michal listened breathlessly. She really heard it—a faint sound, far-away yet deep. She turned to her hostess. "It's beautiful," she breathed.

"I knew you would enjoy it. I listen to it always when the sound of the wind in the long grass I can no longer endure."

"Then I mustn't take it. Mother wouldn't like me to."

64

"No, it is yours. I no longer need it!"

They drank fragrant tea from thin cups and ate dainty slices of the cake. "This is much joy for me!" Louise Oulette said happily as they finished.

"It has been fun," agreed Michal. Even so, she felt relieved when she saw that the load was nearly ready. She rose. "I must go now," she said politely. "Thank you for such a lovely time," hoping she sounded just like Mother.

Mrs. Oulette smiled, well pleased. "Do not forget to take your little present," she reminded her. "So young, you should be always happy —this may help."

She walked part way to the meadow with Michal. "Tell your dear mother I shall look for her that day she go to Epsweech—or sooner if she can come," she said as they parted.

As they left the hay field, Michal looked back. Mrs. Oulette stood on the flat stone doorstep and waved at her, and as Michal waved back she felt she could not wait to get home. I hope I never go alone to see her again, she thought; but even so, I love her.

As the loaded hay wagon creaked ponderously up the hill from the ravine, Michal's own home reached out to her, warm and safe. From the yard she smelled the smoke of a fresh wood fire in the cookstove. Faith and Rory came running to meet her, and as she went inside Baby Brother gurgled from his quilt on the sitting-room floor. Mother turned with her slow smile. Impulsively Michal started to pour out her bewilderment, then stopped. Only Uncle Fred could explain about Mrs. Oulette. Perhaps she could ask him if he came for the hunting in the fall.

Michal excused herself from the supper table as soon as she dared. Tiptoeing to her bookcase drawer, she hid the shell under her apron, slipped out the front door, and ran to the pigweed patch. She sat down on her little box, leaned her head forward, and putting the smooth lip to her ear, listened. The faint sound came. It was wonderful, like the magic carpet, she thought, to go so quickly from the prairie to where —as Mother often sang—

> "The rivulets gushing in coral caves,
> At intervals dripped in the dark blue waves,"

as she heard once again—faintly—the far-off sound of the sea.

65

IX

By the first of July the prairie roses were nearly gone, and bees bumbled over the thistle blooms in the pasture. Michal brought home bouquets for the house—great bunches of purple and white prairie clover with coneflowers from the hills.

The long days of haying season were over. The barn mow was full to bursting, and in the hay yard near the barn three immense stacks—fragrant and well cured—were stored, each anchored against the danger of being blown apart by lengths of rope thrown over them at regular intervals, the ends of each rope weighed down by large rocks.

Oulette's slough was almost dry now; the tall wiry grass had been cut for a month, and when the news leaked out that Haar had rented the rich alkali-free land for the fall there was much amusement and speculation.

"Wonder what that furriner's up to now?" asked Gus of Hetty. "He sure wouldn't be crazy enough to plant winter wheat in Dakota Territory—besides, it's too small for that."

"I'm not a-sayin'," returned his wife, "but mebbe you'd best wait an' see before you call him too crazy. He seems to be doin' right well, what with his woman workin' like a Percheron mare and all the young uns hoeing potatoes, besides him takin' milk and eggs to town every week."

Haar gave out no information. He broke the slough bottom, dragged and disked the black silty bed, and sowed something in it.

By the time early goldenrod brightened the hills, the grain needed rain badly. Dry weather was very well for haying, but all the hay was cut. As bright day followed bright day with the same blue sky and brassy sun, and never a trace of cloud shadow to darken the earth beneath, the homesteaders began shaking their heads as they squinted toward the shimmering horizon.

The little seedlings on the tree claim were hard hit. Glen transplanted a load of those still alive down to the dam, where they took courage and began putting down roots in the black dampish soil.

66

"See how my willow's growing, Father; it'll soon be tall as the trees in the picture of the Lazy Dog."

"Seems as though your tree's the only thing on the place that's done what we thought it would," said John Ward bitterly.

The garden began to wilt; Gus hauled barrels of water on the stoneboat from the lower well and gave it relief. Then the wheat stalks began yellowing at the base, and the well in the lower pasture went dry. Panting birds with outstretched wings rested fearlessly in the shade of the buildings.

On a warm sticky Sunday in mid-July, the Wards were finishing breakfast. In spite of the heat that made his dark hair curl damply about his rosy face, Little Brother was bubbling over with joy as he sat in his highchair and tried to feed Rory his mush.

Father looked up from a volume of the *Encyclopaedia* as Mother spoke:

"Let's make that trip to Ipswich this week, John. If what I suspect is true, it'd be as well to have a family group taken; and it would be such a relief to get off the place—it has been about a year now," she finished wistfully.

"I ran into Doc Broome on the street yesterday, Mavis. He said this heat's been hard on babies—four died of summer complaint lately. We'd better wait till this infernal heat lets up; I'd rather have a live boy than a fine photograph."

Mother reached over quickly and covered Little Brother's fat hand with her slender one. "I'll take no chances with him," she said, her eyes darkening. "We'll wait."

That afternoon, like huge dragons breathing, hot winds came, crisping the prairie grass, wilting the garden, withering the remaining little box elders and willows on the tree claim until they looked like dead twigs stuck in the dry ground; and, worst of all, shriveling the glutinous wheat kernels.

At night a sunburned moon shone warmly over the prairie. The dragon winds stirred in their sleep; breathing lightly over the desolate wheat fields, they rattled the faded, brittle stalks.

Mrs. Tannyhill sat in the sitting room and fanned her red face with her slat sunbonnet. "It's hotter'n all Gehenna, ain't it, Mis' Ward? I come over to tell you I'm leaving the country."

"When?"

"Just as soon as I can get packed."

"How long will you stay?"

"Oh—I'm going for good. It's bad enough with the cold winters, but when the heat cooks my potatoes right in the hills that's too much."

"But your place—and stock?"

"Don't you worry about them—Herman Haar has been at me and at me to sell him my relinquishment—so I did, yesterday; the cow and chickens too," she added with great satisfaction.

"I'm sorry; we'll miss you, and I'd looked forward to having—" She broke off suddenly and turned to Michal, "Will you ask Hetty to bring us a pitcher of cold water and glasses on the tray?"

Michal came back as soon as she could. Mavis was saying, "Of course, I wouldn't have chosen February, but . . ." Her voice trailed away.

"If I'd stay for anybody in this God-forsaken country, I'd stay for you. But I can't stand another month of it!"

"I don't blame you. Well, it'll mean Ipswich for me. I know how you feel about the prairie, but John doesn't see it. He's taken the death of the trees harder than the loss of the grain. In his dreams of our future he's always seen the Tree Claim as a place of quiet groves where our neighbors would come for picnics and Fourth of July celebrations."

"They'll never be any trees in Dakota Territory," said Mrs. Tannyhill with sweeping finality. "Did you ever find out who stole your wheat that time?"

"Only the one they caught, Matt McGuire."

"I think it was that bunch of riffraff down southwest. They left that place they'd rented, kit and kaboodle, and ain't never come back—what's that smell?" she interrupted herself to ask, sniffing audibly.

"Hetty's wild stubble-berry pies; we'll have some, with coffee."

"Stubble berries? You mean them little purple ones? They're poison. Maw used to call 'em deadly nightshade! I wouldn't as much as touch 'em."

"Michal," Mother said pleasantly, "will you please ask Hetty to serve us cookies and tea before Mrs. Tannyhill goes?"

As they ate and drank, Mother half apologized for the flies. "What do you do about them? They seem to creep in somewhere in spite of the mosquito bar at the windows."

Mrs. Tannyhill looked carefully about the room. "Flies? Say, Mis' Ward, you don't even know what flies is. You should see them at my

68

house! Every mealtime a solid rim of 'em are around every dish. Only thing I know is to shake a weed over the table while vittles is on."

"They're awful. I can't bear them about food and I hate having them near the baby."

"My, but he looks well—almost too well. Are you sure that flush on his cheeks ain't fever?"

"He's always had good color," said Mavis, but she lifted the boy to her lap, where he cuddled down contentedly and presently slept.

"They's more poison around this place than stubble berries," remarked Hetty gloomily after the midwife's departure.

"You mean her?" asked Michal, but Hetty shook her head and smiled grimly with a meaning look out toward the desolate west wheat field where the black ox was peacefully grazing with the other cattle. Hetty still didn't mention him in the presence of Mr. Ward, but by her mutterings she had given Michal to know that she was still brooding about it.

The morning after Mrs. Tannyhill's visit, Little Brother was fretful and languid. His cheeks were flushed, and when he refused his breakfast John Ward said, uneasily, "We'd better have Dr. Broome, Mavis."

"Let's do," said Mother slowly, "particularly since there are so many sick children now. He hasn't been himself for several days—but it's just his teeth, I think."

"I'm not going to town until he's better. I'll send Glen."

Dr. Broome was there before noon. "I see no cause for immediate alarm," he said noncommittally, after a brief examination, removing his eyeglasses and dangling them from a black silk band. "He's teething and seems to have some temperature. Give him one of these powders dissolved in a little water every three hours. If he is no better in a day or so, I'll come out again."

"I didn't like his manner, did you?" asked Mother anxiously after the doctor had gone.

"Not particularly, but he's always been a pompous old duck," said Father; then, seeing how pale Mother looked, he patted her hand. "Don't worry, Mavis; those powders'll bring the boy out of it."

Two mornings later Michal woke to the whirr of the coffee mill as Hetty ground the roasted berries for breakfast. She vaguely recalled that the night had been full of murmurs, quiet confusion, and Little Brother's fretful crying. Mrs. Tannyhill was there, insisting that Mother lie down and rest. "You've been up all night, poor dear, and I can take over."

"Thank you, but I won't leave my baby," said Mavis quietly. "There's the doctor now. John, bring him in, will you?"

After Mrs. Tannyhill had left with Faith to do her own chores, Michal wandered nervously into the kitchen.

Hetty was slumped in a chair by the table, her face hidden in her hands. Michal shivered. The house was filled with some new terrible thing.

She was tiptoeing from the room when Father strode in. "The doctor wants a spoon—what's the matter with you, Hetty?" he asked irritably.

Hetty Perkins sprang to her feet and burst into a wild torrent of words. "What's the matter with me, you ask? Well, I'll tell you! You know I told you, John Ward—I said nothing but bad luck and death would come of a black ox. I knew it, and I told you to get rid of him. I'm going crazy—I can't stay here any longer. That baby is going to die—I know it!"

John Ward grasped her arm roughly. He spoke slowly, each word like a little piece of ice. "Go, damn it! But for God's sake stop your blather! Hasn't Mavis enough to bear without you making a fool of yourself? Pack your things and get the hell out of here."

He went to the cupboard, took a silver spoon from the spoon holder, and quickly left the room. Then the door opened softly, and Mavis came in. She crossed to where the distracted woman stood and put her hand on her arm. "Hush, Hetty," she said gently. "I don't know what we'll do without you, but you mustn't stay if you're unhappy."

Hetty wiped her eyes on her apron, threw her arms awkwardly around Mavis's neck, and sobbed: "No, Mis' Ward, I can't leave you like this. If you can stand it I oughta be able to stick it out."

Michal sidled out, called Rory, and started over to the hills across the ravine. The buffalo grass, as brittle and dry from drought as it usually was after heavy frosts, was crisp under her tread. She made for a boulder on top of the hill and, resting on it, looked about. In all the country she could see from the hill there were only two green spots—the little trees down by the dam and the slough bed Haar had planted, now showing the vivid tender green of young plants.

Rory wandered off after ground squirrels and she did not call him back; she might as well be all alone. There were no flowers; only a few

70

ragged stalks of what had been prairie asters and the whitened plumes of goldenrod gone prematurely to seed. She sat a long time until the prairie's withered desolation filled her with a feeling of emptiness and complete aloneness. Then she went slowly homeward.

The doctor's rig was in the yard. He came out as she neared the place, Father with him. Michal veered so she need not meet them—they were both a part of the aloneness. They shook hands and the doctor drove away. Father, head bowed, went slowly back inside.

Michal went down and sat behind a haystack out of sight of the house. Rory came, panting, and threw himself at her feet. Down by the dam a solitary killdeer teetered and swayed over the cracked muddy earth only lately covered with water. All the ordinary familiar sounds of living had stopped. Michal could hear the silence, punctuated only by the plaintive pe-ep, pe-ep of the killdeer searching for food. She sat while the constant peevish pe-ep, pe-ep, pe-ep, pe-ep, over and over, pe-ep, pe-ep, pe-ep, pe-ep, rang in the silence. Except for it, all of life seemed ended. Before the red sun sank below the far-off rim of the dun prairie, the monotonous cry of the bird drove her to the house.

The silence and loneliness followed her; tiptoeing to the door of the bedroom she turned the knob softly and saw Mother stretched face down on the bed and Father leaning over her. They did not see nor hear her. Maybe she could find Hetty. But the back bedroom was quiet. Tapping, she listened, then entered. The shades were down; on the bed was something covered with a sheet. Michal tiptoed over, lifted the sheet and looked into the face of Little Brother. He was sleeping with his hands folded on his breast. The sleep was still. His little face and hands were like Mother's white wax candle—but Little Brother wasn't there at all. The room was empty. Michal quickly replaced the sheet and went out.

The day of the funeral the Haars came early, and Herman Haar said to Mavis in his broken English, "Mine Frau vould mit you speak vonce?"

Mavis went into the room with the huge woman; Michal followed.

Mrs. Haar handed Mother something wrapped in a spotless white cloth and pointed to the little casket. Mother unwrapped it—a tiny pillow made of softest down and covered with a linen case in the exact center of which, against a light blue silk background, a square of beautiful old linen lace was knitted in a pattern of the Christ Child with Mary

71

in the manger, while Joseph, leaning on his staff, watched the shepherds kneeling in adoration. Above hung a great star.

Mavis stood looking at the lace picture, traced it with her finger as though memorizing it, then moved to where Little Brother lay and carefully put it under his head. Then, as she looked up at her neighbor in mute thanks and saw the big tears rolling down the tanned cheeks, she turned suddenly, hiding her face on the other's shoulder. For the first time since Little Brother's death she sobbed out her pent-up grief, while the German-Russian woman patted her shoulder tenderly and quieted her with little soothing words Michal could not understand.

The funeral was held in the sitting room. Mother wore her black cashmere dress with white ruching at the throat. She seemed to be sleeping with her eyes open, for she didn't notice anyone.

Many people came whom Michal did not know. Faith wanted to sit by Mother, but Mrs. Tannyhill held her, and she was too shy to try to break away. Mrs. Oulette sat opposite Michal. She wore black. She did not once look up or even bow her head when the minister prayed, just sat with her hands folded tightly in her lap, looking straight ahead, her face as still as Little Brother's.

The minister, a tall frail man from Ipswich, talked a while, but said nothing interesting, Michal thought. She watched him closely and with flattering attention, however, for his arms and legs were much too long for the rest of him, and whenever he walked or waved an arm in gesture it gave him the appearance of being about to fold up—like Father's four-bladed jackknife.

Finally he sat down, and two men and two women who had come with him from town stood up and sang mournfully, "Go, Bury Thy Sorrow," while another woman played the organ. All the women except Mother and Mrs. Oulette cried.

As the procession of carriages started away from the house, Michal still felt alone, even though she sat between Father and Mother. Mother didn't hold her hand; she seemed in some awful dream that Father shared with her.

The long line crossed the ravine, reached the top of the hill, turned west, and near the very boulder where Michal had sat alone so long the day before, the little grave was waiting. They all left their carriages and gathered near the grave, the family nearest, the others apart—and farther away, the men with heads bared. The minister read something, the same four sang "Nearer, My God to Thee"; then, as the minister said something about ashes and dust, a man dropped a few clods from a shovel into the grave.

Michal's heart pounded. They were leaving Little Brother here alone. She groped for Mother's hand; but, as before at dusk that first night at the homestead, Mother's hand reached hers first and held it tight. Then Mrs. Oulette was running toward the man with the shovel, crying hoarsely, "No! No!" and clutching his arm, gasping "No!" when her husband reached her, gripped her firmly by the arms, whispered something to her, and almost dragged her, still struggling, to their carriage and drove quickly away.

Others followed, and as they left Little Brother and started home, Michal, looking back, saw that two men were already shoveling earth into the grave.

Mrs. Tannyhill helped Hetty, and they soon had supper nearly ready. They made Mother lie down, and Hetty set the little round table in the front bedroom where the four of them could be by themselves. Michal was restless—she wanted to do something to make home seem less lonely. Then she remembered what Mother had said about the potpourri, "To be opened in times of great joy or great sorrow." Going to the mantel she took off the covers, stirred the contents with a spill, and replaced the pierced top. Then Hetty called her to supper. Mother could not eat; but after the rest of them had finished, Michal went over and stood by Father's chair. Though he had Faith on his knee, he leaned over and, putting his arm around Michal, drew her close. She looked up and met his gaze, and saw that he was really seeing her again. The tenseness left her, and she sighed her relief as she relaxed. The spicy fragrance of the potpourri filled the room.

X

The weeks following the death of Little Brother were monotonously dry and hot; occasional grasshoppers, their black wings bordered red, flew with shrill nerve-rasping noises over the dead wheatfields where cattle had been turned to forage. Earlier this year than usual, Glen worked on firebreaks. He plowed two wide parallel strips along the

73

boundaries of the place, burning off, on calm days, the grass between them.

By the middle of September, the stock had finished the shattered grainfields, but a fine large hay crop was stored in long stacks behind the barn; the garden, when dug, revealed many, if small, potatoes, some carrots, beets, and onions. The rest of the late garden stuff had not been worth gathering. Hetty had had plenty to say to Michal as to why conditions were so bad, and Michal began to wonder if there might not, after all, be something to her ideas about the black ox.

On a windy Sunday in September, John Ward, after a late breakfast, sat by the table taking account of the year's work.

"How have you made out?" asked Mavis, pouring a second cup of coffee.

"Not too well; the Percherons and the binder cut into my profits."

"Haar told Gus he did rather well this year. Do you think you did as well as he?"

"There's no comparison," returned John Ward, a touch of irritation in his tone. "In the first place he sells all his eggs, most of his milk and cream; they drink skim milk and churn the little cream they keep; then he's selling those winter turnips he raised in Oulette's slough to everybody for miles around. I'll have to admit that was a very good business deal for him. But he works his wife and children like slaves, and they spend practically nothing for food and clothing—just scrimp and save from one year to the next. He'll make out, all right!"

"Will you make it, John?"

"Why not? Haar's done better this year, but in a contest between modern and primitive methods there's no chance for him in the long run. Next year I'll show him."

"But what about this year?"

"If it hadn't been for this blasted drought," impatiently, "we'd be in fine shape. There was an A-number-one hay crop; and since no one answered my advertisements about the black ox he was what you'd call a gift from God. Then I have all the latest equipment. We can't expect luck to always come our way. With this free land and plenty to eat, in a few years we'll be living like lords."

By now a stiff breeze was blowing; Michal excused herself and ran down by the dam to look at her willow tree. The leaves were shedding, sailing like tiny golden boats on a sea of wind. When she stood against

74

the trunk, she saw that, despite its slanting, it had grown. She rushed back to the house to tell Mother.

Mavis was looking out of the front window. Across the prairie huge tumbleweeds, wind-driven, rolled clumsily in mad haste over the ground; but Michal knew she was not noticing them—her eyes were fixed on the hill across the ravine. She didn't turn or give any indication that she knew of Michal's presence. The girl stood beside her mother until she could no longer stand the silence. "What's wrong?"

"So lonely. Last year I had Louise Oulette and—" She broke off, then went on in a low voice: "Today, back home, people are walking to church. They can hear the sound of church bells. And there are trees instead of tumbleweeds."

"We'll soon have trees here, too," Michal spoke eagerly. "My little willow is tall now."

Mavis did not answer but placed her hand on her daughter's shoulder, and they stood looking out at the erratic procession of the tumbleweeds.

Suddenly Mother drew in her breath sharply. "John, come here!" Following her gaze, Michal saw far off to the southeast a dust devil spiraling faintly black against the horizon.

Father took one look, then, followed by his wife and daughter, started for the barn; Gus and Glen were running toward the house. Gus pointed and said briefly, "Good thing we did the firing on them breaks —looks like we'll have use for 'em right now." The spiral was larger now, and nearer, and Michal saw that it was not a dust devil but the black smoke of a prairie fire rushing toward them.

"It's heading for up the ravine—that's where the grass is thickest," said Glen, excitedly.

"Well, we're all right, and Haar finished backfiring yesterday. Ol' Lady Tannyhill's place is protected by ours—how about Oulette's?" asked Father.

"I dunno. We'd best go over an' see."

Gus loaded the buckboard with barrels while Glen hitched the high-steppers to it. John Ward found gunny sacks and threw them in the buckboard, then began drawing water from the deep well and filling the trough barrels. By the time the men had the barrels filled Hetty came out with jugs of water mixed with vinegar, sugar, and ginger to refresh them during the hard, thirsty work of fire fighting. Glen—in

75

spite of his protests—was delegated to stay home and patrol the east side so that no burning tumbleweed or whirling disk of dried cow chip could roll across the barrier and start fires on the Ward place.

The high-steppers were off, and the grumbling Glen filled two barrels on the stoneboat, covered them with gunny sacks, hitched the black ox and white bull to it and went, still muttering, down to the southeast line.

"Michal"—Mother turned to her, her face flushed and her words coming with a rush—"let's climb the knoll at the southwest corner of our place and watch the fire."

"Don't you do it, Mis' Ward!" implored Hetty. "Supposin' the fire'd jump the break—any kind of bad luck can happen around here these days."

"There's not a bit of danger. Glen is patrolling. Besides, I'm worried about the Oulettes. The knoll is just opposite their house, and I'd rather go there now than wait until the men come back with news."

"Well, if you feel that way, I'll do the work and look after Faith—you go along."

By the time they reached the top of the knoll, the air was full of acrid smoke. Jackrabbits were loping up the ravine, and a cottontail scuttled past them into the west wheatfield. Then small gold serpents of fire writhed through the short crisp prairie grass and struck with hissing tongues at the tops of the longer grasses in the ravine. A large crouching animal with tufted ears ran ahead of the crackling flames. "A lynx!" Mavis exclaimed, pulling Michal back; but it only glanced at them with big round eyes and snarled without pausing in its flight. Close behind it bounded a half grown antelope fawn, the first Michal had ever seen. Rory trembled and whimpered and strained at the leash.

A solitary whooping crane, stately even in the haste of fear, ran from the covert of dry rushes that rimmed Oulette's slough and took off ponderously, uttering deep hoarse notes of alarm. They watched the great white bird until it was lost to sight and its sonorous clamor faded into silence.

The flaming serpents whirled and twisted in fury up the ravine, leaving a charred path behind them from which rose small smoky spirals where dried cattails still burned along the rim of the slough.

"Look! Their place is safe!" exclaimed Mother.

The smoke was lifting, and the men were still beating out small fires with wet gunny sacks.

76

"There's Louise Oulette coming out of the house now."

"Maybe she's seen us and is coming over to talk. I've missed her this summer."

"So have I."

But Louise Oulette had not seen them. She was looking west up the ravine as though watching the retreating fire. Then, throwing her arms above her head, she laughed—not the low liquid sound Michal knew, but strange, shrill laughter that carried to them across the distance.

"Mother! What—"

"I don't know; I'm afraid this excitement—"

"Should we go to her?"

"No!" Mother spoke decisively.

"Why not?"

"The doctor won't let her have callers."

They looked again; the smoke had cleared now and the woman was dancing, her slight figure moving lightly over the blackened earth from which wisps of smoke spiraled thinly like gray veils. The men watched as Mr. Oulette led her into the house.

"It might be as well not to mention that we came up here today," suggested Mavis as they turned away.

Michal nodded.

The men, smudged and grimy, reached home shortly after them. As they gathered around the table to enjoy Hetty's good dinner, John Ward told them what had happened. "When we got to Oulette's, Pierre had just finished backfiring. He took us in for coffee; then we went out to watch for burning tumbleweeds—their firebreak is only half wide enough anyway, and it made me uneasy. We had a hard time of it when the fire came roaring up the ravine after it passed the slough. Twice it jumped the breaks, but we were lucky and pounded it out with wet sacks. Then as the wind veered a little and the fire rushed past and away I heard a sound behind me. It was Mrs. Oulette."

"Was she awfully upset?" asked Mother.

"God, yes! First she stared up the ravine after the fire, then gave sort of a scream and began dancing in the smoke and all. She kept moaning about the wind in the grass—over and over. Damnedest thing I ever saw." Father blew his nose violently, then went on quietly: "Be-

77

fore we left, Pierre thanked us for our help, then took her inside. I felt for him."

"Pity the poor woman, John. She has no business here on this prairie."

XI

By November the ground was frozen. This year John Ward had not objected when Gus had banked up to the window sills of the house with fresh straw and horse manure. Nor did he seem to mind other little economies. The Dutch oven in the dining room was in use now, and from the stack of slough hay Gus twisted huge skeins that burned up fiercely. That helped save the hard coal for the extreme weather.

One dark leaden morning Michal lay listening to the familiar sound of Haar's geese calling hoarsely after a late flock going south. Mother and Father were talking quietly; then Father's voice rose impatiently.

"I tell you, Mavis, I want you to go to Ipswich this month or next at the latest. The snow'll be here any time now, and I'd like to feel that you're settled safely close to a doctor."

"John"—Mother's voice was amused—"the baby isn't due until February. I wouldn't think of going so early. The girls would be lost without me."

Michal sat up with a jerk. A baby! Another baby!

"I don't like it. Hetty can take good care of the girls. What if we're snowed in? What if—"

"You know I always go—go full time."

"Yes, but—"

"I tell you"—Mother's voice was tense—"I'd go mad in a hotel room with nothing to do but think of—everything. And I'd worry so about Michal and Faith. They need me. I can't go now." Her voice broke. "I can't. I just can't."

"There, there." Father's tone was soothing, and Michal relaxed. "I didn't know you felt that way. You needn't go until you want to. How's that?" Heartily.

Mother's voice was muffled. "I promise to go in January sometime. That'll be a month early. But I can't go sooner."

Michal sank back, reflecting. So there'd be a new baby. Mother had been moving more slowly these days, the way she had when they'd first come here. And she was bigger through the middle, too, now that Michal thought of it—like she'd been before Little Brother was born. It was strange she hadn't realized.

When the weather grew cold the last week in November, Father decided it would be safe to butcher. The day the men worked butchering the hogs and yearling beef Michal stayed in the house and stuffed her fingers in her ears whenever the agonized squeals pierced the quiet.

For days Hetty was busy grinding sausage and making headcheese and lard; the house smelled of sage and cracklings. Finally the meats were all stored in the granary—all but half the beef which Haar took as his share. Later he would butcher a beef and give John Ward half of it.

Then, early in December, the snow came—feebly at first—feathery flakes drifting aimlessly. With them came snow buntings, whirling in little eddies with the wind like dead leaves from some great tree. By night the snow was coming straight down in small business-like flakes.

When John Ward went to town and they were short of oil, Mavis thawed the frost from the windowpane with a warm flatiron, put a twisted rag in a can of grease in the window, and lighted it to guide her husband over the snow.

One night he came home with news of Mrs. Oulette. "I saw Pierre in town, Mavis; he was taking his wife on the afternoon train to Yankton."

"Oh, no!" Mavis paled. "Is it—"

"Pretty bad; two women from the institution were there. It took them both."

Mavis's eyes were bright with tears. Finally she said quietly, "The wares of this prairie country are sometimes too dearly bought, John."

"Well, it's a pity; but people go off everywhere," said Father matter-of-factly. "Oulette is selling out to Haar. And his grocery store to Lightener. He's going back to Canada."

Michal slid her head under the covers as tears slipped down over her cheeks into her ears. Something terrible, something she didn't quite understand, had happened to Mrs. Oulette. She would never see her again. Never hear the liquid voice so like the ok-a-lee of the blackbirds.

79

Later that month, after the kerosene accident, Father tried once more to persuade Mavis to go to Ipswich. The storekeeper had sold John Ward gasoline by mistake. When the lamp flame flared up, Mavis had risen awkwardly, lurched against the table, and had then fallen heavily just as Father grabbed the lamp, ran to the front door, and flung it violently out into the snow.

There had been another kind of excitement. Mother had cried out and bent over suddenly, her body making a big clumsy shadow on the wall.

"Maybe I better take her to town." Father had spoken frantically. "My God, we can't have anything happen here! No doctor—no midwife even."

But Mavis was calm. "John, control yourself." She bent convulsively, relaxed, then went on: "If anything is going to happen, going to town won't help. You and Hetty will have to manage, that's all."

Hetty boiled water and Father paced nervously, but that was all. For hours Michal lay listening. Hetty and Father kept watch, while Gus slept so that he could carry on with the next day's work. By midnight the pains had stopped. Hetty left then with a final, "Now you call me, Mr. Ward, if anything starts again."

Once, Michal heard Mavis's voice, "I don't think I could bear it if anything happened to this one—I just couldn't bear it."

"You'll be all right." Now that the danger seemed to be over, Father was quieting Mother. "By God, we won't let anything happen to this one." Then, confidently: "You'll go to town, Mavis? It'll be hard, but you see now it's the only thing to do."

"No. I'm sorry to be stubborn but I've never had my babies early, and this one won't be either. I'll be extra careful now and stay in bed more. I'm not going to Ipswich until January." From the sitting room Michal heard Father's sigh, as sharp as a curse.

This was the winter of the deep snow. Father had to dig steps from the door of the stormshed up to the surface one morning after new snow had fallen on the already deep drifts about the house.

After the half darkness inside, the only touches of color were the red gash of barn under the eaves and the red brick chimney of the house, out of which a delicate blue-gray feathering of smoke wavered and thinned away. Rory gamboled about, warm as toast in his heavy red-bronze coat.

80

One end of the Ward pighouse was crushed, and eleven shoats were killed. "I wonder how much the Haars lost," observed Michal.

"If Haar lost anything it'd be his family, not his stock," observed Father bitterly. "That barn of his would stand through a cyclone."

"Shouldn't you make it over soon," asked Mavis hesitantly, "to see if they're all right?"

"I saw smoke coming from that direction today, but I'm going to send Gus over. Don't worry about them. They may even be living in the barn, but they're safe."

Michal thought, Father doesn't make fun of Mr. Haar any more.

After they were all in bed Michal heard Mother ask, "Then we'll have to make everything for Christmas, John?"

"I'm afraid so. It's a shame, but there's no help for it."

"Well, Hetty and Michal and I can do a lot. We'll center things around Faith." Mother's voice thickened a little.

"We'll give her a bang-up time of it," Father said hastily, then: "You can see now, Mavis, why I wanted you in town. This snow makes me nervous as hell."

"I wouldn't be anywhere else." Her voice tightened. "We'll give the girls a happy Christmas—then some nice day in January you'll take me in to Ipswich."

"Well, I'll be glad when it's over. By God, I hope we never have another winter baby!"

"We can't always plan these things," returned his wife quietly.

Michal was trembling. Somehow the talk had made her think of Little Brother, in the earth under the deep snow. She was glad his head was resting on the soft pillow with the lace-trimmed cover.

However, Christmas was more exciting than ever. There were rag dolls for the girls made from Father's socks and real hair the exact color of Mother's; wristlets knit of green and yellow yarn; popcorn balls put together with maple sirup; homemade taffy, big gingerbread men, and rock candy just like Father used in his hot toddies.

For the girls there was a homemade sled—carved of wood with strips of smooth metal for runners—and painted bright red. The best present of all was for Mother—a cradle, glowing softly in the dimness of the room. Father and Gus had made it from an old cherry bedstead, and Hetty had used the best sheep's wool for the mattress.

Hetty had outdone herself this year. "At least there's plenty o' vittles," she had said gloomily. "A fine Christmas! No box from Mr. Gordon or the other relatives. Mis' Ward in bed and working her fingers to the bone gittin' things ready." She peered at Michal slyly. "You know why it is, don't you?"

"The black ox?" Michal's voice sank to a whisper.

"Ya. That evil critter. Don't you talk about it to yer father, though."

"I won't. But I've had fun this year."

Hetty shook her head. "There'll never be anything right in this house again till that there black devil's gone—gone or daid!"

After dinner the men went out to do the chores, and Michal curled up in a chair in front of the base burner with the copy of *Little Women* which Uncle Fred had sent for her birthday in the fall, and turned to the chapter "Jo Meets Apollyon."

But something was wrong. Fiery coals were dropping softly into the grate, Faith was asleep, Michal had her book, but Mother . . .

Mavis was sitting quietly, her face set, gazing fixedly at the sofa. Michal looked too. It was quite empty; yet she seemed to be watching something. Then Michal knew. This was just like last year. Only Little Brother had been sitting here, propped up, playing with bright paper. And Mother was remembering. Michal closed her eyes. The day was no longer good. The room wasn't cozy, now, but chilled with Mother's despair.

Mavis rose slowly and seated herself at the organ. After pulling out some stops, she touched the keys gently with her slim fingers and sang softly in her low voice:

> " 'Backward, turn backward, O Time, in your flight,
> Make me a child again just for tonight!
> Mother, come back from that echoless shore,
> Take me again to your heart as of yore;
>
> . . . .
>
> Over my slumbers your loving watch keep
> Rock me to sleep, mother,—rock me to sleep!' "

Fat silver tears were splashing onto Michal's book, making damp marks. She kept her back turned to her mother and made no sound. Mavis was singing something else, but Michal didn't hear. Her tears were still falling.

82

XII

In January, Mavis finally began her preparations for the trip to Ipswich. "I dread leaving," she told Hetty one day, "but Mr. Ward is nervous about my being here even now."

"When do you figger on goin', Mis' Ward?"

"Early next week. I'll have—as nearly as I can tell—about three weeks in Ipswich and at least two or three weeks there after—" She raised her eyebrows and paused, glancing at Michal and Faith, who were watching Hetty as she packed bedding in the bottom of the big trunk. The girls looked eagerly whenever it was opened, for on the cover of the tray was a picture of an alluring lady—brightly colored—in basque, polonaise, and beautiful high bonnet.

"Mother, won't we see you all that time?"

"I'm afraid not." Mavis took a small snowy pile of freshly ironed ruffled baby dresses from a chair and fitted them carefully into the tray. Michal recognized them as having belonged to Little Brother. "We'll do the pinning-blankets tomorrow, and my nightdresses," Mother was saying when Father strode in.

"Well, I'm glad to see you're really packing. I can drive you in any time now."

"I'm getting ready early, John, so I won't forget a thing."

"Mavis"—Father towered over her, his lean brown hands resting lightly on his hips—"I think that I'm going to insist on your finishing immediately and going in with me. This weather may not last. I've been damned patient—" He paused significantly.

Mother's chin rose; for a minute soft dark eyes clashed with hard gray ones. Then Mavis relaxed, and smiled faintly. "Very well. Since you feel so strongly about it, I'll go in early."

"Could you be ready by tomorrow morning? Looks like most of the packing's done." He was watching her closely.

"Well," slowly, "I suppose I could."

"Good!" John Ward whirled to leave the room.

"Even though," Mother added to his retreating back, "I consider it entirely unnecessary."

Father did not answer.

Hetty began to scold. "Mis' Ward, you know you hadn't ought to try to finish today. Now you set right on the bed, and I'll bring everything to you."

"But I feel so well, I'm sure we can do it." Mother's cheeks were delicately flushed, her eyes bright.

By midafternoon the trunk and bags were finished. At first, Mavis stayed quiet, but before they were finished she was moving about briskly, bending, lifting, and shoving in the manner of women packing.

"There!" She closed the trunk, then pushed the dark hair back from her forehead with a tired gesture. "I'm glad that's done."

Faith, who had been watching forlornly, spoke in sudden alarm, "Where are you going?" and started to run to Mavis. But she tripped over one of the bags, fell hard on her head, began to cry, then fell back —limp.

Mavis hurried over, picked the child up, and cried frantically, "Michal, smelling salts, quickly!"

By the time Michal had returned with the thick green bottle, Faith had revived and Hetty was in the room blustering. "Mis' Ward! Picking up that heavy young un! Seems like everything's gone wrong since Mr. Ward came in here with his ideas."

"I didn't stop to think, so don't scold, please. It frightened me, seeing her like that. Are you all right, Faith?"

Faith nodded, and snuggled her head contentedly against her mother's shoulder. Mavis relaxed, then said, "Hetty will put you on the sofa and Sister will read you a story. I'm so tired."

There was color in Faith's cheeks again as Michal read quietly from *Grimm's Fairy Tales.* Hetty was starting supper when Mother called. "Hetty, put on water in the boiler and tea kettle."

"I don't know as there's—" Hetty broke off sharply. "Mis' Ward! You don't mean—"

"I've been having"—she lowered her voice "—pains ever since Faith's fall. I thought if I rested, they'd leave, like the other time. But this seems to be the real thing."

"I'll call Mr. Ward."

"Not yet. There's no need to upset him until we're sure. Just get the water and prepare the bed."

"Mis' Ward, I'm skeered."

84

"Don't worry, Hetty. If it comes to—that—I can tell you what to do. I have easy times, you know."

"Mother"—Michal went over anxiously—"What's going to happen? What's wrong?"

"Nothing is wrong. Just do as you're told." Then Mavis bent suddenly and clutched the arm of her chair.

As Hetty stripped the big bed of its blankets, she told Michal what to bring. Over the mattress she spread a layer of newspapers, and on top of that a torn clean quilt. Michal helped spread a layer of papers on top of that. Over the whole thing Hetty arranged an old sheet, tucking it in tightly.

Mother came in and spoke calmly. "If you're through I'm going to change; then you might braid my hair."

She came out soon in her nightdress and crimson wrapper.

"How many—uh—"

"Only one minute apart now. You'd better call Mr. Ward."

Hetty went out and they heard her shrill cry, "Mr. Ward, Mr. Ward! Come here quick!"

She was braiding Mother's hair when Father burst in. "What in hell is wrong?" irritably. "Gus and I are just finishing."

"If yer not too busy to listen," acidly, "Mis' Ward is havin' pains."

"Pains!" yelled Father, and then swung on Mavis. "You're not going to have that baby here!"

"It may be, John."

"I knew this would happen." He began pacing. "I knew it. But could I tell you? Oh, no!"

Mavis was bending double again; the girls were standing to one side—round-eyed. Hetty drew herself tall. "Listen to me, Mr. Ward. If she hadn't been workin' so hard today, packin' and everything, this would never 'a' happened."

"I'm taking her right into Ipswich," snapped Father. "We sure as hell can't have the baby here."

Mother's voice came tiredly: "John, the baby will be born soon. Control yourself and help Hetty. I'm sorry this has happened, but we've got to make the best of it."

"All right, all right." He gritted his teeth as she sank back, eyes closed. "You girls go eat; then Michal, you put Faith to bed, and stand by to run errands."

He turned and bent over Mavis, saying, "We'll manage somehow, Wife. God, if you were only in town!"

By the time Faith was in bed Mother and Hetty were in the bedroom, and Father was nervously coming in and going out. Gus had fixed himself some food. When Michal went into the kitchen, he asked, "Is your—uh—is something happenin' to yer ma, Miss Michal?"

"Yes, Gus," she returned gravely. "At least, Father and Hetty act like it."

"Yuh don't say!" His blue eyes were bulging. "Yuh don't say!"

John Ward came in. "I want some scissors," he barked. "Hetty says they're in here."

"Anything I can do, Mr. Ward?" asked Gus.

"Not a thing, Gus. Not a thing. Get to bed and get some sleep. No telling how this'll turn out. Michal, for God's sake, haven't you found those scissors yet? How can I give Hetty scissors if you can't find them? A place for everything and everything in its place."

"Here they are." Her cheeks felt hot.

Father left the room. In a moment he was back, still carrying the scissors. "She insists that I put these in boiling water," he grumbled to Gus, lifting the top off the teakettle. "Fool idea, if you ask me, but women—" Still muttering he finished dipping, then left again.

Michal returned to the sitting room and sat down stiffly. From behind the closed door came the murmur of voices, punctuated occasionally by a deep, slow groan. Then Mother's voice would sound—faintly. Once Michal caught the words, "After it's born, wait a bit—before you cut."

At another time Hetty came out, and Michal saw Mother gripping one of Father's hands with both of hers—gripping hard; a great wave of color was washing her face, then receding even as she watched.

Later Hetty was soothing: "It won't be long now. She's in bad pain."

Then Mother's voice, saying clearly, "Oh, John, if I never come back—"

"It's all right, Mavis. It's all right."

"She don't rightly know what she's sayin'."

"If I never come back. If I never—"

"... soon over now."

"If I never come back—"

86

Their voices muffled now and quick—there was hurrying. Father said, "There."

More steps and Hetty's voice, "Now's the time."

A pause. "It's a boy, Mr. Ward!" and over it all a sudden thin wail and Father saying, "Yes, a fine boy."

"You tend him, Mr. Ward, like I told you, amd I'll look to her."

Mother's voice, "Is the baby all right?"

"Right as rain."

Father came out, awkwardly holding a small bundle. "Well, Mike, you've a new brother," he said as he stood in the open door.

Then Mavis's voice came clearly, "Hetty, I'm still having pains."

Hetty was soothing, "Jest the aftermath."

"No, I'm having real pains. John!"

Father looked startled. "Michal, could you hold him? Here. Careful, now."

Michal received the bundle gingerly, placing it just so on her lap as Hetty squawked, "Mr. Ward! They's another baby a-comin'!"

"Oh, my God!"

Father wheeled, ran in, closed the door. The muffled sounds were happening all over again. Michal looked down. It was an ugly thing, and it smelled funny. Long wet black hair. Blotched red face. One thin naked little arm was beating the air furiously. As Michal tucked it back under the blanket, she saw that its fingernails were quite blue.

She went over to the trunk, still in the middle of the room, and, reaching down, took out one of the soft blankets Hetty had packed that morning and folded it carefully about the baby. "Father didn't have enough around you, did he?" she asked soberly. Settling down in Mother's chair by the window.

Even as the baby quieted, a new series of squalls came from the bedroom.

"Another boy!" Hetty's voice held a note of triumph.

The dining-room door opened, and Gus stood there looking sleepy and disheveled. "I thought I heard—" He gazed in bewilderment at the bundle in Michal's arms, then toward the bedroom, out of which a slender wail was rising—then breaking.

"There seem to be two babies, Gus." Michal was glad she could be the one to break the news.

"Well, I'll be danged. Twins!" He sat down heavily.

Faith was still sleeping. When John Ward came out with the second bundle, he said briefly: "Gus, would you lift Faith into Michal's bed? Hetty wants to fix the cradle up as soon as she's through with Mavis." He grinned suddenly and added, "Damned good thing we made it so big."

"Sure is." Gus grinned back, lifting Faith, who stirred, then settled down again in the other bed. "That one a boy, too?"

"Yep. Looks just like Michal did. The other—there—is another Gordon, Mavis'll say."

"How's Mis' Ward?"

"Seems fine." Father's face grew grim. "Looks to me like we've been pretty lucky, though. I said all along—damn it—that she should get to town."

"Oh, well, you know how women are." Gus pulled out his plug and automatically bit off a hunk with strong teeth.

Hetty—pale, and with her bun of hair askew—came out with a great armful of stained papers and sheets. "You, Gus Perkins, help me with this," she ordered sharply, and the room was filled with a strong sickening odor.

Michal and Father went into the bedroom still carrying the babies. Mavis was resting quietly. She smiled up at them, then said faintly: "I'm so tired. Michal, are you all right?"

"I took care of the first baby, Mother."

"I can't understand—twins. There've never been any in our family that I know of."

"Nor in mine either, Mavis."

"Do they seem—strong?"

"Yes, they do. They're smaller than our other babies, but lusty all the same."

"Well, twins would be smaller, I imagine. I must have—miscalculated—somehow." Mother's eyes were drooping.

Hetty was making up the cradle. "Bring me them blankets from the trunk, Gus, and hurry! We've got to get the little darlin's settled."

Mavis smiled, her eyes heavy, her face relaxed.

"So glad," she murmured, "so glad it's—all—over. You're telling me the—truth—John—the babies are all right?"

"Yes, Mavis. Haven't you heard them bellow? I'm going to watch over them tonight so they won't get uncovered."

But she was sleeping. Hetty came to the door. "I'll take 'em now. You two come on out and let her alone."

Father and Michal brought the babies out, quietly, and, "Hetty," Father added awkwardly, "thanks for—everything."

"Aw, now, Mr. Ward, that warn't nothin'. I think I did jest as good as that Tannyhill critter anyways."

"You sure did a good job; good night."

Michal had a hard time going to sleep. All night she stirred restlessly. The room was filled with little cries and the noise of Father stumbling over things as he tended the fire and the babies.

But Mavis slept.

XIII

Mavis had not regained her strength as quickly as usual. "Nursin' two younguns is enough to kill most women," Hetty would say severely. Then, proudly, "That little thing's got enough for both and t' spare."

So for the first time in her life, Michal had to work about the house, dusting, setting table, and keeping the sitting room orderly, thus relieving Hetty for the extra washing and baby tending. Even Faith ran errands, saving Hetty and Mavis many steps.

Mother seemed happy again. Now that the new babies were here, she was even able to mention Little Brother occasionally. "He was too good for this world," Michal heard her telling Hetty once, as she rocked the cradle gently. "Too good for this world."

Michal thought: Then I better not ever be too good. Just enough to get to Heaven.

"Little Gordon here looks very much as Frederick did, don't you think?" Mavis went on, leaning over the small dark head in the cradle.

"A mite smaller and a mite more hair," said Hetty decidedly.

"Y-e-es, I believe you're right. And Philip is another John all over. Even to the temper. I'm glad they're not alike." And she smiled contentedly.

The snow began going in March, the huge dirty drifts shrinking visibly. Far beneath them one could hear the gurgle of imprisoned water running down the ravine. Rains in late March finished the snow, except on northern slopes. Michal found that in many places long strands of grass had grown under the drifts during the thaw. Glen came back just as spring's work was beginning. The harnesses were oiled and repaired, and Glen and Gus were soon working on the land.

One morning in April, Michal hunted pasqueflowers again on the sunny slopes of the little rocky hills across the ravine. Geese were flying north in long thin lines, the raucous clamor of the leaders coming to her pleasantly mellowed by distance.

It was then she saw a top-buggy coming swiftly along the road toward her place. She hurried, but the callers were before her. Father was greeting a man and a little girl whose thick yellow braids glinted in the light.

"Katie!" she shouted joyfully, running up to her, then stopping suddenly in embarrassment.

"Hello," Katie said shyly. She was taller, but still plump and clean looking.

"Come in, Keim—come in." John Ward spoke heartily.

The man shook his big head and said briefly, "No, I must by Leola be at ten."

John Ward insisted. "Come in, man. For just a few minutes, anyway. I've got to hear more about this place you're from—End-of-Track they call it, don't they?"

"Ya—vell, I stop little vile."

"Mavis, this is Mr. Keim—and this is—uh—Katie. You remember she and Michal played together our first summer here."

"Please be seated." Mother smiled and stepped to the dining room. "Hetty, will you bring coffee?"

Mr. Keim sat stiffly on the edge of the horsehair sofa holding his hat on his knees.

"Can you stay?" asked Michal eagerly of Katie.

"Ya. My Fadder goes by Leola on business. I stay von hour here, den go back to mine Tante."

"After your father goes I'll take you down to the dam and show you my tree. I like to listen to grownups talk, don't you?"

"Ya," said Katie primly. Michal wondered if she meant it.

Father was speaking, "You say they're laying the steel?"

"Ya. Train comes in Yuly."

"Place platted yet?"

"No—but soon."

"You think it'll be a good town?"

For the first time Mr. Keim relaxed, and his eyes began to gleam. "Ya. Goot place. Many from Russland come. Buy farms. Raise veat. Goot veat. I vill store haben. Goot place to money make."

Hetty entered with the coffee tray. My father's much handsomer than Mr. Keim, thought Michal looking proudly at John Ward, who had jumped up and was pacing nervously about. I'm glad he hasn't a mustache.

"You know," Father burst out, "if we didn't have such fine crop prospects—if there wasn't so much money to be made here—I'd move to End-of-Track in a flash. By God, I almost believe it would pay me to invest in lots there anyway!" He stopped in front of Keim, who was calmly slurping coffee out of his saucer, holding in his other hand the big blue mustache cup with *Father* inscribed on it in gold lettering. "What would be a good time for a man to go over to look around?"

The other considered, carefully sucking the coffee from the ends of his mustache. "T'ree—mebbe four—mont'."

Father nodded as Keim rose. "I might do that."

Keim grinned broadly. "Come, bring family." He made a sweeping gesture, "Stay by us, ya?"

Father and Mother thanked him, but Mavis's eyes were remote.

Mr. Keim, with a final word to his daughter, "Von hour only," and a cheerful "Gootbye!" left for Leola.

As the girls walked toward the dam they could see Glen working on the new east field. Hitched to a breaker the white bull and the black ox, heads bent low under creaking yokes, plodded slowly and patiently, steadily upturning the tough virgin prairie sod for a flax crop.

"Did you have a nice trip over?" asked Michal politely.

"There vas much mudt."

"This is a bad time to travel." Michal felt stiff and grown up. "Maybe," she added shyly, "if my father does go to End-of-Track he'll take me, too."

Katie's blue eyes brightened. "Ya, you come stay vid me like mine Fadder say."

"It would be wonderful," Michal went on dreamily. "Just think— forty whole miles. Of course," she added quickly, "I've traveled much farther than that before."

At the dam she showed Katie how much her willow tree had grown in two summers. "We'd better go back to the house. Hetty will give us cookies and milk. I'll show you my twin brothers, too."

Katie sighed gustily. "Babies are much vork."

"Yes, it's hard. Oh, look!"

Out of the sky, silvered by the morning light, they came—lines and wedges of geese, some near, some so far that they seemed like swallows against the sun. Flying low over the west field, their trumpet tones rang louder and louder, and as the leaders settled the girls could see their white throat patches. Still they came, until the great field was covered. As the sentries stood guard, the huge mass moved, seeking grass roots and insects in the newly turned earth.

The whole field quivered like a living thing. Finally Michal said, "I wonder how many geese are there?" She tried to visualize great numbers—her mind hurt—it could not grasp what she was trying to understand.

They watched, silent, until the geese again took flight and the heavy slow-moving bodies hurtled away, diminishing in size until they could no longer be seen—leaving behind only the last faint echoes of their full sonorous cries.

To the south, Haar's geese were calling.

The girls went on to the house, looked at the babies, then ate cookies and drank milk. Mother didn't put out the Spode.

Katie said, "I must go to mine Tante. Thank you for the food."

"I'll walk with you a ways."

As they descended the gentle slope Michal added wistfully, "I wish we would play together often."

"You come see me; mine people from Russland are coming this year."

"When?"

"Sometime dis summer."

"All of them?"

"Ya. All."

As they crossed the ravine Michal decided not to tell Katie about the troll. There was no need to frighten a guest. They climbed to the top of the hill across the ravine. The great spring flight in long wavering lines was still flying high, following their sure course to the north.

As though to investigate the calls of the earth-bound flock, some of the great birds dipped over Haar's place, then, flying low, swooped almost overhead.

With elation, Michal cried: "They've made it, Katie! They've made it at last!" as the leaders mounted higher and the whole flock followed, with loud, sardonic cries of joy, the lines that had gone before.

Katie shook her head. "Dey not go—mine Tante keep always de vings cut."

"Listen."

It came again—that hoarse piteous clamor from the south.

Michal spoke sadly. "I was sure they'd gotten away—I was just sure." Then, resentfully, "But why does she keep them? They're wild things."

"For de fedders from de breast—dey the softest pillows make."

"I mustn't go any farther. Goodbye, Katie. I'm awfully glad you came over."

"Gootbye, Michal. Ven you to End-of-Track come, you stay by me."

"I will." A lump was in her throat as she watched the other walk sturdily along the road, without once looking back.

XIV

Michal was to remember this summer as the most fragrant of them all —the air redolent of sweet growing grain, wild roses, and new-mown hay, mixed inextricably by the wind into the prairie's sweetest perfume.

The water from the deep snow had filled the ponds and had brought many sandhill cranes to Oulette's slough. Michal, as she had done often before, climbed the highest hill across the ravine, hid behind a boulder, opened her copy of *Little Women*, and waited for the great gray birds.

They came soon, walking Indian file up the hill, then scattered to feed. Michal read, one wary eye on the great birds solemnly stalking grasshoppers. The fun should begin at any time now.

In about fifteen minutes, all eight of them came up to the hilltop, so close she could see the pinkish skin on their heads in contrast to the dull gray plumage. Seemingly forgetting their nests in the slough below, they began bowing elaborately to each other. Bowing, turning, hopping, they danced awkwardly on the hilltop, reminding her of the

93

time she had seen people dancing in a street pavilion, at Ordway one Fourth of July.

Later Michal closed her book and walked toward the Oulette place. She had shunned it all summer, but she wanted to go there once more, this last day of haying.

Haar had planted the land well—wheat and oats on the plowed fields and flax on the breaking. The once neat shack looked dingy; the tarpaper was faded and hung in untidy shreds. She walked up the stone-rimmed path to the door. Here and there a few bachelor's-buttons bloomed among the rankly growing weeds, accenting the disorder. Tumbleweeds flourished beside the gray-white boulder Pierre Oulette had left as a seat. Here his wife had often rested, watching the sunset and waiting for her husband's return on the Ipswich road. Michal brushed off the dust and sat down on the boulder in the shade of the shack. The slow, warm midsummer wind washed her cheek; from the slough the liquid *ok-a-lee* of red-winged blackbirds brought back memories of Mrs. Oulette's voice.

Rising half fearfully, she opened the door. What had been a home for the Oulettes was now a storeroom for Haar. Empty sacks and a rusty plow littered the floor, while a worn horse collar and part of an old harness hung from the wall. A mouse scuttled under a gunny sack in one corner. No morning-glory vines twined over the west window to keep out the hot sun. Instead, a big bluebottle fly bumbling lazily against the cobwebbed pane sounded loud in the silence.

Michal shut the door without entering and ran down the hill. She felt as she had the day they had left Little Brother's open grave.

XV

The wheat in the west field stood tall and proud, only the heavy heads bending with their burden. The hot milky smell of the plump grains came tantalizingly to Michal's nostrils. The warm breeze riffled the wheat's green surface, already changed on the higher stretches to tawny gold. The family had finished a leisurely Sunday-morning breakfast at the round walnut table beside the open window in the sitting room. Mother was reading the Bible.

94

"Another week of this weather and it will be ready for cutting," said John Ward suddenly, coming to look over his daughter's shoulder. "We're due for a bumper crop, at last, Mavis."

"It must have been on a Sabbath day like this that Jesus, walking through a field like ours, plucked and ate of it," said Mother dreamily.

"Uh-huh," returned Father indifferently. "Mavis, I'm going to make that trip to End-of-Track this week. Why don't you come along?"

"You know I couldn't take two nursing babies on a forty-mile ride."

"No, I suppose not. How long is it, anyway, since you've been off the place?"

"Almost two years." Mother's lips curved down a little.

"Well, if you'd rather I didn't go, I won't." Father's voice held a note of self-sacrifice.

"I want you to. It may be a chance for a sound investment."

"I know it is." John Ward began pacing, and Michal burst out: "Let me go with you. Please. Mother, may I?"

"Let her come, Mavis. She can stay with the Keims. You could see for yourself how clean they were. It'll be company for me, and a treat for her. The grain'll be ready for cutting in about ten days, so I want to get this trip in before then."

The week brought perfect weather, hot and still, with no wind to lodge the heavy yield in the depressions.

Father was in high good humor on Friday as he and Michal in the light top-buggy, drawn swiftly by the Hambletonians, handsome in their new harnesses, skimmed over the prairie—now carpeted with thick curly buffalo grass—toward End-of-Track.

Michal relaxed beside Father, not saying much. Occasionally he would point out with his whip a shack, barn, or wheatfield. "We're not the only ones who'll have a bumper crop this year. Look at that stand."

They ate lunch by a spring, the air fragrant with crushed bergamot. Before they left, Father pointed out an old buffalo wallow several hundred feet away and a trail leading to it on a swell of hill beyond the slough.

Hours later he said, "Here we are!"

Michal sat up and rubbed her eyes. She must have dozed. To the west the sun was sinking richly behind dust veils settling like mist over the land. Evening primroses were unfolding their pale petals.

Michal saw tents, a few shacks, and one large red building—all huddled together on their side of the railroad tracks as though for mutual protection against the pitiless prairie. "Father!" her voice rang with disappointment, "Is this all?"

"What'd you expect," irritably, " a full-sized town?" He pointed the whip. "That red building there must be the new railroad station."

Michal, feeling hot, sticky, and tired, murmured, "I wonder where Katie lives."

"I'll ask the first person we see." The puffing engine of the mixed train was shunting freight cars onto a siding, and the Hambletonians shied at the crossing.

On the west side of the tracks John Ward stopped the horses beside a large woman, who, carrying a huge bundle, was charging briskly down the middle of the road.

"Where's a hotel?" he asked, taking off his hat.

"Right there." She pointed back to a haphazard-looking building on the right-of-way.

"That?" Father exclaimed involuntarily.

"Well, it's the best they can do till the town's platted," she snapped, then added proudly, "Considerin' that 'twas built in one or two days, it's pretty good."

"It's a wonder the Chicago Milwaukee Railroad let them build it there."

"Ain't done nothin' about it. O' course, when the town's platted they'll build a new one on the other side o' the tracks."

"Where do the Keims live?"

"That way," she pointed west. "First house—you can't miss it. Only two finished houses in this place. Keims are mighty fine people. He aims to have a store. You fixin' to move here?"

"Like to. We live on a farm south of Leola. Bumper crop this year. Otherwise I'd be tempted."

"Well, if you ever move here and need any washin' done, jest ask for Achsah Klunk. Everybody knows me," and as she moved away her laughter, rich and deep, floated back.

They drove on until they came to a tiny house set well back from the road. Father tied the team. As they walked to the door Michal caught the thick fragrance of flowers, now hidden by the gathering dusk. Mr. Keim came to the door, his heavy figure outlined darkly by the light from the lamp that he held.

96

"Mr. Keim, it's John Ward, who lives south of Leola near Haar's."

"Oh, ya, ya. Goot. Come in."

He ushered them into an immaculate room. Mrs. Keim, a bulky edition of her daughter, came forward, followed closely by Katie, who was staring curiously; then her round face broke into a delighted smile.

"Michal!"

"Hello."

"You have kum to stay by us?" Mr. Keim's broad face was beaming.

"My daughter, yes, if she may. For tonight and tomorrow. I'm staying at the hotel."

"You must stay here by us. We have much room."

"No, thank you. I have a man or two I must see tonight and early in the morning. But if Michal may stay, I'd be thankful."

"Ya. But you stay by us for supper."

"Well, yes, I'll be glad to. Maybe you can tell me some things I want to know."

As the two men sat down Mrs. Keim said, "Katie vill show you vare you vash." Then she turned and Michal saw that one whole cheek was covered with a purplish red birthmark.

Katie led Michal to a neat little outhouse in back. Why, this is just as clean as ours! she thought in surprise. There was a big hole, a middle-sized hole, and a little hole—like the story of The Three Bears. On one side was a small box filled with ashes and a little shovel. When Michal was through she carefully put a shovelful of ashes down the hole before joining Katie, who was modestly waiting outside.

"Have your relatives from Russia come yet?" she asked casually as they returned to the house.

"Not yet, but any day now."

Michal felt disappointed. She wondered if Katie were just imagining that they were coming. After all, she herself made up things that she wished to happen. But there was that picture, of course. And that dark boy. It must be true.

Frau Keim was fishing small green pickled melons out of a cask when the girls entered the kitchen. "Kum." She smiled at Michal, who smiled back, trying very hard not to look at the blemish.

After Michal had washed, Katie led the way to the *Stube* where the table was set for five. Father was talking rapidly to Mr. Keim as they

97

ate *Kaffeekuchen* and rich noodle soup in which floated immature eggs the hens had never lived to lay.

Now that she was washed Michal felt wide awake, and as she began eating she looked curiously about the *Stube*. Behind the stiffly starched Nottingham curtains petunias were blooming—the identical color of Mrs. Keim's birthmark.

Father was saying, rather irritably, "Then in a way this whole trip has been useless."

Mr. Keim shrugged. "If you vished to buy lots, ya. The town is not yet platted."

"Well, it was the only time I could get away, so it can't be helped. Anyway, I'll get an idea of the place." He rose from the table abruptly. "Excuse me, but I want to see Becker tonight, so I'll be off." He turned. "Thanks for the meal. And for taking care of my daughter."

Katie had her own little room, small and neat as a pin. This was the first time Michal had ever spent the night away from home. As she opened her little bundle to take out her nightdress, she said, "This hair ribbon is for you, Katie."

"Thank you," answered Katie shyly, but her eyes gleamed as she took the crisp blue ribbon.

Michal had never slept in a featherbed before. It felt smothery, and for a fleeting instant Mother and home seemed very far away. Even if Katie does have her own room, I'm glad that I'm me and not a foreigner, she thought sleepily, and that my mother is beautiful and doesn't have a red mark. I mustn't forget to ask Hetty what that mark can be.

The next morning after breakfast Michal was surprised to find that Katie quite matter-of-factly started the housework while her mother kneaded down bread dough. The work seemed never ending. Katie went cheerfully from one task to another—bedmaking, dusting, sweeping, polishing, with her guest trailing along politely, helping as best she could.

After they had gathered the eggs, they walked over to look at the garden. The garden was a mixture of dill, potatoes, dwarf melons, onions, garlic, saffron, cabbages, four o'clocks, and immense blood-red poppies—the whole enclosed by a hedge of Russian sunflowers, the heads fourteen inches across.

"It's like a house in a fairy tale," Michal told Katie seriously. Then, turning, she glimpsed a spiral of smoke—slim as Indian pipe—far to the south.

"Look!"

"Ya, the train!"

"Could we go see it come in?"

"I'll ask Mutter."

Mrs. Keim sat near the windows crocheting an intricate pattern of white lace. She handed her daughter a piece of white thread. "Same as latst time," she ordered firmly, and Michal thought impatiently, She just doesn't want us to get there, as they hurried down the road toward the station.

"Do you have to buy the thread *before* the train gets in?" she asked as they hurried over the tracks well ahead of the engine, which was now whistling lustily for the crossing.

"Ya."

The train pulled slowly into the station as the girls reached the store. While Katie bought the thread, Michal counted the cars—ten freight and one, two, three yellow passenger coaches—a long train for such a little town. People spilled out and spread over the platform, then began to trickle across the tracks and down the road past where Michal was standing. There were a few Americans, but most were foreigners. Katie joined her, and the girls stood watching.

The Rooshans came up the street, the men ahead dressed in sheepskin coats, tall astrakhan caps, baggy breeches tucked into high boots, and carrying sacks. "Seed veat," whispered Katie. The women, large and shapeless in gathered skirts and loose blouses, with gaily bordered black head shawls tied under their chins, carried bulky bundles, pillows, and featherbeds. Many children, small replicas of their parents, followed in their wake.

"Why do those men wear sheepskin coats this time of year?" whispered Michal scornfully.

"There is no odder vay to carry them. They must use their hands to carry their seed veat."

"The women dress just like Mrs. Haar."

"All the vimmen from Russland dress dot vay."

Michal tugged at Katie's arm. "Let's go up to the station and look at the engine . . ." Her voice trailed into silence.

Another family was approaching. The man, blond, stocky, walked beside his wife—a well built strong-looking woman dressed very decently in black, a black silk cashmere head shawl, fringed with a border of red roses, circling her shrewd determined face. Behind her were two girls, as blond as Katie but older, giggling nervously.

Michal was not looking at them, but at a tall dark boy who was walking confidently a little ahead and apart from the others. Although he was wearing the boots, sheepskin coat, bright red sash, and tall Russian astrakhan cap, he wore them easily and becomingly.

As they passed he looked at Michal, his piercing black eyes flicking her arrogantly as he strode along. Her cheeks burned with resentment. Who does that Rooshan boy think he is? her thoughts ran angrily —then paused. "Katie!"

"Ya?"

"I've seen that boy before. In the picture you showed me that time. Aren't those—" She broke off as Katie looked at the group more closely, then cried out, "Mine Tante and mine cussings!" and ran after them there in the dusty road.

Michal saw Katie speak to the woman, who nodded her head, then stooped and embraced her. The man stepped forward and said something, in answer to which Katie pointed in the direction of her house.

Michal hesitated. Katie seemed to have forgotten her. She didn't know whether to join them or try to find Father. As she stood there, uncertain, wondering what was the polite thing to do, she heard a familiar clip-clop, clip-clop, coming smartly, then slowing for the little group in the middle of the street.

"Father," she called, running forward.

"I was just going out to get you. What in hell are you doing down here? Get in."

"Katie's relatives have come. I can't leave her, can I?"

"Tell her goodbye. We're leaving."

"But I thought we were going home tomorrow."

"I got through early. If we leave now, we'll make it home tonight sometime." He scowled irritably. "Tell her we're sorry we don't have room to take her relatives to the house. Hurry."

Michal walked self-consciously over to the group, which had moved to one side. They seemed to be waiting for her. "Katie, Father and I are leaving for home right away. He is sorry we can't take you all to your house."

As she spoke she was conscious of the boy who was standing very straight nearby, his dark gaze on her as she made her goodbyes to Katie.

Then, as she ran back to the buggy and climbed up, she was suddenly aware of how fine they must look in their shining carriage, the proud team, the new harnesses, and her handsome lean father at the reins. As they flashed down the road to Katie's house for her things, Michal held her chin high.

She ran up through the yellow sunflowers to the door of the *Stube*. Mrs. Keim went out to talk to Father, and when Michal hurried back Katie's mother was peering eagerly down the road, as though she had already forgotten them.

"We're off!" said Father with satisfaction as the Hambletonians trotted briskly toward the crossing. Michal did not answer. She was watching the little group walking toward them, already on the west side of the tracks. As they sped by she waved to Katie, but her eyes were on the boy. He was striding along, head high, eyes straight ahead. Katie waved, but the boy didn't seem to notice them at all.

Michal settled back. "Did you buy any lots, Father?"

"Can't until the town's platted. That's why I got through so soon. Saw the men I wanted to see and that was all."

"I wish we might come here to live."

"Well!" John Ward looked in surprise at his daughter. "I thought you didn't like the place."

"I like Katie. We are *Kamerads*."

"Ump," he snorted.

Michal looked back. The little group had reached the gate, but even at this distance she could pick out the boy. He still walked a little apart from the others.

XVI

The ripe wheat, dull gold in the sun, stood waiting—ready for harvest; quietly proud, heavy bending, not a breeze stirred its gleaming splendor.

After early breakfast, Michal waded out into the west field with Father and Gus as they tested it. Picking heads here and there they rubbed them in their palms, then blew off the chaff and chewed the grains reflectively. "We'll begin cutting tomorrow," said Father expansively. "Be sure everything is ready by tonight. I'll be home early. We'll start with the uplands, since that'd shatter first."

By noon the machinery was inspected and oiled, and the work horses were brought up from the big east pasture and put in their stalls where they'd be handy at daylight. The pantry shelves were covered with fragrant pies, and the hot kitchen was filled with the smells of fresh rolls and chicken simmering on the back of the cookstove in a huge black kettle. Hetty was dog tired but in good humor.

When the men went down to oil the harnesses, she said, "It's boiling hot, Mis' Ward. Why don't you go take a nap now? I'll redd up—they ain't much to do."

Michal took this chance to ask about the blemish. "I tried not to look at it, but it was so large and so awful it was all I could do to be polite and not stare at her."

"A birthmark," said Hetty sagely. "It was her mother's fault. When she was carrying her before she was born, that is—her mother thought of beef liver or some such awful thing and"—lowering her voice dramatically—"she marked her child."

"What do you mean—carrying her before she was born? How could her mother carry her before she had her?"

"She carried her in her body—didn't she?" Then Hetty turned snappish. "Run along now. Can't you see how busy I am."

Michal wandered in to lie down beside Faith. It was hot and sticky, with no breeze, and she was tired. Mother was still sleeping when she woke. Tiptoeing out to the kitchen, she found it clean and still.

"Sh-h-h!" warned Hetty, finger on her lips. "Let yer maw sleep. I declare to goodness I wish it'ud stir up a little breeze."

Michal started for the granary. The back yard was covered with A-coops in each of which a fussy hen scolded as her chicks ran heedlessly in and out. Yet when a hawk soared as he saw the girl, and his lengthened shadow floated along the ground, the long-drawn alarm call, Ker-r-r-r, sent the chicks scurrying each to the protection of its own mother's wings.

The granary smelled of neat's-foot oil.

"Hello," greeted Gus. "Just set yourself down 'til I get this harness finished, and by then it'll be cool enough for us to go down to the lower pasture to see if they's enough water for the stock."

"I'll just sit out here and watch the chickens. I don't like the smell of oil on a day as hot as this."

Hetty had had wonderful luck with the poultry—angular half grown chickens, slender graceful turkey poults, and ducks, diving and dibbling in the shallow muddy water of the dam. On their way to the lower pasture, "Seems like it never will cool off," complained Gus, wiping his sweaty face with the back of his hand.

Then it was that Michal noticed the stillness. It was strange, for even on the quietest summer days little breezes were always wandering here and there, stirring the grasses; now not a leaf quivered on her willow tree, and every grass blade stood straight as though listening.

Suddenly she felt fear—the same strange prick of fright she had felt that first night when they looked down over the fields and the weird wavering cry of the plover had come to her at dusk. The rasping flight of a huge grasshopper, loud in the silence, startled her out of her mood. Gus was watching a cloud that had appeared—a huge dark boiling cloud with angry yellow-gray edges already blotting out the sun.

"Let's hurry, Miss Mike," he said quickly. "We might have wind."

They ran over an earth suddenly covered by deep shadows, and reached the house breathless. When the storm struck, Gus was helping Hetty close doors and windows; then he rushed to the barn to help Glen with the animals.

With the first wind came a drumming as though many hands were throwing rocks on the roof. Faster and louder, then *crash! smash!* More rocks, larger, more violently hurled.

Michal ran to Mother's room. She turned from the window, her large dark eyes staring from a face pale as milkweed blossoms. Hailstones were bouncing high in the yard. The twins were both asleep in the cradle. "Where's Faith?" Mother couldn't hear her for the drumming on the roof. Moving close, she repeated her question.

"She was here a minute ago," said Mavis, looking about the room. "Surely she wouldn't have run outside." Even her lips were pale now.

"No, I'd have seen her as I came in." Michal spoke reassuringly, and began looking—behind the big chair, in the wardrobe, then—"Here she is!" She reached under the bed.

Faith was crowded far under, close to the wall, and lay flat with her face buried on her arms. Michal called, "Come out, Faith. Come out!" but she either did not hear or pretended not to. Mavis rolled the bed out, went over and picked her up. The child clung to her mother, arms tight about her neck.

"Let's lie down, girls, until it's over." And they threw themselves crosswise on the big bed. Rory, unrebuked, jumped up beside Michal and lay still, whimpering.

The pounding lulled; then came the swishing sound of rain, and through the dusky light thin pale fingers of lightening clutched like witches' claws at the prairie, and thunder followed like the fearsome roars of giant dragons. Faith cowered and cried; Rory whimpered and nuzzled Michal's hand.

"It's letting up, Mother." The tension in the room was leaving. The lightning fingers ceased their frantic clutchings; the thunder growls were dying away in the hills.

They found Hetty in the sitting room, seated in the middle of four great goose-feather pillows in the center of the room. "Why, Hetty, what—"

"Well, you see," she said, getting up sheepishly, "feathers don't conduck lightnin', and it ain't never like to strike in the middle of a room." She picked up her pillows and, sniffing, walked out with dignity.

Although the sun shone again it was cool—almost cold. Michal shivered as she opened the door and looked out. The only sound was a dull roar where the ravine ran full, and a *drip—drip—drip* of water from the roof into the brimming rainbarrel, the overflow from which had plowed deep runnels through the yard.

Where only an hour before great fields of wheat had flaunted their tawny beauty in the sunshine, now was desolation. Even the stubble had been pounded into the ground by the merciless flail of hailstones that still covered the ground and were piled high in house corners.

Michal picked her way down to the chicken house where Glen was wading through the hail and helping Hetty pick up the grown poultry and chicks, poults and ducklings that, battered and denuded of their feathers, lay where the hailstones had struck them down. Some few had reached the shelter of the chicken house. On the higher ground six of the slatted A-coops still stood firm, and bedraggled mothers hovered anxiously over their loudly chirping young.

"Pick up any of 'em that's alive and bring 'em up to the house," gasped Hetty, rushing past, her big gingham apron full. They made trip after trip to the house where Hetty, sleeves rolled up, worked to save any she could. The smaller ones she put in the oven—still warm from the noonday meal. The room was so stifling with the awful smell of heat and wet chicken feathers that Michal left.

She went down past dead poultry to where Gus was working with the hogs. Most of the grown ones had run into their houses—a few young pigs lay battered down in the pens. Genevieve, the huge Tamworth sow, was safe in her private quarters, shared with her latest litter of ten; five of the piglets had escaped; the rest were drowned.

John Ward reached home late; he had waited an hour to ford the ravine, and even so the water had reached the hubs of his rig. After making the animals comfortable for the night, he, Gus and Michal went out to inspect, by lantern light, his acres.

The storm had followed the ravine, cutting a straight swath through the Ward homestead. No damage had been done on the south side except to a small part of the Oulette wheatfield owned by Haar. East of the Ward buildings it had spent its force. The dam was out, but Michal noticed by the wavering light of the lantern that the little willow, though scarred and tattered as to leaves, was already standing upright.

They went last to the lower pasture where the young cattle had been running, along with the white bull and the black ox. During the storm they all had huddled in the fence corner by the gate nearest the barn. Lightning had followed the barbed wire and the ground was heaped with great piles of seared stock, among them the white bull.

Father raised the lantern high and swung it in an arc. "I don't see the black ox—" he began, then stopped abruptly as, far to the left, the dim glow caught the soft gleam of metal—wide-spaced—like golden eyes. Brass guards tipping horns and the dark inert bulk back of it. "He's dead, too. God damn it!"

John Ward stood for a moment, holding the light and looking carefully at the dead stock. Then, without another word, he turned abruptly, walking away so fast that Michal and Gus had to hurry to keep up. He said nothing until he reached the house; straight to the sitting room he hurried where Mother, her beautiful hands held slack in her lap, sat waiting. There was a white line around Father's mouth as he said: "Well, Mavis, begin packing the things we least need, tomorrow. We're moving to End-of-Track."

"But this place?" Mother's voice was anxious.

"Don't worry about that. Haar is crazy to own it; he'll buy it, and at my price, too, by God!" He whirled. "And, Mike, if he comes snooping around—and he will—you keep your mouth shut."

Mavis rose, went quickly to the clock shelf, took the covers from the potpourri, and stirred the contents with a paper spill from the vase beside it.

XVII

The morning after the hailstorm, Michal watched excitedly for Haar. Before noon she saw him come over the hill. Instead of crossing the ravine, he turned off toward the lower pasture where Gus and Glen were skinning the dead stock—"Might as well skin 'em and at least get something for the hides," Father had told them after chores that morning.

Michal ran down the back way and sauntered to the fence corner. There she carefully selected a place within hearing, where the breeze blew away from her, and she could avoid the sight of the already bloating cattle.

"I thought you wasn't comin' down here," said Gus glancing up briefly, but not pausing in his work.

"A person may always change her mind," said Michal loftily, settling her skirts and looking disinterestedly away toward the eastern horizon.

Herman Haar clumped up, chewing a blade of grass. "Bat luck for Yohn Vard, no?" he remarked casually.

"Well, I wouldn't eggsactly call it good," said Gus, straightening and rubbing his back.

"Sefen yahr back same t'ing by me kum—all crop lost. He vanting to sell iss?" asked Herman carelessly, leaning over the gate.

"I ain't hearn any talk of it. Why don't you go up to the place an' ask him?"

"Ya," he agreed, turning back toward the road.

Michal got up quickly and started toward the haystacks, not answering Gus's parting remark, "Mighty short call you made us, I must say."

She ran to the barn, then—just ahead of Mr. Haar—strolled up to where Father had dug a deep hole beside the piles of dead poultry. He

106

paid no attention to Michal, but looked up and nodded indifferently as Haar joined them.

"De hail—she get you bat, Yohn," he remarked dolefully.

To Michal's surprise Father smiled. "Yes," he said cheerfully, straightening up and climbing out of the hole. "Pretty bad to have a year's work and a crop like that one wiped out in ten minutes or so."

"Ya, ya!" agreed Herman shaking his head.

"But next year I'll make it up."

Mr. Haar's face fell. "Aber if next yahr gifs no rain?"

"Well, of course"—Father began shoveling poultry into the hole—"that's a chance we farmers always have to take—you know that."

"Better you sell—I could a little more land haben."

"Yes, I'd sell if I got my price—but nobody around here will pay that." Father smiled grimly and shoveled faster.

"How mooch?"

"You know—same price I quoted you last spring." Father spoke carelessly and shoveled the last of the draggled blood-stained chickens in with the rest and began covering them.

"Ach, Gott! Iss too mooch."

"Sure! I told you nobody here'd pay me for it. But that's all right. I'm not going to give the place away. You know how high lumber is now, and you know, Herman, that there isn't as well built a house in the township. When Fred Gordon does anything he does it right. The barn is well put up, too; except for your new one it's the biggest anywhere around. You're proud of your barn, but your Frau would be just as proud of a house and it'ud save you plenty of time and money if she could move into one like this—all built and ready. She likes it too."

"Ya, dot iss so—but iss too mooch." As he moved away, he called back over his shoulder, "I gif you half dot."

"Like hell you will, Herman," said John Ward cheerfully, and tamped down the earth with his shovel.

"You didn't tell Mr. Haar the truth today, did you, Father?" asked Michal at dinner.

"Are you calling me a liar?" he countered, leaning back in his chair and smiling.

"Well, aren't you," she asked seriously. "You spoke of being here next year and acted as though you didn't care whether you sold or not."

Mavis shot a triumphant glance at Father. " 'Out of the mouths of babes—' "

Father nodded; then, turning to Michal, "Well, I guess I did stretch the truth a bit," he admitted, "but there are two situations when a man's justified in that: one's when"—and he smiled at Mavis —"he's courting a woman like your mother; and the other when he's horse trading. I call this business with Haar a sort o' horse trade."

The following week was one of happy confusion. Hetty tore into the work—and there was plenty—with more cheer and animation than she had shown in months. "It's a good thing I made all them pies— they're comin' in mighty handy these days," she said as she packed Mavis's best clothes in the big trunk.

"I'm glad you take this move so happily," said Mother, bringing another load of clothing from the wardrobe.

"Well, I don't mind telling you"—Hetty lowered her voice and looked toward the door—"I do feel like a new creatcher since that black ox was kilt. We'll make a fresh start in a new place an' things'll be better," she observed piously, carefully folding Mavis's best black basque—passementerie side out.

"I'm glad too. I've tutored Michal long enough. She needs school, and it'll be lovely to live in a peaceful little village where I can hear church bells ringing and stand in the door and watch the girls going to Sabbath school in their best clothes. Here are my toque and kid gloves; see if they'll fit into the upper corner of that top tray, will you, please?"

Herman Haar did not come back. By the end of the second week the buoyancy of the first excitement had given place to a tension that Michal was quick to feel running beneath the surface of everyday affairs. Hetty, still cheerful, went about her usual work; but Mother seemed anxious and Father increasingly irritable.

"What if he doesn't come back?" said Mavis suddenly, apropos of nothing, as the family sat out in front one evening in the gathering dusk.

"He'll come back, all right. Just give him time."

"But shouldn't you be over there at End-of-Track now?"

"I can't do a thing until End-of-Track is platted; I left word with Becker, the banker, to notify me in time to get good lots. In the meantime I've got Brooks all lined up to take over my Ipswich business, but we're keeping it quiet until Haar takes this place. Getting anxious to leave?"

"I can't wait, John." Her voice was tense but low.

"Well, for once we're agreed about moving; that's a relief, anyway.

Haar is a shrewd buyer; he's waiting for me to approach him. If I don't, and he thinks we're staying on here, he'll come across—don't you worry," and he leaned over and patted Mother's hand.

More than half of September was gone, and as golden day succeeded golden day the tension increased; each morning Michal wondered, Will he come today? and her waking hours were chiefly spent watching for Haar to appear across the ravine.

On the evening of the twentieth, Father came home early. "I had a letter from Becker, the banker, today. He tells me to plan to be there soon—things are looking lively and plenty of enterprising businessmen are looking over the place for locations. I've got to make it quick now."

He was quiet all through supper, and afterward, instead of settling down to read, he paced up and down the sitting room, scowling. Suddenly his face cleared; he stopped and smote his clenched right fist into his left hand. "I've got it!" he declared; then, as Gus came in and hung his lantern behind the kitchen door, Father called, "Gus, come here!"

"Yes, Mr. Ward."

"I want you to take the plow and begin on the west side of the west field tomorrow morning early; at the same time have Glen take the breaker and begin on the west side of the north pasture. Except for chores, plow and break steadily all day, and be sure that both of you stay on the west sides where Haar can see you from his place."

"Yes, Mr. Ward." Then a slow grin spread across his face and he winked.

"That ought to fetch him, eh?" Father returned jovially.

The next day the men plowed until time for evening chores while Michal from various vantage points watched for Mr. Haar. But he did not come, and Michal felt so sorry for Father that she met him at the ravine. "He hasn't come yet," she said, but he answered only, "Hello, Chicken," abstractedly, and they rode up the hill in silence.

Michal fiddled with her food—it was hard to swallow. She excused herself as soon as she could and ran to the window. No sound. It was almost dark; a few stars winked at her as she slipped unnoticed out of the front door and ran quickly across the west field to the knoll where over a year before she and Mother had watched the prairie fire. She'd take just one more look. Then she heard the clatter of hoofbeats from over the hill across the ravine. She stood listening. They rang clearer and louder, and she flew across the field and burst into the house. "He's coming!" she gasped, and while Father said:

"Everybody keep quiet and let me handle this—Hetty, make a pot of fresh coffee," Michal hurried to wash her flushed face and smooth her hair.

Her hand shook with excitement as she took *Little Women* from the shelf. The house looked very cozy as Haar knocked. The glow of the best lamp showed the open cottage organ in the far corner; and Mother, her mending basket beside her, was quietly working. Father sat reading in the dining room under the hanging lamp; the chenille table cover was littered with papers and magazines. From the kitchen came the clatter of dishwashing.

"Well, good evening, Herman." Father opened the door wide, "Come in. Gus, take his horse to the barn. What can I do for you?"

Herman Haar came in, blinking in the bright light. "It is nottings mooch," he said casually, sitting down in the chair Father indicated. "Mine Frau, she broke today mine shofel—she cuts *Kuhmist*. I vonder if you me one gif bis I to Epsweech go."

"Why, of course; we have two spades—they're better for cutting than shovels. Mavis, have Hetty bring us hot coffee."

"I see you plow today the vest side." Mr. Haar said politely, after Mavis had excused herself and gone to the kitchen.

"Yes," Father's voice was casual. "I had almost decided to rest that field next year, but I got to thinking it's my best wheat land and hasn't been used too long, so I'm plowing it deep this fall and planting it to wheat again next spring."

"It give goot veat, dot field," said Haar indifferently.

"Yes, you saw that stand of wheat. I figured I could spare half of the north pasture too. I had Glen start breaking it today, and I'll sow it to flax next year."

Haar seemed to have lost all interest in the land. "Nice house," he said without enthusiasm, eyeing the sitting room. "Var do Goost and his Frau sleep?" he asked suddenly.

"In the back bedroom—like to see it?" Then, as Mother came in followed by Hetty with the tray, "Do you mind my showing your room to Mr. Haar, Hetty?"

"Of course not, Mr. Ward; come right along. I'll light the lamp for you first," putting the tray on the center table.

"Not yet—we'll drink our coffee while it's hot and see the room later. There's no hurry."

Mavis poured coffee, and Michal watched in wide-eyed wonder as

110

Herman Haar poured it into his saucer to cool it, then drank each saucerful down in one big *whoosh!* After the third helping, he wiped his mouth on the back of his hand and asked carelessly, "Vot you take for dis place now?"

Father paused a moment before answering, then said calmly: "I told you last spring just what I'd take, Herman; it's worth that to me, and more."

"Iss too mooch," answered Mr. Haar flatly.

"Yes, probably you're the only one in the township who could pay that price, but you've made enough off the Oulette and Tannyhill places to afford it; it's worth that to me. It's the best of land, and we're very comfortable in this house."

"Mine Frau vood dis Haus like." Haar spoke as though to himself. "Effer since I de big barn bilt I hear notting but 'Haus, Haus' " and he smiled ruefully.

"Tch! Tch!" said Father seriously, shaking his head. "Women all want houses—they're queer that way."

"Ya—she say I mine horses und cows like more as her and the Kinder. Voman's iss fools!" he observed.

Father nodded his head sympathetically.

"Dot room of Goost—I nefer see it yet."

Father got up slowly, and spoke amiably. "Oh, yes, I nearly forgot."

Michal heard the mumble of their voices, and as they came out Herman made no reference to the room. Instead he asked abruptly: "For vhy you break dot nort' pasture, Yohn?"

"Well, I can spare it—it's one of the best pieces of land I have; level as this floor, well fertilized with all the stock running over it so long, and no stones to speak of. It'll make fine wheat land after a first crop of flax on the breaking."

Herman Haar did not sit down; he started for the door.

"Good night, Mr. Haar," said Mavis graciously, looking up from her mending. "Come again."

"Wait a minute until I get my hat—I'll go out with you—you mustn't forget that spade."

Michal's heart sank. He wasn't going to take it after all! They'd stay right here; she wouldn't mind, but Father and Mother would be very disappointed. Besides, she had decided she'd like to live in a town —it would be exciting, and there'd be Katie and that awful boy.

Father came from the kitchen with his hat, and Herman Haar put his hand on the doorknob—then turned back abruptly, put his hand in his pocket and drew out a big greasy pocketbook. "I take it—pay t'ree hundret dollars down until ve tomorrow by Leola papers make." And he counted out the money in wadded bills.

"It's yours! I'll write you a receipt." Then they shook hands, and as Haar started for his horse Father called: "Wait a minute Herman. You're forgetting that spade."

XVIII

For a week Michal stood on the fringe of a happy confusion. Father and Mr. Haar estimated and figured on shingles and scraps of paper, for Father was selling him the machinery, and livestock—even Genevieve and her surviving piglets. The horses, however, John Ward was keeping. Haar cast covetous eyes on the work horses but did not want the Hambletonians. As Father explained apologetically to Mother: "I've an idea there'll be an opening over there for a livery stable. I may start one and keep it until I'm well established in my machine business. I can always turn it over."

Mavis smiled.

Finally the dickering was over. John Ward spent another couple of days in Ipswich finishing his deal with Mr. Brooks, most of which had been done quietly right after the decision to move. Hetty spent a hectic day helping Mavis get Father off for End-of-Track, then settled down in earnest to finish packing. Every day the house seemed less like home.

Then Father's letter came asking Gus to meet the train at Ipswich, late afternoon on Thursday. By Friday evening they were all ready to go. Michal was glad, for the place seemed strange and lonely. Haar had taken the milch cows and all the hogs and poultry the hail had spared. The house was bare, the furniture crated, books boxed, and carpets rolled. Mavis herself packed her best Spode set, the potpourri and other cherished pieces in apple barrels, wrapping each dish tenderly in newspaper. Hetty had fried chicken and made roll jelly cake for lunch on the trip, and the house was fragrant with the smells of the last hearty meal they would eat at the Homestead; for tomorrow morning early they'd start the long forty-mile journey west to End-of-Track.

That afternoon Michal ran down to say goodbye to her little willow tree. It was the thing she most hated to leave—grown so tall and bright and shining with golden leaves, now beginning to fall. She might never see it again! Then she heard the steady *clump-clump-clump* of a work team, Herman Haar with a load of bedding, a carved chest, and a tall wardrobe. "Mine Frau, she could not vait. Ve pring dem in?" He was asking Father.

"Of course, Herman; come in, come in. No, don't let your wife do that work—Gus will help you. Just put them in the dining room."

Mrs. Haar was excited. She smiled broadly and talked in German, looked around the room, waving her hands in an effort to make Mavis understand. Hetty made fresh coffee while Mavis took Mrs. Haar through the rooms, enjoying her exclamations of pleasure. Then back in the sitting room, as she said "Ach" and poured out another avalanche of German words, Mr. Haar sheepishly explained to Mother, "Mine Frau, she is glat so big house mit vood floors to haf."

There was a new, strange smell in the house, Michal noticed, since the Haars had arrived—a strange earthy smell. Then Hetty brought coffee, and she heard Mother say to Mr. Haar: "Tell her I'm very glad the house is going to someone who will enjoy it so much. It makes me glad too; I hope you may be very happy here."

After they had gone, Mavis said to Michal: "I'm going over on the hills a while. Want to come with me?"

Michal was puzzled; Mother almost never walked on the prairie. Only as they climbed the big hill did she realize Mother was going to Little Brother.

Mavis seated herself beside the little mound; she did not cry—just sat with folded hands. Michal leaned against the boulder behind her, silent; she felt choked by embarrassment and pity. For a while she watched the evening cloud shadows slide over the prairie, and the cranes feeding down along the ravine. Perhaps Mother would like to see them, too. She glanced at her, but Mavis still sat as before, and seemed not to know that Michal was there.

The cranes finished feeding, and with much clumsy wing flapping took off; then, with necks stretched full length, legs straight out behind, they began climbing high in great progressive circles and their

113

weird throaty cries of somber lamentation came back to her, clearly at first, then more faintly as they reached the far heights. She wondered if Mother heard their calls—if so, she gave no sign.

The sun was nearly down and Michal was cramped and tired before Mavis stirred, rose to her feet, took her daughter's hand, and without a word or backward glance went slowly down the hill. The little chicory blossoms along the road were tightly closed before they reached the ravine.

That night Michal lay in her bed, made up on the floor. She wondered: Why couldn't the Haars have kept their things in their own place until we are gone? I wanted tonight to be ours and the smells to be the smells of our house. That earthy odor would be the dugout. But the sharp tang mixed with it puzzled her. She sniffed, then remembered. It was the same smell that came from the mosquito smudge when Glen tucked dried cow chips under the green weeds to hurry the fire. Damp earth and cow-chip smoke. They could have the house! After all, she was going to a town—excitement—people. She and Katie would play together often. She'd get acquainted with that strange Russian boy, too —the smarty! He thought he was so much. She'd show him!

Michal shifted uneasily. She should have been asleep long ago, for tomorrow would be a long day. It might be exciting to sleep on the floor, but the bed was hard. The room was filled with shadows in unfamiliar places, and there was still that annoying smell.

The moon was high now, and its light sifted down through the window into her face. She would look out and see her little willow tree once more. Getting up softly so as not to waken Faith, she tiptoed to the window. There it stood, alone, gleaming pale gold, giving its light to the dim sleeping prairie just as the moon gave its brightness to the far dim fields of the sky.

There was no wind—the whole night seemed to be listening. Michal leaned on the sill and listened, too, until presently, growing drowsy in the soft light and the silence, she crept back into bed.

From the direction of Haar's place came the mournful howling of a dog. It would be little Tan Ears, awake, and baying at the moon. Then faintly from the hills far beyond Little Brother's grave, a coyote answered; three short yelps and a long-drawn desolate wail.

Michal thought hazily, I wonder if the Haars will take good care of my little tree.

114

Part Two

END-OF-TRACK

I

1887-1890

The Wards dressed and breakfasted by moonlight; as gray dawn dimmed the stars they were on their way—west again. For hours the little caravan, following the faintly defined road, lurched over the prairie that rolled ahead in immense yellow-gray waves. Before sunset they glimpsed End-of-Track in the distance.

Shadows were gathering and the eerie cry of a solitary killdeer floated plaintively through the thin air. Finally, as pinnacles of pale gold lingering in the west were faintly reflected behind a mauve and lavender afterglow, they entered the town.

End-of-Track was not the place Michal and Father had visited a few months before. It had grown. Instead of the dusty road paralleling the track there was now a business section where Market Street bisected Main. Along these streets sizable box-elder trees had been planted, each neatly enclosed in its protecting fence, and hitching posts stood before the new buildings that raised their true story-and-a-half heights still higher with false fronts. Everywhere buildings were going up; sidewalks were so new that the yellow boards were still beaded with drops of amber pitch.

Father suggested that they go to the new hotel—the Stuyvesant —but Mother said: "Since we have the cradle and bedding in the prairie schooner, Gus and Glen can set up beds tonight. I'd rather stay in our own home, John." And he agreed, well pleased.

As they drove into the heart of the town, Michal busied herself watching the passing people—businessmen, brisk and hurried; women in bustled skirts and tight basques; and everywhere, lonely and apart, the foreigners, avoiding for the most part the sidewalks for the middle of the street.

The house was a terrible disappointment—a large new rectangular building propped up on great wooden blocks back of the livery stable but facing on Second. It wasn't like the house of Mother's song—no jasper or pearl about it—it wasn't even painted!

Swept by the same depression she had felt on first seeing the Homestead and Tree Claim, Michal asked, "Why is our place up high on those stilts?"

"This was the only house I could buy. It was meant for a store, but it was solidly built and so I took it and left it here."

"Will it always be like this?"

"Of course not! It's too close in for one thing. I've bought forty acres of land"—he gestured with his whip—"on that hill to the northwest. Next spring we'll move it out there, put a good foundation under it, finish the upstairs into bedrooms. In the meantime it's handy to my work."

As Father helped Mavis and the younger children out of the carriage, Michal climbed down, then glanced curiously at a neat wooden cottage directly across the street. Framed in the window between starched white curtains was a girl about her own age, her face pressed against the windowpane. Michal smiled, but the girl moved back, made a horrible face, and thumbed her nose. In Michal's present mood she could really show that girl something. Putting her index fingers under her eyes and pulling down, and her little fingers in the corners of her mouth and pulling out, she stuck out her tongue, and as the girl stared open-mouthed, Michal turned with great dignity and marched into the house.

Within the hour Father, Gus, and Glen had lugged in the cradle, bedding, and a couple of chairs while Mavis and Hetty—having turned the twins over to Michal and Faith—made up crude beds which would serve for the night.

Everyone was cross and hungry by the time Hetty hauled out the picnic basket which still held a few chicken sandwiches and cake left over from lunch. Mavis had just retired to the front bedroom to nurse the twins when a rich voice at the door boomed, "Open up, somebody, my hands is full," and Michal recognized the voice of Achsah Klunk, the woman she and Father had seen on that first trip. She was carrying a large brown earthen pot, from which flowed the heavenly odor of baked beans.

"When I seen you come this evening, figured you'd be starved fer somethin' hot. These'll stick to your ribs."

"You bet they will, Mrs. Klunk," agreed Father heartily, taking the pot from her with alacrity. "You must live close by."

"The little shack right across the alley."

"Mis' Ward's nursin' the twins but she'll want to thank you—" began Hetty.

"Don't bother her. I gotta get right back." She poked Michal playfully with an elbow. "The look on yer paw's face was thanks enough," as from the kitchen came the sound of the men already dishing up.

Later, as Mavis helped undress Faith, Hetty handed the bean pot to Michal, saying: "Tell Miz Klunk we licked the platter clean. Why, even yer maw took two helpings."

Though it was dark, Achsah was sitting on her tiny porch when Michal crossed the alley. "Jest put my wild cucumber vines to bed," she said cheerfully. "There'll be frost any time now, and gunny sacks make good blankets."

"Everybody said to tell you those were the best baked beans they'd ever tasted," said Michal handing her the jar.

"Oh, I can cook, all right. Cooked fer railroad graders fer years before I started washin' for 'em. Sit a moment, child." As Michal seated herself on the top step, Achsah went on: "This is my favorite time o' day, with the dark siftin' down and the smell o' raw lumber and dust and smoke. In daytime the town looks sort of nekkid; but come night it's real pritty with the stars shinin' and lamplight makin' little gold squares. Glad you folks of come. Lotta riffraff round a boom town, and I don't mean Rooshans. Nights, that big house so empty and all, give me the creeps."

"Who lives in that place across from us, Mrs. Klunk?"

"The Pratts. Amos and Abigail and a girl about your age—Fanny."

"I saw her today. She—I mean—well, we made faces at each other."

Achsah chortled. "I'll bet. Most people here is fine, but Abigail Pratt is a snoop and a gossip. She's the kind knows a woman's in a family way before the husband has his pants buttoned. And I wouldn't trust that Fanny far as I could throw a bull by the tail."

Michal sighed. "Mother'll probably expect me to play with her some. But my real friend is Katie Keim."

"Good," approved Achsah. "She's a nice girl. And her folks are salt of the earth. Poor Mr. Keim. Since he built his new store he's been rushed to death, and looks awful tired. The Rooshan farmers are hauling wheat in now—streets are clogged with 'em—"

"Is that why it's so dusty?"

"Yep. Well, as I was sayin', Mr. Keim litters hay on the floor of his store nights and some of his best customers from 'way out spread coats or blankets and sleep there. Even sleep on the counters. Poor man looks run to death."

"Do the children help haul wheat?" asked Michal, thinking of Katie's cousin, that dark boy.

"The older ones do. You see 'em at noon eatin' fat pork—Schweinefleisch, they call it—spread on thick chunks o' bread."

Michal shuddered. "It sounds awful."

"Oh, them Rooshan kids is healthy as horses. And fine lookers too, some of 'em. There's one girl, Frieda Baur—folks live out a ways but more money than you can shake a stick at. She's a corker—yellow braids clear to her hips and thick as my arm. Eyes blue as flax. Then there's a boy, a relation of Keims, I think. Real dark and tall, he is. Don't look like the rest. He'll be a heart smasher one of these days."

Michal rose hastily, feeling uneasily that the woman had read her mind. "I guess I'd better go now."

Achsah Klunk picked up the bean pot and stood up also. "Glad you set a while." Michal began to edge away politely, but the woman went on: "Oh, you'll love this town, child. It smells good, sort of clean and new, and it looks good. It even sounds good. Listen tomorrow for the sound of the blacksmith hammer. First a loud clang—and then softer ones, and finally the little long-drawn-out sound like a silver thread. Like music it is—"

"I'll listen," said Michal softly. "Good night." For a moment she lingered in the shadow of her own house, reviewing all that Achsah Klunk had said, particularly about that boy. It must have been Karl she was talking about. She pictured their first meeting, herself aloof but pretty in one of the new dresses Mother had promised. Perhaps she'd

120

smile and nod, or maybe she'd pretend not to see him at all. Then Mavis came to the door and called, and Michal went in thinking, Anyway, when I see him I'll make him notice me, even if I have to take him down a peg or two.

II

By the time the cries from an early flock of geese traveling south floated down to the little town on the prairie, the new house began to seem like home. Everyone was busy, for along with the influx of newcomers and the constant building, grain was pouring into the town. Every day the streets were crowded with wagons—many drawn by oxen, their heads bowed under heavy neck yokes; some by horses; a few even by a horse and an ox—streaming from dawn to dark over the delicate tracery of trails that webbed the prairie for sixty miles around.

Hetty, grumbling constantly about the dust kicked up by "them infernal teams," nevertheless admitted one afternoon: "I don't see as how it could be any cozier, Mis' Ward. Except I don't like a house on stilts. I'll be mighty relieved when Mr. Ward gits it fixed. 'Twouldn't surprise me to see some varmint crawling up through that trap door any time."

"He'll have it done next week, Hetty."

"You know, Mother," confided Michal, "it'll seem funny to call the town Eureka. We've called it End-of-Track for so long."

Mavis smiled. "I don't care what they call it so long as we're here. Hetty, I feel like a new woman. My husband satisfied. The babies thriving. There'll be church again. And people. I'm sorry there's no school yet for the girls. It'll mean my continuing to help Michal a while yet. Faith, too, is ready to start."

Hetty nodded then glanced out the window. "Here comes Achsah." She paused, then added sharply, "Something's wrong! She's cryin'."

As Michal ushered their guest in the back door she saw that, sure enough, Achsah's eyes were red and almost swollen shut. The big woman sat down heavily at the table without even waiting to be asked.

"Been bellerin' like a calf all morning. Thought some of Hetty's good coffee might help."

As Mavis poured a large cupful, she said gently, "Tell us about it."

"My wild cucumber vines. Somebody sneaked up last night and tore them down. I haven't even had the heart to clean the mess up yet —lying there all wilted and dead, my little vines."

"That's the meanest thing I ever heard!" exclaimed Michal, hurrying to the window. The airy leaves that had softened the small empty porch were strewn in a limp puddle over the well scrubbed steps.

"It's frightening," Mavis said slowly, "to think that anybody would do such a vicious thing."

Achsah wiped her eyes, blew her nose, then took a large gulp of coffee. "That's what got me, Miz' Ward. I know the killin' frost is due any day now, but why couldn't they of taken a poke at me 'stead of my cucumbers."

Hetty snorted. "Cuz you'd poke back, that's why. Some sneaky kid, probably."

Michal spoke up. "It's like the time Matt punched the eyes out Father's picture."

By the time Achsah had drunk her third cup of coffee and had heard the whole story of the wheat stealers told dramatically and with great relish by Hetty, the other woman had relaxed.

"Just remember, Mrs. Klunk," added Mavis, "you can grow bigger vines next year."

"That I will, Miz' Ward. And I'll clout anybody who lays a hand on 'em."

A few hours later Hetty, peering cautiously through the lace curtain in the sitting room, hissed, "This is our day for callers. Here comes that Pratt critter with Fanny."

"Please, Hetty, try to like Mrs. Pratt a little. After all, her husband and mine are partners in the livery stable now, and we've got to get along."

"Do I have to play with Fanny?" demanded Michal. "Katie and I—"

"Yes, you do." Mavis spoke tartly. "Every time I turn around Katie's here or you're there."

Mrs. Pratt, plump and voluble, began talking before Mavis had closed the door. "Just dropped in for a chat. Fanny, go sit by Michal.

Now that our husbands are partners, our girls should be best friends, don't you think, Mrs. Ward?"

Mavis smiled. "I'm glad about the partnership, Mrs. Pratt. The men seem congenial."

"Well, Amos wanted to buy him out, you know."

"John considered it. But I'm rather glad he kept part interest in the livery stable. This way he can give his best to the farm-implement business and still go to his office in the tack room, smell the saddle leather and neat's-foot oil and talk horses. Besides, John's always happier when he has more than one iron in the fire."

As Mavis began pouring coffee, Abigail Pratt rose suddenly, tiptoed to the window, pushed the curtain back, and whispered: "There goes that Klunk woman. It don't seem decent, a woman like her living in the same block with respectable folks. In Salem, Massachusetts, it couldn't happen; but a body kin expect anything in this hole. Why"—coming back and sipping coffee rapidly—"she's almost in your back yard."

"She's been kindness itself to us," Mavis replied quietly.

"She'd better not be kind to me," snorted Abigail. "Funny, I say, when a woman makes her living washing for railroad men. They's apt to be something besides washing behind it. Every decent woman in this town is talking about her. I don't envy you having that eyesore of a shack right across the alley from you either. Y'd think she'd paint it, at least. And having your innocent children—"

Mavis interrupted, "You know, somebody tore down her wild cucumber vines last night."

Abigail was deflected. "They did? Now who—" She was off. As the women discussed the vandalism, Michal was aware of a curious intentness on the part of Fanny. Turning to look at her, she saw something flicker like a living thing in the bright brown eyes before they slid away from her own. In that instant she knew the culprit as clearly as though she'd been told, and her skin crawled with disgust.

Mavis was pouring more coffee. "Do you dread the winter as much as I do?"

"Something awful. Don't you hate your house up on stilts like it is? It'll be terrible cold, come December."

"Next week the men are going to put a tarpaper and wood base around it and then bank it high for winter. It wouldn't pay us to put a stone foundation under it, when we're moving it next spring."

123

"No, of course not; but still I'd be afraid of it setting up so high—the draft could give you joint pains. Only one agony is worse"—she lowered her voice—"bein' in the family way—and personally I'd rather be in Tophet with my neck broke than that!"

"I never mind," said Mavis gently. "I always feel so very well."

"I felt terrible—just terrible! If you ever have another"—she stopped and eyed Mavis curiously—"you'll call in Dr. Kelp?"

Mavis smiled. "Well, as Hetty says, there's no one else to have."

Mrs. Pratt leaned forward, her sharp voice softening. "I'll swear by him. He certainly helped my misery—besides, he uses such elegant Latin words."

Michal remembered seeing him drifting along the street—dressed in clothes too large for him and smoking a long cigar.

"And not only does Mrs. Kelp not go to church"—Mrs. Pratt again—"but I've heard that she smokes the same black cigars her husband does and drinks her whisky like a man. The poor doctor! Of course, she don't mix with people a-tall. But I'm goin' to call on her some fine day and see a few things for myself."

Hetty came to the sitting room door. "Gus wants to see you a minute, Michal."

"Then you girls might stroll about and get acquainted," Mavis suggested, and Michal knew Mother was relieved at their going.

The girls found Gus out by the back door, holding a tomato can. "Look what I found down by the marsh."

Fanny took one look. "It's a snake!"

"Ya. Cute little garter snake. I'm dinged if it don't look just like them garters I give Het for Christmas—all black and gold and blue."

"It's no bigger than a lead pencil," exclaimed Michal, peering at it. "Is it for me?"

"Who else? I gotta hyper along now. Better not let yer maw see it."

"Thanks, Gus. Look, Fanny, it coils right around my wrist like a bracelet."

Fanny peeked again cautiously, then shrank back. "How can you touch the slimy thing?"

Michal, beginning to enjoy herself, drew her hand out of the can dangling the snake. "Don't be silly. They're cool and firm, not slimy. Anyway, it's just a baby. Let's go show it to Katie."

"I wouldn't be seen dead talking to Katie Keim."

Thoughtfully, Michal replaced the snake in the can and then turned. "And why not?"

124

"Ma'd skin me alive! Besides, I'll have no truck with any dirty Rooshan."

"Katie's not dirty! She's cleaner than you are!"

"She ain't either."

"She is, too."

"She ain't! And I'll tell her so."

"You do and I'll drop this snake down your neck!"

Fanny took off in a cloud of dust with Michal hot on her heels. Careening around the house, she saw that Fanny was headed in the direction of the Keims', weaving in and out of sidewalk traffic and finally darting across the street just ahead of a team hauling a load of grain. Michal plunged recklessly after her, heedless of people, horses, or anything else. She was gaining ground by the time they reached Keim's store, when Fanny stopped suddenly, wheeled, and stuck her foot out. Michal plunged to the sidewalk, dropping the tomato can and crying out as she felt a sharp twist of pain in her ankle. "You nasty little sneak!" she shouted furiously, then went mute as Fanny darted behind a tall boy—Karl Gross—and beside him, her blue eyes round with amazement, Katie.

"Don't let 'er up!" squeaked Fanny, clutching his arm. "She's going to put a snake down my neck!"

"*Dummkopf!*" He shook her off irritably, then looked down again at Michal and smiled faintly. "*Vas ist los?*"

Fanny forgotten, Michal saw herself as she must look to the others —one braid loosened, her dress dusty and torn. She felt her face go crimson, knew the dark, bitter taste of humiliation.

Katie knelt down. "Your hand, it iss bleeding."

"Must have cut it on the can when I—Katie," she cried, "there goes my snake! Get him for me."

Katie shrank. "Gott, no!"

"Will you?" she appealed to Karl, who—scowling—reached down and pulled her to her feet, and, then, without a word, walked into his uncle's store. Fanny smoothed her shiny dark curls and scuttled in after him. Michal turned just in time to see a flash of black and gold as the snake wriggled into the weeds under the sidewalk. "It's gone!" She looked at Katie, shrugged, brushed the dust off her skirt, and began braiding her hair. "That boy—your cousin—he might have gotten my snake for me."

"Karl is too busy to catch snakes for anybody."

"Probably afraid."

"He's afraid of notting," firmly. "You are limping."

Grimly Michal tested her full weight on the hurt foot. "I just twisted my ankle a little. That's why I didn't go after the snake. Whew! I hope Fanny doesn't tell Mother. She thinks I'm too old for this sort of thing."

"You are," replied Katie calmly. "Soon you'll be putting the hair up and liking boys—even," slyly, "boys who won't chase snakes."

"If you think for one minute that I could like that awful cousin—" began Michal, then paused as she noticed a tall woman who had just come out of the store and who was eyeing her severely. "Are you Michal Ward?"

"Yes, ma'am."

The stern face softened slightly. "I'm Prudence White. I've been meaning to call on your mother, but wanted to wait until she was settled. Would you tell her that church services are going to be held this Sunday in the depot."

As the woman talked, Michal studied her carefully—the pale face and strong chin accented by a dark mole; coal-black hair parted exactly in the middle and worn smoothed down without a thread out of place. I wonder what a fly would do if it tried to light on her head, she thought, and giggled inwardly as she pictured it skidding helplessly down the shining black surface.

She introduced Katie, but Mrs. White gave the blond girl only a cool nod and strode away. Katie didn't seem to notice the snub, for she said thoughtfully, "She has a son, Yoshua."

"Who's he?"

"He iss telegraph operator."

"Oh, him. You mean that boy at the depot, sort of pretty with curly brown hair and big blue eyes. He looks like an awful sissy."

Katie's face turned pink. "He's a goot boy," she announced firmly. "Do you know him?"

"He has sometimes to our store come. Den lately I meet the trains each day because Grossmutter come from Russlandt and we don't know just when. He talks with me and makes eyes efen."

"Katie likes Joshua, Katie likes Joshua," chanted Michal under her breath.

Katie's blush deepened. "He is old—seventeen years," loftily— then, with another sly look at Michal, "Karl is not so old."

126

"What do I care how old Karl is!" violently. "Even if he is your cousin, I hate him!"

Katie smiled demurely.

Fanny came out of the store bouncing a chocolate candy mouse up and down by its long rubber tail and keeping a cautious eye on Michal. "Did you catch your snake?" she asked sweetly.

"If I had you'd be on your way home this minute, Fanny Pratt."

"Wait'll I tell your mother, smarty."

"You tell on me and I'll tell Achsah Klunk something I know— and you know what."

Fanny licked her tiny rosebud mouth nervously, her eyes terrier bright and scared. "I'll get even with you someday, Michal Ward; see if I don't." Then she turned and ran.

III

As Michal opened the kitchen door a medley of tangy smells greeted her. A kettle of spicy pumpkin splattered lazily on the back of the stove next to the reservoir. Hetty was mixing boiled beef, suet, apples, raisins, molasses, and cider vinegar in the big chopping bowl for mincemeat. "Some people don't know when to leave," she whispered, as Michal walked through to the sitting room where Mrs. Pratt was still holding forth, not noticing how tired Mother looked. Then the door opened suddenly on Father, who exclaimed, "Well, Mavis, I've—oh, how are you, Mrs. Pratt? I didn't know I was interrupting a tea party." He looked annoyed.

"Never mind, Mr. Ward; I was just going anyway. Mr. Pratt is a quiet man, but he likes his meals on time. Drop over often Mis' Ward. It's only a step."

John relaxed only after he had closed the door on her. "Mavis, I've sold the Percherons to the drayman—$600 cash and Starlet, the sweetest little buckskin filly you ever saw, to boot. She rides easy as a rocking chair. You and Michal can use a saddle pony."

"I'd love a good horseback ride. Next spring we'll go evenings," said Mavis dreamily, settling down to nurse Gordon and smoothing his dark curls absently. "I'm glad you're rid of the draft horses, John. Wasn't that a very good price?"

"Yes, but they're worth every cent of it. I've got to leave right now. The sheriff has to go to Hillsview and wants me to take him."

"Why can't one of the men go?"

"Glen took a man up north to look at a piece of land and may not be back before morning. Gus will look after the business. Tell Hetty he'll sleep in the office tonight. Besides, the sheriff wants a close-mouthed man. He might need a deputy."

"But, John, your supper."

"I'll eat in Hillsview. Take care of this money." He thrust a roll of bills into her hand. "The buyer paid me after the bank closed. The revolver's loaded. Keep it handy—it'll make you feel safe. Don't expect me until you see me."

He kissed her and strode out.

"Michal"—the heavy roll of bills seemed almost to weigh down Mother's slender hand—"will you please tuck this money back of the pendulum of the old clock in my bedroom?"

When Michal reentered the kitchen Hetty was saying gloomily, "Mr. Ward sure has an almighty faith in somethin' to leave us defenseless women and children here with money in the house."

"Hetty, please don't talk that way before the girls. We're perfectly safe with the gun. I'm rather a good shot. John taught me target practice before we were married."

"Humph!" snorted Hetty.

"Besides"—Mavis's dark eyes twinkled slightly—"the black ox is dead. There!" She handed sleepy Gordon to Hetty—modestly covering her breast with the shawl—then began coaxing Philip, who was crawling rapidly over the floor, his blue eyes brimming with mischief, as he evaded his mother.

Hetty scooped him up firmly and handed him to Mavis as Faith, eyes wide, looked up from the table where she and Michal were eating, to ask, "Can anything hurt us, Mother?"

"God takes care of his own."

"God was sure watching over these blessed babies when he give 'em a mother with milk spillin' from her buzzums like a fountain," remarked Hetty proudly.

Mavis blushed, lowered her eyes, then winced. "His teeth are sharp," she murmured, looking down tenderly at the baby who was

128

nursing violently, kneading his mother's breast with one fist and pushing away the shawl with the other. "John must have been like Philip at this age."

Michal relaxed. Imagine Father ever being a baby! The room was fragrant with the scents of mincemeat, dried-apple sauce, freshly baked bread, and a faint sweetish smell from Gordon, who had thrown up a little milk.

"Hetty, I think I'll let you change the babies and get them settled for the night. I'm going to walk a little before I eat."

"We'll come, too," announced Faith, and Mavis smiled assent as she handed over Philip, put on her dolman, and helped the girls into their cloaks.

As they began their leisurely pacing—up and down, up and down—in front of the house, a man slipped out of the shadows and hurried through the alley.

"Mother, he was looking in our window," whispered Michal.

"Probably a railroad man taking his dirty clothes to Mrs. Klunk," returned Mavis. "But it did almost seem as though he stepped out from beside our house," she added, half to herself.

"Mother—"

"It's all right." Mavis spoke quickly. "We're just nervous because of what Hetty said. Remember that she is superstitious, even though she is our good practical Hetty."

A little wind was rising, and the moon, clear as a frozen bubble, was poised delicately over the deepening horizon. Mavis shivered. "We'll go in now. Michal, you hear Faith's prayers, please, while I eat my supper."

IV

By the time the girls were in bed the house had settled down into the now familiar pattern of night noises—the twins' murmurs in their sleep, the ticking of the clock, the house creakings, and over it all the muted outside sounds—a dog yelping, a baby crying somewhere, occasional soft footsteps; the faint wind weaving all these sounds together.

Michal lay tense, listening. From the kitchen came the murmur of Mother's and Hetty's voices. Finally, the door opened and she heard Mavis say, "Well, it does seem strange with our men both gone, Hetty."

"If it weren't fer all that money it'd seem good, like I told Gus when I took his supper out to him."

"Where's Rory?"

"Why, he's sleeping behind the stove, Mis' Ward. What's the matter? You're nervous as a witch."

"It's silly, Hetty, but we saw a man outside the house when we walked tonight, and he seemed to be looking in the window."

"They's a heap a riffraff around a new town. Now, you git to bed and I'll lock up good and tight and bring you some hot milk—that'll put you to sleep. You'd best have Rory sleep in your room, too."

"Never mind about Rory. I'm going to put the revolver under the pillow."

Michal woke with a start and sat up. It seemed as though she had heard Rory cry out, but she must have been dreaming. The striking of the clock startled her—*whir-r-r*, one—*whir-r-r-r*, two—*whir-r-r-r*, three.

The room was bright with moonlight. From Hetty's room came the sound of deep steady snores, each ending in a piercing whistle. Sleeping on her back again. Faith stirred. Michal thought she heard a footstep. Probably the wind. After all, Rory was on guard.

But it came again, muffled—the clump of heavy feet moving stealthily in the dining room. She stiffened, then relaxed. Father, of course, home early.

Outside, the faint wind quickened. The curtains stirred, and a wave of shadow washed across the brightness and broke against the wall. Strange not to hear Rory's tail thumping against the furniture and Father quieting him. But it was Father, all right, because he was moving clumsily into his and Mother's room. From the other bedroom came Hetty's snores—louder now and still ending on that high note.

Then Mother's voice came, oddly, as though caught in a sob—and Father was answering, hoarsely, almost like somebody else. Something was wrong.

Michal slipped quietly out of bed and tiptoed through the dining room and sitting room. It was bad to spy, but she couldn't sleep now until she knew that everything was all right. The room smelled queer

—like the breath from a saloon. Surely Father hadn't made a hot toddy in the middle of the night!

Cautiously she pushed the heavy green velours portiere a little to one side, then caught her breath. How lovely Mother looked sitting up in bed in the clear moonlight—dark hair tumbled about her shoulders, beautiful hands tensed over the bedclothes she had pulled up over her breast! But her eyes were black and wide as she stared up at the bulky figure towering over her—not Father. Again—more overpowering now —came the sharp stench of whisky.

"I seen her bring the money in here. Where'd she put it!" The voice was coarse and strange.

"In the clock there." Mother's lips seemed hardly to move.

As he opened the clock Michal saw Mavis's right hand go swiftly under Father's pillow, then return to her lap.

The man turned, holding the roll of bills, and said thickly, "John Ward will miss—" He took a step, then paused. "Not bad—not bad at all."

"You have the money—get out of here." Her voice was caught in her breath again.

"Maybe I kin take something from John Ward besides the money —eh?" He moved forward, staggering slightly. "Git him two ways."

Mavis whispered, "I have a gun."

He stopped. "Gun?" Another step forward. "A little thing like you wouldn't shoot a man."

"You're drunk. Don't make me shoot!" The moonlight glinted on the shining barrel. He took another step. Then, as he lunged, the room was jarred by the sharp report.

"Mother!" Michal tore back the portiere. "Mother!"

But Mavis didn't hear. Her eyes were fixed on the dark form sagging, settling, then lying motionless on the floor in the bright moonlight. One of the twins cried out, then settled back into sleep.

Hetty's voice rose from the back of the house. Michal ran, flinging herself against Hetty's sparse frame. "Come quick!"

"I dreamt I heared a shot."

Mavis was out of bed. "Light," she whispered, slipping into her wrapper.

"What's the—my Gawd, Mis' Ward!" She recoiled violently as she almost fell over the mass on the floor.

"I've—killed—a man, Hetty."

131

"I'll git a light." She rushed out.

"Mother, where's—" A shriek rose from the back of the house. Mavis and Michal rushed to the kitchen. Hetty, holding the lamp, was standing over Rory, limp and silent on the floor by the trap door. "He kilt Rory," gasped Hetty; "the dirty bastard kilt Rory."

Michal ran over and kneeled down by her dog. He was quiet. She touched him. His body was still warm, but Rory was dead. Michal raised her face, drained of all color. "Mother."

"Michal, I'm going back to the bedroom."

"Mother."

"I can't help you now. I can't help you tonight."

"I'll get Gus." Hetty threw on her cloak and hurried out. Michal stood up. She was trembling and didn't know where to go. A loud knock sounded.

"It's Achsah Klunk. Kin I come in?"

Michal walked stiffly over and opened the door.

"I seen yer light. Trouble?"

She nodded mutely and pointed toward Rory.

Achsah looked at the dog, then spoke sharply. "Child, yer shakin' like a leaf. Here—" she pulled off her large gray-fringed shawl, wrapped it firmly around Michal, then took the red-checked cloth off the table and draped it gently over Rory. "Now, where's yer ma?"

"In the bedroom." Michal's teeth were chattering. "There's a man in there on the floor."

"God a'mighty! Show me the way, child."

Achsah marched briskly into the bedroom behind Michal. Mavis— face still set—was rocking the cradle automatically.

"What's all this, Mis' Ward?"

"Good evening, Mrs. Klunk. I've killed a man," Mother said tonelessly.

"Have you now?" said Achsah matter-of-factly, squatting by the figure on the floor and peering into its face.

"He's dead," Mavis continued stonily.

"Dead as a herring," agreed Achsah heartily. "What was he after?"

"Money—and—" Mavis stopped abruptly as Hetty and Gus, followed by Dr. Kelp, entered the house.

"Thisaway, Doctor." Hetty's voice was breathless.

"Good evening, Mrs. Ward." Dr. Kelp spoke unctuously as he

drifted over to the still figure, knelt soundlessly, and put his big fat hand on the outflung wrist on the floor.

Then he rose. "Respiration has ceased. There is nothing I can do."

Gus spoke up sharply. "It's Matt McGuire!"

"Matt McGuire!" Hetty squawked. "I'm glad yuh kilt 'im, Mis' Ward."

"Hetty!"

"Yes, I am. And jest t' think 'twas me who wanted to kill 'im and you who done it," she finished admiringly.

Dr. Kelp was already drifting toward the door. "If—ah—there is no other service I can perform, Mrs. Ward—"

"Thank you, Doctor. Goodbye."

"I'll git back now," said Gus, hurrying out. Then Michal's heart gave a leap as Father's voice came from the other room. "Gus, what in hell are you doing away from—"

"I'm a-gittin' right back," Gus said hastily. "They's been a shootin'."

"Wait a minute." John Ward strode into the bedroom. "What's this?" He walked over to the middle of the room and looked down.

Mother walked up very close to Father. "John, I shot Matt."

"Matt McGuire! Gus"—he pushed the portiere aside—"get the sheriff. At the Stuyvesant. Then 'tend to my team."

Achsah Klunk stepped forward. "Let's get this blessed woman out of this here room. A good toddy is what she needs."

Mavis stiffened; her chin rose. "I never touch spirits, thank you."

"Achsah and I'll make a big pot of coffee," said Hetty cheerfully. "We'll have it in the kitchen. Oh, I fergot"—with a glance at Michal—"the dining room, I mean."

"I want the babies out of here." Mother's voice was tremulous.

As Achsah and Father lifted the cradle and carried it carefully into the sitting room, Michal tugged at Father's sleeve. "Rory's dead, Father —out by the trap door. He killed Rory."

John Ward's face turned red and he began to use words that Michal had never heard before—words delivered with such clipped intensity that Michal shrank back and Mavis, pale as a candle, interrupted sharply, "That's enough!"

A knock sounded, and without a word Father wheeled and let in the sheriff. They talked a moment, then went into the bedroom.

The scent of fresh coffee drifted comfortingly through the rooms.

133

Michal heard Hetty saying busily, "—jest can't git over that Kelp critter not even askin' what'd happened. It ain't nature not to be curious."

"Him and his wife are strange ones, all right." This was Achsah.

Father and the sheriff came in and sat down. Hetty and Achsah brought in bread and butter, cups, and the great coffeepot. Then Hetty poured and passed the steaming cups—even Michal was given one. The sheriff took a loud slurp of coffee, then leaned forward. "If you would tell us about it now, Mrs. Ward."

"He must have come shortly after you left and watched us through the window"—Mother stared straight ahead—"because when I woke he asked me for the money. He didn't use his gun, never dreaming I had one, I suppose. Besides, he was drunk. Anyway, I told him where the money was. When he turned I reached under the pillow for the revolver. He took the money . . ." Mavis's voice faltered. "He took the money—"

"Then, Father," Michal continued impatiently, "he said, 'Maybe I can take something from John Ward besides the money.' Do you suppose he meant Mother's cameo?"

"I see." Father's voice sounded queer and his hands kept opening and shutting as he stood up and began pacing.

The sheriff stood up, too. "There's a $100 reward offered fer him, Mrs. Ward. And it's yours."

Mavis shuddered violently.

Achsah Klunk leaned over and patted her shoulder. "Killin's too good fer his like, Mis' Ward."

"The Bible says, 'Thou shalt not kill.' " She turned toward Father. "Here on the prairie"—her voice trembled—"I have broken one of the Ten Commandments."

"You had no choice, Mavis." Father took her hand. "By God," he went on violently, "if I'd been here I'd have ripped him apart!"

"Miss Michal," Hetty said, frowning, "how come you heard what that skunk said to yer maw?"

"I thought I heard Rory cry out." Michal's eyes filled with tears. "Then I thought I heard Father come. His voice sounded queer, so I tiptoed in and saw."

"How come yuh never called me?" demanded Hetty.

"It happened so fast—" She turned to Father, bewildered.

"You couldn't have done a thing. Well"—he turned to the sheriff —"shall we get on with it?" He nodded significantly bedroomward.

134

"And"—Hetty gestured toward the kitchen, then squawked—"My Gawd! Look'a there . . ."

Rory, weaving unsteadily and looking very sick, stood in the open door, the checked tablecloth still dangling from his stern. Michal collided with Father as—at the same time—they reached the dog, whose plume waved vaguely in greeting.

"Riz from the dead!" exclaimed Hetty.

"But he *was* dead," said Michal, smoothing Rory's head gently as Father ran his hands expertly over the dog's body.

The sheriff, leaning against the door and picking his teeth, nodded wisely. "A thing like thet happens once't in a while—if they's hit just right. Stunned so's they'll seem dead. A dog jumped me once't and I kicked it over the heart. Sure thought it was a goner, but it come to in half an hour or so. Valuable critter, too. But a dog shouldn't never jump a man."

"That's probably what happened to Rory," said Father. "Well, Michal"—for a moment his gray eyes softened—"you've got your dog back. Keep him quiet for a while," he finished as he and the sheriff went toward the bedroom.

Michal, sitting on the floor with Rory's head in her lap, tried not to hear the dull thuds as Father and the sheriff moved slowly through the sitting room. As the front door slammed after them she said slowly: "If Rory had died, I'd never have seen him again. Is that what death means—never seeing again?"

"In this life."

Achsah spoke gently. "Yer paw would 'a' got you another red dog."

"There could never be another Rory."

And Mavis said, "If we hadn't come to the prairie this would never have happened."

V

The day following Matt's death, Michal realized fully how much better for Mother it was to be living in a town instead of a lonely homestead on the prairie. All morning the house was like the time of Little Brother's death, with Father in the bedroom comforting Mavis and the rest of the family tiptoing about nervously.

Then with afternoon came the callers, and Mother had to receive them—Abigail Pratt, Prudence White, and Mrs. Crum, the minister's wife. The talk revolved quite naturally around the shooting, with every woman agreeing that Mavis had no choice but to defend herself against —and here the voices were always lowered and eyebrows raised significantly. Listen as she could, Michal heard no word given to express this nameless horror.

When John Ward saw the color returning to his wife's cheeks he went to work looking relieved. Mrs. White managed to outstay Abigail, and Mother seemed to enjoy her more than anybody she had met so far; but Michal snorted inwardly when she heard the woman say firmly, "Joshua has never in his whole life given me a moment of worry or questioned any decision I have made for him." How could Katie like that milksop!

As Mrs. White was leaving, she mentioned church. "Not a very fancy place for worship, but I know that God's spirit will join us even in a railroad station, particularly when He knows that we'll have our building soon."

"Thought of the services helped me through last night," said Mavis simply. "We'll be there."

And so except for the twins, the Ward family—even Father—went to church that Sunday. The expectant hush in the waiting room of the little red depot was broken only by the rustle of silk dresses as the women settled themselves on the improvised seats—rough planks resting on beer kegs.

Just before the services began, a drayman and his helper brought in a melodeon, placed it near the front, and retired on tiptoe. The pastor, head bowed, sat behind a large center table Michal recognized as belonging in the lobby of the Stuyvesant Hotel. As he rose to announce the first hymn, a small, thin woman neatly dressed in green cashmere took her place at the melodeon.

A breeze, straight from a million acres of dry virgin prairie grass, blew gently through the west windows as the congregation rose and sang:

> " 'I've reached the land of corn and wine,
> And all its riches freely mine. . . .' "

136

After droning a long prayer, the minister announced the second hymn. They were singing

> " 'There is a Happy Land
> Far—far—away' "

when with the soft slither of surah silk, in came the Gorgeous Vision. Michal was not the only one who thought her so. Most of the congregation forgot the far-away happy land to stare—the women frankly, the men with secret sliding glances. Not only was her bustle the most outstanding and her sparkling black passementerie trim the most elaborate, but the splendor culminated in a shiny black straw bonnet over which nodded red rosebuds, like prairie rosebuds, but much, much larger.

Mother never took her eyes off the preacher, but the sermon was lost on Michal, so absorbed was she in the fashionable young woman ahead. During the final prayer, however, Michal peeked at Fanny, who was sitting primly between her mother and a small, meek-looking man —Amos Pratt—Father's new partner in the livery stable. Fanny was peeking too, and the girls exchanged hostile glances before bowing their heads piously for the final Amen.

The services over, the pastor, a large blond Scot, a network of tiny purplish veins mottling his red cheeks and nose, came and introduced himself as Reverend Crum. Then others gathered, first Mrs. White introducing her son Joshua, who murmured politely, and then the Pratts. Father clapped a big hand on Mr. Pratt's shoulder, nearly knocking him flat, "Amos, here, is my new partner, Mavis—"

"Yer lookin' better today, Mrs. Ward," interrupted Abigail volubly. "I'll drop over tomorrow again to cheer you up and keep you from thinkin' too much about yer awful tragedy. I'll make you twice glad as we used to say in Salem, Mass."

She took her husband's arm and reluctantly passed on to make room for the Gorgeous Vision, preceded by the tiny birdlike woman who had played the melodeon, her mother it seemed, for, "Mrs. Cutter and Miss Cutter," introduced the pastor.

"I like Mrs. White, John," remarked Mavis as they walked out, Father trying to suit his long quick stride to Mother's.

"Uh-huh. Seems a fine person. She's from Bismarck—a widow."

"I noticed the fashionable Miss Cutter casting sheep's eyes your way," remarked Mother tartly.

"Don't be foolish," snorted Father. "Listen, here comes the train.

137

Must be a real big bunch of Rooshans for them to be running a special on Sunday."

"Please, may we watch?" begged Faith and Michal in unison.

"Well, for a minute or so," good-naturedly. "Look over there, girls —real newcomers for sure." And he gestured toward an ox-drawn wagon halted beside a great pile of bleached buffalo bones along the siding on the right-of-way. The box of the wagon was piled high with buffalo bones.

"How can you tell, Father?" Michal glanced sharply at the big man and the half grown boy—no, it wasn't Karl.

"No crop to haul, so they pick buffalo bones from the land and sell them for $10 a ton."

The train was puffing importantly into the station—fifteen freight cars and three yellow passenger coaches, the latter soon vomiting forth the usual horde of foreigners. Michal watched, fascinated as always, as they came up the street, the men in front, carrying their sacks of precious seed wheat; the women and children trailing behind with their burdens of featherbeds, goose-feather pillows, and boxes. They plodded along the dusty street, heads down, like beasts of burden.

Just then Michal's eye was caught by a little old woman who, although stooped and frail, was moving briskly around the station with the aid of a stout black cane. For a moment she wondered—could that be Katie's Grossmutter—then dismissed the thought. After all, there was no sign of the Keims or the Grosses.

Mavis took Father's arm. "Isn't it strange that when all these people come, we're so indifferent. If they were Americans we'd be all excitement, want to know their names, where they came from, where they'll live. As it is they might be so many cattle."

"And we're gawking at them as though they were cattle," said Father irritably. "Let's go."

"Wait a minute," said Michal. "I think that might be Katie's grandmother over there. I've been watching her, and she's beginning to look scared."

John Ward wheeled impatiently, but even his grim face softened at sight of the old lady—dressed all in black except for her head shawl which was bordered with red roses—standing very straight and terribly alone. The air of briskness that Michal had first noticed had given way to bewilderment as she searched with pathetic eagerness the faces of the few Rooshans left on the station platform.

"She is frightened," Mavis said gently. "Michal, you know a little German. Come, we'll speak to her."

"Be quick about it," snapped Father. "I'm getting hungry."

"*Guten Tag*," said Michal awkwardly. "Iss *Grossmutter* to Keim —to Gross?"

"*Ja, Ja.*" Clutching at Mavis and Michal with small, work-gnarled hands, she poured out a torrent of German.

"Come with us," Mavis said quietly, motioning to Michal to pick up the bundle tied in a black-fringed shawl. Then as they started to join Father and Faith, Michal exclaimed, "Here's Katie!" as her friend hurried up, cheeks scarlet from running. She and the old lady embraced; then Katie thanked them, took the bundle, and piloted Grossmutter homeward—the latter tapping along with her cane as spiritedly as she had when Michal had first seen her.

Just after dinner Katie arrived at the Wards' carrying a large loaf covered with a snowy dishtowel. "Mutter say thanks for speaking with Grossmutter," she said handing the fragrant bread to Mavis, then speaking excitedly to Michal. "My Fader take Grossmutter in the buggy out by Oncle Wilhelm's—he and Mutter ask if you come mit?" she asked eagerly.

Mavis looked worried. "But it's way out in the country—and on Sunday, too? Wouldn't you like to stay here and look at pictures in the big Bible?"

Katie, looking bewildered, smiled uncertainly.

I must go, thought Michal. "Please, Father!" she took his hand, "it'll be such fun!"

"Oh, let her go, Mavis." His voice was persuasive. "It'll help her get acquainted with the country. She'll have to stay in plenty and look at pictures all this winter."

"All right," and Mother sighed resignedly. As they left the house Michal heard her say, "It wasn't the acquaintance with the country I was worrying about, John."

Katie's parents and Grossmutter greeted Michal cheerfully, and soon the two-seated buggy was jogging along the main road west, taking them nearer and nearer to the Gross farm.

The girls chattered volubly. "Faith and I have a bedroom all to ourselves now and a new brass bedstead." But when they turned north, then angled northwest onto the already well worn road leading to the home of the boy, she thought but did not say—I'll see him again soon.

When Katie pointed out the place, Michal said, "That?"

"Yes, that; it is goot for such a little time," Katie insisted.

"Yes, it is." But her tone, though polite, was not convincing. It is really terrible, she thought.

A few cattle grazed along a hillside behind two haystacks and a huddle of buildings. The land sloped from the hill south to a slough.

Katie pointed to the right. "Dere dey sleep!" she explained cheerfully. A rude dugout built into the side of a knoll was covered in front by a wagon box leaning against the entrance. "Dere dey eat." She pointed triumphantly to the left, to a small sod building no larger than a claim shanty. Smoke poured briskly out of the tin stovepipe.

"But what's that?" Michal nodded toward a long rectangular building ahead, only partly built—the framework of peeled logs open to the weather and one-third of the far end sodded to the eaves.

"Dot? De big house."

"Why don't they finish it?"

"It takes much vork." Katie's voice was reproachful. "First dey go to Missouri River, t'irty-six mile for trees," and she pointed to the roof. "Now dey finish dot end—de barn, so cows and horses are varm in vinter. In middle vill be chicken house, and dis end real house."

"And they'll live like this until then?"

"Sure! If it gifs goot vinter vedder dey haf it by von, two mont' finished."

"But it's built crooked." Michal had noticed that the long building stood northwest by southeast.

"All farmers builds like dot so ven de nortvest vind blows it takes snow past easy."

As Katie's father stopped the team in the yard, the door of the cookhouse opened; Frau Gross came out followed by her more leisurely moving husband and the two blond daughters, Anna and Susanna. Karl isn't home, thought Michal, and felt a disappointment so keen it angered her.

While Mr. Keim tied the team to the hitching post, the rest of the group clustered about Grossmutter, who was—Michal knew by the gestures—retelling the moments of her arrival. Then Katrina Gross took her mother's arm and pointed to the dugout, but Grossmutter hung back for a moment, speaking Karl's name. Katrina shook her head. Grossmutter nodded, then took Anna's arm. As they started for the sleeping quarters of the dugout, Grossmutter lifted her piercing black eyes. Michal smiled impulsively, and the old woman smiled back, a fleeting impish smile, as she passed.

Katie whispered to Michal, "Even Tante Katrina minds Grossmutter—but she iss now tired and vants to sleep."

Then the men drifted away, talking and inspecting the improvements, and Frau Gross led the way back to the cookhouse. As she opened the door, heat rushed out with a smell compounded of damp earth, dry cow chips, and cooking. The light was dim after the brightness of the prairie sun, for the only light inside came from one small four-paned window in the south side of the thick sod wall. Already, thrifty slips of geranium and fuchsia were growing in tin cans on the broad sod sill beside Frau Gross's knitting. The room, though crowded, was immaculate—the ceiling and walls whitewashed, the earthen floor water sprinkled and freshly swept. At the far end, on a shining cookstove, the tin lid rose and fell, releasing from a huge black kettle the rich tantalizing smell of beef soup. The center of the room was filled by a plain heavy table, homemade, as were the long benches flanking it. To the left of the door stood a large wardrobe. The women, talking busily, drew a bench to the side wall, and the girls seated themselves on the other. Michal listened to the stream of German, picking now and then a word she knew, and to Katie—pausing politely to interpret anything she thought important. "Mine Tante now tells mine Mutter she very happy is for de cookstof we gif her for present ven she come. You see, most farmers' Fraus first have ovens make of clay and stones."

As the men came in, the women rose and, followed by the girls, went out to inspect the big house. The cattle were straggling home now; one cow had already entered the barbed-wire corral in the lee of the nearest haystack.

Michal heard barking, and from over the hill, silhouetted against the Indian-red sunset, she saw Karl and a large dog bringing in a beast that had wandered from the herd. It stopped and with lowered head pawed the dusty earth.

"A bull?"

"Yah."

"Isn't Karl afraid?"

"No." Katie shrugged. "He afraid of notting. Dot bull, he does not like de dog. Anna goes now to tell him about Grossmutter."

Michal gave her full attention to the approaching group until the bull was safely shut in the corral. Then she sighed with relief and turned. Karl's mother was watching her intently. She doesn't care for me. She looks at me the way Mother does at Katie.

Karl greeted them all quietly as he and Anna came up with an impersonal "*Guten Tag*." Then he glanced at the team and started for the dugout. Katrina Gross spoke quickly; he veered then to the cookhouse.

Mrs. Gross was showing them where she intended having her garden the next year, when the men came out. The women started toward them. Karl—the big dog at his heels—pulled Katie's braid, then looked at Michal.

"Hello," she said.

He smiled faintly. "*Guten Tag*," formally.

"Tell him," Michal said to Katie, "that I like the new house."

Katie interpreted and Karl spoke briefly. She turned back. "He say 'T'ank you' and tell you he understand when you say 'house' in English."

Michal looked at him quickly. He was still watching her, the same faint smile on his lips. Remembering the snake episode, she felt her face flush with pleasure tinged with embarrassment. "I'm glad you understood," she said, and as the group neared the buggy Karl strode forward and walked beside her, so close that once his arm brushed her shoulder. She was warm with happiness. He stood beside her through the goodbyes.

As Katie climbed into the buggy Michal leaned down impulsively and patted the big dog gently. Instantly Karl called the beast back, speaking sharply in German—his dark eyes angry.

Katie interpreted quickly, "He say dog for vork—not petting."

Michal spoke hotly. "You're a mean boy; a dog needs to be petted," and climbed up beside Katie in the back seat.

Then she felt someone staring, and turned to find Karl's mother watching her again intently, an unpleasant smile on her face, not troubling when discovered to turn her eyes away.

Katie waved goodbye and the blond sisters waved back. Karl—face impassive—had stepped back, but he was still watching. His mother—her hand on her son's arm—was looking too, that same smile still on her lips.

I'm sorry I came, Michal thought miserably, not even waving. We walked together and we quarreled. His mother doesn't like me and I hate him. I wonder if he's waiting for me to wave. She risked one last look.

The Gross family had turned and were walking slowly back to the house. Katrina's hand was still resting on her son's arm.

VI

Although she thought of him often, the days and weeks passed without Michal's seeing Karl again after the day at the Gross farm.

By the time the last geese had flown south the delicate trails had become roads—deep, rutted, dust covered—each with a high weedy hump in the center. Then snow fell and the town settled down to the long prairie winter. Building went on slowly when weather permitted. At first Michal did not mind it. She and Faith played and studied indoors, enjoying the snug sitting room with its bright clean fire of hard coal. Father discontinued his morning tubs and, except for Saturday, sponged himself in the cold bedroom.

After Christmas, Michal grew restless. The twins were always underfoot; she and Faith were short-tempered with each other. Studies, games, books, pasting were not as absorbing as before.

One bright January morning at breakfast she spoke up irritably, "Mother, may I spend this afternoon with Katie?"

Mavis hesitated, then "Why not go over to Fanny's for a change?"

"Fanny!"

Father grinned. "Amos Pratt's a fine man, but I can't blame Michal for avoiding Fanny and that b—"

"John!"

"—mother of hers. After all, there's not much choice. Later there'll be more playmates for her. Besides, Keim sends me business. However"—he bent a stern look on his daughter—"don't forget, Mike, that they're foreigners; and, by God, don't ever let me catch you looking at any of those Rooshan boys!"

"Even though she is past thirteen, John," Mavis interjected dryly, "I hardly think you need begin worrying about the opposite sex yet."

"Well"—Father's ears turned red—"she's growing up fast. It doesn't hurt to have some things understood—once and for all."

"Then I may go to Katie's?" Demurely.

Mavis sighed. "All right. But play with Fanny next time," she finished gently.

Father rose, looked at the calendar, reached for his coat. "Talk about Dakota weather—don't know that I ever saw such a day near mid-January so like spring. Believe I'll have Glen haul in a few loads of that slough hay from the stack over west."

Michal did her room, dusted the sitting room—with an eye on the twins who were just learning to walk—then settled down with a copy of Longfellow's *Poems* and was soon deep in the wanderings of *Evangeline*. She did not hear the knock, but heard Faith say, "She's in there," and Katie, crisp and clean as always, came in smiling. She picked up Philip, and asked, "How can you sit here on such a fine day?"

"I've been watching the twins while Mother writes letters. Are you all through with your morning's work?"

"Ja." Katie dimpled. "I came to ask you to my house over for dinner."

"Well," hesitating, "I was planning to come this afternoon."

"Goot. Karl is in with a load of flax for the warehouse. You come this afternoon, and we'll have more time for ourselves." She put down the wriggling Philip, and glanced innocently at her friend.

Michal closed her book, yawned elaborately. "Maybe she'll let me go now. I'll ask anyway."

Mavis was writing by the window in her bedroom. "Mother, could you spare me this morning? Katie has asked me for dinner."

"All right, but come home early. Tell Faith to watch the twins until I've finished here."

"May I wear my best dress?"

"Of course not; this isn't Sunday."

"Then may I unbraid my hair and put on my circle comb?"

"Yes, but why?" Mother looked puzzled.

"After all, this is an invitation to dinner," hurrying out before other questions might be asked. "Come, Katie, while I put on a clean apron."

She loosened her heavy hair, darker gold now, and wavy from the braids. Katie smiled as she carefully adjusted the blue circle comb, then, mischievously, "The blue apron, too, with that?"

"It goes best with this dress." Screening with her body the bottle of scent, she lifted from it its silver stopper and dabbed perfume on

144

the front of her dress. "There. That didn't take long." She put on her apron, tied it, then tossed her head, enjoying the feel of her flowing hair.

As they picked their way along the street toward the sidewalk, they heard Gus shout jovially to Glen, "Looks like an early spring this year."

"Yeah, meadow larks'll soon be singing. Good day for hauling, anyway," returned Glen, urging the horses to a trot. He stood erect at the front of the rack; his cheeks were red and the breeze blew back his overcoat, exposing the lining of bright Scotch plaid. He waved and called "Hello, girls," cheerfully as the hay wagon rattled up the street.

"Oh-h-h," sighed Katie rapturously.

Michal turned to find her friend's gaze riveted on a slim young man who was coming toward them.

"Hello, there." He seemed self-conscious.

"Hello, Yoshua." Katie was laughing up into his face. Michal saw that she had broad, shallow dimples and lovely even teeth. Why, Katie's awfully pretty! she thought with sudden surprise.

Joshua blushed, fumbling awkwardly with his cap, shifting from one foot to the other, his lashes making dark shadows against his pale cheeks. "Where are you going?" he asked, shooting another glance at Katie.

"Just happened to be passing," returned Michal loftily. "What are you doing out of the telegraph office?"

"Had to deliver a wire to the hotel. The train's about due. I must get back. So long."

"You sure are stuck on him," remarked Michal, glancing sidewise at Katie, "and did you flirt!"

"Of course. I like him so I flirt. Shall we play outdoors?" she asked, as they opened the gate, "It is so warm."

"Why don't we start your scrapbook?"

They settled down to cutting and pasting. Frau Keim had just finished baking, and the house was warm and fragrant with the pleasant smell of fresh bread. She sat down in her big chair by the sunny window and picked a withered leaf from the fuchsia plant, trellised now, and heavy with showy drooping blooms, purple-red like her birthmark. Then she relaxed with her crochet work.

The clock struck ten. Presently, "Here iss Karl," said Mrs. Keim from the window, and Michal's heart quickened as she heard the team pass back toward the barn. But she was leaning over the table, a picture of complete absorption when, after unhitching his team, he entered through the kitchen. Her heart was beating fast. She had given up hope of seeimg him before spring. For a moment she heard him pause in the door before she raised her head and smiled. "Hello, Karl."

"*Guten Morgen,*" gravely. He was even taller than she remembered, and Michal, dropping her eyes quickly under his dark gaze, felt a slow blush creeping up her throat into her cheeks. Frau Keim spoke to him in German, and they talked earnestly. Michal listened curiously but could understand only single words here and there.

Katie whispered, "You look nice today," and Michal, feeling oddly shy, risked another glance at the boy. His aunt was talking fast now, her crochet hook moving as rapidly as her lips; but Karl, lounging carelessly in the doorway, was looking steadily at Michal. For a moment she stared back, catching the image of a smile in the deep-set black eyes before she dropped her own.

He knows I'm here, she thought. He knows I'm here as much as I know he's here. He can't help it, either.

Mrs. Keim's voice rose, arguing some point with her nephew. When Michal looked at Katie questioningly, she said: "Karl say it is only ten, so he have time to go home and get one more load flax before dinner. We go out to the barn with him?"

As they hurried after the boy stalking ahead, Michal's temper rose. "Let's go back," she whispered fiercely. "He doesn't care whether we see him off or not. Besides, it's getting awfully cold." Pulling her cloak closer, she shivered, staring resentfully at the lithe figure striding ahead. The wind had risen; the sun was paling. Above it a rainbow-tinted band brightened the sky; and on either side of it sundogs sent out colored streamers.

"Look, Katie! The sky!" But Katie, ignoring her, trotted after her cousin. Michal shrugged her shoulders and followed. As she entered the barn a huge dog rose from between the horses in the stall, the same mongrel with the coarse wolf-like coat.

"Kum," Karl's voice was abrupt as he tried to back the team, still in their harnesses, toward the barn door.

"Katie—come here!" Michal led the way out beyond the wagon where she could get a good view of the sky. "The wind has changed. Look!" The wind was blowing colder from the northwest, where a bank of sullen gray clouds was boiling.

146

Katie's blue eyes turned dark. "Blizzard!"

Michal jerked her head toward Karl, who, inside the barn, was still working to back the horses out, "You'd better tell him to wait."

Katie hurried in and spoke rapidly.

" '*Rausmit!*" he spoke harshly, as Michal came inside. He tugged and pulled impatiently as the horses moved forward reluctantly.

"We'd better go back to the house. If he wants to stay out here and —" She broke off abruptly. Karl was scowling furiously down at the dog, which, crouching, refused to move.

"Kum!" His voice held the quiet arrogance of command.

Teeth bared slightly, the dog still crouched as the wind deepened. With an oath, Karl kicked him squarely in the ribs. The dog did not cry out, only growled deep and crouched lower.

"How dare you kick that dog!" Fury was thick in Michal's throat.

"*Dummes Esel, sei still!*" His dark eyes were cold as his voice.

Blind with rage Michal pounded her fists against his chest. "You are the dumb mule! Start for your dugout and die!"

Karl slapped her cheek—hard—just as Katie cried, "It kums!" and the storm clouds—like a stampede of white-maned buffalo—enveloped the town. Karl pulled the two girls back and tried to close the door. Michal fought him, whispering, "Let me go!" and broke past him and through the open door.

The wind and the white cold seized her, held her lightly for a moment, tore the breath from her body, then flung her roughly to the earth and left her lying there, helpless in a violent white void. Something stumbled over her. Then as she felt herself grasped, lifted, Michal turned her face in against Karl's shoulder. A few steps and they came up against the door. He felt his way along until they were blown out of the white blindness into the darkness of the barn—into the warm darkness of familiar objects, the fragrance of animal warmth, leather and hay. Karl dropped her and, throwing all his weight against the door, closed it slowly; then leaned, panting, against it for a moment, shattering a crystal fan of snow at his feet, before he turned. His eyes now held no anger. Katie was crying silently.

The horses and dog had moved back into the stall. Already the blizzard was sending pale fingers of cold into their dark haven. Michal, snow drenched, felt a thrill of pure terror as she recognized in the long bleak cry of the wind the lost voices wailing, and felt more violence around her than on that other long-ago night.

Karl's voice cut the gloom. "We had nothing like this in Russland. How long will it last?" He spoke in German and Katie answered in the same tongue.

"Two hours, two days. *Ich weiss nicht.*" Michal understood both well enough to think, I'll soon be able to speak their language.

"We must get together for the heat," said Karl, and Katie pointed silently to two buffalo robes in a corner. "Goot," said Karl briefly. "Kum."

Leading them to a stall where the girls knelt on the straw-littered floor, he tucked one of the robes around them, then, kneeling, drew the other about himself, the edges overlapping.

"It's like a Sioux teepee with our heads sticking out the top like poles." Michal spoke for the first time.

Katie nodded. Then they were silent, listening. Even though the barn was tight, fine snow, as delicate as their own frosty breaths, sifted in. And over the lesser sounds—the muted clumps as the horses and cows moved restlessly in their stalls, the scratching and whimpering of the wolf-like dog, turning round and round to make a warm nest in the straw—over all these was that high sharp keening. Michal thought aloud, speaking softly: "I wonder about the folks; and Glen, hauling prairie hay. What if any of them were caught in it. What if—"

"It does no goot to wonder." Katie's voice was cool as an icicle.

"Aren't you afraid?"

"Karl vill take care of us."

"I can take care of myself."

As the warmth of their bodies blended, Michal, relaxing, began imagining how it might be. Would they be found, after the storm, frozen to death here in the stall—huddled together under the buffalo robes? Tears filled her eyes as she pictured Father—white and silent—and Mother, weeping over her coffin.

She sniffed, then stiffened as, feeling Karl's eyes on her, she turned to meet his gaze—her thick hair darkened with melted snow, blue eyes tear-washed and lashes clotted together into long curved black points. Under his steady look her own faltered, and as a fresh blast of wind shook the barn she trembled. Deliberately he put his arm round her. "Nu, nu—" He spoke quietly, as to a small child; then, turning to Katie, he said in German, "Is there any rope?"

"*Ja.* Back there." She pointed, finger close to her face.

"Enough to take us to the house?"

148

She nodded. Karl went back and lifted the two long picket ropes, which, carefully coiled, hung from spikes. He pulled the picket pins out, deftly knotted the two ropes into one, then firmly secured one end to a scantling near the door that held harnesses.

"Maybe the storm will be over soon," Michal said, dreading the cold outside. "Father was caught in a blizzard once, and it was blowing nearly as hard as this one minute, and the next it was over."

"Karl t'inks we go in before we get too hungry and too cold," Katie returned simply, watching her cousin who was cinching the buffalo robes securely on the horses with surcingles. Then he filled all the mangers with hay, and rejoined the girls.

As he came up, Michal spoke, indicating the robes, "Shouldn't we put these around us? It's awfully cold outside."

Katie translated her message. Karl listened impassively, then flashing her a glance of quiet scorn as he replied, began tying the loose end of the picket rope about his waist. "He say robes too heavy for us to walk in. Horses cost much money—goot team. Need robes more as we."

Staring coldly at Karl, she made no reply. He spoke to Katie, who again relayed his words. "Karl say we hang on behind him." Michal gripped the rope and, thinking, I'm not afraid if they're not, took a deep breath as he opened the door. Struggling against the pressure of the wind, they moved out of the narrow opening, then slowly rolled the door shut. Karl veered to the left following the length of the wagon, then plunged out. One step—two—three. Michal felt her fingers numbing in her heavy mittens, felt the rope slipping. A million tiny crystal knives were cutting her face. She bent her head lower, then stumbled over something and, reaching out with her right hand, felt only emptiness where Katie should be.

"Karl!" She screamed, jerking on the rope, but the wind snatched, scattered, and dissolved the sound of her voice. She felt the rope slacken. Karl, supporting Katie, put his lips to Michal's ear and shouted, "Stall!"

Barn. Back to the barn. Back along the wagon, along the wagon to the door. With all her might, Michal pushed. Then Katie and Karl were pushing too, and a slit of warm fragrant darkness opened to them.

The dog rose to greet him as Karl strode to the harnesses and, working rapidly, took the reins and returned to the girls. Making loops, he tied them firmly about the girls' waists and then tied the ends of the rope about him.

"Karl say, hold on to him." Katie's voice was tired, her face pale, and her brows and lashes thickly clotted with snow. Michal smiled and patted Katie's arm reassuringly, then nodded at Karl and, gripping his arm tightly, helped with the door. Once more the storm caught them. Along the wagon, along the length of it. Then the plunge out into the cold foam of storm. Karl was holding Michal's arm so firmly that, head bent, eyes closed, she was able to move forward.

They were lost now—bound to the real world by a slim rope. Michal quit thinking, only moved forward—one foot ahead of the other—nothing else mattered. Their progress was broken sharply. Karl pushed sideways, making an arc in an effort to bump into the house.

She was the one to hit it, stumbling against a drift, then feeling real solidity under her groping mittened hands. For a moment all three leaned against the hardness—resting. I never want to move again, Michal thought wearily. I want to lean against this house forever.

But Karl was moving again, feeling his way. They reached a corner, made the turn; then Katie stumbled and all three fell over the back steps. Afterward, Michal always remembered how beautiful Frau Keim looked standing there in the doorway in the warm golden shower of lamplight at noon, tears splashing down over her cheeks, over the purple birthmark. She managed to hug all three of them at once, although Karl pulled away and began unlooping reins and untying knots. Before closing the door that shut out the cold—the piercing, numbing cold—Mrs. Keim tugged hard on a rope, explaining briefly to Katie, "Your Vater look for you," as she filled a pan with snow and commanded them to rub their noses and fingers well. Katie's father, a broad snowman, came stamping and blowing in, coiling his rope. He gestured to Karl, and they went into the Stube, where Michal could hear them discussing the storm.

Even the heavenly warmth of the kitchen and the rich chicken noodle soup failed to take the chill from her bones. Later, when they went to bed, she noted vaguely that Katie's nightgown was too short; but she didn't feel like giggling about it as, teeth chattering, she sank gratefully into the deep feather bed and into deeper sleep.

Through that night and the next day and night, the small town on the prairie huddled, helpless under the storm. Michal dozed feverishly through most of it, only waking long enough to worry about her family. Then Mrs. Keim would soothe her with quiet words, force her to take broth to allay the nervous chills that made her teeth chatter, and she would relax and rest again. Uneasily.

For the winds never stopped—but wailed on. Sometimes savagely —snarling deep like the wolf-dog out there in the barn. Other times, muted—like little voices calling softly. Many little voices. Then Michal would toss, remembering the lost ones in all the blizzards that had ever been. All the lost ones calling—their voices now part of the wind.

Vaguely she was conscious of Karl and Mr. Keim talking in the *Stube*. Once it seemed as though Karl stood by her bed, looking down at her—tall and dark and silent—but on waking she knew that it must have been a dream. And over it all—the warmth and kindness and the muted guttural voices—was the storm boiling over the prairie from the unbroken wastes of the north.

Michal wakened to an awful stillness. It's over, she thought. I'll go home now.

As she stirred, Katie entered the bedroom. "Your Vater came early —he takes you home in bobsled."

Michal rubbed her eyes. "I've had a long rest."

"You haf been sick all two days. How do you feel?"

"A little tired." She stepped out onto the floor, weaving slightly as she began dressing.

Katie, eyes modestly downcast, continued, "Karl has already eaten and with my Vater is digging into the barn—there's a drift the door over."

"I suppose he's anxious to get home." Her eyes darkened, and she put her hand quickly to her cheek. "Even if he is your cousin, even if he saved our lives, I don't like him."

Katie shrugged, "Is all right—other girls do."

Michal turned her back, slowly tying the sash of her blue apron. She didn't want Katie to see her face, to guess the horrible new feeling rising inside her. Worse than rage. Worse than fear. Other girls!

A loud knock, then, "Is she ready?" Father's voice.

"Father!" Michal hurried out. He picked her up as though she were a child.

"Hello, Chicken," holding her close, stroking her face, her hair.

"Everybody all right at home?"

"All accounted for now but Glen. I'll get you right back to Mother, then go help find him." Turning to Mrs. Keim, "Many thanks for all you have done for my daughter." He shook her hand heartily. "Here's Gus. We'll see you folks later."

As they drove for home in the heavy sleigh, "It looks like a different town," Michal exclaimed.

"Wind and snow do queer things to a place. I'm glad you weren't out in it."

"But I was." Eagerly she outlined her story.

He scowled and said unreasonably, "You had no business outside." Then, sharply: "Isn't that boy new to the prairie? Seems to me I heard Keim say—"

"He came here just before we did."

"For a Rooshan, he certainly used his head." Father had Gus stop by the back door, free from drifts, and helped her down, saying, "May not be in until dark."

Mavis and Hetty pulled her in, hugging her, both talking at once. Then as Hetty plied her with food, Michal—thoroughly enjoying herself now—retold her experiences, omitting only her quarrel with Karl and her flight into the storm.

Mavis was pale when she finished. "That's what I was afraid of. It was such a lovely day. I prayed you were not out playing on the prairie when the blizzard struck. God answered my prayers."

God and Karl, thought Michal guiltily.

"I want you to rest in Father's big chair today. It sounds as though you almost had lung fever. I must thank Mrs. Keim for everything."

Faith, who had been standing shyly in the background, brought all the favorite books, then herded the twins away, while Mavis, arranging pillows and blankets, told Michal: "Father had just come in for dinner when it struck. I was so worried about you that he started to Keims, but could make no headway."

"Where was Gus?" Michal asked, leaning back comfortably.

"At the livery stable. It was a blessing too, for although he didn't have much to eat—some peanuts and two apples in the office desk— he had the stove for heat and could watch the horses. Of course, we're concerned about Glen. Father thinks that he must have been close enough to some shelter to make it in time."

All day Michal read and listened to life quickening again outside. She could imagine people coming out of their homes, like gophers cautiously emerging from their burrows in spring. Mrs. White, and of course Mrs. Pratt, both paid calls for a few minutes—but Mavis entertained them in the dining room so that Michal could rest.

Underneath everything ran a hidden current of all the untold things in her story. Of Karl lifting her so easily from the snow. Of Karl's putting his arm about her deliberately—as though, Michal thought, his doing anything depended only on his wish to do it.

Unbidden, other pictures rose to the surface—of Karl just as deliberately striking her and—face dark with anger—kicking his dog. She pushed those images away—back far beneath the surface—and tried to remember whether she had dreamed that he had stood by her bed the day before, looking down at her. Then she heard Father in the kitchen —heard him saying, "No, Mavis, not a trace. We found the outfit— both horses dead—half a mile from the stack, but Glen must be lost."

"Father!" Michal called out, and he and Mavis, with Faith, came into the sitting room.

"Is there any hope at all, John?" Mavis was pale.

"I doubt it. It's hard to say what a man can do in a blizzard." Father sat near the base burner, unbuckling and removing his gum overshoes, then pulling off his felt pacs. "Faith, bring my slippers, will you? What I figure is that he didn't give the horses their heads in time."

"Was Glen the only one lost?" faltered Michal.

"No, Mike! A lot of them won't be found before spring. Too many were caught out in it, like Glen, because it was such a nice day. That young fellow, Josh White, the telegraph operator, said last reports claim about three hundred people are missing in Dakota Territory alone, and no reports yet on stock losses."

"Father, did it hurt Glen to die?" Faith's hands were trembling as she gave him his slippers.

John Ward lifted her onto his lap. "No, not much, if any. He just felt drowsy and went to sleep."

"He's with God now." Mavis's voice was tender. "John"—she stood behind his chair and rested her hand on his shoulder—"you look so tired."

"I saw terrible things today, Mavis, enough to last me a while I can tell you. Gustaf, the blacksmith, will probably live, but he'll lose both legs below the knees. He keeps begging to die. Mutters the same words over and over. God!" Father shook his head.

"But Gustaf always tosses Faith high up in the air." Michal spoke in bewilderment.

153

"He'll never do that again, Mike." He settled his long figure into a more comfortable position. "The worst thing—and I can't get it out of my mind—was a woman and child they brought in from a few miles out. New to the country, I guess; at least I didn't know them. Found them forty feet from their shanty. The girl was about Faith's age, and"—he paused—"she had on a little coral necklace. Looked like a doll, lying there with frost shining on her cheeks."

"If we didn't have God, we couldn't bear these things, John."

"Umph," muttered Father, but he reached up and patted Mother's hand that still rested lightly on his shoulder.

"But why does He let things like that happen?" Michal burst out violently. "I liked Glen. I saw him just that morning. He stood so straight and tall in the rack and smiled and waved to Katie and me."

Mavis's large eyes were serious. "Remember,

" 'God moves in a mysterious way,
His wonders to perform;
He plants his footsteps in the sea,
And rides upon the storm.' "

"But what good does that do Glen, or the little girl?"

"We can't understand God's will, Daughter. Perhaps in His infinite wisdom he took them while they were young and happy."

"But I still don't see—"

"That's enough, Mike," interrupted Father, but kindly. "By the way, did you hear about that remittance man, the dude who lives at the Stuyvesant?" He was grinning now. "It seems he had just left the bank when the storm broke. Somehow, he wandered along the street, missed the buildings, and headed east—ending up at That House"—he paused slightly, raising his eyebrows significantly—"out by the race track."

"How awful!" exclaimed Mavis.

"He was damned lucky. Nearly done in when he got there. Anyway," went on Father, "we went out in that direction first this morning and caught him sneaking into town. He didn't relish being picked up or the remarks of the rescue crew. Slunk into the hotel in a hurry."

"And Achsah heard," burst out Hetty, who had been standing in the doorway listening, "that the whole time he wuz there he just sat back and kept his little mouth all squinched up like a hen's behind."

"Hetty!" moaned Mother, as Hetty retired quickly in red-faced confusion and Father's roar of laughter filled the room.

"Great God," he gasped finally, wiping his eyes with his big hand-kerchief, "I can just see him, in the midst of—"

"John!"

Father relaxed, snorted again, then sobered. "Well, it's over. A lot of folks will have cause to remember January, 1888."

"Poor Glen! Did you wire his folks?"

"Yes. I'll write them tonight." He rose. "You've got to be tough to survive on the prairie, Mavis," he said wearily. "When do we eat?"

VII

After the great spring thaw, on a day when southwest winds carried the fresh smell of moist earth over the prairie, Michal hurried to Katie's. Mother thought the excursion was to be a hunt for pasqueflowers. And so it was. But Katie had been teaching Michal some of the Roo-shan dances; today they could practice out in the open on the floor of the prairie.

Mrs. Keim came to the door.

"Good morning, Mrs. Keim. Is Katie home?"

"She is de bet in—kum." She opened the door wide.

"Sick?"

Frau Keim shrugged and smiled. "Vell, no," and preceded Michal into the neat bedroom. "Your *Kamerad*," she said briefly, pointing her to a chair.

"I'm sorry you're sick. I have the whole day off and wanted to spend it with you; what's the matter?" She broke off anxiously as the door closed behind Frau Keim.

"Oh, notting." Katie smiled mysteriously.

Mrs. Keim bustled back in with a warm flatiron wrapped in a towel. She threw back the covers and, taking one from beside her daughter, carefully adjusted the other in its place and left the room. Katie drew the covers snugly back, but not before Michal noticed that where the yoke of her white nightgown was trimmed with rows of hand-crocheted insertion it was rounded like Mother's instead of being flat as it had been the night she had stayed with her the year before. Katie was different.

"I'm sorry about your stomach-ache." She spoke awkwardly.

"Cramps I haf—not stomach-ache." Condescendingly, as to a much younger child.

If she wanted to be like that, "I'd better be going," she said stiffly.

"No—sitz awhile." Hastily, then giggling, "I must tell you—a boy in our *Kirche*—you know, dot Baur boy?"

"You mean Frieda's brother, that fat Adolph who lives north of the Gross place?"

"He not so fat. Besides, they're rich—his *Vater* mooch land has."

"He's still fat. What about him?"

Katie giggled again. "He all time looks at me while our *Prediger* speaks. He vait by door and valk home mit me latst Sunday, and mine *Mutter* ask him for dinner."

"You mean your mother let a *boy* come to see you? Why, you're just a little girl yet! My Mother wouldn't think of letting a boy call on me!"

"No?" Katie's voice was cool. "Mine *Mutter* glad. She ask Adolph. I be married in t'ree, four year now."

"To him?"

A shrug. "How can I know?"

"What about Joshua?"

"Yoshua!" she returned indifferently, but the red crept up from her throat and covered her face, and she changed the subject abruptly. "You should see once how de girls all are crazy over Karl. Look at him like a calf. Adolph's sister, Frieda; she is lofely—long t'ick braids gold like ripe veat. Blue eyes. Skin vite like snow. Red cheeks. She haf vite dress all hand embroidery red and blue around neck and skirt. She look at Karl, too, but like you, when no one see."

Michal rose quickly. "I really must go now."

Leaving Keims', she thought uncomfortably that Katie somehow knew more than she. She turned toward Fanny's, then changed her mind and hurried toward the home site on the hill. Between the site and town ran a ravine that wound westward to a large reed-fringed pond, now full of water from the spring runoff. Already Michal had chosen her retreat there—grassy with a large boulder in the middle, where only a month before water had swirled on its way down.

Today she'd go the long way by the railroad tracks and avoid mud. Three blocks past the depot, and she would be in the country.

The ponds on each side of the high grade were filled with water;

there was a new softness in the April air and the smells of a moist, quickening earth. At the ends of the big culvert on either side of the track where water gurgled, Michal caught faint whiffs of new grass, long bright green strands that had begun growing weeks before under the protection of the drifts.

She found no flowers as she angled northwest, climbing the hill, then hurried to reach the top where already piles of lumber showed that work would soon begin. Four stakes marked where the house would stand with four smaller ones inside for the cellar. She and Faith would share a bedroom upstairs on the southwest side, with a window on the west where, as Katie had teased, Michal would be able to see the Gross place.

To the north the barn site, high and dry, had been well cleared and was as smooth as a dance floor. Lifting her skirts and humming "When I Was a Maiden," Michal circled lightly, practicing the steps of the Rooshan dances. It was like birds flying or clouds in the wind, she thought as she sank breathless to the ground, wondering again why Mother thought dancing a sin.

A pebble, thrown expertly, whizzed over her head and lit with a sharp sound on the lumber beyond. She jumped to her feet and turned to confront a boy of about her own age with bleached brown hair and hazel eyes, who grinned sheepishly as he said, "Scared you, didn't I?"

"What are you doing here?" demanded Michal sharply.

"Just exploring. I've found a fine place in that ravine down there, and then I heard you singing."

"That ravine just happens," loftily, "to be my own place."

"Does your father own it?"

"No—but I intend to go there when I want to get away from people; I picked it out the first time I came here. We're moving out soon."

"Well," reasonably, "if your father doesn't own it legally, it's no more yours than mine."

Michal ignored this. "Who are you anyway?"

"Lewis Reid."

"Oh, the new lawyer's son!"

"Yes. We moved here a month ago. We live in the house a block east of where they're building the schoolhouse."

"You mean the new white house with the big bay window?"

"Yeah. I know who you are. Your name's Michal Ward, and you never stay to Sunday school but leave right after church."

157

"I nearly had lung fever during the big blizzard, so my mother has made me keep quiet since."

"Does she know that you come up here to dance?" he teased.

"No, she doesn't, and you'd better not tell!"

He flushed. "I'm not a tattletale! What kind of a dance was that, anyway?"

"Rooshan. My best friend Katie Keim taught me."

"Is she a foreigner?"

"Of course."

"Does your mother let you play with Rooshans?"

"She doesn't really like it, but she has never forbidden it," Michal returned coldly.

"But Rooshans—a girl like you?"

Michal's quick anger flamed. "Katie may be a foreigner, but she's still the nicest girl in this town," she said with finality.

"All right—all right—don't get so excited," he said quietly. "Play with Indians if you wish; it's your own business."

Michal relaxed. He wasn't so bad after all. Far against a rise to the west a man was plowing—Wilhelm Gross, no doubt. From the top of the next big hill they might see the Gross place. She spoke casually, "I want to find some pasqueflowers for Mother. Would you like to come?"

His face lit up. "My mother's hobby is flowers; she's planning on a native garden, so I'll surprise her and start it today."

Carefully skirting the depression between the two hills, they began the long climb north up the south slope of the boulder-strewn hill, enjoying the faint scant warmth of the sun on their backs and finding from time to time a few fuzzy pinkish-blue pasqueflowers huddled among the withered buffalo grass.

Lewis dug two clumps with his jackknife and carefully wrapped them in a clean white handkerchief. Michal watched, well pleased, thinking, Katie should see me now. She may have her fat Adolph and Karl may have his new girl. This boy is nicer than any of them. He's like us, and he likes me already. I can tell.

She ran ahead to the crest of the hill, paused a moment, then called excitedly, "Lewis! Come see what I've found! A buffalo wallow on top of a hill! And the biggest rock you ever saw!"

He came running, and they stood looking down into the depres-

158

sion from the exact center of which a huge solitary boulder lifted its immense rounded dome high above the rim.

Michal held out her flowers to the boy. "Here, hold these for me, please; I'm going up." She found footing and scrambled to the top of the stone and stood up looking west. "I can see all over the prairie from here. Come on up."

Lewis hesitated. "I've got my good coat on."

"Dude."

"No, I'm not. I walked the scaffolding of the schoolhouse yesterday and I'll do it again with you, if you like. But I won't climb that thing just to show off to any girl! Besides"—he looked about curiously—"I don't like this place."

"Why not?"

"It's bare—and lonely. I like the ravine better."

Michal thought, I'm glad! as she stood erect, looking at the fluffs of clouds patterning the blue skies. A wavering line of wild geese speeding north was passing over, flying so high their honking clamor reached her only faintly. This place is mine—my Place of Rocks. No one else shall come here.

Lewis had already lost interest, she noted, and, leaving the flowers by the rim, had wandered over the crest of the hill. He turned, and called: "There's snow still over here. Let's have a snowball fight."

Michal climbed down. As they ran down to the long white drift that filled a narrow draw, "Some man left his shoes here," called Lewis, "and his pants, too," he added, stopping suddenly.

"That's queer." Michal went close and, stooping, poked the overalls tentatively with one finger. They were not empty. There was something that gave slightly to her touch. She drew back, then glimpsed a piece of plaid, bright under the snowy glaze of ice just above the overalls.

"Lewis," she whispered, and felt dizziness flowing over her, "Lewis, it's Glen."

"Who's Glen?"

"He worked for my father," stammered Michal. "He was lost in the blizzard."

She gave one more look, then turned and fled. Lewis overtook her at the crest. Downhill; uphill again. Then down toward the grade. Michal lost her rubbers in the mud but did not stop. Panting, half falling,

159

they finally reached the depot, then stumbled along to John Ward's office. He was in the yard showing plows to a farmer.

"Father!"

He looked up, irritated at the interruption, "What—" he began. Then, as she staggered to him, sobbing, he held her close. "There, there, what is it?"

"Glen," she whispered.

"Where?"

"North side—second hill—back of our new place. In the drift—his legs sticking out of the snow."

He glanced sharply at Lewis. "Who's this?"

"Lewis Reid."

"Good. I know your father. Rest before you go home. Come, Jake." And, followed by the farmer, Father had on hat, coat, overshoes, and was gone.

Lewis spoke only once on their way home. "I told you I didn't like that place."

But Michal felt in no mood for talk. She was remembering how alive Glen had looked that morning of the blizzard, the plaid lining of his coat bright in the wind.

VIII

The Wards and the Reids became great friends. Michal loved to go to Lewis's house, not only for the exchange of books which went on constantly, but because of the cheerful, uncluttered atmosphere. No racks of photographs, no Turkish corners here. Light green matting on the floors. The walls—covered with heavy unfigured ivory paper and woodwork painted the same shade—were bare except for a few Japanese prints in slit bamboo frames. Against two walls were open shelves filled with books.

Alice Reid, a tiny fragile woman whose ash-blond hair and large blue eyes were striking against the black richly embroidered Oriental robes that she affected, spent most of her time reclining on a lounge near the bay window which contained an orderly riot of greenery—ferns, begonias, and a profusion of sweet blooming heliotrope filling the room with an exquisite fragrance. These were no ordinary house plants, but thrifty ones, all free of dust, with no dead leaf, and washed clean as though just sprayed by misty rain.

Even though Mrs. Reid and Mavis were much alike, they were different. Mother seldom paid much attention to fashion or looked in a mirror. But whenever Mrs. Reid passed the full-length mirror in her sitting room, Michal noticed that she paused, pulled her robe a bit closer, lifted her chin, and smiled at her own reflection.

James Reid, Lewis's father, was a slender man whose eyes, the exact color of his red-brown hair, were twinkling. He always kissed his wife on the forehead—it was a habit, Michal thought.

Even though John Ward seldom had time for social contacts, he and Mr. Reid enjoyed talking business and politics. Besides, they were both Masons.

In April, Gus took the banking from the foundation of the house, but not until late May was the ground solid enough for the move to the hill. Then early one morning the movers came, placed heavy rollers under the house, and started their teams. The building trembled, then slowly and with many halts began to creak along, while Michal looked nonchalantly out of her bedroom window, just as though they always lived this way.

It was slow going after they began the ascent of the hill; the sun was setting before they reached the site. Michal took Faith and Rory and ran up well ahead of the house. She had not been there since that awful day she and Lewis had found Glen's body on the hill beyond. Now the cellar and well were finished, the barn and corral almost completed, and a windmill was pumping water into a huge new trough.

The hilltop was thickly sprinkled with clumps of yellow violets shining like stars in the carpet of green prairie grass. Faith gathered a handful of them while Mother watched.

"I've never seen anything like it. It must be an omen of the happiness waiting for us here," she said reverently.

While Faith was arranging her flowers carefully in the cornucopia vase that formed the top of the big silver castor, Michal called Rory and ran down the swale to her place in the ravine. It was still too damp for comfort, but the cool sweet wind of May was blowing, the grass was green, and thistle and milkweed plants were growing sturdily in a thick hedge about the place. The large blue violets were blooming. She picked a few with their leaves. Then, as she saw Father going up the hill toward the house, she ran up the swale to meet him, and they went in to supper together.

Father cut the roast and dished up the vegetables. "Well, Mavis," he said as he passed Mother her plate, "this is the most painless trek we've had. It isn't often a family eats breakfast on the old site, dinner at their own table halfway, and supper in the new location. That's what I call expert moving. Tomorrow the men will begin putting in the stone foundation. In another month or so things'll look better around here, particularly—"

A loud knock interrupted him. Hetty went to the door. "Here's a telegraph for you, Miz Ward, but he won't give it to me," she whispered shrilly, closing the door.

"A telegram! Somebody's dead!" Mother, her face white, half rose from her chair.

"You come sign for it, Mavis. I'll take it."

He handed her the yellow envelope. Mother turned it over and over. "I wonder who it's from," she said faintly.

"Why not open it?"

"Of course." She read the few lines, dropped the message, and crumpled in her chair. "Oh, John! Fred is dead!"

John Ward took his wife tenderly in his arms, then picked up the wire and read it aloud: " 'Fred died Yucatan May tenth. Yellow fever. Will write from Denver. Leaving tonight. Phyllis.' "

"There, there, Mavis. There, there," he kept saying gently, crooning as though she were a child.

"He died unsaved." Her voice held a hopelessness beyond grief.

Michal stumbled from the room, out of the house, and walked quickly toward the hills. The afterglow was dying as she reached the Place of Rocks and for the second time climbed the boulder and, seating herself on a depression near the top, leaned back. The huge stone, still faintly warm from the heat of the sun, gradually relaxed her. Someone was plowing late, far off to the west on a sidehill. As she sat listening vaguely to the faint querulous pe-e-e-nt of a solitary nighthawk high overhead, the awful loneliness of the prairie overwhelmed her. She thought: I'd been saving so many things to ask him. But dying means never seeing him again.

What did Mother mean, "He died unsaved"? It had something to do with his being a freethinker and not going to church every Sunday.

162

But Uncle Fred would surely go to Heaven. God couldn't help liking Uncle Fred, who was so kind and who understood all the things a person wanted to know, particularly things Mother and Father couldn't answer.

She remembered that other evening, their talk in the soft half-light and the deep-toned notes of the trumpeter swan. Always she would have that to remember.

Although it was almost dark the man was still working on the hillside. As Michal climbed down and left the Place of Rocks, she thought: *But it isn't enough. It isn't enough.*

IX

Michal, absorbed in her own grief, did not at first fully realize what was happening to Mother. She lingered in the quiet of the ravine one summer afternoon until the last drowsy bumblebee zoomed away through the warm, cobwebbed twilight. Then with lagging steps she started up the swale.

The house loomed dark and quiet on the hilltop, and her steps quickened as, with a touch of fear, she saw that there was no glimmer of lamplight. She hurried, thinking, I shouldn't have stayed so long. Then the kitchen lamp gleamed out at her; and, relieved, she loitered again, looking away at the hills to the north, now fading to dusty purple. I'd better go in, she thought; and, looking up at the west window as she passed, she saw Mother's face staring out without seeing her, pale against the darkness of the room. Suddenly the warm dusk became unfriendly and full of shadows. As she opened the door a bird cry came from the hills to the north; and for the first time in many weeks Michal remembered Louise Oulette.

The house seemed dead. Even Hetty tiptoed quietly about her cooking while keeping an eye on the twins.

"Mother"—Michal made her voice cheerful as she went into the sitting room and lit the lamp—"I'll go to prayer meeting with you tonight."

"All right."

"What dress shall I wear?"

"That one's all right." Apathetically, not looking up. Michal knew she was not listening, and turned away to the south window. She saw the glint of Father's lantern coming up the hill and ran to meet him. How tired and discouraged he looks! she thought as he took her hand.

"A little hard these days, Michal?"

"It's awful."

"I know. But give your mother time, Chicken. First Matt. And now Fred's death was a terrible shock to her." Then, more heartily: "But in another week or so she'll be herself. We'll just have to be patient. If she doesn't come out of it soon, I'll ask the reverend to call on her one of these days. Church is the only thing she shows the slightest interest in, and he might be able to help her."

But long twilights came to the prairie, the wheat paled to gold; and Mavis sank even deeper within herself. She still sat most of the day, pale and apathetic, looking out over the prairie. Father had begun staying downtown until bedtime, and often did not come home at noon for dinner. When he was there he was so irritable that Michal wished herself out of the house. She longed for the old days when a comfortable murmur of talk and occasional laughter had come from the front bedroom in the morning and after bedtime at night.

One day in late summer Michal lay in the hammock on the front porch listening to the distant hum of threshing machines and wondering if they had reached the Gross farm yet. The drone of the machine soothed her, and her tense body relaxed. The dun prairie was covered with sheaves and the pale gold of stubble fields.

"Good morning, young lady." It was the Reverend Crum. She went forward to meet him, confused at not having heard his arrival. As usual his well brushed plum-colored wool suit, white collar and cuffs, and satin cravat enfolded him in pontifical dignity.

Mother greeted him courteously, going through all the motions automatically. Besides her work basket and a silver framed photograph of Uncle Fred, the center table contained a tray and a cut-glass pitcher of cold lemonade which Hetty had just made. The Reverend Crum glanced at this rather quizzically as he settled himself comfortably, and became a dignified part of the room.

Mother poured lemonade for the three of them, and as the pastor leaned back, Michal admired the picture he made—his graying blond hair waved back from his forehead, his mustache and muttonchop whiskers well brushed, well trimmed, the hand that held the glass ornamented by one heavy seal ring. He sat pleasantly at ease, yet concerned as a clergyman should be for the spiritual health of the bereaved lady parishioner. Having disposed of the lemonade, he cleared his throat, and leaned slightly forward, his fine hands clasped before him, the tips of his fingers touching. "You are going through a fiery trial, my dear sister. I have noted your faithful attendance, your deep absorption, your great need."

Mavis's face was a pale mask, her eyes dark pools of despair. "And yet I have found no comfort. No hope."

"But God is our comfort. God is our hope."

"I can't find Him, Reverend Crum. I've lost touch. I can't find Him."

"God is testing you." He spoke smoothly, Michal noticed, as though he had repeated these same words many times before. "Surely you have realized that since moving here the Lord has been testing you."

Mavis bowed her head. "It may be. I don't know. I don't know . . ." her voice trailed off, her eyes cooled to apathy once more.

Michal leaned forward. "How do you know that God has been testing her, Reverend Crum? What right has He to treat my mother that way?"

Reverend Crum frowned slightly. "When you are older, my dear, these things may be revealed to you. If you keep your faith."

"How old?"

"Perhaps tomorrow. Perhaps next year. Perhaps ten years from now."

"But what must I do in the meantime? Just wait?"

A faint note of irritation crept into his voice. "Just trust in Him and"—he paused, glanced about, pointed to a geranium blooming in the window—"and grow. Grow like that flower in the sun," he finished triumphantly.

"But—I'm not a geranium!"

A brisk knock at the front door interrupted her. Michal opened it to admit Abigail Pratt, who, breathless from the climb, dashed in, heading toward Mavis. "Good morning, Mrs. Ward. I know it's early and you're not seeing much company; but I just had to hyper up and tell you—" She broke off, noting the pastor for the first time. "Well, I'll declare I didn't see you, Reverend. It's so dark in here after the light outside. If I'd a known you were here I'd not a come in my Mother Hubbard. Ain't it a lovely day?"

"Ah—it is indeed, Mrs. Pratt." Then, rising: "I must take advantage of it to make a few more calls. Good day. Good day." And he made a relieved departure, forgetting in his haste to ask them to kneel in prayer.

As the door closed behind him, Abigail Pratt burst out, "Mrs. Ward, I called on that Mrs. Kelp, the doctor's wife, finally—you know I've been a-meanin' to." She leaned forward, her bright eyes snapping. "She has the queerest house. Nice furniture and carpets, but lots of bookcases full of queer books and the table all littered with magazines —not regular magazines like the *Ladies' Home Journal* and *Comfort*, but strange ones with no pictures. I tried to visit, but she just sat there with a frosty smile and didn't give me any help. And while I was telling her about the lovely new stained-glass window in the church she actually"—Abigail paused, then hissed, "you'll never believe this—she actually picked up a big lacquered case full of cigars—and passed it to me."

Mavis looked mildly interested.

"Did you take one?" asked Michal.

"You very well know I didn't, young lady. But she did. Lit it, crossed her legs, sat there smoking like any man, streams of smoke coming out o' her nose just like out of a dragon's." And Abigail clipped her lips together.

Michal noticed that Mother was smiling faintly. "What did you do?" she asked.

"Just what any Christian woman would do. I couldn't get a thing out of her—so I got up and said, 'I guess this is no place for me,' and she didn't even say I'm glad you came or ask me to come again. And when I got up to go she smiled for the first time and asked the cute little hired girl with the white cap and apron to see me out."

She paused for breath and looked a little nettled, for Mother had turned her face toward the prairie and didn't reply. Abigail leaned forward, then, and spoke firmly, "I wonder if I could have a little private" —with a glance at Michal—"talk with you."

Mother turned as though she found it hard to bring her thoughts back. "Of course, if you wish," she said quietly, and looked at Michal. "Will you please have Hetty bring coffee?"

Michal went to the kitchen and saw that Hetty already had the tray set and fresh coffee brewed. Hetty looked up and grinned. "I know

—I know. I wonder why that Pratt critter had to come a-leggin' it up here this morning, and me so busy ironin'," she grumbled, lifting a twin away from the stove.

Michal shrugged, went determinedly to her room, took her manicure scissors from the bureau drawer, and climbed the stairs. I'll find out what she's up to, she thought, tiptoeing her way carefully past trunks and boxes and old chairs across the arms of which lay Father's portrait—the one Matt had mutilated. Finally she knelt on a rag rug directly above the sitting room. "Not so fast, my black fellow," she whispered as a cricket hopped from the rug. Cupping her hand over it, she wrapped it in her handkerchief and put it carefully in her apron pocket. Then, flipping back a corner of the rug, she found what she was looking for—a knothole in the floor. When she heard Hetty bring in the coffee tray, she carefully cut with her scissors the wallpaper and cheese-cloth foundation around the knothole, and pulled back the flap. I knew this might come in handy some time, she thought as she glued an eye to the opening.

As Hetty left the room, Mrs. Pratt leaned over and put her hand familiarly on Mother's knee. "I just had to see you right away, Mis' Ward. I've been strugglin' with my conscience for weeks—ever since I seen signs of it; but after what I saw this morning with my own eyes, I knew that for your own good I must 'break my long silence,' as they say in the stories in *Comfort*."

She paused, drew a long breath and, as Mavis said nothing, went on. "Far be it for me to see a fine family broke up for lack of warning. Mis' Ward, your husband is untrue to you!"

Mother's body stiffened, and her hands grasped the arms of her chair. Then, "What did you say?" she asked, with more animation in her voice than Michal had heard since Uncle Fred's death.

Abigail Pratt, pleased at gaining her attention, nodded. "Surely" —she paused, took a sip of coffee, then went on slowly, each word coming with great relish—"Surely, you must have noticed that a certain young lady in this town has always made eyes at him? Kit Cutter."

"Well?" Mavis's question came like the crack of a whip.

"Now, mind you, I'm not blaming you. The whole town knows how you been troubled, broodin' over that burglar and your dear brother. But—you know how men are—they like their wives to take an interest in everything they do; and, well, if they don't there's always those who do. Everybody's a-talkin'," she finished darkly.

167

"I'm sure I don't know what you mean," Mother said, lifting her head proudly.

"Is dinner ready, Hetty?" John Ward's voice boomed from the kitchen.

"I must be going right away." Abigail Pratt rose hastily. "I didn't know it was so near noon!"

She's afraid of Father, thought Michal in disgust. I'd like to hit her—the old—the old witch. She put her hand in her apron pocket where the cricket still struggled in her handkerchief. Carefully she took the shining black insect from its prison, held it over the opening, and dropped it just as Hetty came in for the tray. It hit Mrs. Pratt's shoulder, gave a little hop, and then, to Michal's satisfaction, disappeared in the open V of the visitor's Mother Hubbard.

It's even better than I hoped, she thought as Abigail, clutching her bosom, shrieked, "A spider—inside my dress!"

"Let me help!" Mrs. Pratt fidgeted while Mother unbuttoned the wrapper and explored. "It's only a cricket," she said presently, "but I wonder how it got there."

Hetty glanced up at the ceiling, smiled broadly, and left the room abruptly.

Michal hurried downstairs just as the door slammed. John Ward peered cautiously in. "Has the old pelican gone?" he asked. "She always comes at the wrong time."

"After all"—Mother's voice was cool—"why shouldn't she come this morning, as well as anybody else?"

"Well," lamely, "I thought I saw the reverend headed this way."

"He was here, but he left after Mrs. Pratt came."

Father spoke irritably: "Doesn't she even have sense enough to stay away when you have your pastor calling? I really came early to say I'm taking you and Michal with me after dinner on a collection trip."

Mavis sank into her easy chair, and her voice again held the apathy they had heard so long. She leaned her head back wearily. "I don't believe I feel like leaving the house today."

"I insist." Father's voice was cold. "You've got to begin facing yourself."

"All right, if you wish."

By one o'clock they were speeding along on the northwest road in the surrey. This is luck, Michal thought. I might get a glimpse of Karl.

168

Mavis was sitting stiffly beside Father in front, and Michal, lounging on the back seat, was enjoying the rhythmic *clip-clop, clip-clop,* of the Hambletonians.

Michal broke the silence. "Who are you going to see today, Father?"

"A man named Schultz. Fairly new to the country. He made one deposit on a breaking plow and has never come back. Thought I'd look him up, though I don't know just where his place is and neither does anybody else, apparently."

Michal leaned back, then sat up expectantly. They were nearing Gross's place now, passing a field of rusty-gold wheat ready for cutting. The never ending prairie wind was dozing, but erratic breezes stirred the heads of the wheat, heavy with grain, and the huge blood-red poppies planted along the edge of the field. She sniffed deeply of the ripe grain smells which were mingled with the warm, languorous scent of the poppies.

"I think Schultz's place is somewhere around here," said Father. "But it wouldn't be this one on the left—he got here too late to plant wheat."

"That's the Gross farm," Michal broke in eagerly. "Katie's relatives. Haven't they a nice stand of grain?"

"Umph," grunted Father. "Those Rooshans have the damnedest luck."

"There's somebody, John. Maybe he could direct you."

"Good idea." The horses, brought up quickly, reared briefly and plunged to a halt. Michal leaned forward. Off in the distance Mrs. Gross was using a hoe, and not ten feet away from them Karl was cutting weeds at the edge of the field. He paid no attention, but kept on working—his back to them. With quick pride Michal noticed how easily his dark muscular body moved with each stroke of the scythe.

Father's neck was turning red. "Boy, there. Boy!"

Slowly Karl straightened, turned. His face was impassive. In the distance Mrs. Gross leaned on the handle of her hoe, watching.

"*Ja?*"

"Does Schultz—Franz Schultz—live on this road?"

"*Nein.*"

"Where does he live, then? Where do I turn to get to his place?" Father's voice was clipped.

Karl shrugged, and John Ward bellowed, "For God's sakes, are you foreigners deaf, dumb, and blind?"

"John!"

"Look," Father's voice turned mild as honey. "Schultz, Franz—" Then out of the field—crouching—crept the great wolf-dog, and sprang at the horses.

"Kum!" Karl's voice was quiet and the dog retreated; but the Hambletonians plunged, reared high—plunged again. Father worked silently, skillfully, until they were under control.

"If that God-damned cur ever crosses my path again, I'll kill him!"

Karl Gross straightened, and his head lifted with an instinctive, terrible arrogance. Deliberately he spat, then turned back to his work. For one awful instant John Ward's hand gripped the whip, and Michal thought surely he would lash out. Then, with an oath, he let the team go.

Pure rage shook Michal as she leaned forward, crying: "That's the boy who saved Katie and me in the blizzard. You had no right to act so."

Father seemed not to have heard her. "By God, he'd better not get near me again!"

Michal leaned back thinking, Karl got the better of it, somehow. But the day was a dead thing now, lifeless under the hot sun and the thick rich odor of wheat and poppies.

Then Father said suddenly, almost cheerfully: "There's Schultz's team coming now. I'd know that crow bait of his anywhere." Michal hardly noticed. She felt spent, as though she had run uphill for a long time.

As John Ward slowed, then stopped the team and talked in broken German to Schultz's broken English, she brooded over the events of the day, from Abigail Pratt's horrible gossip to the encounter with Karl, and Mother's stiff silence since. How could she enjoy things if her family kept on the way they had this summer? And now Karl and Father!

She roused a little as Father said. "Till after harvest then. Goodbye." And he waited for Schultz's team to start before turning around. As the familiar rhythmic *clip-clop, clip-clop,* lulled her again, she heard him say cheerfully: "Well, we were in luck after all. Might have chased out a dozen turnoffs without finding him."

"Yes, John." But Mother's voice was remote, and Michal tensed again.

As they whirled by Karl, who gave no sign of their passing, Father growled: "That's one Rooshan who'd better get over his uppity ways. If I'd been alone today, I'd of thrashed him within an inch of his life."

"It seems to me that before you sit in judgment on others, you'd best put your own house in order."

Father checked the team slightly. "What do you mean?"

"Don't pretend to me you don't know what I'm talking about, John Ward."

"By God, I've never bothered to pretend about anything!"

"Very well, I suppose you don't know that the whole town is—gossiping—about you and—a woman."

"And may I ask"—his voice was smooth as steel—"The name of the woman?"

"Since you choose to put it that way"—stiffly—"Kit Cutter."

"Well, I'm damned!" The team quickened its pace, and Michal watched the dark blood creep up Father's neck and ears. "That female newspaper! So that's why she snaked out of the house so fast this morning."

"I see you don't trouble to deny it."

"And I see that you have fine wifely faith in your husband." Bitterly.

"I didn't. At first. But you've acted—strange."

"And well I might, after the summer you've put me through. I'm human, you know. As a matter of fact, Miss Cutter has happened by the office a few times when I stepped out at noon. So we walked along together and talked. I could hardly ignore her. This morning she happened by the post office as I was coming out. If passing the time of day with her is causing gossip, the town can go to hell."

"It would be like a man to believe that she 'happened' by." Michal had never heard Mother talk like that before.

"And it would be like a woman to make something of it. Don't be like Abigail Pratt," snapped Father.

Then Mavis did a strange and terrible thing. She leaned her face into her hands and began to sob—deep sobs which shook her whole slight body. Father stopped the team abruptly and drew her into his arms. "Now, now. Now, now."

Slowly, slowly, she relaxed. Gradually her breathing grew even again. They had both forgotten Michal, who was crying great silent tears in sympathy and scarcely breathing for fear of disturbing them. As light from the afternoon sun mellowed into deep gold, Mavis drew a long sigh. "Oh, John. This terrible summer. Until Mrs. Pratt came this morning, I didn't think I could care about anything ever again. I just didn't care."

"I know." Father spoke heavily. "Matt's death—"

"Yes, Matt. Then Fred dying unsaved. My dearest brother. Even if we did disagree so. Somehow my faith in God began to crumble. I didn't know I could still care about anything until this morning."

"How do you know Fred died unsaved?"

"He was a freethinker. If he did believe in God, it wasn't the God I know."

"Rubbish! Everybody has a different idea of God. Fred was one of the finest men I've ever known—bar none. He damn' well better be in Heaven or I don't want to go there."

"I don't either." Mavis spoke seriously. "God has been testing me. Reverend Crum spoke of that this morning. And I've failed Him, myself, and my family miserably—" Her voice broke.

"Nonsense. You just had too much strain. All those years on the homestead. Losing our boy. Mrs. Oulette. Matt, Glen, now Fred. Well, it looks like Abigail Pratt did me a good turn, after all."

Mavis blushed. "I hate to think that—common jealousy—should—"

"Well, as the reverend said once, 'All things work together for good.'"

"I'll be all right now." She touched his brown cheek softly. Father tilted her chin up, put his mouth on hers, then crushed her close in a slow, deep kiss, yet held the reins firmly even so.

Michal relaxed and drew a long sigh. It was all right again—between Mother and Father, at least. Mavis stirred, turned. "Michal. John, we forgot her."

"I guess Mike'll be glad we have," he said jovially, releasing Mother and letting the restless horses go.

Michal said nothing, only leaned back contentedly. The prairie was fragrant again. He's forgotten Karl, too. She relaxed, watching the swelling earth dipping and falling away to the edge of the sky.

As they swung into the long driveway—the edges accented by the green of the small box elders—Rory dashed out to meet them and the horses shied. Then Michal heard Father mutter, "That damned Rooshan," as they sped toward the house.

172

X

By fall Mavis was herself again, and Michal and Faith were counting the days until school would start. Best of all, Katie said Karl would be there part of the time. "Mine Tante and Onkel have big fight about it." She giggled.

"You mean, Mr. Gross doesn't want him to go to school?" Michal asked incredulously.

"He say Karl's place is on farm. She say Karl go to school. So"— she giggled again—"Karl go to school. He just stay out to help with hauling and butchering."

The whole town was proud of the new rectangular white school snuggling firmly against the prairie, clean windows gleaming and bell cupola perched on top like a jaunty red cap. It was really an up-to-date building with cloakroom extending across the entire front and a shelf on the center wall holding a large shiny water pail, brimful, with a long-handled tin dipper hanging near it. The seats and desks were of light oak, the latter with hinges that could be raised or shut down and locked at night.

Mrs. MacVey, the teacher, sat behind a desk on a raised platform that extended across the full width of the front. She had a fat baby whom she nursed at recess and noon, then placed on a quilt on the floor. It was a good baby and slept most of the time; but Michal had heard Mrs. Pratt raving to Mother about "innocent children seeing a baby nursed and changed. In Salem, Mass., things were different, believe me."

Michal wondered what she'd think if she knew that Fanny was already known as the school flirt, for Fanny's eyes turned bold and bright whenever any boy, but most particularly Karl, looked her way.

By the end of the first week the children were settled in place and the school routine had begun in earnest. It was odd to see small Faith in the same row with teen-age Rooshans—Karl among them—who would stay there until they could speak and read English well enough to go on. A girl named Lily Lumpkin, whose yellowish eyes peered suspiciously out from under a thatch of unkempt hay-colored hair, was

173

the only one in Fifth. Lily's faded dress was soiled, and her pock-marked face was startlingly clean in contrast to her dirty neck. No one shared her desk.

"I don't like Lily Lumpkin," Fanny Pratt announced at recess one day.

"Why not?" demanded Michal, forgetting that she didn't care about her either.

"Well, she's dirty. Her mother scrubs and takes in washing. And she's got lice!"

Michal stole a look at Lily, who was leaning against the wall of the schoolhouse, watching them circling as they sang:

> " 'Water, water, wineflower, growing up so high—
> We are all young ladies, and we are sure to die—' "

Lily's yellow eyes were burning with a desperate hunger. "We ought to ask her to play," Michal said slowly.

"Well, I certainly won't." Fanny Pratt shook her head arrogantly. "She always scowls and mutters, 'What's it to you' if I speak to her."

As Michal beckoned to the girl, who came slowly forward and took the extended hand, Fanny exploded, "Count me out, and you know why!"

On a crisp November morning after Karl had been absent a week, Fanny sweetly asked the question Michal herself had been dying to ask. "When is Karl coming back to school?"

Katie shrugged. "Soon. Hauling is now done and hogs want to be butchered next week."

Butchering! Michal shuddered, remembering a day at the Homestead. Fire burning under the great iron scalding pot; water steaming; the rude scraping bench; the hog stunned by a sledgehammer blow between the eyes; the awful gurgling squeal after he was stuck; the limp body scalded in the vat; the scraping; the hoisting with the windlass; the disemboweling; the sickish smell of fat guts slithering into the waiting tub.

Fanny was saying, "He'll fall behind."

"He study at home."

"Even if he is a Rooshan I like him," said Fanny boldly. "Don't you, Michal?"

"No," said Michal rudely, wishing Fanny would be still.

174

"Well, I'm going to give him a lovely valentine on Valentine's Day," announced Fanny as the bell rang, swaying her hips as they walked toward the door. "I'll bet he gives me one, too. I can tell he likes me."

Katie giggled. "He's never heard of a valentine."

"Then I'll explain it to him. Don't tell my mother, Michal."

Michal's face was pink with rage. "You know I'm no tattletale," she hissed, "even if she is," she muttered to Katie under her breath as they filed in.

"Vy do you care if she likes Karl?" asked Katie innocently.

"I don't. If I sent any boy a valentine, it would be Lewis."

That night after supper Michal settled down by the base burner, glad that Faith and the twins were in bed. "Mother, if a person prays hard enough for something will God make it happen?"

"If you pray with faith and it is His holy will. Remember how a few Sundays ago Reverend Crum preached from Matthew 17:20: 'If ye have faith as a grain of mustard seed, ye shall say unto this mountain, Remove hence to yonder place; and it shall remove; and nothing shall be impossible unto you.'"

"Then"—Michal's eyes were shining—"if a person has faith enough, he can make anything happen."

"Yes." And as Mavis smiled again, Michal thought, How beautiful Mother looks these days! A little plumper, too.

John Ward stirred and glanced up from a volume of the encyclopedia. "Isn't that rather a strong statement?"

"Christ made it, not I."

"I prefer the motto of another great man, 'Read not to contradict ... nor take for granted ... but to consider!'"

Michal didn't hear. Inside herself—over and over—she was chanting silently, "Lord, I have faith in you to make Karl give me a valentine instead of Fanny Pratt."

XI

The days were shorter now, and Michal enjoyed the sharp metallic sound of horses' hoofs striking on the frozen ground. On a day when snow slanted with the wind, Karl returned to school. Better still, he spent the school week with the Keims, going home only for Saturdays and Sundays. However, he was so deeply engrossed in his studies that he seemed more remote than ever.

But Michal was content. Any lingering doubts as to whether God was listening to her prayers were completely dispelled when the Reverend Crum preached about the cup of bitterness—the drink of vinegar mingled with gall; and when he asked, "Are ye able to drink of the cup that I shall drink of?" Michal got the idea. They had the very thing at home—in Mother's bureau drawer. The quassia cup! They had always had it—a little smooth wooden goblet of good plain design. Once when Michal had had a fever Mother had filled it with cold water which had become bitter from the quassia wood, and had insisted Michal drink it. She had never forgotten the terrible taste. This sermon, then, was God's way of telling her that if she wanted that valentine and would drink of the bitter water, He would know that she was willing to suffer for His sake in order to do her part.

Each night after Faith was sound asleep, she knelt beside the bed, first praying earnestly, repeating her wish solemnly, then taking a good swig from the cup of bitterness. Even as she gagged and sputtered into her handkerchief, she could feel God's benevolent presence and knew that He was with her. So strong and sure did she feel, that Karl's very indifference became a sign of his desire to give her the finest valentine in the room.

She was no longer disturbed when Fanny went as far as the sidewalk with him, running to keep up, looking up slantwise with her bright brown eyes, moistening her little buttonhole mouth. Fanny chased after all the boys. She sought Lewis, too, but always with a careful eye on Michal. Sometimes she flirted with Adolph, and even Burt Brattle, who lived near Lily on the other side of the railroad track.

As holiday season approached, the edges of Michal's faith began to crumble. Karl seemed completely unaware of her. One night she took an extra large swallow of bitter water and was violently sick. To make matters worse Faith woke and caught her refilling the cup, and she had to give up her bottle of cologne as a price for silence, no questions asked. It was beginning to look as though God was angry or, at least, losing interest. Karl's indifference might be real indifference. She began to look for a hopeful sign. During Christmas week it came.

In the center of the sitting room ceiling had been carefully pasted

176

a huge bright star of shining gold. The hanging lamp depended from the exact center of this shining thing, and at night when it was lit the opaque milky shade gave the star a heavenly radiance. When during Christmas week the Reverend Crum preached from II Chronicles 16:9, "The eyes of the Lord run to and fro throughout the whole earth," the star had suddenly, as by a miracle, been transformed into the Eye of the Lord. She had since then spent much of her spare time—not kneeling— that would have been too noticeable—but seated on the rug in front of the base burner, repeating her wish: "Lord, I have faith that you will make Karl give me a valentine." The Eye of the Lord glowed down warmly on her and she was comforted.

Everything went better after that. When Fanny started the trouble with Lily, Michal felt that she passed the test with flying colors.

It began one afternoon just before they broke step as the line marched out, when Fanny sang softly:

> "Lily Lumpkin killed a louse
> And hung it in the slaughterhouse."

Some of the others took it up, stamping hard to accent each beat:

> "LI-ly LUMP-kin KILL-ed a LOUSE
> And HUNG it IN the SLAUGH-ter HOUSE."

Lily broke from the line and ran swiftly away. She didn't look back.

For several days they sang the song every night—softly lest Mrs. MacVey hear it. Then one morning Lily did not come to school. Just as the last bell rang, Achsah Klunk came striding up and asked to see Teacher. They talked in low tones for a moment, then Mrs. MacVey —her long beautiful jawline more clearly defined than usual—spoke to the school: "No one of us, I am sure, means to be unkind; but we have been really more than that—we have been cruel."

Achsah turned quite red. "Her mother works so hard cleaning and scrubbing for other folks I had to come in her place. I think Lily could have stood it if somebody hadn't made up that nasty little song about her."

Mrs. MacVey spoke quickly. "Shall we ask Mrs. Klunk to see Lily at once, tell her we are sorry and that we want her to give us a chance to show her we are sorry? All in favor say, Aye!"

There was a roar of assent. Automatically Michal glanced toward Fanny; she was looking very virtuous and shouting with the rest.

That afternoon, just as the last bell was ringing, Lily Lumpkin came in and took her seat. Her hair was combed. She kept her eyes on her work and studied all recess to make up her morning lessons.

At recess Fanny said: "I don't care what they say; I'm not going to be friendly with her. My ma wouldn't let me. In Salem, Mass.—"

"You started it." Michal spoke coldly. "The least you can do is to be decent. I'm going to walk part way home with her tonight." Then, with a flash of inspiration, "I'm going to be her friend."

Fanny gasped. "Your mother won't let you!" Shooting a glance toward Katie, who was gossiping with some of the Rooshans in another part of the yard, "It's bad enough for you to play with Katie."

"You're not too good to want her cousin for a beau," flashed Michal.

"That's different. All the girls make eyes at Karl." She paused. "Or do you want him for your beau, too?"

"No, I don't," Michal lied coolly. "I just wanted to remind you that I'm not the only one who likes Rooshans. As for Lily, my mother always wants me to do the kind thing."

That afternoon Michal and Katie taught Lily to chant

"Hippity hop
To the barbershop
To buy a stick of candy."

Just before they parted, Lily, after glancing quickly about, dug deeply into her faded pocket and brought out something in her clenched fist. "Lookit," she whispered reverently. "It's a white penny. Achsah Klunk give it to me. You're the only ones I've showed it to."

They looked. It was only a nickel, an ordinary five-cent piece.

"Why, dot's—" began Katie, but Michal trod on her toe sharply. "Thanks for showing it to us."

Lily's yellow eyes turned shy. "It's all right. Well"—she yawned— "I gotta get home. My back teeth is floating." She held herself proudly as she left.

"Don't you see, Katie? She'd never had a nickel before. Imagine! I'm glad we played with her." They watched the figure disappear. "What'd she mean about her teeth floating? I wonder."

Katie shrugged. "I don't know."

Michal skipped all the way home, remembering the look in Lily's eyes and the proud way that she had walked. She couldn't wait to tell Mother.

But when Mavis came in from Ladies' Aid she was not pleased. "Michal . . ." It wasn't like her to fumble for words like this. "It isn't that I'm not glad you were kind to Lily. It's just that—I'd rather you didn't become her playmate."

Michal turned slowly to stare at Mavis, coolly, as though, almost, she were a stranger. Sitting there in her black silk dress with the black silk tasseled braid, Mother was every inch a lady, even though her body had thickened with the new baby. Most of the women were wearing their hair parted in the middle and creped; hers was done plain and piled high to show the narrow strip of white which ran back from her forehead like a white satin ribbon. "The Gordons turn white early," Mother always said proudly, almost as though it were a royal symbol.

"Mother"—Michal spoke slowly—"when you were a little girl didn't you ever play with anybody like Lily?"

Mavis shuddered. "Goodness, no. I always felt"—with a level glance at her daughter—"that my parents knew best."

"But Lily doesn't have any playmates."

"But, Michal, if she has—ah"—Mavis paused delicately—"vermin —you might get them, too."

"Wouldn't it be better for me to get lice than for her to get that awful look in her eyes again?" reasoned Michal. "It isn't that I like her so much. It's just that I can't bear that look she gets."

Mavis's lips quivered. "I don't understand you. With all the nice children there are to play with, you choose Rooshans—and now a girl like that." Nervously she picked Gordon up.

Michal's blue eyes filled. "Well, I can't understand you, Mother. Reverend Crum preaches about being kind to all God's creatures. And you say what a good preacher he is. And then you don't like it if I try to do as he says." She gave a loud martyred sigh.

"We just don't see things the same way, child. Play with Lily if you think it wise. But I hope you never forget"—her chin lifted—"that you're a Gordon."

"I won't," dutifully.

Mavis relaxed into a hurt silence, but Michal didn't notice. She had sat down in the corner and was looking up at the Eye of the Lord. Under her breath she was saying, "Oh, God, help me to understand my mother. I need my Uncle Fred." Resting her chin in her hands, she stared fixedly at the star until—to the accompanying soft thuds of falling coals—she felt her faith strong within her once more. "And God—don't forget the valentine."

XII

The first bell was ringing when Michal and Faith left the house on Valentine's Day. Faith had made red paper hearts for everyone in the room, but Michal was giving to the girls only. "Why should I give any old boy one?" she had demanded the night before, when Fanny had asked.

The room was already thick with chalk dust and chatter as the girls entered. Michal's first glance was for Karl, but as usual he was studying and apparently unaware of the big paper-covered box, with the wide slot in it, on Mrs. MacVey's desk. Just for a moment Michal's spirits dipped low before she thought, He doesn't want anybody to guess.

"We'll have our valentines just before school closes this afternoon," announced Mrs. MacVey as Michal and Faith dropped theirs in.

Fanny Pratt whispered, "Look what I'm giving Karl Gross," and held out an elaborate square dotted with blue forget-me-nots, the whole edged with a fringe of blue silk.

Michal shrugged and slipped into her seat.

"That Fanny Pratt is boy-crazy" she whispered to Katie. "Did you give any valentines to boys?"

Katie dimpled. "I sent one through the mail."

As the day wore on, tension mounted. Even Mrs. MacVey's baby —usually contented on its blanket—fussed and cried until it was nursed, soothed, and finally turned over to one of the older girls.

At last the big moment arrived. Michal and Katie were appointed to distribute the missives, and they worked rapidly. Mrs. MacVey's desk was soon covered; and Michal noted with satisfaction that her own and Katie's desks held a good number.

She delivered several to Karl, but he ignored her completely as he glanced carelessly at the valentines. He doesn't want even me to guess, she thought, as she turned to deliver her own nice one to Lily Lumpkin.

Lily was smiling, a fixed awful smile over the emptiness of her desk.

Now as Michal handed her the square white envelope her face relaxed as she clutched it. Next year I'll give everyone a valentine, Michal thought fiercely, as she saw that Faith's little red hearts were in some cases the only ones on otherwise vacant desk tops.

Katie was already opening hers, and as Michal sat down she saw what she was looking for. It was on top—a large heavy cream envelope. Involuntarily she turned and smiled at Karl, who, caught off guard, was regarding her with his level dark gaze. Michal thought she caught an answering flicker before she turned to her pile, sorting them in order of size with the cream envelope last.

She opened them slowly, handling each one delicately, whispering thanks to Katie for her filigree one and turning to flash a smile at Lily for her crude painted effort. The white candy heart with I Love You in red must have come from fat Adolph, because as she lifted it out of the envelope he hit her on the cheek with a spitball and smirked meaningly. Michal smiled faintly then caught Lewis's eye. He winked and grinned impudently, hazel eyes sparkling.

She stared coldly. Lewis hadn't given her one. As she turned back to open the heavy cream envelope she thought angrily, "If he'd saved half the money he puts into those candy pipes he might have bought me as nice a one as Karl." The big envelope contained a smaller one, and the contents were soft to the touch.

"Open it," whispered Katie excitedly. Fanny was watching, too.

Eagerly Michal drew out the vision of beauty. On a white quilted satin background edged with rich uncut loops of red silk fringe was a painted card. Down a path between trees faintly green, on a conveniently low bough on one of which a pair of cooing birds perched, walked a boy in buff coat and doublet and hose. Clinging to his arm a maiden looked coyly down while her free hand, encased in long black mitts, daintily held her Kate Greenaway skirt from too close contact with the path. As though all this were not enough the picture was outlined in red silk braid exactly matching the fringed edge. Under the picture was printed in gold letters "From You Know Who."

Yes, she knew. As Mrs. MacVey said, "Attention. Monitors pass," Michal folded her hands, only vaguely conscious of wraps being passed, the last-minute shuffle. When Lewis punched her and whispered mischievously, "Where'd you get that?" pointing to the valentine, she only smiled dreamily and whispered, "It's beautiful," then, rising, floated to her position in the line and marched out with the others.

Katie ran to Karl as soon as the line broke to see his collection, teasing as she came to the blue one. Michal followed more slowly, lost in a soft mist of shyness.

"Karl." She touched his arm gently. "Thank you."

"For vat?" he asked sharply, staring down at her.

"Why—for this—you know," gesturing with the valentine.

"I haf not a valentine given."

Katie giggled. "Karl care nottings for valentines."

"But—Karl gave me this—I *know*. He had to." Her voice held bewilderment and a horrible growing fear.

"No." He was still standing there quietly, watching her.

Then Fanny ran up to them, and Fanny was showing Katie and Karl her valentines and was saying: "Lewis gave me this. Of course, he gave Michal the prettiest, though. I saw him getting it at—"

Then Michal was running blindly for home.

Mavis was playing the cottage organ softly as Michal stumbled in.

"Why, you're all out of breath! Where's Faith?"

"I—don't know." She spoke stupidly. "I ran all the way."

Hetty marched in carrying tea things, set them down, then glanced sharply at Michal. "I declare, you look as if a ghost wuz walkin' over yer grave. Didn't you git no valentines?"

"Oh—yes." She handed them over, then sank down in Father's big chair.

"My, my." Hetty shuffled through them rapidly. "You done all right. Lookit this un, Miz' Ward."

Mavis read the verse out loud. "This is lovely, really elaborate. Who gave it to you?" she asked quickly.

"Lewis."

"How very nice!" Her face brightened as John Ward burst in the door—a twin under each arm.

"Philip here is a born horseman, Mavis. Kept saying, 'Make 'oss run.' Damnedest thing I ever saw." Father put the boys down, then asked sharply, "What the devil's all this?"

Mavis was placing the valentine prominently on the lambrequinned mantel. "Lewis gave it to Michal." She smiled, "Our daughter's growing up, John."

182

Father gingerly touched the fringe, read the verse, then said slowly, "Well, I'll be double God-damned."

"Dubbo Dod-dammed," piped Philip rapturously.

Father snorted, then blew his nose violently as Mavis cried out, "There, John, you see?"

"Yes, Mavis," meekly. "Oh, Mike, here's a letter for you. From Rochester."

"Phyllis?" Mavis asked quickly.

Michal tore open the envelope slowly, without curiosity. Inside herself she was back in the schoolyard and Karl was saying abruptly, "I haf not a valentine given," as she removed another sealed letter and a note.

"It's from Aunt Phyllis," Michal said quietly. "It says:

" 'DEAR MICHAL:

" 'As you know—after your Uncle Fred's death I went to Denver City to settle his affairs, then on to Virginia to visit my sister and family. On my return early this month to Rochester I found this letter to you from Fred in a book which had been sent up with some other things after my departure. He must have written it shortly before he was stricken and never mailed it. So I'm sending it on to you now.

" 'How are your dear mother and father? Give my love to the whole family.

" 'Hastily,
" 'AUNT PHYLLIS' "

Michal lifted the envelope which bore her name: "Miss Michal Ward, Eureka, Dakota Territory, U.S.A." in Uncle Fred's firm handwriting. There was no return address.

Everyone—even the twins—stood quiet, watching her. Then Hetty gave a loud sniff, wiped her eyes with the edge of her apron, and whispered, " 'Tis a voice from the grave."

"Mother"—Michal turned—"would you mind if I went off by myself to read this?"

"Of course not," Mavis said quietly, and Michal hurried out.

She walked quickly, head bowed, turning naturally toward the Place of Rocks. It would be cold there, but she could be alone and there was much to be thought out, much to try to understand. Uncle Fred hadn't written often, but his notes to her had always been gay

183

and interesting. She wondered if Mother had understood her wish to get off by herself.

Wintry winds had swept the hill bare of snow, and from the dead grass a few brittle skeletons of last summer's purple coneflowers swayed gently. As Michal seated herself on a ledge at the foot of the tall old rock, she heard quick steps, crunching louder as they neared her hideaway. Irritation filled her. Surely Faith hadn't seen her come this way, and followed. But it was Karl who stood there on the rim looking down at her. Karl's tall body made taller by the high black astrakhan cap; the jaunty, full-skirted, black astrakhan coat belted with a vivid home-dyed scarlet sash; and high Cossack boots—all made a dark stroke silhouetted briefly against the deep silver of the prairie sky. His packet of valentines was jammed carelessly into one of his smaller books.

Michal shrank back as he walked slowly down into the old snowy hollow. It was too soon. She hadn't had a chance to think it out. It was too soon to see him again. "How did you know I was here?" She shoved her letter deeper into her cloak pocket and rose to face him.

"On my vay home"—he gestured toward the west—"I see you. I kum."

"Why?"

He shrugged. "I vant to."

For a moment they stared at each other. She had never before noticed that his eyes were guarded by heavy lashes, and that his mouth was wide and full—the upper lip scalloped down a little. "You always do what you want, don't you?" she asked curiously.

"Ja." He leaned easily against the boulder. "Vy you t'ink I haf you a valentine gifen?"

Michal tensed. As always when she was with Karl, the day had sharpened. The pale earth, the dry rattle of dead coneflowers, the faint smell of sweat and horses—and over everything the blur of her own despair. "I was—testing my—faith." In her concentration she frowned. "It was a bargain that I had—with God, you see. But now '—she stumbled—"I don't know whether my faith was too small."

Karl scowled. "What does Gott gif about valentines? Dey are silly stuff. For Kinder."

Michal scowled back. "They're not silly and they're not for children only. We always give them here in America. "Why"—her voice lifted triumphantly—"it's even the day birds choose their mates."

184

Karl spat deliberately. "Dot is not so." His black eyes narrowed. "Vy you ask Gott for a valentine from me?"

She blushed. "Because, you—because if you sent me one it would be like moving a mountain with faith—as it says in the Bible."

"So?" He smiled, his dark eyes flicking her lightly.

Michal flinched, then, and blazed. "I don't think you even understand what I have been saying—or why I'm mixed up. You couldn't help me." Her lips trembled. "You wouldn't even try. If God—"

Karl straightened. "Gott is for *Kirche*. Valentines and Gott"—contemptuously—"you little Englisher."

"You're just too stupid to understand anything." Michal was furious. "Maybe they are silly, but Lewis Reid saved enough money to buy me the—the most beautiful one in town. It's in the middle of our mantel at home. My mother put it there."

Karl's brows made a straight black line. "Dot Lewis is an *Esel*." With a violent gesture he pulled out and tore his packet of valentines in two, tossed them carelessly to the wind, then strode to the rim and disappeared without a backward glance.

Trembling, Michal sank down at the foot of the great stone. Leaning her head against it, she closed her eyes and tried to steady her breathing. Tears rolled slowly down her cheeks and splashed onto her cloak. I want to die, she thought miserably. Nobody knows nor cares how I feel. If I died Karl and Mother might be sorry.

The vision of Karl and Mavis bending sadly over her revived her a little. Brushing away the tears with her mittened hand, she pulled out Uncle Fred's letter, and opened it.

"Michal, my dear," it began.

She closed her eyes for a moment. It came back then—picture clear—that beautiful evening in the pigweed patch. He was smiling at her again, his dark eyes warm and understanding.

The coneflowers were rattling gently still, and a fragment of valentine wavered on the rim of the hollow, then blew out of sight, flashing blue forget-me-nots against the pale sky.

"MICHAL, MY DEAR,

"I intended writing you at some length tonight, describing this strange country and the way I feel about it. But I'm tired and quite dull-witted and shall consequently spare you the quaint nonsense that people usually feel impelled to write when in a foreign land.

"Instead, I'll save it all to tell you. My client and I plan to leave in a few days for the coast and take a nice slow (very slow, so we can catch up on sleep) boat to New York. Then I'll go home to Denver via Dakota. I want to hear the wingbeat of the upland birds and watch cloud shadows on the prairie once more. This jungle shuts out the sky.

"So—tell you father to oil his guns and your mother to place a light in the window for me. As for you, Michal, I'm sure you already have a secret place where you go to think. Perhaps you'll take me there and we can talk things over as we always have.

"Often I've thought of our visit in your pigweed patch when we listened to the song of the Trumpeter Swan. Did you guess, I wonder, how much you helped me that evening? Grownups get confused, too, you know. Just keep the way you are and you'll be all right. See you soon.

"Love,
"Uncle Fred"

Folding the letter carefully and replacing it in its envelope, she rose stiffly and brushed the snow from her cloak. The prairie sky was paling into twilight as she climbed to the rim of the hollow. The wind carried the cold fragrance of snow and frozen earth.

As she began the descent Michal thought of how he'd come, after all, to her secret place—all the way from that "strange country"—and not as he'd intended, but with words of comfort when she needed them most. The wind quickened and Michal hurried—away from the Place of Rocks and the dead coneflowers rattling gently there on the hill.

XIII

Spring came early. By the first of April huge bluebottle flies buzzed over the steaming manure pile back of the livery stable, and from the prairie ponds came the sad slender plaint of killdeers. Farmers were busy breaking new land for flax and plowing for wheat.

The townspeople were busy, too—new saloons, a new store, more rough board sidewalks and hitching posts under the thrifty box elders along Main and Market streets; while two new churches lifted their white spires bravely, like pale index fingers pointing upward.

By the time school closed, Mavis and Hetty had everything ready for the new baby, who was expected sometime soon. John Ward was no help at all—nervous, as usual, before the event, and increasingly irritable over the dry weather and consequent fall-off in business.

But nothing could dim Mavis's serenity, as she calmly awaited her confinement, ignoring Father's frequent, "Well, at least, we're in town near a doctor this time," and Mrs. Pratt's sympathy: "I'd rather be in Tophet with my neck broke! How do you do it so easy, Miz Ward?"

"Eat sparingly so the baby will be small and stay in bed for two weeks afterward."

David, born on a hot windy day in June, was large and blond like his father. Michal had never realized until now how excited people got over new babies. She and Hetty were kept jumping as they entertained a steady stream of callers, all bearing gifts. Even Lewis's mother called, who rarely left her couch. She was beautifully dressed in a carriage cloak of black lace over violet silk, her little lace bonnet trimmed simply with bunches of violets. Everyone lingered over the exquisite gifts she had brought—a christening robe of finest material, elaborately pintucked and trimmed with delicate lace, and a jardiniere holding hyacinth plants, with spikes of bloom so heavy they were supported by thin wooden strips.

The day the Reverend and Mrs. Crum came, Michal surprised Father and the reverend in the dining room hastily but cheerfully drinking a toast to the new boy.

"Every time I've called here I've admired your fuddling cup," the reverend was saying as he carefully set the old English drinking cup down—six squat vases so connected that to drink one was to drink all. "My father had one. On this hot day I've had the capacity."

Later, his breath smelling strongly of cloves, he gave a rather long, emotional prayer of thanksgiving for the safe arrival of the child. Mrs. Crum seemed in a great hurry to be gone, and Father caught Michal's eye and winked.

By late June there was still no rain, and farmers and businessmen alike were beginning to look for clouds and shake their heads as the sky remained ominously clear. Hardly a day passed without a gray plume of smoke from a distant prairie fire against the horizon. Father gave orders that the children stay within the town firebreaks.

As the long summer days dragged on, Michal was filled with a new queer restlessness, her moods changing as quickly as cloud shadows passing over the prairie. A silver bird call, or the sight of Mother nursing David, could send her into a bright glow bordering on ecstasy. Yet an hour later she would be swept into strange dark despair. She did a good deal of crying.

Her whole summer was ruined the day Father snapped, "No, for the last time, you can't have a new dress for the Fourth of July celebration."

Michal's heart sank. "Then I shan't go at all!"

Now she'd be at home all day. Wouldn't see the sackraces, the three-legged race; she'd miss the greased-pig catching, the bandstand music. Worst of all, she'd not be able to stand inside the pavilion with Katie and watch the Rooshans dance. She wouldn't see Karl dance.

She'd visualized herself in a thin white dress, light-blue sash, and a new leghorn hat encircled with a wreath of asters as blue as her eyes. She'd visualized Karl's look of rapture as he swept her into his arms and they whirled to the wild Rooshan music.

But Mavis was saying: "I don't see why both the girls can't have new dresses, John. I know business has been slow with the drought and all, but surely—"

Father pounded his fist on the center table and roared: "All right, I'll tell you why. I traded some horses for land on the Missouri River last winter. I was going to drive the family over this summer and surprise you with it. This spring the river changed its course and wiped out my land."

"But how could a river change its course in a dry year?"

"Well, it did. We're not going to have money for new dresses or new anything for a while."

Mavis was very pale. "You might have told me sooner, John. You might even have asked my advice about doing such a silly thing."

"Silly!" shouted Father, strangling on his own rage. "Oh, God!" and he slammed out of the house so violently that David wakened and began to cry.

Mavis sighed and rose to her feet, "Well, Michal, I'm sorry about the dress. We'll lengthen last year's and buy fresh ribbons."

Michal burst into tears. "I'd rather die!" and rushed to her room. As she flung herself onto the bed, she cracked her head on one of Faith's dolls. Snatching it by its wig she swung it onto the floor, smashing it to bits.

As suddenly as it had come, her anger was gone. Somberly she stared at the wreckage, the sprawled dead thing there at her feet. Kneeling down, she picked up the limp rag body, headless now. "Poor little doll," she whispered. "I wonder why I did that."

XIV

On Fourth of July Michal stayed in her room and wrote a long poem entitled "Bury Me Under the Weeping Willow," while Father, meek as milk, took Faith and the twins to the celebration.

That evening Katie dropped by to tell her how she'd met Joshua there and they'd spent two whole hours together, watching the races and the dancing. Even though she didn't say so, Michal knew that this was their first real date. Once more she felt Katie's condescension, tinged this time almost with malice as she described how handsome Karl and Frieda Baur had looked as they danced together.

As the long summer days dragged by, Michal avoided Katie and spent most of her spare time with Lewis. When time for house-cleaning week approached, she had about decided that Mother was right—it was best to be with your own kind.

On Saturday morning of house-cleaning week Michal relaxed in the hammock on the front porch thankful that the hectic time was over, the fence and clotheslines no longer sagging under the weight of bedding, portieres, and rugs; the house free of Father's curses as he barked his shins on misplaced furniture.

Today the house was shining, walls, woodwork, cupboards; the well beaten carpets stretched and tacked down over heavy layers of fresh straw and newspapers; and the striped bedticks washed, plumped with stuffings of clean wheat straw, and decorously buttoned down their middles ready for another six months' service.

In spite of the September heat and constant rasping of grasshoppers, Michal was so absorbed with the passing of Little Eva that she jumped when Katie called softly from the carriage block, "Hey, Michal!"

"Tie Poddy, and come in out of the sun."

"I can't stay, but I need you to help me—come to my Tante's with me."

Michal hesitated, "Why?"

"I'll tell you vhile ve ride—please come! I vait for you here."

"I'll have Gus put a sidesaddle on Starlet. Wish we could wear pants for riding. Men have the best of it."

They rode in silence through the front gate, and angled across the dusty prairie toward the Gross farm. "Well, Katie?"

Katie seemed to find it hard to speak. Finally, "Susanna forgot her earrings—so I take them out to her today."

"That's nonsense! You don't need me for that. Besides, I shouldn't be riding horseback today—I'm not very well."

"You, too?" Katie eyed her shrewdly. "When?"

"Since last January. Mother was at Ladies' Aid, and Gus and Hetty had the children in their room when it happened. I thought I was bleeding to death. I was terribly scared, and went outdoors and got a basin of snow to stop the bleeding."

"But your Mutter"—Katie's voice held surprise—"had she not told you?"

"No."

"Gewiss! My Mutter told me when I was ten. What did you do?"

"I put on Mother's heavy wool shawl and hurried down to Achsah Klunk's, and she explained everything—and told me what to do. You're very lucky to have a mother who tells you things."

"Ja, I know."

They rode in silence over the sere prairie until again Michal asked, "Well?"

Katie's flushed face was stained a deeper red as she said hurriedly in a low voice: "It's Yoshua; you know he is a fine boy, but that Mutter of his will nefer let him go with me. Michal, we must see each other, so today I meet him."

"So that's why you're all dressed up and look so nice?"

Katie nodded, smiling shyly.

"Where?"

"In Switzer's house on hill. It is empty now."

"But, Katie, aren't you a little young—"

190

"I'm a year older as you," with dignity.

"That's so. Well—what can I do?"

"I take Susanna's earrings home; we stay a while, then ride away together to the hill back of your place—the place where you and Lewis find Glen. Then you ride home slow so there can be no talk. I stay short while with Yosh and go home, back around by your place."

Michal noticed as they rode into the Gross yard that it was as neat as though just swept; the main building, long since finished, as well as the summer kitchen, was freshly whitewashed with vivid blue trim under the eaves and at the door and window frames.

Everyone was busy. Anna was out west gathering cow chips. Susanna and her father were cutting *Kuhmist* down in the cattle corral. After harvest the bricks of earth, straw, and dung would be stacked until dry, then the whole daubed with fresh cow dung to keep out rain and snow. This was the equivalent of coal to the farmers. The earth slowed the burning process and gave the smoke a turfy tang.

The girls tied their horses in the shade of the cookhouse and went to where Tante Katrina and the lovely Frieda were shredding cabbages for kraut, in large tubs.

Katrina greeted them in German, suggested that Anna could use help with the cow chips, then continued in animated conversation with her young neighbor. As Katie turned to go, little old Grossmutter hobbled briskly out. Smiling a welcome, she grasped Michal's hand, led her through a neat picket fence enclosing the flower garden, and motioned her to a bench against the wall near the door. On either side of a rock-rimmed path ice-plant carpeted the ground. Grossmutter puttered about the flowers, pulling a few weeds from the marigolds, stirring the earth about the four-o'clocks and blue bachelor's-buttons, gathering and putting in a large paper sack a few ripe saffron flowers, and picking ripe pods from the poppy plants. The poppies grew beside the bench where Michal sat. The heavy-headed blooms, dark red like splashes of blood, gave out a sickish sweet smell which first soothed her then made her drowsy. Finally Grossmutter had the plot tidied to her satisfaction, and beckoned her to the cookhouse.

It was neat and cool inside, and dark after the sun glare. The elder woman briskly dusted a corner of the bench by the table for Michal, then pouring two glasses of homemade raisin wine, with a flourish put one before the guest, raised her own glass high, and they both drank to Grossmutter's "Gesundheit!" Michal thought of what Mother would say, but she knew now that at least one member of the family really liked her.

Karl's grandmother went to the stove and peered, sniffing, into a big black pot, then added water; Michal, feeling rather dizzy, strolled out to meet Katie and Anna, who were slowly walking in with two bulging gunny sacks hanging down on either side of Poddy.

Susanna had joined the kraut workers and was washing her bare feet in a pail of cold water by the hogshead. Then Karl, driving a work team hitched to a sod breaker, came around the corner, the coulter clattering on the dry earth. He paused at sight of the women, picked up the heaping tub of cabbage, and dumped it into a huge hogshead nearby. Michal's heart skipped a beat. "Hello, Karl." She and Frieda spoke in unison.

He gave them a brief glance. "Hello," he said soberly.

Susanna pulled the back of her skirt forward between her legs diaper fashion, then beckoned her brother. He steadied her elbows and helped her into the hogshead, where she stamped, tramping the kraut down firmly. She didn't wash her feet carefully nor clean her toenails, thought Michal. Remembering the *Kuhmist*—I'll never eat homemade kraut again.

Then little Grossmutter was calling them for dinner, and Michal thought, I can understand and speak their language almost as well as Karl does English, when Katrina said to Katie in German, "Is she staying?"

Michal felt hot blood rush to her face, but before she could turn to go Karl strode to her side and faced his mother. "She stays," he said quietly in English.

"Here speak we German," flashed Katrina, glaring at her son, who —taller now than she—returned her look with iron composure.

"I speak as I wish," he said, and, leading Michal into the cookhouse, sat down beside her at the table. When Frieda, her face becomingly flushed from the heat, seated herself by Susanna, her eyes sought Karl for a moment. Then she looked away quickly, and Michal thought: She feels as I would if he had chosen her. But I am the stranger in this house.

The table was set with a huge round loaf of bread at one end, and at each place a deep white galvanized soup plate, cup and saucer, fork and spoon. There were no napkins. Grossmutter lifted the loaf to her bosom and with a long sharp knife cut toward herself and put the thick round slices in each plate. Then, with a triumphant flourish, she brought from the stove and placed in the center of the table a large rose-decorated chamber pot, cover and all.

Wilhelm Gross proudly lifted the cover and ladled out soup on the bread in his plate, then speared a floating lump of fat with his fork. Michal, smiling a fixed smile of embarrassed horror, gave Katie opposite her a glance. Katie, blushed, squirmed uncomfortably, and looked away. Michal sobered suddenly, for Karl's mother was watching her like a lynx, and she swallowed with the horrible fear that she might not be able to keep down her food. The others were finishing, but Michal knew wretchedly that Katrina was still watching her.

When dinner was finished, Grossmutter went to rest, the girls did the dishes, and Katrina—after giving Frieda her recipe for *Apfelstrudel* —left abruptly, with no parting word for Michal.

Katie was restless. "We could ride a while before we go home," she said innocently, and Michal knew that she was impatient to meet Joshua. "How do you like Frieda?"

"How should I know. I've never even talked with her." Then she exploded. "That wasn't a soup tureen—it's a chamber pot! Why don't you tell your aunt?"

Katie's face turned brick-red. "I have, but she says it gives a good big soup dish and cover keeps it hot. Many others think the same. My Father sell many to farmers. They do not have chamber pots back in Russland, so—how can they know?"

"So that's why she watched me like a cat all through the meal?" She looked up. Karl was standing behind them, and by his stern face and set jaw Michal knew he had heard. He looked directly at her, eyes smoldering; then, without a word, he turned and went to the corral where Wilhelm was working.

Michal spoke miserably. "I should never have come here today, Katie. Staying when I wasn't wanted, and now criticizing that chamber pot—and Karl overhearing."

"Hist! Here comes Frieda."

"Michal, you come with Katie sometime to my house?"

She is lovely, Michal thought, and speaks English better than Katie.

"Thank you, Frieda." But the girl did not hear her. She was looking at Karl. She lingered, admiring Starlet, stroking Katie's horse, and waiting.

Then Karl was walking back toward them swiftly. Ignoring Michal and Katie completely, he grasped Frieda's arm. "Come," he said in German, "I have a new-born colt I want to show you," and Frieda went blithely off with him to the barn.

Suddenly Michal wanted to be free of Katie. The whole day was spoiled. Mother was right. She had no place in the lives of these people. "I want a drink of water, then let's go."

"Cold water is in big house. Be still, not to wake Grossmutter."

Tiptoeing into the clean empty winter kitchen, Michal took a dipper of water and, sinking into a chair, closed her eyes and felt the nervousness leave her as she sipped the cold water. Katie was waiting, and she must go. But before leaving, she must thank them. Rising quietly, she walked to the open door of the *Stube*, pausing at the threshold to accustom her eyes to the subdued light.

The large orderly room was cool. The ticking of the big clock on the wardrobe seemed loud in the silence. The afternoon sunshine slanting down through the single many-paned window filtered through the snowy Nottingham lace curtain. On the deep window ledge a sturdy geranium flaunted its compact red blossoms. Framed against this sat Karl's mother, quietly knitting. On her bed in a dark corner Grossmutter was lying sound asleep, a ray of light touching one small bare foot, the long toe nails yellow as horn.

The white *Kopftuch* covering Frau Gross's hair threw her features into bold relief—a strong face, deeply lined, but in repose showing remnants of the girl she had been. She was beautiful! thought Michal. I have never really seen her before. Beneath her sun-browned hands fell a panel of fine white lace, and her agile fingers worked surely and her lips moved as she silently counted stitches.

The clock whirred and struck—once—twice, and the spell was broken. Katrina looked up and saw Michal on the threshold. There was no apparent change in her face as they appraised each other. Imperceptibly the expression changed until a stern woman with implacable eyes faced Michal.

The steady ticking of the clock filled the room; and after what seemed a long space of time, Michal turned and walked swiftly from the house, thinking, I'll never come here again.

194

XV

In November, 1889, the Territory was divided into two states—North and South Dakota—but Michal hardly noticed; for the winter of 1889–1890 was a bleak one for the Ward family. Father's speculations, combined with the drought and crop failures of the year before, had finally caught up with him. There was still plenty to eat, but there was little cash for extras.

Michal and Faith went to school in last year's dresses, lengthened and freshly trimmed. Michal didn't mind the old dresses as much as she did her scuffed shoes. Faith had outgrown hers and had to have new ones; but Michal's feet had quit growing. She had turned fifteen in September, and to her disgust she was able to wear the old pair.

Mavis said very little, but once Michal saw a flash of the deep bitterness she felt. "Your Father is a good businessman, but he'd be a better one if he'd talk things over with me once in a while instead of acting first and then telling us about it."

"But Father says that it's a woman's job to run the home and a man's to run the business."

Mavis smiled faintly. "True. But he makes decisions about my job, too, without consulting me. For instance, you need shoes, but instead he bought that churn Hetty's using right now." And from the kitchen came the muffled plop of cream as Hetty turned the handle of the new barrel churn.

There was one comfort, however. The Ward girls weren't the only ones making-do this year. Lewis and the Baur children—fat Adolph and lovely Frieda—were the exceptions, but everyone knew they were just plain rich.

Since the day at the Gross farm Michal and Karl had ignored each other completely. Occasionally she surprised him studying her with the old inscrutable gaze, the only sign that he was aware of her existence. But Michal knew that he had not forgotten her remarks about the chamber pot. Well, she hadn't forgotten that day either.

By spring of 1890 everything pointed to another dry year. Farmers and businessmen talked of nothing else, while women let down more hems and made things do. Even the Indians were affected—rumors coming that when on travois they were cooking dogs and ground squirrels in their stew. It was even whispered that they were dancing great ghost dances to the Great Spirit for a return to the days when the prairie teemed with buffalo and the skies were black with ducks, geese, and whooping cranes.

Talk of hard times and Indians bored Michal. She was still possessed by that queer restlessness and a new feeling of expectancy—of something exciting about to happen yet not happening, like a hoped-for letter that never comes. She lived in a dream world centered passionately around Karl—a world where they met frequently, always accidentally, and engaged in furious arguments which she won with ease and brilliance.

In the cold light of day at school his indifference to her came as a shock, so real was her imaginary relationship with him. At no time did he make the slightest attempt to see her alone, either during the winter days when he stayed at Keims' or the soft sweet days of spring. Sometimes he left the school yard with Frieda Baur. Michal retaliated in the only way she knew—by seeking out Lewis, who was always there and glad to be with her.

By the time Mrs. MacVey announced a picnic as a celebration ending the school year, Michal felt more like her old self. Even though going out on the prairie usually meant pushing David in the baby buggy, being outdoors again after the long confinement of winter released her from thoughts of Karl. Still, she held a faint hope that if she looked nice enough at the picnic, he would notice and think of her during the long summer that lay ahead. Even if she couldn't have a new dress, Michal was determined she would look pretty enough to make him look twice at her.

Hetty added a blue flounce to the hem of her old thin white summer dress, and Mavis bought a wide blue ribbon sash. She would have given anything for new summer shoes, but Father snapped irritably: "In a month or two, Mike, you can have a good pair. Your next ones are going to have to last a long time if we have another year like the last one."

Michal didn't argue, just bent her head to hid the hot, quick tears of disappointment. If only Father knew how awful she'd look in a summer dress with high-top black button shoes. But Mother understood.

"Since everybody is to meet there, why don't you leave early and be sitting down when the others come? The dress looks lovely, even if it is old; and the skirt is so full it will hide the shoes when you're sitting down."

"What if we play games?"

"Just say you're too tired."

Michal mulled this over as she headed for the slough on the day of the picnic, swinging the heavy lunch basket. Lewis would be mad when he got to the house and found her gone, but it was more fun to go by herself; and besides she could always make it up with Lewis.

In spite of the shoes—resoled and polished—she was pleasantly aware of her slim waist, tightly sashed, and her new lovely breasts filling her dress front. The prairie was warm with late spring sunshine. From the south side of town the hum of the flour mill came, dimmed by distance like the hum of a giant bee. The slough was smaller than usual, for there had been less snow the winter before and still no spring rains. It was pleasant to see the white stars of crowfoot anemones opening on the pond bank, and the arrowhead's spongy leafstalks unfolding their shining spears in the shallow water. Red-winged blackbirds were trilling and nest building in the cattails at the water's edge; ducks were nesting; and huge dragonflies, their wings glistening in the sunshine, skimmed low over the water. Far out in the marshy section three pairs of sandhill cranes were arranging dry reeds into bulky nests. For a time Michal watched them from behind the reeds. Then, as she turned reluctantly toward higher ground, she caught her breath and sank back again behind her shelter.

Above her on the rim of prairie west of the slough, a giant whooping crane that had been leisurely feeding now stood motionless, startled by sight or sound of her. Like a snowy image he stood—so close she could see the long cruel yellow beak, the orange eye set in the red triangle of feathers along forehead to cheek, even the black strip along the rear edges of his great wings. The sound of a reed crackling was followed by a soft splash, and he was off—running at full speed, his wings half extended, until he left the ground; then, mounting higher and higher, spiraling steeply upward and on to the north, his hoarse clamor came down ever more faintly after her eyes had followed him out of sight.

Only then did she see what had startled the crane; it was Karl standing on the opposite bank watching her—silent and dark as an Indian. Michal's heart began to pound, and she rose to her feet in a panic of shyness as he came around the pool, lithe as a cat, his eyes never leaving her. As he strode up she saw that for the first time in months he was smiling at her.

"You are early, Michal."

"So are you."

"I was here and watched you; then I threw a stone in the water to make the bird go."

"It's the first time I've ever had a good look at a whooping crane! Why'd you have to scare it away?"

"You watch that silly bird like it iss the only thing in the world. I want you to look at me!"

"Why?"

He didn't bother to answer. Under his steady gaze she quailed inwardly and started to pick up the picnic basket.

"Stop." He gripped her arm, then went on slowly: "You are not like our women, who think only of us. You watch a wild thing like it is important." He shook her slightly. "You are not like the others, even your own kind."

Michal jerked her arm free. "I am too like everybody else. Do you know why I came early today, Karl Gross? I didn't want anybody to see my shoes; that's why!"

He stared at her in amazement. "Vat?"

"I'll show you 'vat.' Look!" Recklessly pulling up her skirt a few inches, even exposing the lace edge of petticoat, she poked one foot forward. "Who ever heard of nasty old black shoes with a summer dress? I'm going to sit on my feet so nobody can see them, and Katie or Frieda or Fanny or anybody else would do the same thing in my place."

For a moment his face was impassive. Then he began to laugh. He slapped his thighs and yelled with laughter. He tried to speak and was shaken by fresh spasms. For a moment Michal watched open-mouthed. It was the first time she had ever seen his iron composure broken. Then she saw it as Karl must, a picture of herself sitting primly on her feet all afternoon—she who was seldom still—and she began to laugh, too.

Karl wiped his eyes with a bright red handkerchief, grabbed her arms and shook her again. "You silly American! Who looks at shoes? Your face—" He touched her flushed cheek lightly, and they stared at each other, uncertain, yet swept by this new thing, this strange warm tide between them. They were so quiet that the wild birds, stilled by their laughter, burst into song again. Karl spoke softly, "It iss your face

I see, not the shoes." He was breathing quickly, as though he had run a long way. He was drawing her close and his eyes were on her mouth. Then, at the sound of voices, Michal tried to pull away. "They're coming," she whispered.

He scowled. "They come too soon. Someday I finish vat I start."

Drawing away, Michal picked up her lunch basket just as Katie and Adolph Baur, followed by Frieda, hurried over the rise. Frieda paused a moment, looking down, and Michal caught her breath at the picture she made standing there—her heavy braids hanging well below her waist. The ribbons banding her skirt were red and purple, accenting her bright blond beauty. If she was surprised at the sight of Karl and Michal, her face gave no hint of it.

Soon the slough was live with children, the younger ones playing games, the teen-agers chatting. Lewis came late, and he was angry. "I told you last week I'd come by for you."

"Mother suggested I come early—" She paused, and stole a glance in Karl's direction. He was sitting off by himself, staring moodily at the water. She would not tell Lewis about the shoes or how Karl's laughter had freed her from thought of them. She hardly understood it herself or the emotions churning inside her. When she got home perhaps she could sort her thoughts and feelings into some kind of order.

"I'm hungry; let's eat!" yelled Adolph Baur, untying Katie's sash and ducking hurriedly as she swatted at him.

"Mrs. MacVey isn't here yet. We've gotta wait for her—"

"Here she comes," said Lewis.

"Children!" They all looked up. Their teacher was standing on the knoll, her face pale and stern. "I'm sorry to tell you that the picnic has been canceled. Fanny Pratt has diphtheria, and you have all been exposed to it at school. You are all to go straight home."

XVI

Although she had a bad case, Fanny Pratt recovered. Through May and June there were no other cases, and parents relaxed their vigilance, relieved that it had not become epidemic. Once more talk centered on drought, crop failure, mortgages, and abandoned homesteads.

Then in July the barber's little boy died suddenly of the awful choking croup, and fear again stalked Eureka. As new cases developed, careful parents kept their children off the streets and peered through the curtains at an occasional pathetic little procession threading its way toward the cemetery south of town. Mavis kept her family close, for the disease was peculiarly fatal. By the middle of August the number of cases lessened, and once more the tension began to relax.

One hot day Michal asked, "Mother, could you spare me for a while today; I'd like to go to the ravine."

"So long as you stay away from town."

Michal ran, light as thistledown in moccasins she'd traded with an itinerant family of Indians for a bucketful of eggs. Her braids loosened, and she shook her hair free, enjoying the feel of the wind and the smell of the hot sun. The retreat seemed cool and remote after so many days in the house. Flinging herself down in the shadow of the boulder, she rested her flushed cheeks against the shade. A bronze and black butterfly uncoiled its spiral "tongue" and inserted it deep down to the thistle nectar, lazily opening and closing the gorgeous tawny tapestry of its wings as it dined.

"Heap fine scalp for Sitting Bull wigwam."

Michal jumped, then scowled as Lewis grabbed a fistful of her heavy brown-gold hair and jerked smartly. "What are you doing here, Lewis Reid?"

He chuckled. "Been coming every day. Knew you couldn't stick it much longer, and figured you'd come."

"It's been awful, hasn't it? I don't suppose we ought to be together now."

"There haven't been any new cases for several days. It's all right. You look pretty—your cheeks so pink, eyes so blue, and with your hair all down that way."

Michal blushed, lowered her lashes demurely, and began braiding her hair. "Let's look for Indian pipe. I found a clump here last year. What's happening in town? Father hasn't brought much news lately."

Lewis leaned nonchalantly against the rock, watching her swift fingers. "Well, even though Dakota's a state now, it hasn't seemed to change anything. Talk of drought, crop failure, mostly. A lot of Americans are leaving, Dad says, but the Rooshans are sticking it out."

200

Michal deftly secured the end of her braid, then rose. "Come on."

The clump of Indian pipe was there. "Look." She touched, then recoiled from the snake-cold flesh, each thick translucent stem supporting its shell-like solitary flower. The waxen blooms were swaying slightly against the dark earth. But the whole clump was tinted a delicate pink.

"It's an omen," breathed Michal.

Lewis studied the plant curiously. "Did you know this has other names—corpse plant, ghost flower?"

"Bad luck." Michal shivered. "Blood on the ghost flower."

"You've been listening to Hetty and her superstitious rot. Or Katie, maybe. She's dumb enough to believe in omens."

"I've hardly seen Katie this summer!"

"Well, Rooshan, hired help. What difference." He grabbed her hand as she jumped up. "What's wrong?"

"Why talk about it?"

He stood up, too, staring at her, his frank blue eyes puzzled. "You get mad so easily. I always say the wrong thing."

"You know perfectly good and well what you say. Katie's my best friend, yet you talk about Rooshans as though they aren't people."

"But Michal, now that we're practically grown up you must know that they're not like us. You're fifteen. In a few years you'll be married. You're not going to have your children playing with Rooshans and maybe speaking English with a German accent."

Michal stamped her foot. "I'm never going to get married."

He grinned. "All right. But you're my girl and don't you forget it."

"I'm not anybody's girl!" She knelt and snapped off a stem of the ghost plant.

"It'll turn black," warned Lewis.

"I want Mother to see it." And she ran up the swale without even a goodbye.

As she cleared the hill she saw Dr. Kelp's rig by the carriage block. Michal hurried around to the back door. The kitchen was stifling. Hetty was ironing furiously as she recounted "Jack and the Beanstalk" to Faith, Philip, and Rory sitting solemnly on the floor.

"What's Dr. Kelp doing here?"

Hetty brushed her forehead wearily, sweat drops splashing onto the cloth folder and sizzling on the sadiron. "Gordon's took sick."

Michal leaned against the door. "Oh, Hetty."

"He don't seem bad, but I dunno, I been expecting this."

"Why?"

"Yesterday I spilled the salt. And this morning a cricket chirped in my room. Couldn't find him. Then, yer maw leaves the bedroom winders open at night and lets all that poisonous night air in."

"I'm going in. Mother may need me."

Dr. Kelp was just leaving. "Positively no malady. A slight irritation of the delicate texture of membrana muck-osa."

"You're sure it's not membranous croup, Doctor?"

"Very sure, Mrs. Ward. Good day." And he drifted out of the door.

Michal relaxed. "Then it's not serious, Mother."

Mavis started. "Don't come in here. We still don't know. John, what do you think?"

Father was pacing. "We know damn' well Kelp's no doctor, Mavis. I think I'd better bundle the boy up and take him to Aberdeen to the specialists."

Mavis's face cleared. "That might be best. Then we'd know. I'll be glad when we get a real doctor here."

From Mother's bedroom Gordon whimpered, and Mavis hurried to him, calling back, "Help Father get ready, then keep the children quiet and out of this part of the house."

As she returned to the kitchen Michal remembered the ghost flower. It was on the dining-room table where she had dropped it. The pink had turned black.

Two hours after Father and Gordon had left on the afternoon train, Faith and Philip began to ail. Mavis's face was set as she hurried from Faith's bedside upstairs to Philip's below. Michal tended David then hurried in to her mother. Mavis was wiping Philip's face with a cloth dipped in cold water. "Is it the same thing as Gordon has?"

"I—don't know. It doesn't seem to be. It's more like summer complaint."

"Should I go up to Faith now?"

"You'd better help Hetty care for David, and stay away from the sick rooms. I can't have all my children down." For a moment her voice faltered, but her hands were steady and her back straight.

Michal lingered. "You can depend on me, Mother."

Mavis raised her head. "I know, dear," and Michal noticed that the narrow ribbon of white through the dark hair was wider than it used to be. Mother is getting old, she thought as she hurried out to David. I don't want her ever to be old.

Father returned next morning with good news. Gordon had stood the trip well. There had been a consultation; it was decided that his condition was not serious. However, to be on the safe side—since they weren't sure of the nature of his illness—he was to be kept isolated in the front bedroom.

Mavis, magnificent as always during illness, moved tirelessly from room to room, administering remedies, cooling the flushed little faces, and soothing Father.

For two days after Father's and Gordon's return from Aberdeen, nothing changed. Then, in the middle of the third night, Gordon choked suddenly and died.

XVII

Afterward Michal knew that Faith's and Philip's summer complaint was a blessing. Mavis was so busy caring for them, and so relieved that their trouble was not diphtheria, that the full impact of Gordon's death was softened.

She planted asters on the small grave, and her face held a new sadness; but this time she had her minister and her friends to comfort her. And Gordon's grave was not a lonely mound on the vast prairie. Only once did Michal see her break down. On the morning when Hetty, sniffing loudly, fumigated the rooms with a shovel of burning sulphur, Philip came in with one of Gordon's battered toys and searched the house for his twin, calling anxiously as he looked in all the familiar hiding places. The rest of that day and even into the night Michal listened to the terrible muffled sound of her mother's grief and Father's voice soothing behind the closed door of their room.

The girls were taking music lessons now, and it was a relief to Michal to put in her hours at the organ practicing, to escape Mavis's restlessness. She wakened often to hear her mother moving quietly about the house, smoothing blankets or standing by a window looking out into the dark. Sometimes she would creep into the sitting room to her favorite chair, and Michal knew that she was grieving for Gordon in darkness unrelieved by lamplight or starlight. Dimly Michal sensed—as once or twice before in her life—the awful loneliness of the human soul.

Sometimes she slipped out of bed quietly, so that Mavis would not hear her, and sat by the window. Nearly always far out along the horizon she could see, reflected against the night sky another prairie fire. One night she saw three separate glows; and when she heard Mavis tiptoe into Philip's room Michal joined her and together they watched until Mavis said quietly: "Most of the fires are fifty, sixty, or even a hundred miles away, so don't be nervous. These drought years have made a tinderbox of the prairie, but we're well protected by our own as well as the town firebreaks.

"I'm not afraid of prairie fires, but I always remember Mrs. Oulette and they make me sick."

"I know. When we lived on the Homestead I don't know what I feared more—the winter blizzards or the spring and fall fire danger. Even here in town, I spend hours when you're all asleep, watching to make sure that that glow in the sky is not getting brighter. So go back to bed and don't worry."

During these days Mrs. Pratt came with all the latest gossip. Mostly, however, she lived and relived Fanny's illness and what her life might have been had Fanny died. Also, with great relish, she kept Mavis informed about the Rooshans, their fear of the great Indian dances, and the possibility of an uprising. "Why, only last week some Rooshan thought the Indians was coming and he threw his flour and live hog down the well, loaded his kids in a wagon, and come tearing into town. When they got here they found one of the boys was missin' and found him a mile or so back where he'd bounced out. Some ways I think they're right. Maybe Sitting Bull will massacre us all."

"John says those days are over."

"Humph." Mrs. Pratt blew her nose. "Ain't this smoke awful. Makes a body's eyes burn somethin' fierce. If the Injuns don't git us the prairie fires will."

"It is smoky today. John says there've been no reports of anything close, so it's drifted in from some far-off place."

"Maybe he's right." The familiar avid note crept into her voice. "You're bearing up mighty well under your grief, Mrs. Ward."

Mavis answered seriously. "Gordon was too good for this world.

God answered my prayers for Philip and Faith, so I must be content."

Michal, who had been pretending to read in the dining room, rose and slipped outside. Mrs. Pratt always came around to Gordon's death sooner or later. It was hot outside and fuzzy with smoke haze, but the air felt good. It seemed as though she could still smell sulphur in the house. That awful woman with her talk!

She would go down by the turntable; there might be a few gentians or asters left. It was a lovely place, east of the depot, isolated by the tracks on one side, and on the others by a shallow kidney-shaped pond curving around it. It formed a retreat shady and cool in summer, its tall grass threaded with little long-stemmed flowers. Supported on high pilings, the plate and platform made a latticed roof. In May she had found violets—little yellow ones with purple veins and large blue ones just outside, and leaves and pink blossoms of sorrel. On a bright day only last winter she had found a white owl that had taken refuge there, apparently dazzled by the snow glare.

A girl in a faded dress, searching for something, turned, startled at Michal's step. "Why, Lily. I haven't seen you all summer. What are you looking for?"

"Piss-a-beds."

"What?"

"You know. They make good eating."

Michal watched her toss the dandelion greens into an old tin pail. Lily paused and removed a large lump of gum from her pocket. "Want half?"

"No, thank you."

"Fritz Geiszler gave it to me. He said his jaws was tired anyways."

"You mean he had chewed it first?"

"Sure. Git down quick. Here comes the train."

The engine approached with subdued puffings as it ran from the spur track onto the movable plate, where it came to rest. Then on the wide round platform surrounding the plate high above them, they heard the sweating, grunting men as they pushed the long pole sweeps. When the circle was completed and the engine faced south, they heard a deep voice. "There goes Violet, Frank."

Lily nudged Michal hard and whispered, "Better plug your ears up."

A coarse laugh. "We'd better get back. I've got no time for Violets in the daytime."

"Aw, rest a bit. Pretty high-toned gal, ain't she?"

"Yeah. Tits like an accordion, though. With her corset off they come clean down to her belly."

"God, you'd never guess it to look at her."

"Well, that's a woman for yuh. Everything in her room's purple."

"You don't say."

Michal blushed, and as the engine slid smoothly onto the track and away she said, "Now I know what Hetty meant when she said nobody can be nastier than a railroad man. Who's Violet?"

Lily stood up, brushing at her drab skirts with stained hands. "She comes from the Bad House on the edge of town. She's a chippy."

"What's that?"

"You know—a bad woman."

"What do they do at the Bad House?"

Lily put her hand over her mouth and tittered. "Aw, you know—men go out."

"I know that—I've seen a whole beer wagon full go out," exasperatedly. "But what I want to know is what do they do?"

Lily jabbed her sharply with her elbow. "Ain't you the green one! It's where men go to sleep with women."

"Why don't they sleep with their wives?"

Lily laughed. "Have you ever looked at most wives. I gotta go. I'll walk part way with you."

Feeling depressed, Michal considered these things as they walked toward town, only half conscious of the usual familiar noises—the clang of the blacksmith's hammer hitting the anvil, and the far-off drone of the flour mill.

As they approached Main Street, Lily punched Michal. "Here comes your beau."

Lewis was pale. "Have you seen Dr. Kelp? His wife is crashing in everywhere looking for him. Says she's going to whip him."

"What do you want of him?" asked Lily shrewdly.

Lewis favored her with a cool glance. "I want to warn him. She's got the longest blacksnake whip I've ever seen."

"Good for her," yelled Lily. "Let's go watch the fun."

From the next block came the sudden sound of whoops and whistling, and the three ran to join a gathering crowd on the corner. Mrs. Kelp, with a long heavy whip was lashing her husband, who raised his hands in a vain effort to ward off the blows. Mrs. Kelp, handsome but

206

disheveled, her hair down, her hat askew—her black satin dress glistening as the whip rose and fell—was like a great insect with a black, darting antenna. She punctuated her hits with "You will—will you—you dirty dude—you masher—you quack!" The doctor edged away cringing, but followed. Finally he broke into a shamble, running surprisingly fast for one so bulky. Mrs. Kelp followed him, still raining blows and imprecations on him until they reached their house. As they crashed together through the back door the crowd disappeared with grins and low comments. Lewis had joined a group of boys of his own age, but Lily, who was smiling widely, said knowingly, "I knew she'd ketch up with him someday."

"What do you mean?"

Lily sniggered. "Don't you know? Whenever she's gone, he sleeps with the hired girl."

"Why?"

"There you go again." Coming closer, she said in a low voice: "Why do you suppose dogs tie—you've seen 'em. Why do men take mares and stallions over the big hill west of town? That's why."

Michal took a deep breath. "I've certainly learned a lot today."

Lily was kind. "I can tell you a lot more after school starts. I've gotta go."

As she hurried off, Lewis came over. He was pale. "That made me sick."

"Me, too. What'll happen now?"

"He'll have to leave town, of course."

"I hope so. Maybe we'll get a good doctor then."

"What doctor would come here now?" Lewis's voice was bitter. "All the Americans are leaving the country. There've been two years of drought and crop failure. Even if we are a state, Father says South Dakota is getting a bad name all over the country." Suddenly he turned on her. "How can you be seen with that girl!"

"Too stuck up to speak to her, weren't you?"

"Yes, I am, and you ought to be." Then he grabbed her hand, but she broke away and, yelling, "Snob!" rudely over her shoulder, ran for home.

Ten days later school started, but Lily wasn't there to tell Michal anything more. Fritz Geiszler died first, Lily a few days later. Her death marked the end of the epidemic.

XVIII

Like the days when the haze hung low over the prairie from distant fires
—even so were Michal's thoughts. The life pattern had blurred. In her
mind images drifted as aimlessly as dandelion down, obscuring the
strong clear outlines she had lived by. Now, at night, she crouched by
her window while Mavis slept peacefully, unaware that her oldest child
watched the dim horizon, the far-off glow of fires, thinking confusedly
that the burning questions in her mind were like those fires—for one
put out, a new one leaping to life.

Sleep brought no rest. For the first time in her life Michal was
having nightmares, with the same repeated theme. A delicate iridescent creature, one of the Little People of her childhood, danced carelessly along a cobweb, the near end of which was anchored to a pile of
old shoes. If the delicate creature touched the shoes something Terrible would happen. And Michal would waken screaming in senseless
terror, with Mavis bending over her in the dark murmuring softly, ap-
plying cool compresses, stroking her hair.

Even after school had started, the events of the day with Lily
swirled round and round in her mind like a turntable—the coarse man-
talk, Lily's knowing snickers, and black, shining Mrs. Kelp.

Had Lily's death been a punishment for knowing such things?
Then what meaning could she read into Gordon's death and the death
of Little Brother so long before. One thing was certain—there was
something quite awful about growing up and getting married. The
nightmares were part of her fear. Once she had tried to explain to
Mother about the dreams and how they had started. But at the first
mention of Lily's name and the hint of what she had told Michal that
day, Mavis's face had taken on the old familiar look of reserve; and Michal was ashamed.

Life was awful. Men were awful. Now that she was getting older
she'd be careful not to let any boy touch her. After that day by the
turntable it made her flesh crawl even to think of it. Marriage and birth
lay coiled darkly in a future that had something to do with beer wagons

full of men going drunkenly to That House and of dogs tying openly in the streets.

Yet there was the way she had felt when Karl had drawn her toward him that day by the slough. She hadn't minded that a bit, the touch of his hands on her arms—warm and strong. Her blood had quickened at his touch as surely as the prairie warmed to spring sunlight. Until that day with Lily down by the turntable, she had dreamed over that moment; through the awful days of summer, she had retreated from Gordon's death in wonder at the birth of that strange sweet pulse and the promise, "Someday, I finish vat I start."

Karl had come to school for the first few weeks, over the usual protests of his father. Michal had avoided him as she did the others, Katie, Lewis, Fanny. As the weeks passed she occasionally surprised Karl watching her, almost curiously, as though dimly aware of her confusion and fear. Her eyes always fell first under his steady gaze.

By early fall the prairie was still warm at midday, but the nights were turning chill with the first hint of winter. Once more the wild geese were flying, their calls floating down to the dry buffalo grass, and the stubble of two years of drought.

In Michal's nightmares the shoes and fairy creature had been replaced by two pumpkins, revolving aimlessly in a void; if they touched they would shatter. She was always wakened by her own cries just before this happened. Mavis was there to quiet her, and sometimes even Father, who was more worried than cranky over it all. "It's her age, John," Michal heard Mavis say once, not as quietly as she thought. "It will pass."

Each night she prayed: "Dear God, don't let me dream tonight. I know I was wicked that day by the pond when Karl touched me and I liked it, but please, God, I'll be good if you just won't make me dream any more."

One windy October day Michal closed her English book and looked impatiently at the clock. It was four—time for school to be out. All day the wind had been blowing hard from the northeast, driving dust and bone-dry tumbleweeds before it, and gray-gold clouds before the sun. Mavis was entertaining the Ladies' Aid Society, and Michal wondered idly how many had braved the weather to go. Then, as the children lined up to file out, the mill whistle began to blow—a long steady wail, as though it were stuck and wouldn't stop.

Mrs. MacVey said, "I wonder if something's wrong," and opened the door just as John Ward, riding War, plunged into the school yard. "Now everybody listen!" he shouted, holding the horse in check with difficulty as the children filed out quickly. "There's a prairie fire headed this way from the northeast. You older boys, get out toward the race track to help fight it. Katie and you"—indicating Frieda Baur—"see to it that the younger children go straight home. Mrs. MacVey, you decide that! Michal, take Faith home, then have Hetty fill all the jugs with prairie cocktail and have Gus bring it out to—well, make it the Lumpkin place. Have him bring stoneboat, barrels, and gunny sacks, too." And he was gone, riding recklessly into the wind.

As the girls hurried out of the school yard and up the hill they saw a large pearl-gray plume of smoke to the northeast. It looked far away, but Michal knew that with a high wind flames traveled with the speed of a race horse.

All the Ladies' Aid except Alice Reid had left the Ward house by the time the girls got home, breathless and excited. The women were watching the smoke from the front yard. After Michal had given Father's message, Mavis explained that Gus had already had the team harnessed, and that Hetty had started to mix prairie cocktail as soon as they realized the town was threatened.

"Where's Lewis?" asked Alice Reid anxiously. "I thought he'd come with you."

"Father sent the older boys to help fight the fire."

"I wish he hadn't done that. Lewis is too young. Besides, I need him."

"I doubt that he'll be in any real danger, Alice," interjected Mavis. "Besides, your husband will be there to keep an eye on him."

Michal saw her chance. "Mother, I'm going with Gus. Some of the little kids'll get out there, and the men won't even notice them."

Mavis hesitated. "But we're so safe here with Father the crank he is about firebreaks. Down there with only the town firebreaks between you and the flames—"

"If I'm not needed I'll come straight back."

"Well, at least change to your wool riding habit. That cotton you have on could catch easily."

Michal pelted upstairs, changed, and was down just as Gus drove to the front. As he helped her up beside him, Alice Reid called, "Tell Lewis and Mr. Reid I'll stay on here with Mavis, so they needn't worry about me."

210

And Mavis added, "Stay away from the fire."

Gus glanced sideways at Michal and sang softly:

> " 'Mother may I go out and swim?
> Yes, my darling daughter.
> Hang your clothes on a hickory limb
> But don't go near the water.' "

"Just the same," he added severely, "yer maw's right." As they drove through town and out toward the smoke plume, larger now, he exclaimed, "Somebody's already plowing firebreak between the racetrack and the whore—That House."

Then Michal saw figures, bright and gauzy as butterflies, streaming out of the usually silent place toward the men and boys already scattering along the plowed line. By the time they reached Lumpkins', townspeople—businessmen mostly—and a few farmers were arriving to help. Already another big team of horses hitched to a plow was driving a second furrow.

Gus carried Hetty's jugs and set them on a rude bench by the door. Achsah strode briskly out of the Lumpkin house, sleeves rolled up, ready for action. "Good! I was just fixin' to go pump water. Those men'll be as cross and thirsty as a pregnant fox in a prairie fire before another hour is out. Miz Lumpkin's in town, workin', but she give us leave to use her house till it burns down anyways. Michal, I have a job for you right now." Striding back into the house she returned holding a small dirty tear-streaked boy. "Take this little sinner home, will you? Can't get a word out of him. Never seen him before, but he's scairt to death and his ma, too, most likely—"

Gus took hasty leave as Michal interrupted, "As soon as I get back I've got to give Lewis a message; then I'll come help you."

"They'll be backfiring any time now," warned Achsah. "Stay away from them flames."

Michal picked up the toddler who promptly wet himself, drenching both of them, then subsided on her shoulder, hiccupping gently.

"You're too old to do that, little boy. Now where in the dickens do you live?" As she rounded the house and headed for town, she heard a faint call and saw a woman hurrying toward her from the north. As they drew close, Michal saw that she was a stranger, and not a Rooshan, either, by her looks.

"Thank God he's safe! I've been looking everywhere. With that

211

fire and all—this awful place—you naughty boy." Snatching the child she gave him a couple of spanks, then screamed above the uproar, "Just moved in yesterday up there," pointing to a small new square house on a knoll. "Burned out in the Leola fire last year. Now, our first day here and this. Gotta get back. Our house is safe, anyways." And she rushed off distractedly.

Wrinkling her nose in distaste, Michal dabbed at her sleeve and skirt with a handkerchief, then hurried up the line to where Lewis was standing near a great team of draft horses hitched to the beer dray. Men were unloading stoneboats, gunny sacks, and huge barrels of water. "Can't let that place burn," a red-faced man, steaming with effort, said hoarsely to another.

"Jee-zus, no!"

A few hundred feet away Michal saw Karl, naked from the waist up, walk over to a stoneboat which had just been dragged up and plunge a couple of gunny sacks into one of the barrels on it. Lewis, who was removing his coat, grinned at her as she walked up. "Our friend Karl took his shirt off, but I draw the line at that. He's a muscular devil, I must say."

Michal risked another glance, then shrugged. "Just like a Roo-shan."

"Well! What's happened to you since the time you gave me the devil—" He stopped as a big woman with brassy hair and over-red cheeks strode up, heavy busts and thighs molding the thin rosy material of her dress. The damp gunny sack she held was an incongruous note. The two stared in fascination as the woman spoke sharply. "You kids git. They'll be backfirin' in a minute, and this is no place for you."

"I'm one of the men fighting this fire," returned Lewis courteously, but as she moved away, he muttered, "Who does she think she is?"

When men with rude torches set the backfire, the flames, fanned by a quickening breeze, ran along the breaking. "Look! The backfire has hit the slough." Irritations forgotten, they watched the cloud of smoke rising thickly from where the tough dry grass had caught.

"Here comes the main fire!" Michal pointed to the line of flame, topped by smoke, which had just come into view well beyond the race track. The air was hot and acrid with smoke now, and, despite the clouds overhead, it was bright as midday.

"I'll get back to help Achsah—" She was interrupted by a scream—

212

dimmed by confusion and distance—yet rising, breaking, rising again in unendurable agony from the north end of the line beyond Lumpkins'. Though half blinded by the wind-driven smoke, they saw a pillar of flame—a bright horrible flower, running, running. Then men brought it to earth; as sparks and pale ashes drifted between, Michal plugged her ears against the piteous wails.

Lewis took her hand. "She's stopped now. I think it was one of Those Women. You'd better go home."

Michal gulped, then stiffened. "They'll really need me now. Maybe she wasn't hurt too badly. It didn't last long."

"It doesn't take long," said Lewis grimly.

"Look out!" Michal pointed to a blazing gold disc of cow manure which, wind driven, was rolling toward them. As he ran to pound it out, she headed back toward Lumpkins'. The men who had been guarding the northern end of the line were carrying the burned woman toward the house in a blanket sling. For a moment an awful stillness hung over the prairie as the wind died down; then it howled to life again with new fury.

"Gott im Himmel," bellowed someone, "it goes!"

Up in the unguarded place, where the woman had been burned, several huge fiery tumbleweeds were rolling majestically across the backfire—the breaking. Even as Michal watched, unbelieving, the dry prairie grass beyond caught and turned to pure copper. Then she was running, as were others, without thinking, only knowing what must be done.

"Here!" Somebody handed her a dripping gunny sack, then yelled hoarsely: "Work here! We'll git the new one!"

For the next few minutes Michal pounded the flames, pausing only to dip the sack in a barrel on a stoneboat nearby. Once she glimpsed Fanny Pratt and Mrs. Keim, each armed with brooms, beating the earth grimly. When smoke eddied around her once more it seemed to Michal that she had been fighting this fire forever. The bitter taste of smoke was in her mouth. Her eyes were streaming, and ash clung to her tumbled hair. The earth was hot under her feet and she was gulping for breath. There was nothing more to see, no flame—only smoke. She was alone in a void, dancing, revolving, and something Terrible was going to happen if she reached—if she touched—

She was on the earth and it didn't matter. She had reached the pile of shoes. She had touched the other pumpkin. And nothing happened.

213

Her head was pillowed on her arm, and the smell of burned cloth and the sting of flesh was another nightmare, but not the frightening kind at all.

Somebody was jerking her to her feet, pulling her out of the place. Then she felt the shock of cold water as someone plunged her arm in a barrel clear up to her shoulder. It was Karl, and he was muttering German oaths softly under his breath.

"Michal!" It was Fanny's voice; it jolted Michal back to the prairie, and her eyes cleared just in time to see Karl's face—dark with soot and anger—and to hear him say, "She fell. Take her there—" gesturing toward the Lumpkin house.

For a moment they stood quietly watching Karl as he moved away, beating out small stray outbreaks. Near them a bit of dry grass caught, undulating in lines, golden snakes hissing in the dry grass, twining and twisting as they reached the line of breaking and fizzed out.

As she and Fanny wearily passed new teams arriving with their stoneboats and barrels of water, Michal looked along the fire line. The men were beating out tumbleweeds, rosy with flame, and cow chips which were jumping the backfire in increasing number. As they passed a dray several men dunked gunnysacks into unloaded barrels and ran to help, shouting warnings and pounding grimly, even stamping on the hot ground with their feet. It was still like a dream, Michal thought. I see it. I'm in it. But it isn't real. Far ahead two farmers held a dripping blanket over a pole between their horses and dragged it over a brilliant wedge of fire which had driven a narrow hot tongue across the breaking.

Then the wind shifted, and the low wall of fire turned back on its own path. Smoke rose high, and Fanny breathed a sigh of relief. "It's over."

"Just like that?" Michal asked incredulously.

"The town's out of danger, but it'll take a while to make sure it's all out. Pa and I was out last year during the Leola fire, and we seen a farmer set backfire and save his place just like nothin'. One minute he was in trouble and the next he was safe. Of course, he was on the edge of it and Pa said it was a terrible fire, but I wasn't a bit scared. Ain't you ever seen one before?"

Michal looked down at the blackened earth from which in places smoke wisps still fitfully curled. A small snake, roasted but still coiled to face its doom, met her eyes. She turned her head away, remembering that other fire at the Homestead, the scurrying animals that had rushed from their grassy homes, racing against the bright relentless lines writhing behind them.

"Only a little one," she said quietly.

"I think they're kind of exciting." As they entered the Lumpkin yard, she added, "Here comes Lewis."

"You look awful!" he exclaimed at sight of Michal.

"Well, I fell down," she answered crossly, "and burned my arm."

"Braid your hair and I'll take you home."

"All right. But let me wash my face."

"She was the funniest thing," said Fanny excitedly. "We could see her, beating away at the ground, smoke all around. Mrs. Keim told me to help her—she had to git home—but I knew it was all out, where we were at least. So I was waitin' for Michal to quit when all of a sudden she plopped down, and about that time Karl Gross come runnin' up and dragged her out. He was swearin' something awful. I don't know much German, but I know that much!"

"I didn't faint!" snapped Michal. "And I don't know what Karl Gross was doing down there anyway!"

"A bunch of men come down to put out the fire where it jumped. Too bad it wasn't you, Lewis," she added sweetly. Then at Michal's menacing stare, she added hastily: "I gotta be going. Ma told me to stay the other side of the tracks, so don't say you saw me here."

"Let's go," said Lewis abruptly. "Isn't that the new doctor's— what's his name, Gotthelf—isn't that his rig?"

Sure enough, the doctor's rig was pulling away from the Lumpkin house, and three guinea hens in the front yard were calling raucously as Michal said dully: "I didn't even see the doctor walk by. I guess I'd better get home."

Veering behind the building toward the tracks, they were halfway across the yard before they saw her, and stopped transfixed by the sight. In the open doorway between the porch and the kitchen a figure swathed in cotton batting like a white mummy was suspended upright in a sling that depended from huge hooks fastened to the top of the door. Only the face was free of wrappings—a face topped by brassy yellow hair and punctuated with wide unblinking eyes that stared out unseeingly.

The shock was so great that neither moved until a hand grasped Michal's shoulder. "My God, what are you two doing here?"

It was Achsah. "That's the one"—Michal stammered—"the one who said—"

"What happened, anyway," asked Lewis in a low voice. "We were so far away—"

"She was guardin' against tumbleweeds or cow chips crossin' the break, and one of them whirlwinds come along and swooshed the fire up under the skirt of her dress. If she'd a stood still or rolled in the dirt it woulda been all right—but she started to run, and by the time they got her down her whole body was burned something terrible."

"Will she—"

"Not a chance. Michal, you look stove in, but if you ain't too tired you could sure help. Couple of men scorched their arms. Make 'em keep their voices soft. I'm carin' for this poor woman, and Dr. Gotthelf says she ain't to be bothered."

"Shall I come?" Lewis asked, halfheartedly.

"Well—" began Achsah, but Michal interrupted.

"Our mothers will be worrying about us. Why don't you go up and tell my folks that I'll be a little late? Father's still around here—all over the place like a grasshopper—and he hasn't even seen me."

"You'd better take it easy," warned Lewis as they parted.

The fire was out now, with only a few men patrolling the plowed furrow to ensure against any stray outbreak, but even so the next half-hour was a blur of activity. Man after man, sooty and sweat-stained, straggled in for water or beer. Michal and other volunteers were hard put to shush them, spread oil and bandages on their burns, and furnish fresh towels as they poured water over their heads and shoulders and wiped themselves free of smoke, sweat, and dirt. Several gathered about the beer kegs and began to enjoy themselves, their laughter floating into the dusk. Then Achsah's voice ripped the gloom. "Git. All of you. And I ain't a-foolin'!"

Meek as lambs they ambled away, their muted laughter mingling oddly with the raucous squawks of the guinea hens, still pacing disconsolately about the house.

Alone at last, Michal managed to wash up, braid her hair, roll up her sleeves and spread a little oil on the large red patch on her arm. It was not burned badly, but it throbbed and she was anxious to get home and let Mother treat it.

It was then that Karl strode up. Tumbling clouds and smoke had brought early dusk to the prairie, but even so Michal could see his soot-stained face and torso, greasy with sweat. Without even a glance toward her he lifted a battered dipper filled with water, poured it over his head, then wiped himself with his shirt.

Too tired even to thank him, Michal turned to leave just as Dr. Gotthelf's rig clattered up. As the doctor hurried toward the house, Michal, engulfed by a dark wave of dizziness, grabbed at the doorjamb. The doctor sat her down quickly on the step and pushed her head between her knees. "Young lady, you'd better get home. A good supper, a night's sleep are what you need. You there" he turned toward Karl— "could you walk this girl home? She could keel over pretty easily."

"Ja."

"Good." He clapped a friendly hand on Karl's shoulder, then entered the house.

Michal rested her head tiredly in her hands, not wanting to move, but Karl took her arm firmly and helped her up. "Kum, Michal. It iss not far."

"This way," she whispered, gesturing to the right, so that they'd be spared the sight of the white mummy sightless in its sling. As they rounded the house she added: "You go on. It'll be out of your way."

"Nein. I'm going home tonight, not to Keims'. My people will wonder about the smoke."

Still lightheaded, Michal crossed the yard. Then they were walking on the burn, where the fire had jumped the breaking. The warm earth was still smoking, raising acrid incense to the sullen sky. Michal stumbled, then shrank back before a heap of downy ashes, still retaining the form of a guinea hen that had wandered too far. "Look," she stammered. "One of those cute little—"

Karl dissolved the ghost with a well aimed kick. "See." His voice was stern as he pointed to the house on the knoll—the house of the woman Michal had met earlier. "They lost all but the house, and you over a chicken cry."

Outlined against the sky was the small square house, and beside it crouched three human figures surveying below them the ruins of sheds, haystack, and four iron wheel rims, a skeleton of what had been a few hours before a sturdy wagon. Even in silhouette, the man, the woman, and the child tore at Michal's heart. As far as the eye could reach, from the burned knoll to the east beyond the race track, beyond the hill—all was desolation. The black earth turned the clouded evening sky to pale silver. It seemed as though no green thing could ever grow on the prairie again.

As they crossed the tracks and headed up the gentle slope, a nighthawk swooped down uttering its piercing cry. Michal flinched and Karl caught her hand. "Only a nightbird." His voice was gentle.

Hand in hand they walked together in easy silence, through smoke that sifted like warm fog over the earth. When Karl stopped and took her in his arms, she raised her face quite simply, without thinking. Light from the dying sun, red and cloud-streaked, splintered on his hair, then was blotted out as she closed her eyes and felt his mouth on hers, warm and sure. As his grip tightened and she felt the supple play of muscle as he bent over her, remembrance flooded over her like a cold rain, reminding her of Lily and all the rest. She pushed away, murmuring, "No."

"Oh?" he asked, stroking her hair thoughtfully, his hand oddly gentle.

"I'm afraid."

For a moment he studied her face in the dim light, then took her hand again and stalked abruptly forward. The magic was gone. As Karl's stride lengthened and Michal half ran to keep up with him, she sensed his anger, well under control, but as hot and relentless as the prairie fire he had helped to kill.

Wrenching free of him, she snapped furiously, "Quit dragging me after you!" When he didn't answer, she went on: "What are you mad about now? You're worse than my father. At least when he gets angry he has a reason for it."

"I haf reason." He stood very still and spoke quietly. "You kiss like a child. Like—like a bud tight-closed. Not as our girls at all." Aware of the flame of anger and hot words boiling to the surface, he grabbed her shoulders and shook her slightly. "Nein, Michal. You ask, and I try to tell you. I am angry with myself. Like a snowflake, I haf you—then you are gone. But, like a Dummkopf, still I vant you."

Michal reached up and touched his cheek shyly. "I'm sorry," she whispered. "I know only how to be myself."

He wasn't listening even though he was watching her lips. Fascinated, Michal stared back as—almost lazily—he reached and drew her close, murmuring. He kissed her eyes, the tip of her nose, her mouth—lightly at first, then deeply with fierce tenderness. She felt the length of his hard young body against her own. This was something new—wild

218

and sweet—singing through her veins. This was fire—pure gold and clear—burning away her fears as she returned his kiss as eagerly as he had sought it. Frightened again, she pulled away; but now he was smiling. Even in the dusk she saw the white flash of his teeth. "This time you are not a child." His voice was soft, triumphant.

"I'd better go now." Confusedly, she pushed back her tumbled hair.

"You are tired." Bending he lifted her into his arms and carried her swiftly toward the house which loomed up dark and safe, close by. "Like a feather," he marveled, putting her down. Then he spoke carefully, even hesitantly, for him. "We haf reached the time—when it iss bad to be alone together. You understand?"

"Then why—" She hesitated, not wishing to sound bold.

"Why do I hold you?" He shrugged impatiently. "Because I think of you. Too much, I think of Michal. In school. When I plow. When I walk on the prairie. So if I kiss you, maybe it iss no good. Maybe I think of a good German girl, as I must."

She was too startled to be angry. "Then it is no good, Karl?"

"You know." His voice was rough. "But a little thin Englisher iss not for me. We must not walk together again."

"All right." Her voice was a whisper. "Good night."

"Adieu." Just a moment he held her hand against his cheek, then dropped it abruptly, wheeled, and strode off toward the northwest. Far off, lonely, the nightbird uttered its haunting cry, piercing her heart for what she had found and what she had lost.

Part Three

PLACE OF ROCKS

I

1891-1894

The short bleak days and long cold nights of endless winter had been finally broken by chinook winds that brought the smell of thaw in the air—the pleasant sound of water running under crumbling drifts by day; long-fanged icicles dripping from the eaves, and the eerie crackle and shifting glow of northern lights by night. Later, low-hung gray clouds had dissolved in quickening showers, veiling the sodden prairie in tender green where windflowers huddled in their fuzzy coats through the coolness of April.

Into the dawn of a misty May morning, Michal slipped out of the house. She had dressed quickly, tiptoed downstairs quietly lest she wake the sleeping household, gone into the empty kitchen for her basket packed the night before.

She went to the barn and paused a moment at the box stall of Father's new stallion, Fury. He looked up, snorted, turned his slender head, poised on a snaky, shining neck. At sight of her he wheeled and, with ears flattened back and white teeth bared, lunged toward her. She shrank back; for, quick as lightning, and as unpredictable, he had once killed his groom, and Father knew it before he bought him.

He had owned the stallion a month now. After Sitting Bull's death at Wounded Knee, John Ward had been restless and moody, and complained bitterly that life was tame. When Mavis had rejoined that after all it was good to be settled and at peace, with children growing up in a permanent home, Father had disappeared and returned two days later with Fury, happy as a king.

"Well, what do you think of him, Mavis?" he'd asked Mother impatiently, and she had said soberly:

"Be careful around him, John. He looks vicious."

"You bet he's vicious! But I've got to have some excitement, and taming him'll give me plenty."

Every day since, Father had taken the pacer out and driven him hard. He would come in happy, Fury in a lather but well under control; and Michal realized clearly this morning as she left the barn and headed north that Father needed this daily struggle.

Nearing the Place of Rocks, she wondered about this meeting. "We'll tell our mothers to let us take breakfast there and see the sunrise," Katie had said; then, putting her hand on Michal's arm pleadingly she had added: "Be sure to come early. I must talk with you." Her voice was anxious, her usually placid face pale, almost pinched. Could she and Joshua have quarreled?

Michal reached the hilltop as the sun rose and pierced the mist. She put down her basket and looked over the prairie. After two years of drought the ponds were full again, and wild flowers brightened the thick carpet of green grass. At her feet a late pasqueflower bloomed. Drenched with dew, it was like fog at sunrise, gray-blue flushed pink. The wonder of it swept her—the alchemy which could bring from the earth this sturdy yet delicate beauty.

Far away a prairie cock courted his lady love. She could imagine him strutting, inflating the bare salmon-yellow air-sacs on the sides of his neck, bowing low, calling his echoing Boom—boom—boo, the first two tones deep, the last a half-tone higher. He was answered from nearby, until the sounds rolled over the earth in great waves—mellow balls of music, bounding and rebounding through the hills, dying away.

She arranged the rude fireplace of rocks, and with paper and kindling from home started a fire under the coffeepot, then gathered cow chips to feed it.

Katie came before the pot had boiled. The girls worked silently, spreading a blanket on the ground before the fire and a snowy cloth for the breakfast. They ate in silence. From the valley below came the sound of a cow horn—young Fritz Frankhauser gathering the town herd for the day. Against the distant hills men worked the land—plowing, seeding, dragging.

She looks worried—I'll put her at ease, thought Michal. "The sun is out—it'll be a lovely day."

224

No answer.

"Have you met the new doctor yet?"

"No," apathetically.

"He's nice. Mrs. Reid swears by him. Says we're lucky to have one so up to date. I hear he has been educated both in Germany and this country."

"So?"

"Yes, and Mrs. Pratt called on his bride and then rushed up to our place, and I heard her tell Mother that instead of enjoying her home like most brides—a lovely little cottage chock-full of beautiful wedding presents—there's even a 120-piece dinner set trimmed in real gold-leaf from some relative of the doctor's who owns pottery factories in Germany—she sits with cold cream smeared on her face and moans about the awful prairie winds and this terrible town and makes no secret of the fact she's trying to get Dr. Gotthelf to go back to New York so she may continue her voice lessons—and all that on top of her big wedding!"

Katie spoke abruptly. "She is a fool. That's what I wanted—not a grand one like theirs, but a lovely church wedding. Presents. A little home with Yosh. And now," bitterly, "I'll never have them." And Katie, usually so practical, pulled at her handkerchief with tense fingers until it tore.

"Don't be silly. Of course you will. Mrs. White can't always keep Joshua from marrying you."

"You don't know that woman. Yosh is afraid of her."

"Don't be discouraged, Katie. It'll work out. I've never seen you like this before."

"I've never been like this before. I'm going to have a baby!" She buried her face in her torn handkerchief. Sobs shook her sturdy body.

"Oh, Katie!"

"I'm afraid. I don't know what to do."

Michal drew close and put her arm about her friend, forcing herself to speak calmly. "First of all, stop crying. We'll find a way out. Have you told your mother?"

"No—oh, no! I can't tell anyone but you." She calmed herself and wiped her eyes.

"We must begin right now and get someone to help us. How about Mrs. Gross?"

"No."

"Your father, then."

"Gott, no! He vould kill me!"

"I know! Karl! He'll tell us just what to do. See? He's working on the forty this side of their place. I'll run get him."

"Is too far." But her face had lost the bleak look.

"It's less than a mile. I can run over sooner than it would take me to go for Starlet; besides, that might cause awkward questions. You wait here." And Michal plunged down the hill, heading for the east field. The sun was bright, and far to the northwest clouds rose high like pearly hills against the horizon. As she passed over the height of land between the ponds, she glimpsed the whooping crane standing like an ivory image to her left. Without pausing she went swiftly on her way, glad that the giant bird had not risen but had stood, watching her intently.

Karl did not stop the work horses until Michal had slogged across the field to him, but she knew he had seen her coming, for while she was yet some distance away he had called Wulf back sharply when he leaped toward her, barking. He now came to her, surprise but no displeasure on his face. That gave her courage. She stumbled with fatigue, and he caught her arm, steadying her until the breathlessness left her and she could speak. "Karl. Come with me. Katie is in terrible trouble. She needs you—up there." She pointed. "The Place of Rocks."

"I know," he said quietly.

"Now!" She caught his arm urgently.

"I vill take the team to the barn—you are tired. Rest here." He led her to a boulder at the edge of the field. "Walk slowly back. I vill come soon on horseback. I tell them I to town must go."

Katie, who had cleared away the table and packed the baskets, came to meet Michal as she climbed the hill. "Well?" she asked anxiously.

"He'll come—soon."

"Did you tell him?"

"Of course not—except that you are in trouble and need advice. There he comes now—see—beyond the camp grounds."

Katie clutched Michal's arm in a panic of fear. "I cannot tell him."

"Of course, you can. You can tell Karl anything. He's so practical; he'll know just what you should do."

Karl dismounted, flung the reins over his horse's head, slapped him

226

affectionately on the rump, saying, "All right, Blitz," and approached the girls. "Was ist hier los?" he asked Katie bluntly.

"I am with child." Calmly, also speaking in German.

"By whom?"

"Yoshua White, of course."

"Why, then, have you not married?"

"His mother—she will not permit."

"She was right. It is not goot for us to mix with Englishers. But" —he shrugged—"the business is now out of her hands. You must consider the child."

"But Yoshua fears his mother."

He spat contemptuously. "A man does not fear his mother."

"I—I—might tell him tonight."

"You tell him—but now. I bring him to you here." He left abruptly, and as the girls looked at each other Michal knew that she had gone to the right person for help. Katie's face had relaxed; her blue eyes were almost happy again.

II

A few days later Mrs. White spent the afternoon with Mother. "I just had to come, Mavis; it's too lonely with Joshua gone," she said, pausing to turn the heel of a woolen sock. Then, "He has an old schoolmate, living north of Leola. They've planned to get together all summer. He had a chance to ride with some man driving over on business, and although ordinarily I wouldn't hear of his leaving, I've been worried about him lately. He's really peaked; he has no appetite at all. He asked me so politely if he might go and return with this man. As it was only for three days, I said yes. He'll be home tonight."

Michal, swingly idly in the hammock, heard the talk through the open window, smiled, and wondered what Joshua's mother would say if she knew that Karl on the same day had asked his aunt's permission to take Katie with him on a three-day trip to Leola. He had business with his uncle, Herman Haar, and thought Katie might enjoy the visit, too. "She needs to go, Karl; she has not been the same girl the past weeks, pale and half sick," Frau Keim had said, giving hearty consent. They should be home tonight, thought Michal, and I'll go down tomorrow.

Frau Keim was busy weeding onions as Michal turned in at the little white gate. "Don't get up; I'll just go on in," said Michal. Frau Keim straightened, then nodded and, wiping the sweat from her face with her forearm, went on with her work.

Michal paused uncertainly in the doorway.

"Michal? Come in—my room." Katie was in bed.

"Sick?"

"Every morning—but I stay in bed and it leaves; then I go to rest again afternoons and act sick so Mutter will not know what sickness it is."

Impulsively, Michal went to the bed and kissed Katie. "Shall I come back later?"

"No, but give me a cup of coffee and pour one for yourself; it is hot on back of stove. I feel better. I must tell you all about it."

"Did your plans work out?" asked Michal as they sipped their coffee.

"Perfect. Karl had hired your Father's fast team the night before. He stay all night here, and we ate breakfast while it was yet dark; then picked up Yosh east of the tracks where he waited for us. We reached Leola by noon, get license, go to hotel to eat. Then we were married by a *Prediger*, but not one of my faith." Her face grew wistful. "I was very happy, but I kept thinking how different it was than I had wished. If Mrs. White is not like she is—then Yosh and I would haf been married in *Lutherische Kirche* by my own *Prediger*. I would have wear a white dress, big veil with *Kranz* of white flowers on my hair. Everybody there to see, then a big dinner and presents. But—" Her face brightened. "See?" She pulled a thin chain and from between her breasts drew a gold band. "Yosh bought it months ago, and even though it is not on my finger, I wear his ring—and on my heart."

"Then?"

"We were going to eat at hotel, but the wife of the *Prediger* had been witness and she made us in her home eat good dinner; then Yosh's friend came for him and Karl and I drove down to mine Uncle Herman's. It seemed queer to stay in your old house."

"Had the place changed? Did you see my willow?" Michal asked eagerly.

228

"Ja. Outside is the same only more wheat planted. All the way from Eureka to Leola the wheat looks good. Mine Uncle says best crop he has ever seen."

"But our house?"

"Mine Tante is proud of your house. Of course, it looks different without your furniture, but is very clean. The willow is higher now as your house—the other trees dead. We visit there one more day, then yesterday morning we meet Yoshua in Leola, drive slowly home, stop at spring to eat lunch my Tante fixed for us. Then we rest team a while and sleep, drive into town after dark, let Yosh off east of track; we go on to my house, I get out, Karl take team back to livery stable—and so" —her voice suddenly tender—"I am now Mrs. Yoshua White."

"Does Mrs. White—know?"

"Not yet," hesitatingly. "Yosh has asked me to let it be our secret for a while yet. Each stay in our parents' homes now, but," she said eagerly, "we'll meet at the old Switzer house as before and soon I'll make a nice supper, and you must come eat with us."

"That will be lovely." Michal spoke warmly to hide the chill she felt at knowing Joshua still feared his mother. He was weak—not good enough for Katie. Perhaps, once the break with his mother was made, he would change.

Michal went back by way of the ravine, only half conscious that cheerful buttercups starred the lush grass, blue violets bloomed in heavy clumps, and that in little pools left by the late rains marsh marigolds flaunted their acrid fragrance from inch-wide blossoms. Hurrying up the swale toward home, she did not pause to admire the orange puccoons blooming early this year with blue vetch and lupines, or look up when barn swallows wheeled and dipped, then darted arrow-swift through the lazy sun-warmed air currents above. She was thinking, sadly, He isn't good enough for Katie.

III

The August sun cast a brazen light far over the shimmering hills where blue prairie asters bloomed, as Michal, closely followed by Rory, walked slowly toward the Switzers'. In spite of the midsummer heat, thistle-

229

down and cobwebs floating by her and a hot whirlwind rattling the dead leaves at the base of cornstalks in the field at her left gave first hints of waning summer. Soon now autumn would be succeeded by winter, and then Katie's baby would be born.

Why, Michal wondered, should she be affected by the passing of time? Katie was after all the lawful wife of Joshua, and even Mrs. White herself couldn't prevent the birth of the child.

She paused in passing to stand in the door of the old sod barn where tawny-breasted barn swallows, their steel-blue bodies glinting in the sun, flashed in and out above her head to feed their clamorous young or twittered softly from the eaves near their clay-daubed nests. She remembered a day, long ago, when she and Katie had paused here and the newly arrived swallows—perhaps the same birds—had been flying in and out, busily lining their nests with feathers.

Katie saw her coming and hurried to meet her at the door. "Come in, and bring Rory, too. I am so glad you came early so we can have a good talk before Yosh comes."

As they sat in the clean cool dusk of the shaded room, sipping cold lemonade, Michal relaxed. Soon now all the town would know of the marriage of Joshua and Katie and they would live openly and happily together, as husband and wife.

"How do you feel these days?"

"Better. No more sickness. Now I want to do much housework. Some days when I can't stand it, I slip up here and scrub floors, black the stove. See the cupboard?" She raised the window shade, swinging open the door. "Come smell the cleanness."

"I don't have to. The clean smell was the first thing I noticed when I came in." But she rose, and came close to please Katie. The well scrubbed shelves were covered with new wrapping paper, the edges cut in scallops in a filigree of geometric designs and turned down to show the dishes to advantage. The small array of unmatched stoneware pottery, placed in scrupulous order, and a few heavy goblets, scrubbed and sparkling in the sunlight, were flanked by sugar and flour in shining glass candy jars, the contents protected by covers of heavy glass.

"I wish," wistfully, "I dared bring over the lovely china teaset they gave me for Christmas. But"—her face lit up—"I can wait. Any day now, Yosh will come and tell me."

"Do you meet here often?"

"No, once only in a week. It is hard to slip off, but sometimes I am supposed to be at your house for evening. Yosh takes long walks at night." And Katie giggled like her old self.

"Have you seen Dr. Gotthelf lately?"

"Last week. He says all is fine, and I have told him about everything. He has been most friendly, and yet he is very sad since his wife went back east."

"Wasn't that awful? I don't see how she could do that to such a nice person."

"She must like a big town and her study of music better as a fine man for a husband. Did you hear how it happened?"

"All I heard was what Mrs. Pratt told Mother. Abigail called on the bride—you know, the old nosy. Mrs. Gotthelf sat wringing her hands and talking about this miserable town, the awful wind, the lack of modern conveniences, no advantages, no culture. If Dr. Gotthelf wouldn't move back east with her, she'd go anyway. The doctor flatly refused to leave his practice here. So she went."

"I wish I had dishes like hers," said Katie fervently, "but anyhow, I'm happy with my man. I must cook the potatoes. Yosh should soon be here with steak, and he loves mashed potatoes with steak."

Joshua was thin, and his face showed lines of strain. "Welcome, Michal," he greeted her warmly. Then Katie was in his arms; he kissed her lingeringly and ruffled her bright hair as he teased, "Well, Mrs. White, how does it seem to have our first guest?"

Katie blushed, pushing him away playfully. "Fine. Now, Yosh, you wash up while I fry the steak and finish the table." It was then that Michal thought she saw a pale shadow like a moth linger for an instant at the window where Katie had raised the blind. It was nothing to worry about, she thought uneasily. But as Rory growled low in his throat and half rose to his feet, she pushed him back, went quickly, and lowered the shade. A night moth, of course, she reassured herself. "Shall I help you set table?" she asked to excuse her sudden action.

"No, there is little to do. I tried to bring a tablecloth, but Mutter was in the kitchen, so we eat tonight without one. But we have flowers."

"Busy little housewife, isn't she?" asked Joshua, and Michal, happy to be included in the warm circle of their love, nodded, then stooped to stroke Rory at her side.

"You know"—Joshua's voice was low but full of pride—"every time we eat here she has a special bouquet just for me." Katie brought

231

from the kitchen and placed by his plate a shining glass jar. In it, carefully arranged, were asters lifting from heart-shaped leaves abundant lilac blossoms like clouds of prairie smoke. Nestled near the base of these were two large wilted blossoms.

"What have we tonight?" he asked gaily, looking adoringly at Katie, her round face beaming with joy and perspiration.

"The asters," she said, clasping his hand tightly as she stood beside him. "They are common on prairie everywhere—small, strong, like me. And see the leaves, like a heart—so—they to you from my heart. But these"—she touched gently the two wilted blossoms—"I picked these —large, different, yellow with purple inside. Nefer had I seen any like them before. So I bring them to you, my husband. But after a time" —her voice faltered—"they die."

Michal spoke up quickly. "I know. Mrs. Reid has them in her garden. They are called 'Flower-of-an-hour' because they bloom only at midday."

They lingered over the meal, discussing with Michal their plans for the future. Joshua had just had a raise. The Switzers' mother was still very sick—he would stay abroad with her. If he would sell this place to them they could develop it, get hogs and a cow, make a large garden —enough to feed many children, Katie added enthusiastically.

Finally, "Is there coffee left?" asked Joshua expansively.

"Plenty, if you wish; but I must see if it is warm—" Katie broke off abruptly as a loud knock startled them. Joshua rose, Katie darted to him, and he put his arm about her. But before they could reach the door it burst open and Mrs. White, panting, bareheaded, her satin-smooth hair for the first time in Michal's memory disheveled, stood before them.

"Fanny Pratt said I'd find you here, but I didn't believe her." Closing the door carefully behind her, ignoring the girls completely, she advanced on Joshua. "What are you doing in this place?" she demanded coldly.

Joshua stepped away from Katie, and his arm fell limply to his side. "Katie is my wife now, Mother."

"Rubbish! You are my son. Come home with me at once!"

As he involuntarily walked toward his mother, "Yoshua, stay by me," Katie besought him softly.

"I have to go with Mother," he answered flatly.

232

"But, Yosh, you are my husband." Pleading now, Katie put her hand lightly on his arm, and Michal saw her eyes, wide and unbelieving.

Joshua turned, put both hands on his wife's shoulders, and for an instant rested his cheek against her bright hair. Then he turned away abruptly, and Michal grew cold with fear at the dark despair in his eyes.

Mrs. White, ushering her son out, shot a backward glance at Michal. "I'll take up your part in this with your mother later."

Katie sank into Joshua's empty chair and stared at the cluttered table with unseeing eyes. First I must get her out of here, Michal thought. "Let's go." Then, as the other did not move, she went to her and, frightened by her apathy, shook her slightly. "We must go now."

"No use to go. It is now too late." With the finality of her words, Michal again felt a chill of hopelessness. She is right—it is too late.

Then sudden anger blotted out fear. She would fight. If Joshua was afraid of his mother, she wasn't. "Nonsense!" sharply. "It's never too late. Come home with me."

Katie looked at her now with expression. "First, I must clear away the dishes."

"Never mind them." Impatiently.

"I must. This is not my house." Inflexibly.

Both working rapidly, it was soon done, and Michal had her outside the house. "We'll go by my place first," she said.

"No. I must go to mine own house—to my Mutter."

"All right. We'll go by the tracks. Shorter that way. But hurry."

"It is no use to hurry. It is too late," she repeated dully, but went obediently enough, suiting her pace to Michal's swift stride until they reached Keims'.

Michal ran all the way home.

"What's wrong!" Mother held her needle poised over the sock she was mending.

"Hurry, Father, Mother, to Mrs. White's—something terrible!"

"Sit down, get your breath, then tell us," said Father. Forcing her gently into a chair, he went to the kitchen, and brought her a glass of water. "Now—sip this slowly, then let's hear it."

After Michal had quickly outlined the events of the evening, "I'm not going to interfere," decided Mother. "We can't force ourselves on them at this time. Besides, I'm not dressed for the street."

233

Father spoke up quickly. "I believe Michal's right. There might be violence of some sort—on Keim's part, I mean. He might tackle Joshua. Never know what these foreigners'll do when roused. You'd better change your clothes, Mavis, and don't dawdle about it either. We'll pay a call on Mrs. White. If everything's calm it'll be a short one, I promise."

"But—John!"

"Hurry!"

Mrs. White answered their knock. Her hair was combed smoothly and she was again her calm self as she put her Bible on the table. "Come right in. I've just finished my daily scripture reading. Won't you be seated?" No anger, not even surprise tinged her voice.

Mavis said, "I fear this is an intrusion, but Michal came home so upset after taking Katie home she begged us to drop by."

"No intrusion. I'm always glad to welcome you, Mavis; but really Michal's nervousness is wholly unnecessary, I assure you."

"Did Joshua tell you about the baby?" Michal asked her bluntly.

"He mentioned something, but why should that concern me? The baby is not his."

Father rose. "We'd better go home," he said uneasily. "It's late. Since we can be of no help—"

"Help?" Her eyebrows rose.

"I thought, after hearing the story, that Keim might come storming over here and cause trouble."

"He'd better not!" Her lips went thread thin. "I appreciate your interest and your call. Apparently there was some sort of ceremony—I wouldn't call it a marriage—but you'll all be relieved when I tell you that Joshua has definitely promised me to give her up."

"I don't believe it!" Michal's throat was tight.

"Very well," triumphantly, "I'll let him tell you himself. Joshua!" There was no reply.

"You may carry his message yourself to that—that Rooshan girl, your friend." Scorn thickened her voice. "Joshua, come out please!"

Silence, except for the loud ticking of the clock on the mantel and the chirping of a cricket outside the open window.

"He must have fallen asleep." Mrs. White rose.

"Please don't disturb him. We must go," and Mavis stirred, for Father was still standing, impatiently.

"No, I want this matter settled once and for all," and she moved

234

firmly across the dim dining room and threw open the door of her son's lighted room. At her scream, Father sprang forward, turned, pushed his wife and daughter back—but not before Michal had glimpsed the limp figure hanging in the doorway, and the grotesque shadow it cast across the floor.

IV

The hot sweet days of summer had long since passed, and still Michal had not seen Katie.

On a quiet October evening she climbed the hill to the Place of Rocks. Rory had wandered, and finally to the west she saw him outlined against the vivid ocherous glow of a prairie sunset that transformed the faded stubble to a sea of tawny gold. For an instant she felt keenly the beauty and immensity of the fields and the labor that had produced them, and thought, as she had so often, The prairie is a lovely place. Then she turned to the east. No light fell there. The prairie lay cool and gray, and in the far distance she could see the Switzer house—emptied now of the secret moments, haunted by a soft voice pleading, "Stay by me, Yosh." From somewhere came faintly the slender uncertain cry of a nightbird, and for the first time in her life, there on the sweep of prairie, Michal felt its supreme indifference to those who walk upon it.

For her, night now was something that crouched waiting. In disorderly procession pictures marched across her sleeping mind—the things that Katie must never know. Mrs. White, after her first terrible outcry, started for the door, muttering, "Kill her. Kill her." Then, body rigid, face distorted, she crashed down in a dead faint. And across these images, weaving them all into one pattern, was a grotesque shadow across the floor. Joshua's body had been removed unobtrusively while they ministered to Mrs. White. "Stroke," Dr. Gotthelf had said gravely in answer to Mavis's anxious questions. "She'll probably be helpless, for a time anyway. I'll get the new nurse." He had been the one to break the news to Katie, who had suffered a complete collapse.

Michal turned restlessly toward town. She'd walk home with Father if he were still there. On Main she met Mrs. Keim, whose face lit

235

up at sight of her daughter's friend. "Goot. I haf vanted to see you. Katie vants to see you, too."

"Oh, I'm glad. Then she's better."

"Yes. It has taken long."

"Mother was afraid she'd lose the baby."

"Ve too—at first—but the doctor took goot care. Every day he comes and talks. Latst week she began crocheting a little white bedcover." She wiped her wet blue eyes, bloodshot from many tears. "Her heart—it was broke."

"I'll come see her tomorrow."

"Is Mrs. White still in bed? I ask the doctor but he say little."

"She's better—but it will be some time before she can walk."

Eagerly. "But den—she leaves here?"

"Oh, yes. Next year, probably. When she is able to be about and can wind up her affairs she plans to go to Aberdeen." As Mrs. Keim turned heavily to go, saying, "It vill be better when she is gone," Michal noticed that her face was so pale the birthmark was more vivid than usual.

Soon after Michal's visit, Katie returned quite naturally to her place in the town. She bore her thickened figure proudly, absorbed completely in the future, never mentioning the past. On the whole, people were sympathetic to her. Only once was she cut directly; Mrs. Pratt sailed by the two girls on Main Street with an icy stare. When Michal told her mother of it that night, she added violently: "It's a good thing they've kept away from here. I'd like to kick Fanny all the way down the hill."

Mavis was genuinely shocked. "You sound just like your father. Is that any way for a young lady to talk?"

"Maybe not, but Joshua might be alive today—"

"I've never mentioned this to you, but on the whole Katie has fared quite well, I think. You see, people were talking about her before her marriage became known. Her figure had—changed. Naturally, some thought—"

"Yes, and you know who would be the first to think it. I'll never forgive Mrs. White for what she did—never."

"Those are not the words of a Christian, daughter. Mrs. White is paying many times over for the mistakes she made with her son. I've hoped that she would permit God to open her eyes to her own part in the tragedy; but so far she blames only Katie." She paused a moment

236

and picked up David, bending like a slender reed under his weight as he settled down nursing lustily, then went on gravely—"Ever since this has happened I've wanted to have a talk with you, Michal. Run along, son." She put the boy down and gave him an affectionate spank. "You have reached the age when young men will ask you out and some may try to take liberties with you. Never let a boy touch you or kiss you until you are married."

"Not even if we're engaged?"

"It's safer not to. Let him hold your hand; but remember that men respect and want to marry only a pure girl."

"Was that the way it was with you and Father?" Michal asked shrewdly.

Mavis turned pink. "Yes, dear."

"That man you were engaged to when you met Father—he was very respectful, wasn't he?"

"Oh, yes. Gerald never tried to take liberties. He was a fine young man."

Michal grinned. "Yet you married Father, who tried, I'll bet."

"That'll do." And Mavis left the room.

V

Katie's boy was born six days before Christmas. Michal stopped by for a few minutes on the first day to find her friend sleepily radiant, the baby cuddled close to her, sucking noisily.

Three days later, when she called again, she had heard enough gossip to know that there was great finger counting and tongue clacking. The baby was sleeping in his homemade cradle, and Mrs. Keim's eyes were red as she led Michal to the bedroom. "She is very sad. You help her, *gewiss!*"

Katie was lying flat, crying silently, tears slipping down onto her fat pillow. Michal hesitated in the doorway. "Come in."

"I'll drop by later, when you feel more like company."

"No, I feel like talk."

"I'm sorry you're blue."

The soft lips trembled. "It's Yosh. All day I've thought of him—

how proud he'd be of little Yoshua. And he isn't here to see. He'll never be here to see."

"I know. But he's still alive in the baby."

"It's not the same. You don't understand, Michal. You've got to be married and have a baby too, to know how you need your husband at this time."

"I suppose so."

"Are people talking much?"

"Oh, a little. You know how people are."

"Mrs. Pratt came yesterday."

"She didn't!"

"She looked at Yoshua very hard. And asked many questions."

"Your mother shouldn't have let her in."

"What else could she do? Mutter was polite—not friendly." The plump hand on the cover trembled. "She never came before. Why should she come now?"

"To pry. She'll gossip, but don't you pay any attention. It's nobody's business but yours."

Tears were coming again, fast. "She talked about Yosh. And said it was too bad Mrs. White could not see the baby."

Michal cast about desperately for a safer topic. "Was it hard having a baby?"

Katie wiped her eyes, blew her nose on a large white handkerchief, frowned faintly. "Is pretty bad, yes. With a first one it takes long; that's the worst. Eighteen hours for me. My first pain came in the morning at one. Of course"—sensibly—"the pain is not sick pain—yust hard work. And then when it is all over, you have a baby."

"I'm afraid I won't be so brave."

A faint condescension tinged the reply. "When you have one— you will see."

This was more like Katie. But Michal had relaxed too soon, for the other continued sadly: "At the end I wanted Yosh so. I forgot he was dead and called and called—" Tears were falling again.

Then a deep voice sounded at the door. Katie wiped her eyes, and Michal rose as Dr. Gotthelf came in, snowflakes melting on his dark hair. "Hello, there." His face was pleasant, steel-blue eyes beneath black brows flicking his patient. "As my aunt used to say, 'Old Mutter she picks her geeses.'"

238

Michal rose, and, "With the first snow Mother always says, 'Old Mother Halle is shaking her featherbed.' I'll leave now."

"Why don't you stay?" He leaned over the cradle for a moment, then, pulling up a chair beside the bed, sat down and took Katie's hand. "You can be as much doctor to Katie here, as me." He looked tired, Michal thought, his usually ruddy face pale, the lines in the kindly face deep. "So, the reaction has set in."

"I don't know how to stop crying," sobbed Katie, "since little Yosh came."

"Would you like me to tell you how to get over it?"

Mutely she nodded.

"You'll have these times, you know; when they come, think about the baby and your parents."

"But—"

"Think like this: 'If I cry my baby cries, so I must smile. If I weep my mother weeps; I will not cause her more tears. I will keep my mind on them both.' "

"But I can't—"

"As long as you think of yourself first, Katie, you won't. Remember, it was another person thinking of herself who brought about this trouble. Are you going to start out the same way?"

"Oh, no."

"Then try my plan. Babies can sense unhappiness as easily as older folks."

Michal spoke seriously, "That's what Christ meant, then, when he said to love others as ourselves."

"In a nutshell."

Katie's eyes were round. "I never thought of making little Yosh unhappy."

"Love—especially mother love—brings unselfishness faster than anything. You girls will learn that." He smiled. "That's why I brought you in on this lecture, Michal. Save me time later. Well, I must get on. A few more patients, and then Christmas shopping to finish."

"Will your wife be here for the holidays?" Michal asked impulsively.

He was drawing on his overcoat, and for a moment she thought he had not heard. "You see—I wasn't talking only to you two this afternoon—but to myself. My wife died—yesterday—in New York of pneu-

239

monia. So I'm like you, Katie. Luckily I have others depending on me—as you have. I'll see you tomorrow."

The baby stirred, fussed. Carefully Michal lifted him out of his cradle and put him gently by his mother. From the *Stube* came the muted murmur of voices, then a door closing. The girls looked at each other, then looked away.

The starched ruffled curtains framed a tiny millefiori of white sky and earth and falling snow. For a moment the doctor's sleigh moved through it—a delicate black silhouette. But Katie did not see. Her eyes —soft and blue—were on her child.

VI

Mrs. Pratt made her first call since Joshua's death on Christmas day. Father saw her coming. "Great God, here comes Pratt! I'll be back later." He went out the back way as Mother opened the front door.

"If you can wade through the dining room," Mavis said, indicating the scatter of toys and paper, "we'll have something to eat. Girls, you may join us. Philip, don't let David swallow anything."

Mrs. Pratt looked at the little boys. "If it weren't for the difference in age you'd swear them two was twins—both so fair and lively."

Mavis paled, but spoke steadily, "Faith, will you ask Hetty to bring in coffee and fruitcake?"

"Where's Fanny?" Michal's face was carefully demure.

"She stopped off at Mrs. White's. Such a good girl, always going over to cheer her up. She has the idea that you're avoiding her." Hetty marched in with the tray, set it down and stalked out wordlessly.

"Fanny should know I never avoid her."

Abigail glanced at her sharply. "I've seen Katie's baby. Did she tell you?"

"She did." Coldly.

"Mrs. Ward, I'm surprised that you permit Michal to go there. I've told Fanny I'll horsehide her if she so much as speaks to that girl."

Mavis flushed. "Faith, dear, please run in and watch the boys for me. Didn't Hetty's fruitcake turn out well?"

240

"If that's not a full-term nine-months baby, I'll eat my hat. I took a good close look at it—hair, fingernails, and all. They married in May, wasn't it?"

Michal drew a deep breath and opened her mouth, but Mavis spoke quickly, "It has always been my practice to ignore gossip."

"Well, in a decent community like Salem, Mass., we made such things our affair. You can use soft words, but you've never really liked Michal's being friendly with those Rooshans; in my opinion Katie Kei—White is no better than a fallen woman."

"Mother—"

"I'll do the talking." Mavis sipped her coffee delicately before she spoke again. "I don't want my girls counting on their fingers every time someone is married and has a baby. Katie is bearing her cross now. I'm sure you agree with me that it would be too bad to start an ugly rumor. It would reflect on Joshua's memory, too, and we wouldn't want to hurt Mrs. White."

Mrs. Pratt shook her head. "We just don't see things the same way. Black is black where I come from." She added shrewdly, "For all your words you've never had any truck with those foreigners."

"Most of my friends I've made in church. As a matter of fact, on our way to Reids' today I was planning to stop by at the Keims'. I get out so seldom, you know."

"Why, Mother, I didn't—"

"Well!" Mrs. Pratt rose. "I must go." She opened her bag and took out some packages. "Brought these Christmas things for the children. You folks are awful thick with the Reids these days."

"We've enjoyed them—the few times we've managed to get together."

"He spoils her something terrible. I heard—and I won't mention the source—that he paid every cent of $50 for the mink cape he got her for Christmas."

"Thank you for the presents," Mavis said gently, ushering the woman toward the door.

"By all the signs you'll have Lewis for a son-in-law one of these days. I told Fanny she ought to set her cap for him, but she said, 'You know he likes the tall skinny type, built like a snake, Maw, not a girl with hips like mine.' She's a case."

"Michal and Lewis are children still."

241

"Well, I was married when I was sixteen. They're gone before you know it."

As the door closed, Michal whirled. "Isn't she awful?"

"You mustn't lower yourself arguing with a woman like that."

Faith lifted her lovely curly head. "Well, I don't think Michal should be so friendly with Katie, Mother, and you don't either, really."

"You keep out of this!"

"Girls—girls. Faith is right. My opinion hasn't changed about Rooshans. But ugly gossip is something else I don't believe in."

"Well, now you see why I've never liked to go there, why I've never liked Fanny?"

"Yes, I'm beginning to get your point of view." Mavis's voice was thoughtful. "We'd better get ready to make our call."

"Tall and skinny like a snake," snorted Michal to herself as she climbed the stairs.

Father said: "My God, why this sudden interest in Rooshans? I'll be damned if I'll be a party to any such call."

But his brow cleared when Mother interjected: "Why don't you drive on to Becker's? Then in half an hour come by for the girls and me."

Michal and Faith, pretty in their Scotch plaid Christmas dresses and new high-top button shoes, smiled proudly at Mavis, who, cheeks pink, eyes bright, was giving last-minute suggestions to Hetty.

Picturing the Keim house with its starched scrubbed cleanness—the odor of good food permeating everything—Michal thought, Now Mother will see what nice people they are and why I love to go there.

But as Mrs. Keim, somewhat flustered, led them into the *Stube*, they found instead through a haze of tobacco smoke a room full of people—Karl, Wilhelm Gross, and Mr. Keim waited on by the Gross girls—eating *Kerne* and drinking *Schnaps*. Michal felt her mother pause before she entered and bowed to their hostess' nervous introductions. For a moment there was an awkward silence; then Karl rose to his feet as they continued on to the bedroom. Michal's heart was pounding as always when she saw him. His eyes on her had been cool and level.

Karl's mother was carrying the baby to the bed when they entered. As Michal introduced Faith and her mother, Katie put the baby to her breast, then turned, "He is such a pig. Gobble, gobble all the time. Already when he is picked up he opens his mouth like a little bird."

242

Mavis leaned over him interestedly. "He's a beautiful baby. He looks like you, but I think he'll have Joshua's coloring and eyes."

Katie's smile was radiant. "I'm glad you see it, too!"

"Doesn't Katie look well?" Mavis had turned politely to Katrina Gross.

"Ja." Abruptly she left the room without noticing Michal.

Mrs. Keim spoke quickly. "My sister cooks the dinner."

"We've come at an awkward hour. John should be by for us shortly."

"We are glad you haf come. We do not eat for some time. The men—you know—like their *Schnaps* while their stomachs are empty. They then eat *Kerne*."

Because Mavis looked vague, Faith asked, "What is *Schnaps*?"

"Goot whisky."

"Whisky!" Mavis's brown eyes were wide with horror.

Quickly Michal handed Katie a package. "Something for the baby." As the other took out the quilted, lace-edged bibs, Faith whispered to Michal, "What's *Kerne*?"

"Sunflower seeds," impatiently. "You know."

"Where do they get them?"

"Frau Keim gathers and dries and roasts them and puts them away in flour sacks. They're good."

"But why are there so many hulls on the floor beside each chair?"

"When they get excited they eat very fast. I've tried but I never could do it the way they do. There's quite a trick to it."

Mavis interrupted her conversation with Katie. "I think I hear my husband. Katie, your baby is lovely and you look splendid. Don't get up too soon."

"Dr. Gotthelf, he makes her take care," explained Frau Keim.

"Isn't it a comfort to have such a fine doctor now? Goodbye."

As they reentered the *Stube* Mavis paused and spoke to Karl, who rose again. "Aren't you the boy who took care of the girls in the big blizzard years ago?"

"We were together, yes."

"I've never had a chance to thank you properly." How lovely Mother looks! Michal thought proudly. She could see even Karl's iron composure cracking slightly under her charm. He flashed one of his rare smiles.

243

Faith, who—after a disapproving stare at the two men—had gone to peer out of the window, said, "Mother, Father is getting impatient."

As they took their leave, Michal saw Katrina Gross standing in the doorway, watching. She did not speak as they turned to go—not even to say goodbye.

VII

By 1892 Eureka was the primary inland wheat market of the world. Philip loved to hear Michal tell of the first faint trails in 1887 with directions marked on large boulders; of her first trip to End-of-Track; of the meetings in the depot before their church, with its stained-glass windows and red ingrain carpet, was built.

Mavis sighed because in spite of the W.C.T.U. the worship of Bacchus was preferred to that of God—for with six churches there were well over a dozen saloons. On the streets, children picked their way about the bodies of sleeping men as carelessly as though they were hogs. But there was little if any crime.

More board sidewalks had been built, and many new hitching racks were placed in front of the box elders on Main and Market streets. There were thirty-five elevators and grain houses in active operation. And immigrants still kept coming.

Yet with all the color and life and prosperity, an undercurrent of restlessness sent Father on his first trip to Montana for horses. "Why, John?" Mother had asked.

"Because it's a good business proposition. I'll get a bunch of broncos out there, bring them back—along with three or four broncobusters —and we'll spend a few months breaking them. Choose some for work horses, some for riding, and so forth. Then ship them to Wisconsin or Ohio and sell at a profit. Besides"—he began pacing—"I've got to get out a while. This place is too tame!"

"For me"—she looked out toward the driveway—"it is becoming a real home with our trees growing taller each year. Of course, we had a bad time of it during the drought years, but so did everybody else. I could understand your restlessness if we hadn't done so well lately."

Father swung around irritably. "There are too many damn' foreigners to suit me. I bargained for more good New Englanders when we moved here."

"Well"—Mother was soothing—"perhaps this trip will do you good."

John Ward returned with fifty wild two- and three-year-old horses and three broncobusters. The broncos were run in the north pasture and bedded down in the tall corral. The three men had a bunkroom in the stable next the feed room, and one of them—Danny O'Dell —was especially good. Pete and Bill broke the horses for driving, but Danny worked only with the saddle horses. Grownups and children watched the breaking, fascinated.

The bronco, isolated in the corral chute, saddle tightly cinched, bridle adjusted and Danny up, stood tense or trembling until he called, "Let 'im go, Bill!" And in a second the horse would plunge from the chute, and, kicking, bucking, twisting and turning, back humped and legs stiff, try all his tricks. If a real outlaw, he might even rear up in front and throw himself over backward; that would mean quick action on Danny's part to avoid being crushed. Sitting easily in the saddle he waited until the horse, suddenly stretching his body out full length, plunged madly across the prairie; then Danny gave him his head until the bronco, panting, nostrils widely distended, sides heaving, would appear at the starting point well under control, the first lesson learned.

Father spent every spare moment helping; now that the days were longer he could hurry home and work with the hands until dark. One night he pointed out to Mavis and Michal a small harmless-looking pony that Pete was saddling. "Fleabite. Brought him back for Philip."

"He's so small," said Mavis gently.

"Look at that boy," chuckled John Ward. "A born horseman."

Nearby, Rory, exuding martyrdom, was submitting patiently to having his legs carefully bandaged by Philip—just as he had seen his father do with the trotters. "When you gonna break Fleabite for me, Father?" he asked eagerly, looking up.

"Right now, son!" Still grinning, Father strode to the chute and draped his six foot three inches onto the pony.

"His feet almost touch the ground," giggled Michal, lifting Philip for a better view. "Poor little—" A small explosion interrupted her as Fleabite went into action, twisting, turning, humping, bucking more savagely than any horse they had ever seen. Mavis clutched Michal's arm in quick fear. Then the pony was running, writhing—stopping suddenly. Father's long legs made a windmill until he hit the dust.

From the chute came raucous laughter as Bill, Pete, and Danny whacked one another and rolled on the ground in an agony of mirth. Father picked himself up, looked hard at Fleabite, who was standing placidly nearby, then—ignoring the noise from the chute—walked over toward Mavis. "My God, did you see that?" Then, sheepishly, "Guess we'll pick another horse for you, son."

"Yup." Philip was already back bandaging Rory. "He sure threw you, Father."

"Are you all right, John?" Anxiously.

"Um-hum," he grunted as the broncobusters strolled up.

Danny wiped his eyes. "We bin waitin' fer this. Nobody's ever rid him yet. Those long legs o' yourn—"

"Draggin' the ground," gasped Pete.

Convulsed, they leaned against each other again. John Ward grinned. "All right, boys, all right. You fixed me this time."

Fleabite, looking small and forlorn, ambled back to the gate.

As the Fourth of July neared, Mavis said: "I do believe that this new interest is all for the best. I'm even happy about Fury—as long as all this excitement takes care of Father's restlessness."

Exploding firecrackers woke Michal at sunrise. She ran to the window. Teams were already coming in on the west road, and far-away spirals of dust heralded others from more distant farms on their way to attend the "Yuly" celebration.

All year the foreigners looked forward to the Fourth of July. Every other weekday they worked, but on this one day they did their chores and were on the road by dawn lest they miss any part of the festivities.

Father, on the entertainment committee, ate early breakfast and rushed off, saying: "We still have to get someone to fix the greased pole, and it looked like rain last night so we haven't draped the bandstand with bunting. I'll be back at noon." But he was back in an hour in Dr. Gotthelf's rig. Mavis, pale and big-eyed with fright, met them at the door. "What is it?"

"Stop staring at me like that; I was working on the bandstand and some boy in the street threw a giant cracker. It exploded on my hand —so here I am, damn it."

Dr. Gotthelf helped him to his big chair. "Mrs. Ward, I'll need a

246

medium-sized butter crock—one in which his hand will rest comfortably, with room to spare."

Soon Father, his injured hand immersed in a jar of sweet oil, sat as he would continue to sit for two weeks, day and night. Pale from shock, suffering almost unbearable pain, he fumed and swore, while everyone tiptoed through the house.

Hetty packed a picnic lunch; then she and Gus bundled Philip and David into the buggy and drove out to Schaffer's grove for the day. Faith left early to join one of her friends for the celebration, while Michal hovered solicitously round Father until he finally exploded, "Damn it, I know you mean well, but for God sakes get out of my sight!"

As quick tears filled her eyes, Mavis called her aside, saying: "Faith's stopping by to ask Lewis to come for you early. If the house is quiet all day, I'm sure Father will feel better by evening."

Michal dressed carefully in her dainty new printed muslin, dabbing a little perfume on her wavy bangs, while she cast melting glances at herself in the mirror. Then, hearing Lewis's voice, she hurried down to the front porch where he and Mother were talking softly. When she saw her daughter Mavis looked grave. "Isn't that dress rather short and thin for street wear?"

"It's too hot to wear anything heavier. Besides, short skirts are the latest thing."

"She looks beautiful, Mrs. Ward," Lewis burst out.

"I suppose I'm old-fashioned, but it does seem to me that dresses are getting pretty extreme. Since it's so hot, though—"

"Thank you, Mother. Shall we go?"

As they strolled down the hill he caught her hand. "I'm glad you're slim. You know, the first time I ever saw you—the day we found Glen —I remember the way you looked dancing there in the cold wind, your feet hardly touching the ground, your skirts blowing. I remember my heart jumped a little, and I knew I'd found my girl."

"You didn't either. You threw a rock at me and we had a fight."

"It was a pebble, and besides, at that age boys are supposed to hate girls." He pulled her around facing him. "We're not too young to be engaged, Michal. Please!"

She stood quietly, relaxed in the bright July sunshine. His hand was warm and comfortable. He was nice. And fun, too. Yet as she had dressed this morning an image had been in her mind, one that she'd dreamed of since the prairie fire—of Karl taking her in his arms and whirling her to the strains of a waltz. She spoke carefully, choosing her words so as not to hurt him. "We're too young to think of such things now. You're going away to school. And I may be too."

"Yes, but we could be engaged. I want to be sure of you."

"Let me think about it. And talk with Mother."

"All right." His hand tightened. "Maybe a few kisses sometime might help you make up your mind."

"People shouldn't kiss until they're married." But her lashes were down, remembering.

"Bosh."

As they continued toward town, Michal felt warm and content. When they joined the crowds on the streets she was conscious of people watching him steer her protectively through the throng. She felt apart from them suddenly—not as she had in other years. It had been like that once before—the day Karl had come to End-of-Track and she had flashed by him and his family with Father. These noisy, sweat-stained, red-faced people! They must have known, for some fell back before their leisurely approach.

"There go Dr. Gotthelf and Miss O'Connor, the new nurse. How young he looks today! And isn't she pretty?"

They paused a moment to watch. Lewis whistled. "Those sleeves of hers must be a yard wide."

"Leg o' mutton should be. See, her dress is as short as mine."

"Well, you have prettier feet." He glanced admiringly at her russet shoes.

"There comes Mrs. White. She walks nearly as well as ever. I must speak to her."

But Mrs. White did not seem to see them. She was walking dazedly, instead of with her former assurance.

"Mrs. White. Hello."

She turned vaguely, then clutched them both and spoke hoarsely. "Michal. Lewis. Have you seen the baby?"

"You mean Joshua?"

"Yes. I just saw him for the first time. He was in his buggy in their front yard. Nobody was around, so I walked up and looked at him." She turned abruptly to Lewis. "Is your father home today?"

"Why—yes, I think so."

248

"I'm going to see him. That baby doesn't belong to her. He's the living image of Joshua. He belongs to me."

"I don't think Father would see anybody on business today, Mrs. White."

"Tomorrow then. It doesn't matter. I must go home now to Goldie."

As she limped away Lewis said, "Who's Goldie?"

"Her canary. When it died she had it stuffed and mounted in a glass dome. Since Joshua died she talks to it as though it were human."

"She must be crazy."

"I'm going over and tell Katie!"

"There's no need. I'm positive Father wouldn't touch the case. Besides, I don't think there's a thing she could do—legally—to get the baby."

"Maybe not. But I think Katie should know right away how she feels. Come on."

"Oh, all right."

Katie was standing in the yard holding Joshua and watching—wistfully—the band playing a spirited march as it passed by on its way to the bandstand. She nodded to a group of young people in gay colorful clothes. In the bright sunlight the baby seemed to shine with health and happiness.

As Michal poured out the story, Katie hugged little Joshua close, her blue eyes round with terror. "No! She can't do dot."

"Of course not. But we thought we should tell you."

Lewis spoke impulsively. "Katie, if it'd make you feel better, I'll go ask my father about it."

"Oh, ja, please. I go find Mutter now."

"If you don't mind, I'll wait for you at the pavilion, Lewis. This hot sun is making me dizzy." Then she touched his arm lightly, "Thanks for being so nice to Katie."

He patted her hand and grinned, "Oh, I can be useful on occasion."

The pavilion, floored with rough boards, had a roof and open sides; but branches of box-elder trees from Schaffer's grove festooned along the open sides gave the illusion of a green forest to those inside. Michal felt her heart thump as she neared the booth. She had seen Karl dance here before, but he had never seen her. Today she would watch openly like the rest.

249

Although many of the dancers had risen by lantern light and ridden miles over bumpy roads in lumber wagons, they were fresh and lively in their holiday best. Now they were swaying to the music of a folk song played by the orchestra of harmonicas, accordions, and violins.

The girls wore thin white dresses after the American manner, but trimmed with ribbons—sashes and neck ribbons with long streamers and many bands of varied widths and colors bordering the full skirts halfway to the waists. The men wore their best trousers, shirts, astrakhan caps, and high boots.

Karl was dancing with Frieda Baur, and they were easily the most striking couple on the floor. Karl wore his astrakhan cap at an angle and was looking down at the top of her head. He's proud of her, Michal thought, but then she is one to be proud of—her blond braids so heavy, her dress all blue-and-gold embroidery. Frieda raised her head from Karl's shoulder, smiled, and her lips moved, and as he looked down at her, answering, she hid her face on his shoulder again. Michal's fists clenched in a rage that shook her. She turned away as the dance ended, hoping to see Lewis, but he was nowhere in sight. I'll go meet him, she thought as the music started again, this time not a folk song but a dreamy waltz. Suddenly she felt hands gripping her shoulders, turning her around. It was Karl. He said nothing, but pulled her gently forward.

He was piloting her skillfully on the crowded floor. He dances beautifully; this is easy, she thought, and relaxed. Karl's arm tightened; he held her so close she could feel the beating of his heart. She was floating now, and the girls dancing about her became blurred; their skirts were huge inverted morning glories floating through space in a lovely dream. It was a dream, and when like a dream it ended Karl took her back to her place among the watchers, smiled, bowed, spoke for the first time the one word "Michal," and was gone.

In a daze, she left the pavilion, pushing through the crowd outside. A farmer in a drunken stupor lay stretched across the sidewalk, asleep and snoring. Michal stepped over him without realizing he was there, then almost collided with Lewis. "Hey, where'd you think you're going?"

"Looking for you." She smiled vaguely. "Is it all right—about Katie, I mean?"

"Yeah. I've just come from there. I was right. Father says she hasn't a thing to worry about. The Keims feel much better."

"Good." She sighed restlessly. "I wish it were proper for girls to go to horse races. Father and Becker are racing Euretta and Lillian Russell today."

"Have you ever seen a race?"

"I've climbed up and watched from an elevator window. Father used to stand me between his knees in the sulky and let me hold the stop watch. But then I had to miss the real fun."

"Nice girls don't go to races."

As the afternoon wore on, Michal grew bored. Fireworks, greased-pig chase, band music were not the fun they used to be. When Lewis suggested leaving she said casually, "I'd like to watch the Rooshans dance again for a few minutes."

The sun was down and the long twilight had fallen when they entered the pavilion. The fun was at its height. Eagerly she scanned the crowd. Yes, there was Karl dancing with a girl she didn't know. Not the lovely Frieda, anyway. For a moment she was sure that he had seen them, but his face was fathomless as usual. She tapped her foot in time to the music, thinking, I love it in here. All the color and excitement. I wish Mother didn't think it wrong to dance."

Lewis yawned. "Let's go. If we stay in here much longer we'll smell as though we'd been drinking beer." Then he brightened up. "Here comes Frieda Baur. Whew, what a looker!"

The girl, flushed and lovely, approached and spoke courteously. As they talked, Michal saw Karl speak to the musicians, then turn toward them. He was coming straight to her, smiling a little. She took a step forward as the music filled the room. A waltz. Their waltz. Then Lewis's arm was about her possessively, pulling her back.

Too late she saw the hard anger in the dark face; Karl did not hold out his arms for her, but deliberately swerved, nodded briefly to Lewis, and—without a word—took Frieda in his arms and whirled away.

"Let's go, shall we?" She tried to keep her voice steady.

"Karl Gross has the manners of a pig. He didn't even speak to you," growled Lewis as they left the place.

Michal could not speak; she clung to his arm as he led the way out of town toward the ravine. For her there was to be no more dancing, no blur of morning glories as she whirled in his arms. Had Frieda Baur seen her step toward him? He had known. He had seen her lifted face, her smile of greeting, her step forward. A slap in the face could not have been more deliberate. She never wanted to see him or that girl again—ever.

Falling in with her mood, Lewis was quiet, and as they approached the ravine she found herself quieting. This was as it should be, some-how. Walking in the warm twilight with someone who would never hurt her. Someone of her own kind.

They settled down against the rock and she leaned her head back, listening to the muted noises from the town. The band was playing the new hit: "Daisy, Daisy—give me your answer—do."

Lewis's hand tightened over her own. "This is better."

"Yes."

Gently he drew her head down to his shoulder. "Tired?"

"Rather. The heat—"

"And smells." He grinned down at her. "Never forget the smells."

She was silent, watching balloons of dandelion down float past. In the same light air current a long cobweb caught on a thistle blossom, rose and fell lazily with each pulse.

"Lovely." He was watching her.

"Oh, Lewis." She buried her face on his shoulder.

Tenderly he lifted her chin and, a little awkwardly, kissed her lightly. Then again—more eagerly. His lips were warm and comfortable. Life with him would be like this, she thought. Calm and beautiful—without any hurts. "Do you still want to be engaged?" she asked.

"Yes. More than ever now."

"Then I think we might be, if our parents say it's all right."

"I love you, Michal."

"Yes."

Contentedly she leaned against his shoulder, watching the haze of smoke blend with the haze of evening. Breathing the acrid scent of coneflowers from the swale. The moon—cool as a pearl—floated along the graying sky. Far away. Serene.

VIII

Father was the only one who objected to the engagement. "No daughter of mine can think of getting married at sixteen."

"Nearly seventeen. And of course they won't, John. It'll be several years before they make plans. Alice and I are delighted that the children have chosen each other; they're so well suited."

"Well, if they wait five years." he grumbled, lifting his hand out of the butter crock and studying the blisters moodily.

"It'll be at least that long. Lewis must finish his schooling."

But Lewis had other ideas. "I have news," he told Michal in August. "Do I look different?"

"Well, you didn't wash your face. Your upper lip—"

"That's a mustache. Play something for me."

Seating herself at the organ and pulling the stops, she softly played "Beautiful Dreamer" while Lewis leaned against the instrument, never taking his eyes from her face. As the last note trembled away he said, "How would you like a businessman for a husband?"

"And give up law?"

"Sure. Last night I had a long talk with the folks. Told them how I felt about leaving you and all that. The upshot of it was that Father is going to get me in with Melchoir Jones. He says there's lots of money to be made in wheat selling; if I go in now and learn the business from the ground up, we could be married in two years."

"I thought Mr. Jones had a nephew coming in with him."

"He can't do it. That's what gave me the idea. Father's going to use his influence, so I'm pretty sure it'll work out. What do you think?"

Michal looked down, abstractedly playing a little tune in a minor key over and over—softly, with one hand. "I don't like it. The way you feel about Rooshans—well, I just don't see you dealing with them and I'll bet your folks don't either."

"I can try. After all, this is wheat country. Father says I'd make plenty of money. I thought you'd be tickled to death."

Swiftly she rose. "If you're sure it's right, then of course I am. We'll have loads of fun. Do you mind if sometime I tell Katie of our engagement—as a secret, that is?"

"Go ahead. But why don't you begin to cut loose from Katie now. You won't have much in common with her after we're married."

Michal whirled. "Listen to me, Lewis. Katie'll always be my best friend in Eureka. You can take it or leave it!"

"All right. Suit yourself. She didn't hear any more of Mrs. White's threat, did she?"

"Not a word. Mrs. White is settling her business affairs and leaving. Here come all the children and Rory. Quick, give me a kiss."

She brushed her lips lightly across his; then, as he would have pulled her close, she drew back, whispering, "They might see."

"All right. Remember, only two years more—" He squeezed her hand and went to open the door.

Through the days of harvest Michal spent most of her spare time with Lewis. Each had a bicycle now, and they took long rides on the prairie roads. She saw to it that there were no trips past the Gross farm, however; she avoided every place where Karl might be.

Those were lovely hours. Mostly they looked for clumps of flowers for Mrs. Reid's native flower border—she having everything from the first lavender cups of pasqueflowers, early yellow violets, pink feathery plumes of prairie smoke in April to the last goldenrod, closed gentian and smooth blue asters of autumn.

Lewis had an instinct for finding the best blossoms, and on each trip they carried home some new plant to his mother. "Then, dears, when you have your home you may start your own garden."

Often Michal stayed to supper and Lewis walked home with her through the mellow September twilight, or after the moon rose and shed misty light over the prairie where dust from hauling had softened the hills.

Pete and Bill had gone back to Montana, but Danny still stayed on to help Gus. These evenings after the chores were done he would sit on the carriage block and strum his guitar and sing in his nasal tenor voice the songs of the plains and campfires. Achsah Klunk had taken to dropping by every night or so, ostensibly to see Hetty. Often, lying in bed, Michal heard her deep rich laughter as Danny told her of his home town. "Its right name is Tower City, but the railroad men nicknamed it Sour Titty because there's a spring there; only, the water ain't sour but bitter's gall. Anyhow, it's the flattest damned place on earth, so when I was sixteen I run away to Montana and the mountains and I ain't never been back to Dakota 'til now." Then he'd sing, " 'Oh, bury me not on the lone prairie-e-e,' " always adding, "And mean it, b'Gawd. Give me a grave on a mountaintop."

"Then why do you stay here in Eureka?" asked Faith innocently once.

"Prairie rolls hereabouts. Evenin's like this the hills look sorta like dusty plush. And I like the people—friendly-like—"

And so many a night Michal was lulled to sleep by Achsah's soft deep laughter and Danny's laments of men who rode the plains alone.

During hauling season Lewis went to work for Melchoir Jones—

Flour and Feed. "The glorified errand boy" he called himself. And glorified he was, for to please Mrs. Reid—who still grieved at her son's having given up his professional career—Mr. Reid had presented him with a handsome turnout. The light delivery wagon—green with bright red wheels—was pulled by perfectly matched Arabians, looking exactly as though someone had spilled a sack of flour over their glossy bay coats. A coach dog—flashing black and white—ran at their heels beneath the front axle. "He'd make a lovely house pet," Michal said once, stroking the smooth dappled coat.

"Mother can't abide dogs in the house—but she likes the effect of him with the team," he replied indifferently. "So he sleeps in the stable."

As Michal strolled down to Keims' one warm fall day, she wondered if Karl had seen Lewis in his new turnout. She hoped so, but she would not ask Katie. Joshua was tumbling about on a blanket in the *Stube* while his mother, starched and matronly, stitched a dress for him.

"It is good to see you, Michal. Where have you been?"

"Baby tending mostly. Mother has felt the heat this year. Why haven't you been up?"

"Since—Mrs. White saw Yoshua—I've never left him for long. Mutter is busy, too, and he's so big and strong—" proudly.

"Mrs. White has never done anything more, has she?"

"No, but I still worry."

"Well, she's leaving in the fall."

Michal opened her sewing bag and took out a square of black velvet and began stitching with gold thread.

"You—sewing?"

"Yes. See, it's to be a dragon. There'll be green, red, and yellow with a touch of silver. For my hope chest."

"I've seen you and Lewis go by on your bicycles many times."

"Yes."

"So?"

Michal nodded. "We're engaged. You're the only one I'm telling outside of the two families."

"Then that is why he is working at Yones's place. So you may be married sooner."

"Yes. Although it will be two years at least. Besides, Mother wants me to have a year or so at State Normal School before I marry."

255

"Why didn't you go this year?"

"Father objects to my going at all. Finishing school, but not Normal. Mother thinks every girl should have some training—nursing or teaching. But since David and Philip are so lively, we've put off my going for a year."

Katie shot her an innocent glance. "Karl, too, may go to school. Brookings. Uncle Wilhelm is very angry at the idea. But Tante Katrina wants it. So—if he wants—he'll go."

Michal was very busy with her gold thread. "I thought you told me once that she wanted him to be a Lutheran minister."

Katie giggled. "She did. But, can you imagine Karl a preacher? He is already planning to get land and start for himself a farm. Then next year go to Brookings."

Joshua staggered to his knees, then plopped hard onto his fat stomach, setting up a roar. Katie changed and quieted him before she added, "Karl comes to town every day hauling."

"So does everybody else, it seems. The streets are choked all day with wagons waiting their turn to unload. Lewis said one ox team had come seventy miles. He says they are expecting to reach three or four million bushels by the end of the year."

"Your Lewis knows a lot." She sighed, eyes darkening, and Michal saw that in repose the line of her mouth was sad. "You are a lucky girl, Michal. Will you have a church wedding?"

"Probably. We haven't planned so far yet." She jumped nervously as a team swung past the house toward the back. "Someone's here."

"It's only Karl." Katie smiled serenely, lifting Joshua. "He always comes to play with the baby. Yoshua loves him."

Hastily Michal stuffed her pillow cover and thread into her bag. "I'll go now. Come and see me, when you can."

"Don't run away. He won't bite."

"I'm not running," she snapped crossly. "Mother'll need me, that's all." She patted the baby's cheek. "Goodbye," and hurried out as a step sounded at the back door.

As she walked down the street, skirts swishing pleasantly about her ankles, Lewis drove by. Standing with feet braced apart, holding in the spirited team, he flourished the whip jauntily at Michal in passing. She waved back—her eyes on him proud and tender—and watched him until he was out of sight.

256

IX

Michal was restless. The younger children were all napping; Faith was in the bedroom smearing cocoa butter on her eyelashes to make them longer; and Hetty, dinner dishes done, was resetting the dining-room table. Outside, the wind was rising.

"Be sure to darken the dining room before you close it, Hetty." Mavis sat down by the window. "Michal, you seem nervous."

"It's this wind. I can't settle down to sewing or even reading."

Mavis sighed. "Does it seem to you that your father is less restless now that he has Fury and his trips to Montana?"

"I think so. He's enjoyed the trotting races with Mr. Becker, too."

"This is rather a sad day for me, with Mrs. White leaving for good. Even though I felt her wrong about Joshua and Katie, I've been fond of her. Considering the tragedy of last year, I'm surprised that she has stayed on as long as this."

"From what she said to me once, after the baby came, I think she expected something to happen to Katie—and just stayed to see the fun."

"I don't like that bitterness in your voice, Michal. Remember that she has her side too. After all, Katie is young. She'll marry again and live a full, normal life. Joshua was an only child, and his mother has nothing to look forward to."

"Well, I'm glad she's going. I still have nightmares, seeing that door open, and—" She shuddered.

Mavis spoke quickly. "I wanted to go to the station with her, but she wouldn't hear of it."

She was interrupted by a pounding on the door. Michal opened it to find Katie, white and trembling. Behind her stood Karl.

"My baby is gone. Has Mrs. White been here?"

Mavis stepped forward quickly. "Please come in. Now, Katie, what are you saying?"

"He was sleeping in his buggy in the yard. I was hanging out baby things in the back. When Karl came we went around to see him as al-

257

ways—he was gone. His blanket too." She was wringing her hands distractedly.

Karl stepped forward. "Your friend, Mrs. White, leaves town today?"

"Yes. She came last night to say goodbye. I understood she was taking this afternoon's train for Aberdeen. You don't think she—"

"Yes." He was curt.

Katie sobbed. "My father is at Uncle Wilhelm's. I don't know what to do. I thought she might be here. The key is sitting in the lock, and Mutter is looking in the streets—"

Mavis spoke quietly. "My husband is a deputy sheriff. If you'll go right to him, he'd know what to do."

"Kum." Karl took his cousin's arm.

"Michal, you go with them. Father's at the stable this afternoon."

As they left, Hetty was saying with satisfaction, "I always said, didn't I, Mis' Ward, that 'A wart on the chin is a devil within'?"

When, breathless, they reached the livery stable, Michal poured out the whole story. Father paced—scowling—then interrupted her. "Without a doubt it's Mrs. White. Let's see. The train hasn't left here, yet. She wouldn't be bold enough to leave here on the train with the baby. Probably go to Hillsview. Somebody's helping her. I have it!" He stopped. "Fanny Pratt came in here about one-thirty and hired a horse and buggy. Mrs. White must have grabbed the baby, jumped in the rig, and taken off for Hillsview. Then Fanny will return this evening, innocent as cream. Gus!" he yelled, "saddle a horse for young Gross here. He can ride—they may change their minds and come back, though I doubt it. I'll take the train. That way, we'll be sure to catch them."

Katie clutched his sleeve. "I must go, too. He will be hungry and frightened."

Karl frowned. "Not by horse."

John Ward nodded. "You go with me."

"What about me, Father?"

He considered a moment, casting a brief hard glance at Karl, who returned it steadily. "Put a sidesaddle on the big bay gelding for Michal, Gus. There should be two on the road in case they are returning. Now, Katie, don't worry. We're bound to catch them. Go tell your mother where we're going and meet me at the station. It might pay to notify the sheriff and have them looking, but my hunch is that we're on the right track. Gus, you tell Mrs. Ward to expect us back sometime to-night."

Main and Market streets, alleys, vacant lots—all were filled and overflowing with grain haulers. As they guided their horses slowly through the throng, Michal burst out, "All these people, holding us back!"

"He is in no danger. We shall be in time."

Just ahead a grain buyer running beside a wagon hopped like an agile grasshopper to the top of the load. Immediately he began examining the contents of the sacks and quoting prices. Sitting on the sacks, a little boy listened to his father and the man arguing while he munched raw onion and ate bread and fat *Schweinefleisch*.

A couple of farmers with money in their *Geldsäcke* clumping along the rough board sidewalks hailed Karl boisterously as they turned into a saloon for beer.

As Michal fidgeted, Karl gestured. "Do you know how the hauling goes here? We wheel the sack in hand trucks into a flathouse and dump there. Then wheat is taken from there to the railroad cars. All shoveled by hand. It makes much work day and night for many men. So the streets must be crowded."

Michal shot him a grateful glance. This was a long speech for him. She was relaxing a little already in the shelter of his quiet words. "Thirty flathouses hold a lot of grain."

"Ya. It is a great country."

"Karl, I want to tell you how well you speak English now—with scarcely any trace of accent. Better than Katie, even."

He shrugged, but she knew he was pleased. "To some it comes easier."

They were clear of the town. The prairie, free of the clutter of buildings, stretched before them. The spirited horses shied as huge tumbleweeds and Russian thistles—some of them four feet in diameter—carried by the wind, rolled over and over, scattering their small black seeds. The whole earth was a sullen gray sea—a heaving sea of withered grass topped by the crested foam of the tumbleweeds.

They rode swiftly in silence. Michal's fears were gone. As on that night of the big prairie fire, she felt at one with the earth. Much as she disliked sidesaddle, she rode easily today, as though this were the way it should be.

259

Karl kept a little ahead, his muscular body in beautiful rhythm with his mount. Watching him, she thought, He rides as no Rooshan ever has—as though riding had been in his blood for centuries. It swept over her then like the surge of the wind: Here at this moment, in this place, I know. This is right. Never again to see the earth and my love like this. Just like this. Never the same again.

She must remember the other things—bare feet trampling kraut; his eyes hard as stone that day at the pavilion; the wolf dog growling low. But for the rest of the way into Hillsview the horses beat out in strange rhythm—*Never the same again, never the same again* . . .

Karl led the way straight to the depot. Except for the station agent the place was empty. No train puffed on the siding. No baby in alien arms fretted in the waiting room. "Maybe they didn't come this way, after all," Michal fretted.

"They must." He went over and, after speaking briefly to the man, returned. "They haf not been here. But the train comes soon. They will stay yet a while, then come. We wait here." He led her to the corner near the door where they could see before they were seen.

She closed her eyes, for she was tired. Her cheek came just to his shoulder. It would be good to lean against him for a moment and put her hand in his. Then faintly she heard the far-off whistle of the train. Michal tensed; if they were here they would appear soon. Even as the second whistle sounded—louder now—the door opened cautiously, then Fanny Pratt, carrying Goldie the canary, followed by Mrs. White and little Joshua, entered the room.

As Karl stepped forward, Fanny saw him and started. "Oh!" Mrs. White turned slowly. She said nothing, but she clutched the baby so tightly that he began to whimper; then, wheeling, she walked outside. As they followed, pushing past Fanny, Michal saw that Mrs. White was crooning to the baby, quieting him. She turned. "Why don't you leave me alone?"

Karl spoke curtly. "My cousin wants her child."

"Who is this person, Michal?"

"He is Karl Gross—Katie's cousin."

"You may tell him that I have no intention of giving up this baby. In the eyes of God he is mine."

The steam and smoke of the incoming train blotted out everything else. As it slowed to a stop, Fanny edged out of the waiting room and joined them, standing well away from Michal and Karl. She was still holding Goldie in his glass dome.

When she saw John Ward jump off followed by Katie, Mrs. White's iron composure cracked. "Why don't you leave me alone? Get out of here—all of you!"

Without a word Karl reached for little Joshua. For a moment the woman struggled—then, as Katie ran toward them, she let go abruptly. As she watched the child cuddle his head happily in his mother's neck, her spare frame began to jerk uncontrollably under the weight of harsh sobs. Karl was leading Katie away. Father, looking embarrassed, said, "Let me help you onto the train. Where's your luggage?"

"It came from Eureka with you, John Ward. Go away and leave me. Come, Goldie."

Taking the container from Fanny, she turned without a word of farewell toward the coach. Father spoke impatiently. "Come on, Michal. We've got to get home. Fanny, if you were my daughter I'd horsewhip you. But at least I'll drive you back to town in the rig you hired. Now get."

Fanny got. But Michal, looking back, said, "Wait a minute, Father." Mrs. White had paused at the foot of the car steps. For a moment the girl remembered her face, softened as it had been so many times in the past as she had said, "Here are some wrappers off my tins, Michal, that I've been saving for you." But as she ran up she heard her mumble, "We didn't think it would end like this, did we, Goldie?"

"Goodbye, Mrs. White," Michal called softly.

But Mrs. White did not hear.

The wind was down. Michal and Karl rode in silence behind the rig; Father was driving at a smart clip. Even though it was not yet dark, the moon was up—round as a pumpkin against the twilight sky. The prairie was still, and warmer than was usual for this season.

"Today as we came through town and you spoke of the wheat, I saw that you love the prairie, Karl." Her voice was soft.

"It is a great country." She liked the pride in his voice. "Since I was a small child in Russland, I hear them talk—my people—of this land. Evenings like this after work they would sit eating of the sweet grapes that grow there and reading aloud letters from our people here. And I would look to the sunset and think, *Dort hi naus ist Amerika.*"

261

He paused, "Then we kum, and the earth it is wide and free. My children and my children's children will live here on this rich land. And they will be called Americans—not Rooshans."

Eagerly she leaned forward. "In the Bible it says, 'And they possessed the land and dwelt therein.' That is what your people are doing."

"Ya. It is hard work but goot. I haf bought already one half-section of land—my own."

"Where is it?"

"North and east. I own your Place of Rocks."

"Then I'll have to find another."

"It's not goot for plowing. You are welcome."

"Thank you." She hesitated, "You will marry soon?"

"I must pay my debt first. And perhaps go to school. After that—"

"What will your wife be like, I wonder."

"I know only—she will wish to live on the land. I expect much of a wife. To bear children. To keep my house—"

"And work in the fields—"

"My wife will not work in the fields. But she would be strong enough to if need be."

"Oh, so she's too good for that, is she?"

He turned a dark level glance on her and she met it fully. Then, mockingly, he grinned.

Michal ground her teeth with rage. "Listen to me, Karl Gross. Don't flash your white Rooshan teeth at me. Do you think I give a damn whom you marry? I'm engaged to Lewis Reid and have been since the Fourth of July."

"So." Leaning over, he gripped her arm, black eyes hard. "You think I care? Lewis Reid and his white skin and little yellow mustache!"

She jerked her arm free. "Don't you touch me!"

He smiled. "There was once when I touched you and you were glad. If I wanted I could make you forget that Englisher. You say the Fourth of July?"

"Yes—" She stopped, then, and bit her lip.

"So." He had himself in hand again now. Turning, he said smoothly, "May you be happy with that—Lewis."

"Thank you." Shortly.

For the rest of the trip into town they kept the width of the road apart, and neither spoke again.

X

Michal spent most of the school year of 1892–1893 at State Normal School. It all came about unexpectedly a few days after the kidnaping scare.

Mrs. Reid had been so upset because Lewis had decided to go into the grain business that she finally took to her bed. As a result, his father finally persuaded him to go east for a try at law with the understanding that if he still wanted to continue in business the next year, they would withdraw their objections.

As soon as Mavis heard, she made up her mind that Michal must go to Normal School. She and John Ward quarreled about it. He roared, "I'll have no daughter of mine going to anything but a good Episcopalian finishing school—All Saints' is my choice!"

Mother said, "A girl should have a profession to fall back on and teaching is ladylike. Look at that poor widow in Ipswich left with three children. Now she has to scrub floors and take in washing."

"Michal could always come home to us."

"We won't live forever, John. I wonder if you don't resent the idea of Michal having a more formal education than you."

For once she had the last word; Father, crimson with rage, whirled and strode out, slamming the door. So Michal left the day after Lewis did.

The first few weeks she was too busy making up the work she had missed and adjusting to school life to think much about Eureka. School was a different world made up of new complexities: the mystery of algebra; her roommate's seventeen-inch waist and ruffled corset cover; President William Henry Harrison Beadle; laced shoes versus button shoes; the embarrassment of the morning parade to empty the chamber pails; Emerson's *Spiritual Laws*; the cameo pin from Lewis; the Christmas party, and her mink-trimmed canary-yellow silk dress; her Catholic boy escort Father must never hear about; letters from Lewis; the clippings Florence Knox, her roommate, brought back about the Lizzie Borden Case.

Letters from Katie, Mavis, and Faith brought news from home: Dr. Gotthelf's marriage to Kathleen O'Conner; Kit Cutter's elopement with the traveling man; Achsah Klunk's marriage to Danny, the broncobuster; the suicide by drowning of Violet, the girl from That House and of Achsah's near death when she tried to save her.

But the prairie seemed a far-away place—of lost bird cries and wheat fields of other years, of pasqueflowers long since dead and a willow tree, somewhere. When Katie wrote that Karl was attending church regularly with Frieda, Michal fingered the cameo brooch Lewis had sent her and felt no familiar stir of fear and rage. He was as lost to her as the prairie, and Lewis—for all the miles that separated them—was closer even than before. Michal stored away every event like a nut and then, having embellished it, fed it eagerly to Lewis. They were enchanted with their letters to each other and in love with their new found cynicism proper to all undergraduates.

As the school year drew to a close, Michal felt herself grown up. The prairie would always be a lovely place and she would be glad to go home. Mother was expecting a baby in June or July, and because Hetty was troubled with rheumatism she would be busy. But she and Lewis would have fun. Next fall she would be back in school. And Karl Gross would be one more interesting childhood memory.

XI

Michal wakened to the far-off sound of the cow horn and the closer, more intimate early-morning noises of a stirring household. Beside her, Faith turned restlessly in sleepy protest of a return to the real world, then opened her eyes.

Running her hand through the tousled dark curls, Michal laughed. "I can't get over the way you and the other children have grown. You'll soon be wearing long skirts." Impulsively, she added, "Has Mother talked to you about growing up?"

Faith blushed and pulled the sheet up to her chin. "What is there to talk about? I'll know enough to wear long skirts and do my hair up when the time comes."

Briefly, Michal told her. Faith's eyes grew larger and larger; then she sat up in bed and said soberly: "It's awful. I don't see why you had to mention it."

"I'll tell you why. I don't want you to go through what I did. It's really nothing to worry about. I only wish somebody had told me." She looked out toward the petal-tinted sky, "In fact, there are still a lot of things I wish I knew."

Faith remarked primly, "Mother would be angry with you, just the same."

Michal's voice went cold. "That may be. But at least if you're alone when it happens you won't think you're dying, like I did." She yawned, stretched, enjoying the loose feel of her nightgown—the coolness. "I've got to dress. Before I go to the Reids' for dinner today, I'm going out on the prairie."

"Oh, Michal, you'll get all rumpled and look awful."

"I'll be careful. I've done nothing yet but visit with the family. Then when Lewis came back the other day, we had a year to catch up on. I've got to get out and feel the wind and see the fields—and find if any flowers are blooming."

"I've never understood you." Faith spoke slowly. "Here you've been away to school, gone to parties, worn pretty clothes, met the best people; and now you want to go running over the prairie again. It frightens me to be alone out there even in the daytime. It's so big."

Michal turned eagerly to her sister. "That's just what I love. At school I never feel as though I could draw a deep breath. I like people, but I have to be by myself once in a while. And for me," she jumped out of bed, "the prairie is the place for that."

"Why don't you take Lewis with you?" Faith's voice was wistful. "A whole morning—"

"It won't be. Mrs. Reid asked me to be there about ten o'clock and stay to dinner. That way we'll enjoy the cooler part of the day. Why don't you come with me?"

"No, thanks." Faith got up slowly. "No tramping around in that dust for me."

For a moment Michal's spirits drooped. It would have been fun, now that Faith was growing up, to take her along and show her everything through her own eyes. Then, brightening, she thought, I can go to the Place of Rocks. I'll have the prairie all to myself.

265

On the stony hilltop the curly buffalo grass was sparse. Never had the prairie seemed so desolate. Vague talk of panic, ruin, drought had reached her at school; but as she stood on the great boulder at the Place of Rocks and looked west over dun hills and raddled grain fields she saw—except miles away where on the west road a white-topped prairie schooner crawled toward the Missouri River—no sign of human life. No one was working on the land; no one was picking mustard from the fields spread out in yellowish rectangles. A faint red smudge—poppies, blood red, still bloomed bravely on the edge of the Gross field. . . .

Was Father right? Last night at supper he had said, "Any man's a fool to waste time here—wind, dust, no rain, no trees to bind the soil and hold moisture if we did get it!"

When Mother ventured, "At least, we have a good deep well with a pump and a windmill," he had snorted, "What in hell's one well? The whole East is panicked—the Middle West is ruined—everybody moving out, and you mention a well! The only sensible course is to go to the Far West—to a well watered place with heavy timber—the Flat Head Valley, say, or even"—hopefully—"the Peace River country."

Early as it was, a warm breeze already stirred over the hills, rattling the stalks of the coneflowers on the rim. Down the hill far below her, the only oasis in the desert of desolation, the grass was still green on the tongue of land—the Indian Camp Ground—and the ponds on either side. In the big pond south of it the water was low but the grass was lush and tall. The smaller pond to the north of the camp was dry, and it was filled with Canada anemone plants, their creamy blossoms gleaming like stars against the green of their foliage. She would leave this empty place and go and gather a bunch of the anemones for Mrs. Reid.

Michal reached the gentle slope of the pond's edge and, looking ahead at the flowers, stepped inside before she saw it—the fairy circle! An old Indian ring—so close to the pond's edge that it was ordinarily covered with water—had been transformed overnight. Among the pale boulders, supported on sturdy stems—mushrooms gleamed, from tiny buttons to giants, their caps as smooth and creamy white as the anemone petals beyond them—their delicate pink gills revealed beneath the pileous where the thin protective caul had torn.

If in the hot darkness of night the union of spores and moist fecund earth had produced this miracle of beauty, the prairie could not

266

fail. So vivid was the message to her of renewed hope, of bountiful crops and good years yet to come, that as she turned away she glanced toward the big pond half expecting to see the great white crane. But he was not there.

Michal walked to the big pond and, dipping her handkerchief in the water, wrapped it carefully about the bouquet she had gathered. Then, as she scrambled up the steep bank to head for Reids', her foot dislodged a clod of earth. As it fell Michal saw in the bank a shining black object. She picked it from the ledge. It was the first obsidian arrowhead she had ever found. How had it come here? Had some far distant enemy tribesman thrown it in battle with the Dakotas? Tucking the black shining prize in her corset cover and smiling happily as she thought how Lewis would enjoy it, she hurried toward town.

The soft plink of a banjo greeted her as, discreetly removing the arrowhead from its hiding place, she hurried onto the Reid porch. "Just look what I've found!" she exclaimed, bubbling with excitement.

Languidly Lewis rose from the hammock where he had been lying, idly strumming on his instrument. "You're a little late. Mother's waiting inside."

"I know. But I found a fairy ring down by the pond, and got so excited; then this—"

Mrs. Reid's tinkling laugh greeted them through the cool restful sitting room. "And what have you found now, dear? Oh, lovely anemones!"

"Yes, for you"—handing them to her hostess. Triumphantly Michal held out her arrowhead in the palm of her hand for them both to see.

"Just an old arrowhead! The way you acted, I thought you *had* something," Lewis said scornfully.

Michal whirled on him. "Where's your imagination? It's not only the arrowhead—but how it got there; who shot it; who made it; how long—"

"Anybody would think you were ten years old. Why don't you grow up?" He collapsed into a chair, running his palm rhythmically over the banjo strings.

"Well, I hope I never grow up if it means losing interest in little things, or big things, or just the fact of being alive—the way some people I know have." And she shot him a dark glance as she sat down.

Mrs. Reid's laugh tinkled again as she arranged the flowers. "How good it is to hear you two squabbling again. This house was a tomb all winter. After 'Rica left in April—"

"Is 'Rica gone? I didn't know."

"Didn't Mavis tell you?" She lowered her voice, glancing kitchen-ward. "My dear, *what* I've gone through! 'Rica's mother got sick—lung fever, I think—and 'Rica had to go home. So Mr. Reid found Lisbet." She raised her hands and wrinkled her nose. "Broken English, of course; so I thought I was off to a good start. However, I soon found that she was the outdoor type. She'd work all morning in my flower garden, and insisted on milking and caring for the cow. James was delighted until one day he saw her water Blossom from the milkpail, then sit down and milk her in the same pail. Then there was the day I went into the kitchen for something and found her sitting on the floor peeling potatoes and putting the parings carefully in a pan of water, with the potatoes arranged in a neat semicircle on the floor in front of her." She shrugged daintily. "However, I've trained her and she'll do until 'Rica gets back next month."

A tiny clock on the mantel struck the hour—a delicate chime like a pin on crystal. "Isn't that new?" asked Michal delightedly.

"Yes, James got it for my anniversary present."

As they talked, of Madison, new fashions, the dryness of the weather—Michal became aware that Lewis was watching her intently, saying little. Nervously, she talked on until the sudden clatter of hoof-beats and a loud pounding on the front door interrupted.

Mrs. Reid frowned faintly. "What on earth! Lewis, will you please go?"

He came back in a moment. "Somebody to see Lisbet. I sent them to the back."

Michal peered out curiously as the horses clattered around the house. "Bright rings on the horses. Looks like *Hochzeit*."

"You're as bad as Mrs. Pratt," snapped Lewis. "Peering—"

"Don't be rude, son."

"I'm sorry," he muttered, sinking back into his chair.

From the kitchen came the sound of voices, talking loudly, in German.

"What in the world—" Mrs. Reid exclaimed.

"I'll put a stop to it—" Lewis half rose.

268

"No, no. For goodness' sake don't do anything to offend her now. I'll put up with anything—"

The dining-room door burst open and Lisbet walked in, a broad smile on her face. "I go now, Mis' Reid," she announced gaily.

"Go—now? But tomorrow is your afternoon off."

"I go for goot. I marry."

"Marry?"

"Ja. The man out dere."

"Aren't these men your relatives?"

"Nein. I nefer see dem before."

"But who are they? What do they mean, coming to this house—"

"I haf not ask his name yet. But he haf two quarter-sections."

Lewis rose. "You mean you'd leave us in the lurch—leave here now with a man whose name you don't know!"

She shrugged. "He got two goot claims. If I not take him today he go ask odder girls. Dey get him—and two goot claims."

Mrs. Reid's voice held a beseeching note. "But, Lisbet, you can't do this to me! I never heard of such a thing. Marrying a complete stranger. Besides, you aren't ready. No bedding, no hope chest. You told me that yourself not long ago."

Lisbet shrugged again. "It iss better to marry and not be reaty as to be reaty and not be marry."

"Very well. Lewis, will you pay her? And help her with her things."

"The pay, yes. Dey help me. Gootbye."

"Goodbye. Good luck." She added faintly, sinking back, face tragic, "In all my life I never expected to hear of such an uncivilized—"

"Surely you've heard of *Hochzeit*? Katie told me about it long ago. They make a list of girls and dress themselves and their horses all up. A sort of professional matchmaker goes along—he's called a *Koppelsmann*. They ride to the different places until they find a girl who will marry the boy."

Mrs. Reid shook her head, then said petulantly: "James convinced me that there was money to be made in this frontier town. But every year I realize more clearly that we made a horrible mistake in coming here. Now I'm without help again—'Rica won't be back for a month—" Her voice broke. "Lewis," she wailed as he reentered, "you'll have to go right down and get your father. He's got to find me someone right away."

"But, Mother, Michal has come for dinner—"

269

"Michal, dear, you'll just have to come some other time. You can see—" She waved her hands vaguely.

"Mrs. Reid, why not let me finish the cooking and serve it in here? At home we often have meals on the center table—"

"No, my dear. I could never do that to a guest. I've got to know that James is looking for somebody right away—"

Later, after Lewis had relayed the news to his father, Michal said coolly, "You needn't bother to walk home with me."

"What's wrong with you?" demanded Lewis.

"If you must know, I didn't particularly enjoy being compared to Mrs. Pratt."

He grabbed her hand. "Let's go over to the pond and see the Indian ring. Then I'll explain."

They took the short-cut through the ravine and stopped by the boulder where she had rested her head against his shoulder that Fourth of July evening a year ago. Everything was dry even here; it was not the cool shady retreat of other years.

Nervously, Lewis leaned against the boulder and cleared his throat. "Of course, you're not like Mrs. Pratt. But you have the curiosity about people and a sort of excitement over everything that—well, that you had the first day I met you."

"What's wrong with that? For me you're not as much fun as you used to be because you've lost it."

"Well, but you're grown up now. I want my wife to be above this small-town stuff of peering out of windows. The girls your age back East would never dream of—"

"What you're trying to say is that you want me to change. To be like your mother. And your Eastern girls. Well, I won't. I'm the way I am, and I always will be. And since you don't like it, I'm through." Even as she spoke the words a sudden feeling of relief swept over her.

"You don't mean that."

"I do."

Drawing her close he said quietly, "You're my girl, and I'm not going to give you up."

She stood cool and still in the circle of his arms until, in desperation he leaned his head down against the curve of her neck and shoulder. The small-boy gesture pierced her heart, and with gentle hands she touched his hair. "All right, Lewis. I'm still your girl."

Then he kissed her fiercely and hurried away. Michal watched him go, a tender smile softening her face. He was nice.

She went home by way of the pond in order to see once more the fairy ring. But it was gone, the mushrooms black and dead under the hot midday sun.

XII

The next afternoon Abigail Pratt and Fanny came charging in about teatime. Michal's heart sank. Mother looked tired; her eyes were enormous in her white face. But as always she listened courteously as Abigail Pratt settled down for a good gossip.

"Thanks, Mis' Ward, I will take a cup o' tea; it's quite a climb up this hill and I'm dry as a bone. I was sayin' t' Fanny as we come up, you certainly look awful this time. I'd ruther be in Tophet with my neck broke than be in a family way; but, as I've told you before, you're like a cow havin' a calf—just like that," snapping her fingers, "and no trouble a-tall. Speakin' of having babies, I run in on Mrs. Gotthelf the other morning. When she didn't come to the door, I went around back; and there—far along as she is—she was in a Mother Hubbard, out in the back yard actually mixin' sand and black dirt—topsoil, she calls it— with a shovel. She had on some old drivin' gloves of Doc's, and smiled and ast me to sit down on the washbench and watch her. I said wasn't she afraid she'd strain something, but she said no, it was such a fine morning she felt like gettin' out, and besides, she wanted to plant the first of her imported bulbs—did you ever see such a woman for bulbs— and when she finished she ast me in. Her dishes were done, but her bed wasn't made up and it was all of nine o'clock. She wasn't the least mite embarrassed, either, but ast me to sit down and I did and proceeded to tell her just what I thought of Achsah Klunk and her marriage." Mrs. Pratt finally had to stop for breath.

"What do you think of it?" Michal's voice was curious.

"Just what I told her—the very idea of a woman who washes for railroad men having the gall to deck herself out in white—and with a wreath—and a veil besides!"

"It's her first marriage. What's wrong with white if she wants it, and even a veil and a wreath? She joined the church, too, didn't she?" demanded Michal.

"Yes, and I wonder how she got in—a common—"

"How do you know she's common?"

"Now that's exactly what Mis' Gotthelf ast me—how did I know! Then she ast me if I had ever read somewhere in the Bible something like 'To the pure are all things pure.' So, rather'n argue with her, I went home. I jest said, smooth-like, "I must run along now, Mrs. G., so's you'll have time to make your bed."

"What did she say?"

"Jest laughed and said something about being glad to air it."

When the Pratts finally rose to leave and Mother said, "Do you mind if I'm lazy and don't go to the door with you?" Michal knew something was wrong. The door closed behind them.

"How do you stand it, Mother? Like a cow indeed!"

"After all, I enjoy having my babies. Please have Hetty come help me while you call the doctor."

"Is it—"

"Yes. I had pains most of the time they were here."

"Mother! You usually have so few."

"I know—but this time it's different."

It was. After five hours of hard labor, with father fuming, swearing, and pacing as usual, "Go to bed, Michal, and get your sleep," said Dr. Gotthelf. "Hetty's about worn out, and she'll need you tomorrow."

"Can't I help now?"

"No—I'm sending for my wife, Kathleen."

"But—"

"I know, but I'll see that she doesn't overdo. She's a graduate nurse, remember, and she'll know just what to do. Good night, my dear. Don't worry—it'll be all right with your mother." He smiled and went back into the bedroom.

Reassured, Michal went to bed and finally slept. In her dreams she heard moans and, once, a scream, quickly suppressed. She stole downstairs at dawn. Dr. Gotthelf and his wife were just leaving. Tired as she was, Kathleen smiled. "Good morning, Michal. You have a lovely little sister, plump as a butterball, and your mother is resting well."

272

XIII

Elizabeth was a good baby, sleeping deeply when she wasn't nursing lustily. For three weeks Mavis stayed in bed, but when she did get up her strength did not return. Faith took over the care of Philip and David; Michal almost never left the house, for Hetty's rheumatism was bad and she had more than she could do alone.

However, sometimes on warm evenings she slipped down to visit with Katie, who never tired of discussing her remarkable little "Yosh" and Adolph Baur, who dropped by Keims' often these days. She seldom mentioned Karl, and in some obscure way Michal was glad. Glad too that she hadn't seen him; he always disturbed her and made her relationship with Lewis somehow unreal. Besides, after a year away at school, he would seem crude.

Since their quarrel Lewis had been charming, coming often—taking her for walks when she could get away, talking always of their future, pressing her to set a definite wedding date by next summer at the latest. They discussed the home they would have, not a jumble of lambrequins, gimp, fringe, potted plants, and what-nots to distract the eye and mind, but an orderly place for orderly people. She could slip away in her mind from the heat, fretful children, and her increasingly irritable father, and dream of a cool, orderly existence with her devoted, nice-looking, well-to-do husband. Like a dream, Karl faded more and more from her mind.

One warm windy midsummer morning, Michal slipped into her pink barred muslin, tied the sash, then surveyed herself in the mirror. The dress became her with its simply cut round neck, puff sleeves, tight basque and full skirt which accented her tiny waist. She had worn it the night before when Lewis had taken her to the Kickapoo Indian Sagwa' show; memory of a few moments there turned her cheeks as pink as the pink in her dress.

Michal had been excited by the buckboards, the gaslight, the spieler who, with his long white hair à la Buffalo Bill, roared that he shampooed it with Kickapoo Indian Sagwa'—good for everythin' that ever ailed man or beast.

Lewis had caught her mood as they pushed through the crowd. "You like this, don't you, Michal?"

"It's raw and wild and crazy, and I love it! I love the dark and the heat and the dust and the gas flame and the feeling of being part of it!"

"You are part of it." Lewis gripped her arms and turned her toward him, completely caught in her mood. "You're ice and flame and air and earth and all the things there are. I want to kiss you."

Then he had drawn her away from the torchlight into a pocket of darkness and had crushed her close and kissed her. She had loved it. He had taken her home, presently, with a parting, "I'll see you in the morning."

Secretly, last night in her bed, Michal planned the bedroom they'd have after they were married. Woodwork pale pink like the sky at dawn. Plain wallpaper, silvery green like the tender sage leaves in Mrs. Reid's herb garden. Cool cream Chinese matting for the floor, with hints of pink and green. Curtains of pink cheesecloth—ruffled. A nightgown of muslin with pink rosebuds to match. The creamy pink shell Mrs. Oulette had given her so long ago on the top of her desk. A lovely room, but was it too feminine? It was a girl's room. Karl would look out of place in it, she thought, and frowned as she imagined him looking it over critically, a derisive smile on his face. Now why did *he* have to come into it and spoil everything? Besides, she hadn't thought of him in ages.

When Mavis called to announce Lewis's arrival, Michal started guiltily, fastened a gold heart-shaped locket about her neck, then hurried downstairs, pleasantly conscious of the swish of her lace petticoats.

"Hello." Lewis spoke eagerly, his face alight; and Michal hurried to him thinking, It's still here, what we had last night.

"Where are you two going?" Mavis asked, smiling.

"Nowhere, I guess. The wind's blowing like mad."

"Well, wind or no wind, I need some dried citron, and I need it quick." This was Hetty, in the doorway, arms akimbo, looking belligerent.

"Philip can run down—" began Mavis, but Lewis interrupted.

"We'll get it, Hetty. We won't even have to walk. The wind'll blow us downhill."

Lewis was right. Before they were off the porch Michal was hugging her knees to keep her skirts from blowing above her head. "Let's race." Lewis grabbed her hand and they tore down the hill. As laugh-

274

ing and breathless they slowed down in front of Keims', Katie called from the front door, "Michal, Lewis—come in. See Yosh."

"Come on," gasped Michal, pulling Lewis after her. "I need to rest a minute."

The Keim *Stube* was dark and quiet after the sun and wind outside. As her eyes adjusted to the dimness, Michal saw Karl sprawled in a chair across the room, baby Joshua on one shoulder rapturously pulling his hair. As he rose and the two men shook hands, Michal noticed that he towered over them all—he was well over six feet—and that in spite of his faded blue work shirt and overalls, tucked carelessly into his high boots, he was as assured as always.

"Put Yosh down, Karl," urged Katie. "Now, Michal, watch." Clapping her hands and stamping one foot in monotonous rhythm, Katie intoned, "*Zu Lauterbach hab' ich mein' Strumpf verlor'n.*"

The little boy stood uncertainly, head lowered, lashes down; then in a spasm of shyness turned and ran to Karl, who lifted him with practiced ease and seated himself again. Katie shrugged resignedly. "See. A minute ago he show off, dance and clap like a little monkey. Now—notting. It iss always so!"

"Oh, Katie, that's the way they all are," exclaimed Michal, hurrying over to Karl and Joshua. "You just don't know babies. Here—Josh —come to Michal." She knelt down, holding out her arms, deliberately using soft appeal and restraint. "Come, darling, come to Michal."

For answer Joshua buried his face once more in Karl's chest, yet turned enough to peek mischievously sideways at her. "He's a shy little coot, isn't he?" observed Lewis.

"Shy, nothing!" snorted Michal. "He always comes to me. Karl, will you quit looking so maddeningly superior? All right, stay with him!" And she rose, half amused, half irritated.

Instantly Joshua held out his arms to her. "You little rascal," chuckled Michal as she took him from Karl. "My, but he's heavy. How much does he weigh?"

"Twenty-six pounds," said Katie, trying to look modest and failing entirely.

As Michal sat down she was not unaware of the picture she must make, holding the rosy blond child, her own cheeks warmly pink, her hair loosened from the run downhill. When Joshua spotted her gold locket and touched it tentatively with a fat forefinger, she smiled at Karl.

275

He didn't return her smile, but his moody dark eyes held her own so steadily that for a moment she was pierced by the same sweet wild pain she had felt years before when he had kissed her that dusky evening after the prairie fire.

"It's a good thing you like babies." Lewis's voice and eyes were adoring as he walked to her and gently pushed back a lock of hair that had loosened. "I want at least a dozen. We'd better get that citron or Hetty'll kill us."

Mrs. Keim, exuding warm German hospitality, bustled in as Michal rose. "Katie, you the citron get. I haf *Kaffeekuchen und—*"

"Thanks, but we can't stay, Mrs. Keim. Hetty was in an awful hurry."

"Then the goot raisin wine—a small glass only," she begged.

"Another time, thank you," said Lewis as Katie returned and handed him the citron.

Mrs. Keim turned to her nephew. "The coffee—"

"*Schnaps*," he said curtly.

"Before noon?" Her plump face was raised incredulously.

"*Ja*."

As with much tch-tch-tching and head shaking over the whisky drinker she ushered her guests to the door, Michal—swept by a curious unease—looked back and met Karl's glance fully, and her heart quailed before the naked intensity of his gaze. He's jealous, she thought; he's so mad he doesn't even care if I see it. Then the mask fell. He turned away. But all the way up the hill Michal remembered his face, the dark flesh darker than usual, the jaw set hard as stone.

Pulsing waves of heat, punctured by the rattling whir of grasshoppers—black wings red-bordered—rose from the parched prairie. Michal could not read; her thoughts rose like the heat waves from the earth; and doubts—black and fiery—whirring like giant insects, rasped her mind. She left the chair and perched herself on the wide porch railing. If only Lewis were not so proprietory. If only he hadn't mentioned the twelve babies before Karl. Why did she always forget Lewis and think of Karl when the two boys were together? Why—and this most of all— had this foreign boy, at every chance meeting, the power to disturb her so profoundly? Why? Why? And a mocking echo came as if in answer with hoofbeats from the south.

Karl on his stallion Blitz flashed through the entrance and up the

276

driveway. As Michal sprang to her feet, Karl saw her, swerved Blitz across the lawn, tearing up the grass, and reined him in so suddenly where Michal stood that he reared.

"Karl, are you drunk—or crazy?"

"Both." He leaned forward, hot black eyes burning.

"Why did you come here?"

"You know the custom of my people."

She knew. Blitz was brushed until his coat was black satin; bright ribbons streamed from saddle and bridle; his headstall and reins were decorated with harness rings of blue, red, ivory; Karl himself was immaculate, his astrakhan cap perched at a jaunty angle, a scarlet home-dyed scarf tied carelessly about his blouse; his high Russian boots polished like mirrors. Over both him and the horse was the strong smell of *Schnaps.*

Her heart was pounding. "Get out of here before somebody sees you," she murmured quickly, walking over to the step and standing below him.

"Vy?"

"They might guess—"

"Ya." He laughed, baring his even white teeth. "They might guess I could haf you, if I vant." He leaned down, and she shrank back before the even fury in his eyes. "Dot Lewis, he is no man."

"You're jealous," she taunted softly.

He shrugged unsteadily. "I haf come to you first."

She curled her lip scornfully. "Are you going from house to house now, asking girls you've barely met?"

"I need go to one other house only. There I shall not be refused."

"Then go to her," she blazed furiously. "I'm not an animal to be bought. You've come here to insult me. And you've done it. I hope you're happy."

Leaning down, he thrust his hand into the heavy knot of her hair and, pulling her head back until she was looking up full in his face, muttered: "I, too, can touch your hair. Not as he does, your Lewis, but as a man with a woman."

She felt her face go bloodless. "My father will horsewhip you for this," she whispered.

"No man touches me." He laughed softly, mirthlessly. "Remember what I haf said, Michal Ward. I could haf you if I wanted." Releasing her suddenly, he wheeled Blitz abruptly and was gone.

Michal, her knees shaking, watched him—frightened by the curious emptiness she felt at his going. At the entrance, the black horse swerved to avoid John Ward. He whirled and looked after horse and rider. Then, as he turned and came striding up the driveway, He can't believe what he sees, she thought; and struggled vainly against a hysterical desire to laugh.

The door slammed as Faith hurried out, looking puzzled. "How long has that Rooshan been here?"

"Just a minute or so. Did Mother—"

"She's asleep." Faith's eyes were enormous. "What—"

"Sh-h-h-h!"

Father came up the porch steps demanding, "What was young Gross doing here, Michal?"

"Just a crazy prank. He'd been drinking, I think."

"I came to the door in time to hear him tell Michal he could have her if he wanted her. What did he mean, Father?" asked Faith.

John Ward's gray eyes narrowed. "By God! I'll put an end to his insolence!" Wheeling, he stalked quickly back toward the stables.

"I hope you're satisfied, Faith. You've really started something."

"What will he do?" Faith asked uneasily, then, confidently, "He'll put that Rooshan in his place, anyway." And the screen door closed behind her.

Michal did not leave the porch. In this reckless, raging mood, Father might do something terrible. Nervously she walked back and forth, listening. She did not have long to wait. Father, up behind Fury, who was hitched to the racing sulky, went skimming down the driveway, heading for town.

Her thoughts were swift. He will go south through town, west for over a mile, then north. If I cut across the prairie I can make it.

She darted down the hill. The sun was low, and it was cooler now, but she ran until her heart hammered and she was breathing through her mouth—great gulps of air. As she skirted the edge of the pond she heard—far off—the quick hoofbeats. Father has him under control, she thought, as she ducked down on the rim of the pond behind the high bank screened by reeds and cattails; then, while she recovered her breath her ear caught the hoofbeats, closer now, the distinctive rhythmic swing of the born pacer.

Peering out, she caught glimpses of the powerful forequarters of the big bay horse swaying smoothly and evenly along, approaching at

278

a swift clip. She was slipping—looked down to find a secure footing—and in that instant the pattern of steady rhythm changed to a wild, irregular staccato. The big bay was rearing, lunging from side to side of the road, a plunging demon, and Father was working grimly to subdue him.

Just opposite where Michal stood, silhouetted sharply against the near-setting sun, Fury stopped abruptly. Had Father really conquered him—and so soon? Then, deliberately, the pacer, lowering his snaky head and looking back at his owner as though taking aim, lashed out with both hind feet, straight at Father's head. Father never took his eyes from the horse. He dodged the blow, working hard in the meantime with the reins to raise Fury's head. Then Michal's heart sank and her body chilled with fear. For she saw now that Father had, when harnessing, in his anger, either forgotten or deliberately neglected to put kicking straps on Fury—and the checkrein was hanging loose, or had broken in the struggle.

Fury's head was still down. Again he turned, looked back at Father as though taking deliberate aim; again the vicious hoofs lashed out; again John Ward dodged, pulling back hard on the reins. . . . Again and again the scene was repeated—the crafty stallion diabolical in his rage; John Ward coolly anticipating and parrying every thrust of the plunging heels so close to his head. All this Michal saw against the red ball of the near-setting sun. She could not stir—dared not cry out. Father needed every sense alert, sharpened, if he were to win.

For what seemed unending time she stood, tense with fear, waiting for the outcome of the struggle. Finally it seemed that Fury was tiring. Blood-flecked foam testified that the bit was cutting the stallion's mouth. He tossed his head high; Father pulled the reins taut, and now could ply the whip.

As suddenly as Fury had gone into his rage he recovered. Head high, he paced beautifully to the north fork of the road, responded obediently at the command to turn, and took his master smoothly, swiftly, back over the road he had traveled before. Father was safe, and he had not gone to the Gross place. There would be no quarrel, no violence. There would be no—she had to admit it—struggle within herself as to where her loyalty would lie. It had been a furious fight, but not a long one, for the sun was just disappearing on the western horizon.

Michal relaxed her clenched fists and expelled her breath in a loud, deep sigh. Her palms were sore where her nails had dug into them.

She was out watching Gus clean the padded box stall when Father, now in excellent spirits, brought the bay stallion home. Together they went out to meet him.

"Some workout you musta give him this time, eh?"

"Plenty strenuous workout, Gus! I drove him on the road for miles and twice around the track besides. I'll help you."

The big bay stood tractably for the rubdown. "Seems to me, Mr. Ward, he's taming down a mite o' late—no kicking straps, even."

"Might be," admitted Father with a grim smile. "I'll let him run in the broncs' corral until he wants to go into his box stall. You just put oats in his manger and open the door connecting with his stall so he may go in when he likes. Then you finish the other chores—Mike and I can put him in the corral."

The breaking corral was high and made of strong heavy planks nailed close together. Fury went in without protest. He walked quietly to the far side, turned. Then, deliberately, with head up and tail raised, he paced briskly across the open space, climbed the side of the corral and—still pacing beautifully—headed northwest for the brow of the hill.

"God, Michal—did you see that?" Father's voice was tinged with awe. "I never dreamed any horse living could climb that corral."

Fury's hoofbeats, steady and rhythmic, came back to them clearly. As on that long-ago day when they had stood side by side admiring the black ox that had come to them up out of the mist, so again they stood in admiration as the hoofbeats, muffled now by grass and distance, came faintly, more faintly, and finally died away in the dusk.

"You'll advertise for him, Father?" she asked quietly.

"I'll be damned if I do. After all"—his voice was wistful, almost sad—"he's going west where he belongs. He may go clear to the Peace River Valley for all of me."

XIV

As the days shortened to the pale dusty gold of late summer, it became clear that Michal could not return to Normal School. Mavis was up and around again; but she tired easily, and for the first time in Michal's

280

memory her children made her nervous. In addition, Father's restlessness weighed heavily on her mind.

After Fury's disappearance he went to Montana again and came back with more horses and broncobusters. But this time he talked even more glowingly of the Far West, and showed little enthusiasm for his selling trip to Ohio.

Dispiritedly, Michal mailed her letter to Florence containing the final answer: "Mother is still not strong. She needs me." Then she went over to the Reids'. Lewis was packing; he came in when he heard Michal's voice. "Well, I'll soon be on my way."

"It'll be fun getting back—seeing your friends?" She tried to keep the wistful note out of her voice.

Mrs. Reid spoke quickly. "Poor dear. I'm sorry you can't go back. But for your mother's sake—I'm glad you're staying."

Lewis lit his pipe solemnly. "Speaking of school, did you know that Karl Gross is going to South Dakota Agricultural College?"

"No!" Michal turned in genuine surprise.

"Yep. I saw Katie on the street yesterday with her little boy. He's a smart little tyke, isn't he? Well, I stopped to pinch his cheek. Mentioned that I was leaving this week, and she told me about Gross. Rather bragged about it."

"Isn't he a Rooshan boy?" Mrs. Reid asked.

"Yes, a cousin of Katie's."

"Well, I think that's terrible. A foreigner going off to school, while Michal, here, has to stay home!"

Lewis sucked his pipe meditatively. "Well, I'll say this for the beggar, he's bright enough. Arrogant devil, though. I never have liked him."

Michal kept very still. After all, what difference if Karl were going? It meant nothing to her. But as she took her leave she thought, What a dull time I'll have this winter, with Lewis gone and nothing to look forward to!

Walking home by way of the ravine, she sniffed deeply the early fall scents—of dust and drying leaves, and smoke from a far-off prairie fire. The air was thick with milkweed balloons and long trailing cobwebs. The ravine was forlorn, the only sign of life a fusty bumblebee working in a small frostbitten thistle bloom.

As she went up the swale her skirts swished against the dry grass and faded goldenrod on either side. Soon the tumbleweeds would be gray foam in October winds, like that day, nearly a year ago now, when she and Karl had ridden toward Hillsview together. Today the earth gave her nothing—only intensified her feeling of loneliness. From the north came the plaintive call of a plover, pausing briefly on his way south.

Father came back from Ohio in high spirits and loaded with gifts. Hetty was particularly pleased with the brown oilcloth for the kitchen floor. But Mavis said privately to Michal, "What will I ever do with half a dozen pairs of Paris gloves? And Brussels lace curtains, when I so much need a new carpet."

Her daughter eyed her severely. "When I marry Lewis, I'll see to it that I have what I want and not what he thinks I should have—the way Father has always done."

Mavis smiled. "How are you going to manage it? After all, the men handle the money."

"I can handle Lewis. If I need a carpet I'll have a carpet—not curtains."

Through the time of black frost and white snowfalls, John Ward —whenever he was home—paced the floor, and Mother's eyes were filled with shadows as he talked gloomily of the financial situation. "It's no wonder—with Congress considering an income tax! With the country in such a fix the only sensible thing to do is to locate in a place with plenty of water where we can raise all our own food. Dakota doesn't have water. Look what's happened to crops here the past two years!"

Mavis's soft lips tightened. "All right, John. Go ahead. But I'm staying here. I'm not taking this new baby out into the wilds of Montana—away from Dr. Gotthelf . . ." Her voice faltered.

"God damn it, I'm not asking you to! I'm only thinking of the future."

"Panic or no panic, you're earning plenty; we have a comfortable home—even though we do need a new carpet. Michal is engaged to the nicest boy in town. What kind of parents would we be to even consider leaving here?"

"All right. We'll stay here and starve to death. But don't say I didn't warn you."

After that, Father was silent, but he was still restless. In January the whole family came down with heavy colds, Hetty's joints were badly swollen with her "rheumatiz," and Father gloomily read aloud

282

and at length of the Wall Street panic and suicides back East. Even letters from Lewis failed to help, for he seemed cheerfully oblivious of everything but school.

"I feel as though this whole winter has been a bad dream," Michal said in a hollow voice as she mixed a gargle of salt, vinegar, and black pepper. "Florence writes of black satin neckties and umbrella skirts and midnight suppers, and we do nothing but wipe our noses, gargle vinegar, and fight."

Mavis modestly turned her back, put Elizabeth to her breast, then settled back comfortably. "Hard as it's been, it is good training for marriage."

"Maybe. But there are times when I feel like chewing the furniture."

"You're a great deal like your father. It would help you if you would lean more on God. He is my greatest source of strength."

"Religion means a lot to you, doesn't it, Mother?"

"Without it I'd have lost my mind." Mavis spoke quietly, fondling Elizabeth's soft brown hair. "When we buried Little Brother that day out there on all that prairie—"

"I remember," softly.

"If you ever lose a child you'll learn how much you need God. When I was your age I went to church as you do—from habit, mostly. But now church is part of me. I want all of my children to have what I have for the rest of their lives."

Michal leaned forward tensely. "I've never told you this, and I don't know whether I can say it very well; but through the years I've come to feel that it doesn't matter what church one goes to—or if one goes at all. Achsah Klunk tries them all. Sometimes she doesn't go. But she leads a Christian life. If anybody needs her, she's there."

Mavis frowned faintly. "Achsah has done many fine things, it is true. But there is a certain quality about the people in our church. Besides, the Presbyterian doctrine is right."

"Maybe it is. But have you ever stopped to think what would happen if Christ came to Eureka tomorrow? Do you really believe that He'd ignore everybody else and come to our church first?"

"Certainly," returned Mavis crisply.

"I wonder. I can sort of picture Him talking to everybody—people on the street, Rooshan farmers, rich families, poor families, everybody. I think He'd even talk to those women at the Bad House."

"Michal!"

"But it says so in the Bible. I've read it and so have you."

Mavis shook her head sadly. "Sometimes I wonder if you are my daughter. Your whole life, everything you've ever done almost, has been a puzzle to me."

"I'm too young to have it all thought out yet. But someday I'll know, and be able to help you see why I feel the way I do. Meanwhile, I've got to make my own mistakes and do my own thinking."

"You've always done things the hard way, child. God taught me love through tears, and maybe that's how you'll learn, too. If you'd only listen to me, I could save you so much grief. Someday you'll know what I mean. In the meantime, be patient with your father."

And as Father's increasing irritability struck a spark to her own, and they quarreled, Michal turned seriously to God, as she had not done since she had prayed to Him years before for the valentine.

Yet all the hours she spent—earnestly listening to the Reverend Crum, reading the Bible, or praying in her room—went for nothing when Father made one of his unreasonably violent remarks.

"Don't oppose him," warned Mavis. "He's not used to it."

"But last year in school we were taught to think for ourselves. Father doesn't know everything."

"A wise woman keeps her thoughts to herself. Prayer might help you with that temper, daughter."

"I have prayed. Then Father says something irritating and I forget."

Tensions came to a climax one bitter February morning. Father threw down his paper irritably and, rising from the table, began putting on his coat. "My God! Why do they let women around horses! Here's a woman in the North who ran down a child just because she didn't know how to handle a team. Hetty, dip me some warm reservoir water, please."

Michal scowled. "Well, men have runaways and accidents too."

Ignoring her, Father picked up the filled pail of water and went on mulishly: "They twitch the reins. Do everything wrong. Never saw it fail yet."

"I still say that men make as many silly mistakes. Let me tell you, Father, women are coming into their own. Someday we'll have the vote."

284

"See?" he whirled on Mavis. "You wanted her to go to school. And this is what happens—she's telling me."

Michal felt the blood drain from her face, but she turned and faced him. "If I've learned to start thinking for myself a little—is there any harm in that?" She smiled maddeningly. "Anyway, don't worry about women drivers, Father. Lewis says that horses are going to be replaced by those new gasoline-driven carriages."

John Ward's eyes went hard as granite. "One more word out of you, girl, and I throw this water over you!"

"Go ahead—throw it!"

For an instant the room crackled with tension. Then, with a curious little half-smile, Father turned and—without a word—left the house.

Michal sat down by the table, buried her face in her arms, and wept bitterly.

"You shouldn't cross him, and you know how he feels about those gasoline carriages. Whatever got into you?"

"I don't know. He's so sure of everything that it drives me wild."

"Please don't antagonize him." Mavis's voice trembled. "The way he's been lately—it wouldn't take much to give him an excuse to leave here."

"But you told him you wouldn't go, Mother. I heard you myself."

"I said that; but you know and he knows that I always will." As she tiptoed in to the baby, Michal again rested her head wearily on the table. By the stove, Rory stirred in his sleep. Hetty, muttering ominously to herself, began picking up the dishes.

After the quarrel, Mavis insisted that Michal get away from the house at least once or twice a week. Bundling herself and David up against the first slush and mud and damp wet winds of March, they made calls.

Achsah Klunk O'Dell, in the section house down near the mill, was a beaming bride. Michal was ushered through the rooms and was ordered to admire the new organ, complete with plants reflected in the square mirror against the back, and the top draped with cord-ball fringe. "Even Mrs. Pratt come over to see it." Achsah chuckled gleefully.

"Tell me about you and Danny. When I left last year I didn't even dream you were in love."

285

"We wasn't, then. But I liked him and he begun comin' down to see me regular after it got cold and I figgered I was one reason he didn't go back west. Anyway, I'll never forget the day he proposed. It had been a hard day. The Presbyterian Ladies' Aid had gave a chicken dinner and Reverent Crum had tried to get me to jine his church and I wouldn't. I like the Methodist better—and told him so, and so he come out where I was eatin' with Danny and said, half jokin'-like, "What'll you be doin' when you're down in Hell, Achsah?" And because he said it before Danny, and because my corns was hurtin' something fierce account of my standin' all day to cook the meal, I answered, 'Cookin' for Presbyterian preachers, probably, same as here.' Wish you could of heard Danny laugh.

"Reverent Crum was a bit peeved, and says he to me, 'A Christian doesn't talk that way'; and Danny speaks right up an' says, quiet-like, 'I hope Reverent you're not incinerating anything against Achsah—she's the best God dam' Christian in this town.'" At the memory Achsah's laugh boomed out, the full hearty laughter of a deep-bosomed woman. "It done me a world o' good, and so when Danny took me home and asked me would I marry him, well, the kind o' night it was, soft and silvery—when you're glad you're a live woman and wish you had a good strong man to lie with—so, I says, gentle-like: 'Yes, Danny. For years now, come time for frost, I've been puttin' blankets over my wild-cucumber vines, and it'll seem good to marry you. I'm tired of puttin' cucumber vines to bed—I'd rather have a man.'"

"You know, what Danny said about you being a Christian is true. I tried to tell Mother what I felt not long ago—about Christ and what He'd do if He came to Eureka tomorrow—"

"I wisht He would," interrupted Achsah heartily. "I'd like to set Him down to a real good meal and wash his clothes and take him around to meet people and fix Him a soft bed to rest on. Lordy, how I'd love to do fer Him just a little o' what He's done fer me! And someways I think He'd be the easiest person in the world to talk with." Then she rose and rather diffidently straightened a picture a fraction of an inch. "But a course He *is* here all the time. He's a-watchin' the whole kit and kaboodle of us day and night, like I tell Danny."

"Well, you don't have to worry about that."

"Listen, child, I've done some mighty powerful sinnin' in my day, and don't you ferget it. If I can jist squeeze past St. Peter and sorta sneak Danny in too, I won't ask fer nothin' more. And if that blessed saint sez to me, 'Achsah, what you doin' here?' I'll tell him that if Danny and me kin stay I'll scrub them golden stairs till they shine."

Michal giggled. "You've sure got it all figured out."

"The world's my oyster now, Michal. I've got everything."

As Michal went on to call on the doctor's wife, she thought, Achsah's so full of joy some of it spills over for the rest of us.

Mrs. Gotthelf was bending over the baby's crib, and the air in her house was warm and fragrant with the scent of her latest blossom—today a hyacinth—freshly washed diapers drying in the kitchen, and the milky-clean baby smell over everything.

"You enjoy your baby the way Mother does hers," Michal said, watching the curves she made as she nursed the infant—arms, back, breasts curving about the child in warm, contented beauty.

"I want another and then another. My husband, babies, and plenty of flowers. That's enough for me."

Mrs. Reid shook her head when she heard this. "Flowers, yes. But she'll be old and shapeless in ten years if she keeps up that childbearing."

"I don't think clothes matter much to her."

"Poor thing! The clothes and homes that people endure in this town are enough to make me glad I can't get around more."

"Achsah Klunk has the newest sensation. Mrs. Pratt called on her just to see it—a square mirror against the back of her organ, plants reflected in it, and the top of the organ draped with cord-ball fringe."

Mrs. Reid shuddered. "Sounds atrocious!"

"Still"—Michal spoke thoughtfully—"If you hadn't taught me better, I might think it beautiful, too."

"Well, thank goodness I was here to save you, my dear. By the way, Lewis hinted in his last letter that he wants to make plans when he gets home."

Michal nodded. "I know. I've told him not to set his heart on anything until we see if Mother continues to get stronger."

"But she's better—"

"Yes, she is; but—I feel so unready for marriage. We've always had Hetty, and outside of helping with the children and keeping my own things in order—I've never learned much. Mother has always said that she wants Faith and me to look back on carefree girlhoods."

"And quite right she is, too. You'll learn fast enough. Besides, you'll always have servants. People of our class shouldn't grub in dirt

287

and dishwater. Mr. Reid and I will be glad when you two are married. I've had my heart set on this since the first time you children walked in here and I saw how much Lewis liked you. One of these days"—she smiled mysteriously—"there'll be a little surprise for you that may help you make up your mind."

Michal rose. "We'll see. I'm glad you and Mr. Reid approve of me for Lewis. And flattered."

She called to David, then strolled through gray streets. Everything was dark silver and damp with March. Even now the water was melting deep under the drifts, and soon the ravine would be running full. It would be a temptation to marry this year. Perhaps . . . So bemused was she that she almost bumped into Katie, who exclaimed delightedly, "Michal!"

"Katie! How are you? You haven't been up for so long."

The other shrugged, "A baby gifs much work."

"How is your family?"

"Mine—all fine. But Uncle Wilhelm broke his leg last week."

"How did he do that?"

"A fall. Tante Katrine says he wanted to. She is that mad! Because, you see, it means with spring's work that right away Karl must come home from Brookings."

XV

Soon the prairie, except on northern slopes, was bare of snow; again, high above the quiet brown fields that lay patiently waiting, flocks of wild geese patterned the sky in long rhythmic lines of flight.

The mood of winter fell from Michal like a dark garment. And now that she had come alive again, she felt a queer new intensity within herself. Smells of cooking; taste of food; the smooth feel of polished black walnut furniture; the fragrant plumpness of Elizabeth's warm little body. "I feel as though spring had come to me too, as it has to the prairie," she told Mavis.

"You're young and vital." Mother smiled.

"I didn't feel young this winter. Here comes Father with the children."

288

John Ward, smiling amiably, came in closely followed by Faith and Philip. "This came for you, Mike, so I picked the children up at school and came on out."

"Thank you, Father. Hetty has baked cornbread. You boys go and really wash your hands."

Michal opened the small box hurriedly. "Look—my ring!"

They all crowded about her as she slipped it on: a large black opal set in yellow gold. "It's the first black opal I've ever seen—I never dreamed of anything so gorgeous!" Michal said softly.

"Hetty says opals are bad luck." But Faith's eyes were envious.

"Superstition." Michal's voice was sharp, then it softened as she saw the tears ready to fall. "Better eat, Faith, or you'll be late for school."

After dinner Michal read Lewis's letter to Mavis: " 'You told me once that you liked opals best of all. Mother gave me this old family ring, and I brought it back with me to be put in a modern setting. Personally, I'd rather have gotten you a diamond or sapphire. But, knowing you, I believe you'd like something unusual. Then, somehow, it reminds me of you.

" 'Darling, you said you wanted a wide wedding band like your mother's. I saw a beauty the other day—heavy, very plain. I am bringing it home, hoping that this summer I may put it on your finger. And I don't want you ever to take it off. Write me that this may be true, as—' "

She broke off, blushing. Mavis smiled. "Lewis has shown his usual good taste. Now, why don't you take the rest of this beautiful day off and celebrate as you please?"

Michal's face brightened. "I'll go on the prairie. All this sun must have brought more flowers out. And down by the big pond there may be violets. It's so warm today, I'm going to put on that thin muslin summer dress—the one Lewis likes so. 'All-over-blue-flowers' he calls it. I want the feel of sun on myself."

"Better take a shawl in case a wind comes up. You know"—Mavis sank down in her chair by the window—"everything seems to be coming right again. Father hasn't said a word about Montana for quite a while. Hetty is better—and I'm well."

"Your cheeks are as pink as ever."

"But my hair is graying. It suited my purpose not to get well too quickly." Mother spoke slowly. "Your father must learn that we can't pull up roots the way we used to. And I think he's beginning to realize it, after what I said last year. What are you going to write to Lewis?"

"I don't quite know. What do you think?"

"You're still very young. Yet, somehow, I'll be glad when you're married. You have that restless quality of your father's, and marriage will settle you."

"That word 'settle' has an awfully final sound, Mother."

Rory rose to go with her, but Michal sent him back. She must be alone on this excursion—there was much thinking to be done. All the hills lay drying in the long sweet breath of spring. The best violets would be down by the big pond.

Heavy on her finger lay the ring. Marriage would be good. Better to tend her own babies, have her own house, her own problems. It would be a relief, in a way, to leave home; get away from the noise, confusion, Father's irritation, Mother's way of doing things.

The mess, for one thing. When she had a home, she'd keep everything in its place and teach her children to do so. And her children would mind better than Philip and David minded Mother. Yes, and she would manage Lewis far better than Mother had ever managed Father. Mother had made a great mistake there. No man would ever run her.

As she approached the pond, Michal moved softly until she saw the water lying cool and faintly ruffled. A few mud hens and a small flock of mallards on the far side were the only living things visible.

Kneeling by the pond's edge next to a little green carpeted hollow where blue violets dipped on long, frail stems, she picked a few, tucked them in her hair, then leaned forward and studied her face in the water. Like looking in a mirror in a darkened room, she thought, admiring her large eyes and thick, glinting hair.

Moving back, she pulled the shawl about her and relaxed on the sloping bank. She was alone; this place was hers for the afternoon. From many fields came the indescribable smell of freshly turned loam. Inhaling luxuriously, she lifted her head, listening to the mill, that far-off, steady heartbeat of the town.

Gradually her mind turned inward and she slipped into an imaginary world. There had been many such trips this awful winter—to places inhabited by a girl who looked like Michal Ward and a hero whose face she had kept carefully vague.

She watched the colors in the stone of the black opal change in

290

the sunlight as she turned her hand until the colors blurred, dissolving into formless patterns. Not Lewis. Not ever Lewis and this stone—together. But rather Mrs. Oulette dancing in madness before a prairie fire; a dark troll in the ravine on stormy nights when the water ran high; a black ox with gold-tipped horns moving steadily toward her through a mist. Little Brother's grave—alone, at night—so small; lost voices, calling; Rooshans plodding; Rooshans dancing; black horses, muscled, gleaming; dark riders, free, wild, and fierce; black eyes blotting out the moon; soft kisses in the night—soft strong kisses, lazy, sure—and the skeletons of purple coneflowers on the hills—

Her reverie was broken by a clanging trumpet-like cry. Shading her eyes she leaned back, then froze. A single giant whooping crane was circling above, evidently considering whether to descend or not. Hardly breathing she watched as—satisfied—he began the descent, spiraling down majestically to settle on a grassy patch at the far northwest edge of the pond. As he stood like a white image, resting, she thought, He must be tired to stop so close to a town. If only Lewis were here to see. She watched him until her vision blurred. Closing her eyes she tried to imagine the great flocks of twenty years before—the blue air filled with the white bodies of the older ones and the pure-gold feathered youngsters. Perhaps this had been one of their resting places and this one remembered. They lived to be old, she had heard—sometimes a century or more. He was feeding now. On frogs, perhaps. Too early for grasshoppers.

Was this a sign that she should write to Lewis and say "yes" to his plea for an early marriage? It was her third sight of the crane—he must be the same one—and so a charm. Tonight—at peace within herself— she would write to Lewis.

Her body grew prickly and cramped, but she was too absorbed to notice it. Watching the great bird feed, she thought, If only he had a mate he wouldn't seem so terribly alone. To be only one—where once had been so many. If people like Haars and Wards hadn't come to this country, the skies above the prairie would still resound with the sonorous clanging cries. Of course, Father was a sportsman. He killed for food, and never leveled a gun at anything but ducks or geese or upland birds.

The whooper was becoming restive. For a moment he stood still, listening to something she could not hear; then, with a trumpet-like note, he was running—into the wind, Michal knew, for quick lifting power. He was off, spiraling steeply, powerful wings lifting him higher as his lonely cry resounded, strong, far-reaching.

Then she heard a dull boom, saw the heavy body lurch and one wing crumple—the other flapping frantically—as he fell out of sight just beyond the rise. Michal ran, circling the pond, up the bank and over, then stumbling as, eyes blurred with tears, she saw the prone white body and a tall figure moving swiftly toward it. Karl Gross!

Ignoring him, she flung herself down on the crane. A broken wing might be mended. But no—the snowy breast plumage was stained bright red. He was dead.

Shrinking back, she lifted her face and whispered through stiff lips, "You've killed him!"

Karl's dark eyes were puzzled. "What's the matter? Don't you feel well?"

"You've killed my whooping crane."

He scowled. "It is not yours, but a wild thing. I saw it come as I worked in the field."

"You don't understand." Sniffing, she rubbed her eyes with her knuckles.

In one lithe movement he knelt, took her fist from her face, and forced her to meet his gaze. He spoke softly as though to a child. "You live in town. For you there is much food. If your people had eaten *Schweinefleisch* all winter, you would kill for this meat, too."

Her eyes fell before his black gaze. It was always the same. Even through anger it was the same—the old awareness of Karl sweeping over her. And as her quickened senses reached out, she felt the color rush to her face.

Drawing her wrist away she spoke quickly. "I'd live on hog's meat all my life before I'd touch one morsel of flesh from a whooping crane."

"It is easy to talk!" He was scornful.

"I could talk forever, and you'd never understand," she flashed back.

"I'm sorry you saw," he said abruptly.

"Are you?" Gently she smoothed the soft feathers for a moment. "Then, if you really are—do this." Eagerly she raised her face. "Let's bury him here on the edge of the pond where he rested and fed for so many years. Give him back —to the prairie."

He was staring at her incredulously. "Are you crazy?"

"No, I'm not. Can't you see what it would mean?"

292

"If I had not shot him, someone else would. Grossmutter shall have her broth and we shall eat his flesh." He stopped suddenly, and she saw that his eyes had caught the flash of her ring.

With one decisive motion he picked up the crane, and—face set —turned to go. Michal felt a wild surge of anger such as she had never felt before. She wanted to hurt him as—in some obscure way beyond the death of the bird—he was hurting her. Voice low, and shaking with the repressed violence which had dammed up inside her all the long winter months, she hissed, "Rooshan!"

For a moment she thought he had not heard her. Then, dropping the limp, stained body, and wheeling, he towered above her with a violence which matched her own. For one awful moment she thought he would strike her. She turned to run, but it was too late. His hands were gripping her arms, pulling her to him. Then his mouth was on hers—not gently, but powerfully—his lips forcing hers apart, one hand sliding down over her hips, pressing her to him.

Dimly she was aware that the anger was melting from him—that she was relaxing and that her own lips and body were meeting his as eagerly as his sought hers. His mouth softened, turned warm, controlled now, and his clean breath mingled with hers. She smelled the fragrance of hard healthy flesh, stable odors, and of earth bathed in spring sunlight. Spring sunlight was running through her veins. They two were part of a soft pulsing prairie.

Even as these things swept over her he pushed her away and held her at arms' length. He was pale. "You should not haf said that, Michal."

Low voiced, she answered, "I'm sorry, Karl."

Then, black eyes glinting, he laughed richly—his voice a cup holding male triumph—and as she shrank back he drew her to him lazily. "Little Englisher." He tilted her chin back gently and kissed her as lightly as he would a baby. "Goodbye, Little Englisher." Teeth flashing white as he turned, he swung the bird easily over his shoulder and headed toward the northwest.

Michal watched him go, hand pressed against her mouth, eyes round. "I'd better marry Lewis right away," she whispered into the empty silence around her. Like a person awakening from a deep sleep she turned. Her white shawl was lying on the ground. As she bent to recover it, she flinched at what she saw. Damp red bloodstains of the crane mingled with the blue blossoms on the bodice of her dress.

XVI

Even though these were troubled times—with women demanding the vote and Coxey's footsore army marching on Washington—Michal moved in a dream, committed to the words of the letter she had hurriedly scrawled to Lewis on the day that Karl had killed the whooping crane. "Bring the wide wedding band," she had written, "and sometime in June or July we'll be married."

In her room she had secretly washed out the bloodstains until the pattern of her dress was again clear blue and white. Then, in fresh shirtwaist and dark skirt, she had gone downstairs for supper.

Removing her napkin from its silver ring she said, "I've set the date with Lewis for early summer."

Hetty, in the act of serving, nearly upset the macaroni and cheese. "Not today, Miss Michal! Don't announce it today."

"And why not?" demanded Father belligerently.

"I broke a mirror in the kitchen. You all know what that means!"

"Oh, that can't hurt me, Hetty."

"You'll see—you'll see—" she mumbled.

"Married—married—Michal's gonna get married," chanted Philip.

"Shut up!" snapped Father. "Why the hurry, Mike?"

"I think I know, John." Mother's voice was a little tremulous. "Lewis has been getting eager for a definite date; so I sent Michal out on the prairie today, thinking that the quiet might help her decide. And you see, that is exactly what happened. Could you bring Mrs. Reid up tomorrow? I can't leave the baby. There's not much time and so much to do. Alice will want to oversee the whole thing and—"

"Damn it, I still say they're too young!"

Hetty sniveled audibly and muttered, "Poor little lamb."

Faith alone said nothing, but kept her eyes on her plate as she ate.

Much to Mavis's relief Mrs. Reid took almost complete charge of the wedding plans. "The only thing I ask is that it be kept simple," insisted Michal.

"Spare no expense," added Father expansively, reconciled now that it seemed inevitable.

294

"And I want Katie as my bridesmaid."

"Must you, Michal? With Lewis having that friend of his from Virginia as best man, Katie just wouldn't do."

"Then we'll just have a smaller wedding—or nobody but family."

"Why not Florence?"

"I like her next to Katie and I've invited her. But I want a quiet pretty wedding, with only those we love best with us."

"Of course." Mrs. Reid paused delicately. "I can't remember that Lewis ever cared much for your little Roo—ugh—friend."

Michal pushed back her hair irritably. "The whole thing is getting so complicated. Lewis is bringing the boy he likes best—somebody I don't even know. I want Katie. What difference does it make if they don't quite match? What does it matter what people think?"

Mrs. Reid sighed. "After all, it's her wedding, Mavis. Michal makes her own laws and makes people accept them, too. Now, about your wedding gown—"

"I've always dreamed of a dainty dress of sheer material—plain enough to wear afterward—and perhaps flowers in my hair."

"Well, of course, flowers are good this year—but for a wedding! What about trimming for your dress? I have some exquisite real lace insertion."

"I'd love that."

Hetty, who had been leaning in the doorway, spoke up. "What about the wedding dinner?"

"We'll plan that later. The main thing now is to get her clothes ready."

Then began interminable hours of standing in Mrs. Cutter's sitting room while the dressmaker snipped, pinned, measured. Mrs. Reid managed to drop in nearly every day, tactfully suggesting and supervising.

"I'm beginning to sympathize with Mother after all these years—for having so few clothes," moaned Michal wearily.

"My dear child! Delicate as my health is, I've always managed the strength for fittings. Let's see; sleeves and yokes are being spangled with jet this spring."

"Too dressy. I have my mink-trimmed yellow silk if we go anywhere. Mostly I want plenty of shirtwaists and skirts. And thin summer dresses."

"Now, you must have at least one new dinner gown. Here—look

at this sketch—pale pink chiffon with two deep flounces trimmed with mink."

"But I already have one mink trimmed—"

"You're so slender, it is most becoming—and smart. You'd turn any man's head in this."

"That is lovely. If Mother—"

"Now don't let her tell you it's too daring. Much as I love Mavis, she hasn't a bit of style—"

Mrs. Cutter lifted her thin tired little face. "That's all for today, Michal. Be here as early as you can tomorrow."

"I dream that I'm buried in ribbons and ruffles, and insertion and ruching."

"Um-m-m. Oh, you must have a black velvet coat trimmed with jet and black lace. That's always good."

In spite of herself Michal giggled as she slipped her dress over her beruffled petticoats. "You're going to have that jet on me one way or another, aren't you?"

Mrs. Reid smiled. "I'll admit that your wedding dress is one of the nicest I've ever seen."

"I'm glad you like it. You've been so kind—Mother and I would have been lost without your help."

"It has been real fun for me, Michal. A week from today Lewis will be here!"

"Yes, I know."

Only on sleepless nights did images sweep restlessly through Michal's mind: of violets bending on frail stems and a dead white bird stained red; of the quickening earth and Karl striding over it; of Karl and her anger and Karl and her tears; and the quickening within herself at the touch of him. Then, as her flesh softened at these memories, tears fell, silent tears as night melted into dawn.

Remembering the intimacy of his mouth and hands, guilty color swept her cheeks. Mother's words reproached her: "Never let a man touch you until—" Drearily she thought, There must be something wrong with me that I'd not only permit him but want him to kiss me that way. What ever would Lewis think if he knew—

Tormented, tired, she made up her mind early one morning as she knelt by the bedroom window watching the dawn unfold as delicately as a pasqueflower petal: I'll tell him. It's the only honest thing to do.

296

But the telling was hard. Lewis was a man now—ardent, in a very nice way, and overflowing with plans for their future. "The first thing I'm going to buy you next fall is a fur coat. I saw a beauty that was made for you, at $100." They were sitting in the hammock on the porch, and Mavis had sent the boys away to play.

"That's a lot of money for a young couple starting out," returned Michal soberly.

"Just get this into your pretty little head; we'll always have plenty of money. My father is well off, you know, and"—expansively—"if I do say so myself, I'll always make plenty."

"It still seems wrong to me that they'll support us until you finish school and get established. I don't want you buying me fur coats until you can do it with our money."

"Our money. That sounds good." After glancing around he leaned forward and kissed her quickly. "It isn't as if my folks objected to doing it. They want me to marry you. They want me to finish school. And they are able to make both possible. In the East that isn't uncommon at all."

"Don't be so complacent."

"I feel complacent. Now, look. This winter we're going to plays and parties. School or no school, the winter will be one long honeymoon. If—hey!" He broke off, jumped forward, and grabbed Philip, who was just in the act of loosing a small garter snake out of a tomato can onto the porch. "Here's twenty-five cents if you'll take your snake and disappear until I'm gone."

Michal grinned.

"I remember chasing Fanny Pratt through town once with a garter snake in a can." She smiled reminiscently.

"You were always up to something. Well—are you satisfied now about everything?"

"I think so—" slowly.

"That letter you wrote last spring," he teased—"the one where you consented to be married this summer—sounded as though you had no doubts about anything."

She studied her ring intently. "Lewis, there's something I've got to tell you; if it makes any difference about our marriage, I mean, I'll understand."

He went rather pale. "Yes?"

"It's—that—well, sometime ago a boy kissed me; and—I didn't struggle very hard."

Leaning back and slapping his knee, he roared with laughter. "Oh, Michal, don't scare me again like that. I thought—well, as far as that goes, I've kissed several girls myself."

"You have!"

"I'm hardly the same greenhorn I was a few years ago. Men get around, you know. However"—"I can't say that I approve of what you did."

"Well," spiritedly, "what's sauce for the gander—"

"Oh, no. This is a man's world, even if a bunch of spoiled women do want the vote. Who'd you kiss?"

"Do you want me to tell you about it?"

He lit his pipe before answering. "You know, I don't believe I do. As long as I'm sure you didn't seek it—and, knowing you, I couldn't believe that."

"I— don't believe I did."

"Well"—with mock sternnesss—"see that it never happens again." He squeezed her hand, then grinned. "Somehow the idea of one of these farm yokels or young men about Eureka cornering my girl doesn't worry me very much." He rose, smoothing his fine blond mustache absently.

Michal rose too and faced him, her eyes glinting with amusement. "You're very sure of yourself, aren't you?"

"Why not? I'm coming up tomorrow and take a look at your new clothes."

"Good. Mother bought sixteen yards of black silk and a lot of green velvet trim for a new dress for the wedding. I tried to argue her out of getting black—but she said it would have to do for a long time."

"Just between us, my mother's stylish, but your mother has style. Until tomorrow, then, sweetheart."

"Goodbye." For a moment she touched his cheek with the tips of her fingers. He walked away whistling "The Sidewalks of New York."

In mid-June, Michal set the date for the fifteenth of July. Mavis and Mrs. Reid both objected to the time but she stood firm. "We're all getting cross and tired. And I'd rather we were rested and enjoy it than go dragging down to the church just so I'll be a June bride."

"Michal's sensible," Mrs. Reid said wistfully. "And two weeks shouldn't make much difference."

Engrossed with the pleasant confusion of wedding plans, memories of that day by the pond took on for Michal the quality of a dream. Lewis was so genuinely interested in every detail about the ceremony that their hours together were like lovely bubbles. Each day he had some new and exciting plan to add to their future, and Michal was caught in an enchantment made up mostly of things she had never had and places she had never seen.

"Of course, we've always had plenty, but Father has been the one to take trips. The thought of dancing and hearing good music and seeing plays—Mother's never even suspected that Katie taught me to waltz and folk-dance."

"Oh, that Rooshan stuff! Matter of fact, I'll go dancing more to please you than anything. Wait until we get to New York on our wedding trip. I can't wait to see your face. I'm not entirely sure but that we'll settle there or somewhere in the East, eventually. This is just between you and me. As I've told you, Eureka's awfully dull compared to an Eastern city."

She frowned. "But I love the prairie."

"That's because you've never known anything else. Why, you've never seen a thing."

"I know I haven't," irritably. Then, more calmly: "It's a feeling I've always had—even as a little girl—about the earth. I like the feel of it and the smell of it. I even tasted it once. It's hard to put into words—but somehow I feel as though I should never get too far away from it."

"Oh, you'll change your mind. One winter away and you'll wonder how you ever endured this country."

"I've never 'endured' this country," she returned quietly. "I've loved it. I've been part of it. You haven't the faintest idea of what I mean, have you?"

"Oh, I think so. I like flowers, for instance—you know that."

"Yes, some of our best times together have been out on the prairie hunting flowers. But it's not only the flowers, for me—"

Faith came to the door. "They want you inside to discuss the wedding dinner."

Lewis pinched Faith's cheek. "It's a good thing you're getting married, Miss Ward. This sister of yours is a beauty."

299

"That's right," she agreed, a little startled by the brilliant glance Faith flashed Lewis.

They planned a simple wedding breakfast of breaded veal cutlets, French rolls, chicken salad, potatoes, cake, fruit, cheese, and coffee.

"Hardly enough to put in her eye," grumbled Hetty, stalking to the kitchen.

Mrs. Reid lowered her voice. "Mavis, you really intend to have Hetty and Gus?"

"We can't very well help it."

"But, Mavis—servants!"

"They're more than servants. They've been with us since before Michal was born. I understand your point of view; still, I agree with Michal—it would be awful to leave them out."

"And Achsah Klunk O'Dell?"

"She always stood by us in time of trouble—and Danny came here with John—"

Mrs. Reid shrugged. "Well, that's this country for you. I hope your best man will understand, Lewis."

"Oh, I've prepared him. He can't wait to see the West. Besides, when he sees my bride he'll understand why I put up with her notions."

Michal's expression turned a trifle grim. "If it's a really stylish wife you want, you've picked the wrong girl."

She thought she had had the last word, but as they left he whispered, "Wait until we're married."

XVII

Michal stook looking into the wardrobe at her wedding dress. The fine off-white material was artfully tucked and gathered to accent her small waist and lovely breasts. The real-lace insertion was cobweb-fine. In two weeks now—Her thoughts broke abruptly, sheered away, came back. For the first time since Lewis's arrival, she was at last face to face with some thoughts that had been worrying her.

Everything was perfect that they were planning—the wedding, the bright future. But what about this business of going to bed with a man for the first time? How would she get undressed without Lewis seeing her? Would he leave the room until she was in bed? But then, if he did that how would he undress without her seeing him? That would be just as bad. She couldn't very well close her eyes or put her head under the covers.

Then there was what would happen after that. She walked over to the window, knelt down, and looked off over the darkening prairie, and tried to fit the things she knew into one pattern. She knew about animals, of course. And the things Lily Lumpkin had told her that day by the turntable. Horrible things, dirty somehow, with Lily sniggering and poking and saying, "Ain't you the greenhorn!"

Then there was the way she'd felt there by the pond in Karl's arms. Of wanting more. But more of what? Except for that night at the Kickapoo Indian Sagwa', she'd never felt that way when Lewis kissed her—little quick pecks, usually when no one was looking. The day in the ravine when they'd got engaged had been nice. Comfortable. But it wasn't the same thing at all. Of course, nice boys probably never kissed a girl the way Karl had her. Lewis was nice, and perhaps after they were married she would feel toward him more—

A warm gold slice of moon swung quietly up at the edge of the horizon as Faith entered. Michal spoke abruptly. "Are the children in bed?"

"Yes." She began unbuttoning her shoes. "And Father's gone to lodge."

"I'm going downstairs a minute."

Mavis was reading the Bible. "I thought you were in bed."

"Mother"—nervously—"I've been wanting to ask you something."

"Yes?"

"It's about marriage and the wedding night and all that. Just thinking about it scares me."

Mavis closed the Bible and, rising, put it carefully in its place on the center table. When she spoke her voice was withdrawn. "That is an experience every woman must go through alone. Good wives submit to their husbands."

"But I don't want it to be like that," Michal burst out. " 'Submitting' sounds awful."

"Even though you may endure a certain pain and anguish, you will learn in time to take the bitter with the sweet."

"I'm afraid." Michal's voice was low.

"There are some things we have to learn."

"I see." Michal spoke heavily, then turned to go.

"After you have been married a while I'll give you a book written most delicately; it may help you."

"Can't you give it to me now?"

"Oh, no. That wouldn't do at all."

"All right. Thank you, Mother. Good night."

"Good night. I'm glad we had this little talk."

I would be too if I'd learned anything, thought Michal climbing the stairs. Pain and anguish, pain and anguish. Word fragments from overheard conversations of the past drifted through her mind. "He's a wife killer, all right." "Men are beasts." "What do ya suppose they do? Why do dogs tie?"

Shuddering, she entered the bedroom where Faith was counting strokes aloud as she brushed her hair. "I'm going for a walk."

"At this time of night? It's nearly nine!"

"Listen, Faith, these last weeks I haven't had time to breathe or think. I'll slip out; it'll do me good. Promise you won't tell Mother I've gone. I want to feel free to stay as long as I wish."

"All right. I promise. I know, you want to moon around thinking of Lewis. You'd better take your heavy shawl."

"I'll come in quietly so as not to disturb you."

The house was still as she stole down the stairs, caught up her shawl, and went into a night heavy with the scent of June darkness. Rory started to follow; but she sent him back, then went unhurriedly on her way. In the garden the wide sweet-smelling blades of corn swished gently as she passed. At the back gate she paused for a moment, then headed straight for the Place of Rocks. It would be snug and warm there in the old buffalo wallow, and Uncle Fred would seem close. If he were alive he would help her now. Like the pages of the letter that had come so long ago on that awful Valentine's Day, the blurred faces of white prairie roses looked up at her from the side of the path and their fragrance followed her as she climbed the hill. The great rock gleamed palely in the moonlight.

Spreading out the heavy shawl, she lay back on it looking up at the stars tearing bright holes in the dark immensity of the prairie sky. As from the snug warmth of the hollow she lay watching them, there crept over her the same awful consciousness of infinite number, illimitable space, and human helplessness that she had felt so long ago on the Homestead when the wild geese had lighted in swarms on the damp, freshly turned field.

302

Uncle Fred seemed close, but she had no letter in her pocket now; yet if he were here—gravely filling his pipe, tamping it down, lighting it—he would answer the questions she had put to Mother tonight, directly, without embarrassment. "I wish you had been my daughter, Michal." Over the years the words came back—ghostly—because she could no longer remember the sound of his voice.

Little night noises soothed her: the sleepy trill of a ground bird; the faint stirring of grass bent by wandering breezes; the constant cheerful chirping of crickets nearby. Until they abruptly ceased their song, she did not hear the footsteps. Quickly she sat up.

His deep voice was soft. "Michal!"

"Yes, Karl."

As he sat down beside her she asked, "How did you know I was here?"

"I didn't. For many nights, whenever I could, I haf come waiting for you."

"Why?"

"I want to marry you," he said simply.

"Marry— You're joking."

"No."

"But when—what—"

"Since the last day by the pond."

"That day?"

"Yes. I knew then."

"I can't understand it. Long ago you told me to stay away from you. That we were not good for each other. Why should you change your mind?"

Indolently he lounged back, his profile strong against the pale darkness. Even though the hollow was warm, Michal was trembling. She hoped he wouldn't notice.

"Until I went away to school, I was a German-Russian—to myself and to others. A few months there taught me much. People of separate countries marry and have children. If the parents are different, it does not matter. The children are real Americans. That is the thing I learned. Going from here a few months, I saw that this was true."

Eagerly she leaned toward him. "I'm glad. Uncle Fred knew that, but he couldn't make Mother and Father see it."

"So—we marry."

She drew back. "It's too late."

"It is not too late."

"You don't understand." The moon had swung well up over the rim of the hollow now, and she could see his face—strong chin jutting stubbornly, eyes shadowed. "The plans have been made. I just can't do it—even if I wanted to—"

"If you wanted? By the pond—you wanted to."

Michal rose restlessly and leaned against the stone, relaxing in its faint warmth. The moon bathed them in its soft radiance. She kept her voice low. "I will admit that what I feel for you I've never felt for anyone. I've never understood it. We're different. We always quarrel. I've hated you at times. Yet—"

He was rolling a cigarette. As he lit it, drawing deeply, she saw the firm dark planes of his face, the strong throat. Unreasonably, she wished that she might touch him. He said quietly: "It will be a hard life. We will always quarrel. We will sometimes hate. There will be much work. There will be children. I'll expect much of you, but I'll give much. It will be good."

She looked away. "It's true. But can't you see? It's too late!"

He spoke sharply. "Come here. Sit. All this does no good." But as she seated herself, he made no move to touch her. "If you want to marry me—and you do—then it is right. You think of your family. I haf a family, too. I haf not asked you to marry me to please my mother."

"It isn't only my parents. It's the Reids—all of them. If the wedding weren't so close it would be different." She scowled at him. "Don't you see, it's just too late and that's all there is to it."

He crushed the cigarette into the ground and rose. "I see many things. You are afraid. And you want what he can give you."

She rose also. "That's not true."

"This I tell you. The day you marry him, I marry Frieda who is not ashamed of me, my people, or my God."

In the lambent moonlight they glared at each other. This was the arrogant Karl—the proud man who as a proud boy had walked down the street a little apart from the others. Black eyes hard, he continued deliberately, "And on your wedding night—when he holds you, you will know that elsewhere I am holding her."

"You wouldn't—"

"I would." Coolly he took out his pouch and started to roll another cigarette. Then, for the second time in as many months, she was swept by a blaze of anger as hot and swift as a prairie fire. "Marry her, then! Do you think I care? You walk calmly into my life two weeks before I'm to be married and announce in your lordly way that you've decided that you want me, after all. So no matter how many are hurt I must change my plans. And I'm a coward because I refuse. Why did you wait so long?"

His voice was even. "Because after that day I thought you would feel as I do and could not marry him. A week ago Katie told me. So I have waited for you here. It was the only way."

Abruptly, her anger gone, she leaned against the rock. "I don't know what to do. I'm afraid of marriage to Lewis. I'm afraid of you. Maybe it'll all straighten out when I've gone where I can't see you. I don't know. I just don't know."

"Don't you, Michal?" he asked softly. "Would this help you know?" Gently he pulled her into his arms, cradling her head against his broad chest. Resting there she could hear the powerful beating of his heart. "You fear because you are not sure?" Lifting her, he carried her back to the shawl and put her down easily. All the stars in the sky were blotted out as he kissed her. "You are mine," he murmured, stroking her loosened hair, pushing it back, studying her face.

"You're nice." Reaching up, she touched his cheek shyly. "So nice that I think I'd better go."

"Yes?" Bending, he crushed her mouth under his, parting her lips with his own as he had that other time. Then he was unbuttoning her blouse, her chemise, cupping his hand about her breast, caressing her there. "If you want."

Drowsily she pulled his head down. "I don't want ever to be away from you, Karl."

As she felt the demand of his mouth, felt his muscular flanks against her, pressing, mingling with her own soft warmth, a misty image came to her from far away—of a breaking plow parting the curly buffalo grass and piercing for the first time the prairie soil. Faintly she could smell the dust of the earth, smoke of *Kuhmist*, and sweaty smell of the horse. Then, as she cried out and opened her eyes, the image melted away into a giant pinwheel of stars, and Karl's voice was low and his lips as sweet as honey.

The wind had died down, listening, Michal thought, to the night song of the bobolink. High above, the white moon was watching. Karl

305

was making another cigarette—strong hands deft. After lighting it he leaned back and took her hand. "Were you afraid?"

"No."

"That was because we are for each other. With another man"— he shrugged—"it would not haf been so."

Michal, smiling inwardly at the faint hint of triumph in his voice, did not answer, but lay relaxing in the soft palm of night. Then she asked, "Karl, have you ever thought, on a clear night, that stars are like little silver bells?"

"No."

"Ever since Father was lost in a blizzard once, I've thought of them that way. On some nights you can almost hear them tinkling—"

"Such thoughts do no good." He spoke with finality. "When a woman thinks, she should think of her home, her children, and—at night in bed—of her husband." For a moment she felt her flesh dimple under the touch of his fingers.

"Perhaps first of all, yes. But for me life will always be more than that. The way I feel about the prairie, for instance. A lovely place— sweet as a pasqueflower."

"Maybe to you. To me the earth is a hard place—to fight with sweat over it that we and our children may eat bread."

"It is both. But even though a man and woman see it differently each in his own way—still they should each get glimpses of the other's world. If we marry, I would hope for that."

"If we marry." His hand slid up her arm, gripped her shoulder. "After tonight—do you say if? Think you I would let you go to him now? You may have a child from this night."

"Oh!" She sat up.

"A fine man-child, perhaps," he went on triumphantly, "who will grow tall and strong here in this land—a real American."

"People don't have babies just like that," she protested weakly. "Some go for years and years—"

"Like this soil, we are fertile," he returned simply. "We shall have many children."

She whirled on him. "Did you do this—thinking—"

"I did not. I wanted you. You wanted me. That is all. You could haf gone."

"You're right."

306

"With Katie we shall plan secretly. Your family and mine would stop this marriage if they could. Go to Katie's tomorrow to spend the night and next day with her. After the moon comes up, Katie, you, and I will leaf for Leola in the Keim rig. There we'll be married and kum back. Do not tell anyone."

"This can't be me," Michal whispered. "It's not real." The moon was swinging down again, and the air was turning chill. Quietly Karl folded the shawl about her shoulders, drew her against him as she went on: "I can marry Lewis, go away, never see you again. You can have Frieda." She was crying against his chest.

He waited for the storm to subside before he spoke. "You are afraid again, Michal?"

She drew a long shaky breath. "I'm beginning to think again. To realize what we've done. And I'm all confused. Maybe if I go home now I can straighten it out and let you know."

"If you leave now we will nefer see each other again."

She turned her head, studying the stubborn jawline. "You're strange. Not like the others at all."

"That is true. But I am of them."

"You don't plod along—you walk like an Indian. And you ride a horse as though you'd been born in a saddle. And you're so dark and fierce and arrogant."

She saw the white flash of his teeth. "And you—you are like a wheat stalk in the wind. Thinking yes—thinking no. Bending before every breeze. Crying. Laughing." Tilting up her chin, he bent down and kissed her possessively. "Have you said 'yes'?"

"No." She relaxed against him drowsily. "We'd be hurting too many people. Always between us, you see, would be this. You can't see what—I mean—"

"And always between us would be this." His mouth was on her throat, then her mouth—seeking. His hands were stroking her hair, rhythmically, like wind brushing ripe wheat. And Michal dozed.

The stars were dimming into dawn when she awoke, cradled in Karl's arms. He was looking down at her, eyes shadowed and inscrutable.

"Hello," she said.

His mouth relaxed. "You are rested?"

307

"Yes."

"You slept like a child."

She nodded slightly, closing her eyes.

"And now, Michal, there is not much time."

"Karl." Eyes still closed, she gripped his arm anxiously. "Let me try to tell you why I bend like a wheat stalk in the wind as you said. I want to marry you. In a way it's as though I've always known—ever since that day by the Oulette slough with Katie when I first saw your picture. That part is sure.

"But the other part is the hurting. Ever since I can remember I've hated to hurt or see anything or anyone hurt. And if I marry you there'll be so many. Lewis, first. His folks. Yours. My own. We'd be dealing so much pain to so many people."

"You are right. And if you are not strong enough to do it—"

"Strong enough!" Michal sat up. "You call that strength?"

"Yes." Quietly. "You tell me always how you love the land. But do you only like the part that is good to see? The land is hard. It is not always kind. With too much sun our crops die. Blizzards kill cattle—people. We have lightning unt prairie fires." His black eyes glittered. "Would you kill a whooping crane if your child needed meat?"

Michal shrank back. "I don't know," she whispered.

"What we had this night was goot. Yet if a child is born from this night"—he shrugged—"you will haf pain. Work and love and pain are all the same. Part of living. If your mutter and mine and Mrs. Reid are hurt if we marry, it is too bad—but it is part of life—of hafing children."

"Yes," she said softly. "You must be right. But I don't know it with my head yet. Dear God, what shall I do?"

Then she heard it—far off. The ghost of a deep organ note. She stirred, and he raised his head. "Quiet!" she whispered.

Puzzled, he watched her—as for the second time in her life she listened to the song of the trumpeter swan. It was far away, to the north, not directly overhead. Yet, even so, she shaded her eyes with her hands, trying to see the huge lone bird, listening to hear the sound of his mighty wings. But nothing met her sight, and no sound reached her ears except the faint rich organ note—growing dimmer, dying away. Perhaps it had been a dream. But no. "Once heard, never forgotten."

If God looked down on people, if He looked as far even as a little cup on a little hill on the prairie, then He had sent word. Michal sat up, her face glowing. "I'll marry you, Karl. It's what Uncle Fred would have me do. Almost—" She paused, puzzled, looking east where night had thinned into the first delicate trace of dawn. "Almost it's as though he were watching—"

Karl scowled. "You mean when dot goose—or whatever it was—went by—"

"Yes." Quick tears filled her eyes. "But now I can face Mother and Father and Lewis. I can be strong for you. I'll even learn to kill chickens."

He pulled her to her feet. "It took you long to decide. Much longer, and I was ready to decide for you. We go. You know the plan. We meet tonight. I will do the rest." He kissed her; then, without a backward glance, was over the rim and gone.

As she hurried down the hill, Michal paused for a moment by the clump of prairie roses, their petals misty under morning dew. Gently she picked a few and held the little bouquet against her breast as she hurried toward the house.

XVIII

As Michal came in the back gate Gus called out cheerfully, "Out early this morning." But the house was quiet, and Faith did not stir as she crept in beside her.

Shortly after noon Katie came up, asking Michal to spend the night and next day with her. Mavis seemed pleased. "It will do you good." And Michal knew that she was thinking, Katie will soon be out of her life now.

In the afternoon she went upstairs to rest. If only Lewis doesn't come. But he did, so she closed her eyes and pretended to be asleep when Mavis looked in on her. For a while she heard the murmur of voices, then the sound of a closing door.

Carefully, keeping her mind a blank, she lay quiet for another half-hour. Then she put on her blue-flannel dressing gown and hurried downstairs. Mavis, nursing the baby, spoke gently. "Lewis was here, but asked me not to disturb you."

"Oh. Aren't you nursing that baby too long?" as Mother flinched when the little teeth clamped down mischievously.

309

"If she's to be the last baby I hold in my arms, I want her one as long as possible." And Mavis smiled tenderly down, meeting the enormous, interested blue gaze.

"She's lovely, isn't she? I hope mine will be as pretty!"

Mother's lashes were down, her voice shy. "You and Lewis should have beautiful babies."

"I'm going to have a bath. Will you warn the children if they come in this way?"

Hetty filled the wooden tub from the reservoir, grumbling. "We need a new tub. But you know yer paw. Money for horses, money for everything, but no new tub, even if I have been telling him fer years." And she went out, slamming the kitchen door.

Michal smiled as she filled the large pitcher with clear tepid water and set it on the table. She'd miss Hetty. As she lathered her slim white body thoroughly with her bar of mottled castile soap, she wondered at her own calm. It must be right or I couldn't feel this way. Then, as she rinsed herself carefully with the lukewarm water, she thought, What shall I wear? As she rubbed herself briskly with the turkish towel, Something old, of course.

Standing before the open door of her wardrobe, she looked for a moment on all the new dresses. Then, as her fingers trailed lightly over the soft wedding gown, she knew suddenly that she would never wear it or any of the others. The image of herself with Karl in the mink-trimmed pink chiffon didn't match, and for a moment she looked back on all the dreams that would never be—of dancing in some Eastern ballroom—of fragrance and lovely ladies and idle chatter.

Shrugging, she turned to her other things. The "all-over-blue-flowers" was clean. She wanted to be pretty for Karl. After all, she had worn it that day at the pond.

Quickly she put on ruffled drawers, corset cover, petticoats, dress. Her brown-gold hair she parted in the middle and pinned in a heavy knot at the nape of her neck. In the bottom of her box gleamed the little coral and gold pin Uncle Fred had given her years before. As she fastened it she noticed the flash of the black opal. Slowly she removed it and held it against her cheek before putting it in beside the brooch.

After supper, while she was packing the little bag, a knock sounded on the door and Fanny's head appeared, eyes darting at Michal's startled jump. "I just had to come see all yer new clothes."

"Come in."

"Going somewhere?"

"I'm spending the night with Katie."

"Bet Lewis'll put a stop to Rooshans after you're married. Well, you've got the clothes, all right." Her voice was dripping envy as, ignoring the chair that Michal pulled forward, she peered and poked about in the wardrobe.

Swiftly Michal put in brush, comb, buttonhook, handkerchiefs, cologne. If she would just go!

She jumped as Fanny's voice broke in: "You're the luckiest girl in town! All those dresses. Leaving this hole. Marrying Lewis. Why aren't you happy?"

Michal turned angrily. "What do you mean?"

"I'm no fool. And I've known you a long time. What other girl would go on packing instead of showing off her clothes?"

"I'm late, that's all."

"Is that why you jump every time I speak to you?"

Michal bit her lip, drew a deep breath. "If you'd spent as many hours lately as I have, being fitted for clothes, you'd be jumpy too. And I am late. Why don't you come spend the afternoon with me in a day or so? I'll try on all the new dresses for you, and we'll have a good visit." God forgive me! she added under her breath.

"All right. If you can spare the time."

As they went into the sitting room Mavis said graciously, "Won't you stay a while, Fanny?"

"No, thank you. I'll walk down with Michal."

"When will you be home tomorrow?"

"Probably around suppertime, Mother—if that's all right."

"Try and get a good rest. You—why Michal! Where is your engagement ring?"

Guiltily she looked down. "Oh, I forgot to put it on after my bath."

"Well, run get it. What a start you gave me. I thought you'd lost it."

"Imagine forgetting that," observed Fanny slyly, as Michal re-entered.

"Goodbye, Mother." Impulsively she leaned her cheek against Mavis's soft one.

"Good night." The dark eyes were tender, and for a moment Michal thought: I can't go. Not like this. Not this way, even as she turned with Fanny, walked out, and closed the door.

"Are you stopping in at the Reids'?"

"Not tonight. Lewis was up this afternoon."

"What did he think of your going to Katie's tonight?"

"He doesn't know—" She stopped abruptly.

"Oh. You didn't tell him. Then he doesn't like Katie any better than the rest of the real people here do."

"Katie's as good as any of us."

"Oh, well—she's still a dirty foreigner."

"You may walk by yourself. She's my best friend and you know it!"

"Don't be mad, Michal." Fanny ran to keep up with her. "I suppose I've always been jealous because you've liked her better than me."

In silence they walked down the hill. From the ravine came the lonely call of a bird, blending into the dusk sifting over the late twilight. As they reached town Michal slowed down. "Here's where we part, I guess."

"I'll stroll by Katie's with you."

"All right. If you like." Carefully she held her voice even. "When are you going to be married, Fanny?"

"When Mr. Right comes along, I guess. Ma doesn't want me marrying anybody in this hole." She lowered her voice. "Now that you're going away I'll tell you something if you promise never to breathe a word of it to anybody."

"All right, I promise," indifferently.

"There's one boy I've been stuck on ever since the first time I ever laid eyes on him. You'll never guess in a million years who it is."

"Lewis?"

"No. Karl Gross."

"Karl!" Michal looked at the other sharply. "That's right," she went on slowly, "I'd forgotten. You used to make eyes at him in school. Once you said you'd like to be in a kissing game with him."

"M-m-m-m! I still would. Of course, Ma'd never let me marry a Rooshan. And he's going with that Frieda Baur. I saw her in the store not long ago and came right out flatfooted and asked her if they was going to be married. She blushed and stammered around, said she didn't know. I asked her if it was true he'd bought more land, and she said yes, his mother had told her—his mother, mind you! Frieda's a sly one, all

312

right—that he'd bought the Switzer place—just lately. Got it cheap, too, I guess what with the drought and all."

"He bought the Switzer place?" Michal's astonishment was genuine.

"Hasn't Katie told you?"

"No."

"Well, Frieda went on and on. All about Karl and how smart he is and how because some of the settlers got tired of bad years and moved away, he bought land cheap and how well he'll do when the good years come. She said how when a boy marries he gets 160 acres, four horses, a cow, and some farm machinery—then she shut up. She got so carried away she'd said more than she'd intended."

Michal said nothing. She hadn't thought of Frieda—the beautiful Frieda who loved Karl probably as much as she—being hurt. Feeling sick suddenly at the sure knowledge of more pain being dealt, she quickened her steps.

"Well, you needn't be so stuck up just because you're marrying Lewis. You always have liked Rooshans. I thought you'd be interested. But you've acted very queer all evening. What's the matter with you?"

"Just tired and very bad company, I'm afraid. Here's Keims' now. Good night."

As she hurried into the yard a tall figure crossed the room inside, dark against the lamplight. Karl? She wasn't sure. If so, had Fanny seen him?

Fanny's voice was cool and distinct. "Good night."

Katie's plump face was rosy with excitement as she pulled Michal into the living room. "We were—"

"Pull the blinds quickly. Fanny Pratt's out there."

Karl strode over scowling. "How did it happen?"

She told him, adding: "She noticed how nervous I was—and she may have seen you cross the room. After what she did to Katie, I'm afraid."

Mrs. Keim was twisting her hands. "Ach. This gifs trouble. Your parents vill all plame me."

"We must wait longer," Karl said coolly, "and before we leave I'll look around and make sure she's gone." He turned to Michal, his quick keen glance like a touch. "Your people?"

"They expect me home tomorrow night."

"Goot. Now rest with Katie. We haf a long night ahead."

313

Obediently the girls went into the bedroom, slipped out of their dresses. As Katie bent over little Joshua for a moment, Michal whispered, "Are you surprised?"

"No. You haf always liked Karl."

"Do you think I'm doing an awful thing?"

"You must luff him the way I luffed my Yosh. It would be wrong to marry another."

"What do your folks think?"

"My fadder is still at the store. He does not know. Mutter is afraid of Tante Katrina and your people. Now—let us sleep."

Michal lay tense, her mind a kaleidoscope of shifting patterns. White prairie roses under the moon; mother's face—pale and sorrowful; Lewis; the sound of a closing door; the lonely far-off song of the swan, and far away—over everything—Uncle Fred's brown eyes smiling. Karl's voice and Mrs. Keim's. A dog barking somewhere. And the wind stirring. Always the wind on the prairie. She sat up. "What's wrong?"

Katie was dressing. "It's time to go. You've slept two hours."

"I was dreaming of the wind. Has Karl looked out?"

"Yes. There is nobody about. Here is Mutter's heavy shawl. She wants you to take it." And she bustled out.

Hastily Michal pulled on her dress, crumpled a little already, ran the comb through her hair, rearranged a few heavy wire hairpins. She was pale, she saw, and her eyes were faintly shadowed. Then Karl was behind her, and their glances met in the mirror. He swung her around gently, his hands warm and firm on the soft flesh of her arms. "Are you afraid?"

"A little."

His eyes were smiling. "Of me?"

"Mostly of what we'll face tomorrow night."

Leaning over he pushed the door shut, then drew her close, murmuring: "That will pass. I will help you forget," as he bent to kiss her. Shyly she drew back. "The door. They'll think—"

"You are my wife. A few words mean nothing. When I kiss you, it is not for them to see." He spanned her slender waist with his two hands. "Such a slim one. Not like our women."

She tilted her chin. "It's still not too late if you'd like Frieda."

For answer he swept her to him again until, laughing, breathless,

314

she struggled for freedom. Smiling, he studied her face. "Shall we go and be married? Or are you still afraid, Little Englisher?"

"Let's go."

Mrs. Keim, clucking dismally and shaking her head, saw them to the buggy and handed Michal a large shoebox. "Dis"—she smiled wanly—"is your vedding dinner. It is fried shicken, *Apfelschnitzel, Kaffeekuchen.*"

"All that Karl likes best," remarked Katie with gentle malice.

Karl patted Frau Keim's cheek gently. "*Danke schön*, Tante, for the food and all you have done for us. You know why I haf not told you where we are going? If anyone asks, you do not know. I'll take goot care of your buggy. Tomorrow night we are again here."

"Do you think little Yosh will cry?" Katie asked anxiously.

"Go along mit you. I haf raised a baby too. Gootbye, gootbye."

Karl drove with as much authority as Father, Michal thought as they sped out of town. The air was heavily scented with wheat mingled with dust—the lovely fragrance of a summer night under a clear white moon.

As the team steadied into an easy rhythm, Karl turned. "Try to sleep. It will be a long night."

"I'm wide awake. How about you, Katie?"

"Yes. I'm thinking, too, that it was over this road we came before with Yosh."

"Such thought do no goot," said Karl quietly.

"Still—you will have to face your mutter as Yosh did his. She vill be as angry. And Michal's people, too."

"We will meet that when the time comes. Now rest."

Michal tried to relax, emptying her mind of everything but this moment. Gradually she was lulled by the motion of the buggy, enjoying the fragrant night, watching the stars tremble against the sky. Once she felt Karl look down at her, and she leaned her cheek against his shoulder in reply. As long as he was beside her, she felt safe. It was a good feeling. She dozed.

As they neared Leola, Karl wakened the girls. Gratefully the three ate of the cold fried chicken and coffee cake. Brushing crumbs off her rumpled dress, Michal thought ruefully, And I wanted to be a pretty bride for him!

From the moment they entered the town she moved mechanically, as though caught in a dream. Chilled by Katie's quiet melancholy, she was glad that Karl knew so surely what to do. License signed and folded, they walked to the house where they were to be married.

The quiet little minister led them into a cool dim room filled with massive walnut furniture. "I'll call my wife. Just sit right down. We must have—" He broke off. "Haven't I see you before?"

Katie nodded. "Two years since. I was married here."

"Yes, yes, of course. And your husband, such a nice young man. How is he?"

"He is dead."

"Well, now, that's sad. But the good die young, I always say. I'll get my wife."

Katie, tears falling, spoke in a muffled voice to Karl, who answered quietly in German. Embarrassed, Michal walked across the room where conspicuously displayed on the mantel were two coffin plates inscribed with names and dates— Rosemary 1871–1886 and Patience 1879–1881.

Shivering, she turned away. Katie was blowing her nose as the minister and his wife—the latter nervously patting her hair—entered.

"Now, if you'll just stand here . . ." They were facing a marble-topped center table crowded with family photographs. So, while the eyes from the photographs watched—unseeing—in a dim, unfamiliar room, and to the soft sound of Katie's weeping, Karl Gross took Michal Ward to be his wife.

XIX

As they walked to where the horses were hitched in front of the court-house, they nearly collided with a man who had just come out.

"Uncle Herman!"

"Katie! Karl! Vas ist los?"

"Michal Ward and I are just married."

"Vard." He turned to stare at Michal, who was smiling. He still had hairy ears and nostrils; he was grayer and heavier. "Oh, ya, ya. Yohn Vard's Kind." Then his bloodshot eyes narrowed. "Married? Vere are your families?"

316

"They do not yet know." Karl returned quietly. "We are going back now to tell them. How is your family?"

"Yust fine. Unt soon ve vill be by you in Eureka. For goot. I haf solt mooch landt. The twins stay. The other"—he shrugged—"to school goes. Now ve kum to town."

"That is goot. Come back with us?"

"*Nein.* There is yet mooch to do. Kum mit me." He turned to Michal. "Unt you can your old house see."

"I'd love to—"

But Karl interrupted. "There is no time today. We must go back."

As they parted, going their separate ways down the board walk, Michal said wistfully, "I wonder if my willow tree by the dam is still there."

"Someday we see."

"I could show you the place where I was picking cattails the day I met Katie—the day she showed me the photograph of you and your family. Even then . . ." Her voice trailed off dreamily as they climbed into the buggy and were off. Watching the fields where the heavy stand of wheat—already turning to gold in the higher places—dipped and rose like waves on a green sea before the never ending prairie wind, she heard, for the first time in months, the liquid voice of Mrs. Oulette saying: "Always the wind in the grasses. Never are they still." She remembered a lovely fragrance, and later an empty room.

At noon they stopped by the spring to finish the lunch. Katie was her usual cheerful self again, but Karl and Michal were quiet. As they resumed the journey, after resting the horses, they said nothing.

The sun was dipping in the west when familiar landmarks began to appear. Michal felt a tight knot gathering inside her. The prairie was not a lovely place now, but a thing of heat and dust and awful confusion. "I wish it would be still." She spoke aloud, irritably.

"What?"

"The wind in the wheat. My eyes ache from watching it. I wonder if they know."

"It will soon be over."

She tried to think of other things. After all, this was her wedding trip—through waving wheatfields, now darkening with twilight, but still scented with heat and dust. All day she had ridden beside this silent dark stranger who was her husband. What had he been thinking since he had slipped the little gold band on her finger this morning?

317

"Karl, this ring. Did you get it in Eureka?"

"It was Grossmutter's. Last night I told her of us, and she was glad because she has always liked you."

Michal's eyes stung with quick tears. "Why didn't you tell me before?"

"I thought you might want a new one."

"Not ever." She looked down at the worn little band. "Wasn't it hard for her to give it up?"

He kept his eyes straight ahead. "Yes."

Katie chuckled. "If Grossmutter likes you dot well, you are safe from Tante Katrina."

"I'm glad it fits. I'll never take it off."

They were in town now. Everything looked the same; children were playing late under the lights in the dusky streets. "We'll take Katie home and change to my wagon."

"Then to the Reids'." Michal spoke firmly. "I must tell them first."

"If you like."

As they swung in behind the house, the back door opened and Mrs. Keim's ample figure was silhouetted against the warm gold oblong of light. She did not come to meet them, but stood there until they jumped down and approached her. Her voice was flat. "You are back?"

"Yoshua!" Katie's voice was thin.

"No. Grossmutter. She is dead. We haf kill her."

XX

All the time that Frau Keim talked, Michal tried to listen but heard not one word of what she said. Soon she lapsed into German, speaking so rapidly and with so many gesticulations that Karl and even Katie had to interrupt to understand. Through it all Mr. Keim sat staring gloomily at the little group, occasionally sighing and shaking his head.

Finally Karl rose. "We must go."

"Yes. Thank you, Katie—Mrs. Keim—" Michal's voice broke as she hurried out after her husband. As he worked swiftly, changing the horses, she stood nearby, forlorn.

"Come, Michal."

She hurried to him, gripping his arm with both hands. "Karl, what are we going to do?"

"As we planned. We haf now the hard part."

"Little Grossmutter—" Michal began softly.

"When you work on the land you learn to know birth—and death. Now—" lifting her easily in his arms. He looked down. "You are light as a kitten, my little Englisher. No good to a man—except for this." Bending, he kissed her lightly, then placed her on the front seat of the wagon.

All the way to the Reids' she sat close to him, trying to draw strength for what lay ahead. All he said was, "There is still much to do," as she went in alone.

'Rica led her to the sitting room—the cool, uncluttered sanctuary. As she stood uncertainly in the doorway, Lewis sprang forward. "Darling, what's wrong?"

"I've been—" She stopped, looking mutely from one face to another.

"You look so tired and crumpled." Mrs. Reid indicated a chair. "You know, I've just been telling Lewis that I think a single strand of pearls would be the thing for his gift to you. I don't approve of all the brooches and rings that are worn nowadays. On a young bride just a— *is something wrong?*"

"Yes. And I don't know how—I can't—" She broke down then, and Lewis knelt beside her and wiped away her tears with his big white handkerchief. "Tell us, darling."

Shaking her head she drew the black opal ring slowly out of her little bag and handed it to him, then stood up. "I was married today— in Leola—to Karl Gross."

The little clock struck the half-hour—the chime sounding loud in the quiet room. Pale as wax, Lewis rose to face her. "You're joking."

Mrs. Reid rose also, and her husband stepped quickly to her side. "Yes! What cruel talk is this, Michal?"

"It's true. That's where I've been today, Lewis."

"Wait—" His eyes narrowed. "He's the one who kissed you. You wanted to tell me once just after I got home."

"Yes, he's the one."

"But it's always been us—you and me. It—you couldn't marry that Rooshan."

Mr. Reid spoke for the first time. His voice was kind. "Why did you do it, Michal?"

She faced the three of them. "I married him because, feeling as I do about him, I couldn't honestly marry Lewis. That's why."

Mrs. Reid's voice was as clear and delicate as the little clock chime. "Please take me to my room, James." Even as, leaning on her husband's arm, she swept out, Michal saw the involuntary glance at herself in the mirror.

Lewis sagged into a chair. "I don't know what to say. People just don't do things like this!"

"I know. People don't. Yet I've done it." She was twisting and untwisting the cord of her bag. "I've hurt and humiliated you, broken my mother's heart, and killed Grossmutter. I have it in me to do all those things."

"Yes, and you'll be regretting it before a year is out," bitterly. "Why, he can't give you a thing!"

"No," she said softly, "he can't give me any of the things I'd have had with you."

"What'll I do?"

"Go back to school. Meet a lot of girls. And find one who'll love you the way you should be loved."

"Right." It was Mr. Reid coming into the room. "Here, Michal, take this glass of brandy. Have you been home yet?"

"No. We're going there next."

"Then you'll need this." He turned to his son. "I hate to see you jolted so hard, Lewis, but it could be worse. If Michal loves somebody else, then it's better that you both face it now rather than later. In time you'll see that what I have said is true."

"You don't understand," muttered Lewis, polishing the stone of the black opal mechanically.

Michal rose. "Perhaps I do. I must go." She looked at Lewis, who—face set—had risen as she did. He was looking at the ring. She went up to him, put her hand for a moment on his arm. "I'm sorry, Lewis. Truly, I'm sorry."

"Good night." He didn't look at her, but even in that moment he was polite.

Mr. Reid went with her to the front door. He put his hand on her shoulder. "I'm sorry you're not to be my daughter-in-law."

320

She bent her head. "It would be easier if you'd scold me. Or hate me. You do know, don't you, how I feel about all this hurting everybody?"

"Yes. I know. Now go to your parents. And remember, your father's bark is far worse than his bite."

"Thank you. Good night. I mean"—her voice faltered—"goodbye." And, stumbling, she ran out to Karl.

XXI

Mavis met them at the door. "Come in." She was pale but perfectly composed. "Please sit down. You are married."

Karl answered. "At Leola, this morning."

"Why did you do it like this?"

"It was the only way," he said simply.

"Have you seen the Reids?"

"We've just come from there."

"How can I ever face them again?" Her voice was dull. "If I had known. One day my daughter is wearing another's ring, the next she's married to you—a stranger to us, and, we thought, to her."

"My people, too, will not understand. But there has always been this between Michal and me. I could not let her go."

"But when—" She gestured helplessly.

"Night before last, Mother. Karl has known for years that I sometimes go to the Place of Rocks."

"Place of Rocks? What's that?"

"An old buffalo wallow on the hill. The other night, after our talk, I was unhappy and went there to think. He came—and—persuaded me that we must marry."

Gravely she shook her head. "You know that Karl's grandmother is dead? Fanny came here this morning; she told us her suspicions. I couldn't believe her; but she was so sure that I hurried down to Katie's. Mrs. Keim told me it was so but that she didn't know where you'd gone. Then I went to Father, thinking he might be able to stop you. He raced out to Grosses', sure that they would know everything. You

321

know your Father! Apparently, he thought Mrs. Gross wanted it to happen. When he found that she was as surprised and angry as he—then—well—he was even more furious. The little grandmother spoke in German, and Father said that, as nearly as he could tell, she knew about it and was upholding what you had done. Mrs. Gross said she was going after you, and Father said he was too. Then the little grandmother got out of bed, walked over to them—and fell. Of course, Father came right to town to get Dr. Gotthelf. And all day he's been raging in and out waiting for you to come home."

"We'd better go. I just don't think I can face Father tonight."

Karl rose. "We stay. I face your father. This is between us."

"But Father might hurt you."

"I think not."

"Karl is right, Michal." She paused, then added, "And I want to take this moment—to wish you both—much happiness."

"Mother—"

"Thank you," said Karl. "I would not haf done this to our families, but it was right for us."

Michal lifted her head proudly. Never for one moment had Karl lost command of the situation. He was as much a man as Father. Then, at sound of swift footsteps, Mavis's eyes widened. "Here is John now."

Karl turned as John Ward, stepping slowly now, entered and closed the door with a snap. In spite of her fear, Michal felt a thrill of pride as the two men stood facing each other. The tall blond American, gray eyes like splintered ice; the equally tall dark Rooshan, deep eyes shadowed.

"Are you married?"

"Ya."

"What kind of God-damned business is this, anyway?"

Michal rose to stand beside Karl as Mavis joined her husband and put her hand lightly on his arm. Her voice was clear and calm. "Remember what I said today about violence in this house, John. I meant it."

As though she had not spoken, Karl said, "I haf married the woman right for me—as men do."

"You've stolen my daughter, disgraced your family, murdered your—"

"It's too late, John. In the sight of God and man they are husband and wife."

322

"In the sight of God and man, hell! She's my daughter."

"It is done."

Father turned. "Michal, stay here. It's not too late to end this. These marriages breed death. Look at Joshua."

"I'm no Joshua!"

"Don't interrupt! There's something else you should know. This fellow's mother was furious when I told her. Furious at the idea that my daughter was marrying her son. *My daughter!*"

Karl smiled. "My mother is also proud. She, too, had other plans for me. But she will learn. If not—" He shrugged.

"For the last time, Michal—will you stay?"

"There's no coming back. I love Karl. He's my husband. I'm going with him."

The gray eyes turned bleak. His voice was chill. "Very well. You have chosen. From this night we are strangers."

"John—"

"What you do is your business, Mavis. I'm through."

"But, John—"

"We're leaving. If I find a buyer we'll be out of here in two weeks!"

"Out of here—" Michal turned away from the look in Mother's eyes.

"Come." A hand was on her arm.

"Yes, Karl. Good night, Mother."

Just for a moment she looked back. Everything was the same— the walnut furniture, the Eye of the Lord, the organ, the steel engraving of the Garfield Family, the Bible on the center table. And John Ward—face set—pacing through it all. "Good night, Father."

There was no answer. A stranger walked where he had walked before.

As they climbed into the wagon, Rory trotted up eagerly. "May I take him, Karl?"

"If you like."

"Come, boy."

The weight of his warm silky body comforted her as they rode in silence through the clear night. It was the same still earth, as indifferent to the dark wheatfields and small night songs as to the line of tormented faces she had passed by this evening. The moon, still low, was

323

caught in a cobweb of stars. Michal felt a little of the tension leave her body.

"Where are we going now?" she asked presently.

"To our home."

"Not—"

"The Switzer place. There is enough for tonight. Many nights haf I spent there."

"But what about your people?"

"Tonight I must go to them with Grossmutter dead. But you must sleep. Will you be afraid?"

"No. There's nothing left to be afraid of."

He took her hand. "Someday your father will forget his anger."

"I don't know. He's a stubborn man. It doesn't seem fair for you to go to your people alone—after helping me face mine."

"I will not have you troubled again. My people must come to you."

"Your mother will never do that."

He shrugged. "We shall see."

As they neared the house she looked at him wistfully. "I wish you didn't have to go."

"I must." Then she saw the white flash of his teeth. "But I will come before dawn."

Together with the dog they crossed the threshold of their house. Karl lit the lamp; by its glow Michal saw the same bare rooms where Katie and Joshua had lived out their sad little story together. Only now, soft dust and cobwebs veiled everything. She drew a deep breath and smiled shakily. "By the looks of things I'll have a busy day tomorrow."

Tipping her chin up, Karl studied his wife's face gravely. "You are tired. Sleep well."

Mutely she nodded. steadying her lips to quiet their trembling so that he would not see, and walked to the door with him. Long after the creak of the wheels had thinned into empty silence, she stood listening. Then, faintly, far off in the night she heard the long mournful call of a plover, more like the wind than like a bird's voice—the notes rising, swelling, then falling and dying away. Only now, Mother was not here to grasp her hand.

324

XXII

Karl had been gone for over an hour on his trip into town for supplies. He had not volunteered a word of his meeting with his mother and father. At breakfast, while pretending to sip the strong chicory coffee, Michal had delicately touched on the subject, then retreated sensitively before the powerful reserve within her husband.

The room smelled of wood smoke and hot sunlight—sunlight that shimmered in golden layers. The house was thick with it. Michal wiped the sweat from her face, looked about the dust-cluttered room helplessly, then smiled—remembering dawn, dim, silver and cool, and Karl kissing her into drowsy wakefulness. A soft thrill swept her as she relived those moments. Heaven lives here, Michal thought, and I'll keep it so.

Next year she'd plant wild-cucumber seed under the windows. If there were only one tree to shade us, but other things must come first, Karl had said.

Under the sink, in the scrubpail, she found an old shriveled bar of laundry soap—enough to clean the whole house—windows, woodwork, floor. But the cupboards must come first, the one in the big room, then in the kitchen. She would carry water from the well down by the old barn and heat it.

The cupboard shelves were still covered with papers, yellowed and torn now, but by the elaborately cut edges unmistakably the same Katie had put here so long ago. Suddenly, faintly sick, I must get out of here, she thought.

Hurrying, she drew two pails of water, then put them down to stand and rest a moment in the open doorway of the barn. Swallows, possibly the same ones she had seen there years before—the sun glinting on their shining wings—still darted overhead, in and out of the open door, as they busily fed their clamorous young. Peering into the cool cavernous half-darkness, Michal was relieved to see harnesses hanging from pegs, fragrant new hay filling the mow. The old manure pile was gone, but a fresh one to the left of the entrance testified eloquently that the barn was being used.

She filled the reservoir back of the stove and poured water into the scrubpail for quick heating. There would still be time to look about the outside of the place and plan for next year's garden while she saw what Karl had already planted.

Far to the north of the house a field of green wheat rippled—not as tall this year as usual because of the drought, but, thanks to Karl's methodical care, a fair stand that would give an average yield. Just east of the house was the two-acre garden spot the Switzers had carefully fenced in. Karl had planted much of it to potatoes. She would dig into a few hills later in the day to see if any were large enough to scrub and fry in butter, the way Hetty fixed them.

Beyond the garden, east, were two trial plots of ten acres each planted to hardy dwarf corn recommended by the Agriculture College. Karl had told her at breakfast that he would see which variety did the better. He could use the corn—she'd try it for corn on the cob, too—and the stalks would make fine fodder. The rows were clean and the plants thrifty. Karl had cultivated it until it was "by," and no weeds could take it now. He had certainly worked; the only weeds she saw were a few Russian thistles growing outside the garden fence.

All morning she wiped down cobwebs, cleaned shelves, and polished windows. At noon she stared at her reflection in the old mirror over the sink—hair tumbled, sweat glistening on her upper lip and forehead, her blue-flowered dress, torn on a nail at the well, soiled and crumpled. And she was hungry. Rory padded over and sat on his haunches, leaning against her. Impulsively she knelt beside him and buried her face in his neck, moaning, "Oh, Rory, will Karl ever come? Will I ever be clean again or have this house clean? If Mother could see me now—"

The crunch of wheels brought her to her feet. Hastily pinning up her hair and wiping her face, she peered out. Hetty and Gus were climbing down from the wagon, the back of which was loaded with boxes and bundles, and tethered to the wagon box—Starlet. She went to the door. "Hello. You're my first callers. Come on in."

Hetty turned, took one good look. "Michal Ward! Your face is dirty."

Vaguely Michal touched her cheek. "Is it, Hetty?"

"You poor little lamb. It's about time we got here." Then Hetty was holding her and Michal was hiding her face on the lean shoulder for a moment, wiping her eyes hastily, her smile uncertain. "It's just the excitement, I guess. Hello, Gus."

"Hello, Miss Mike. I'll git these things unloaded and hurry back. By yer leave I'll put Starlet up first."

Michal clutched the wagon wheel. "You mean you've brought Starlet for me?"

"Yer paw said that, by Gawd—beggin' yer pardon, Miss Mike—no daughter of his was gonna be without a good mare even if he had disowned her."

Michal laughed tremulously. "Isn't that just like Father? Tell him thanks."

"Uh—I—hope you'll be very happy with—uh—"

"Karl. Karl Gross."

"Oh, yes. Uh—"

"Now, you, Gus Perkins, quit that stutterin' and get the horse put up and them things in this house right now; them two front boxes first and then all the cleanin' things. Then you high-tail it for home. I gotta git this child fed right off an' then git this house clean by night. What's this?" She was in the kitchen now and had the top off the coffeepot and was sniffing suspiciously.

"Chicory coffee—Karl made it."

"Swill! I'll make fresh while you wash and git into a clean dress—in that first box. You eat a hunk o' this fried chicken I brung, and some of those fresh rolls and drink a cup o' decent coffee and rest a bit while I get started on this place."

After Gus left, Michal, clean, refreshed and renewed by the food, put on an apron. "You tell me what to do, Hetty. I felt so helpless this morning. Not much to work with and not knowing how, either."

"Yer maw has funny notions about bringin' up girls. But you've gotta learn now. Clean out that wardrobe and put yer clothes away. You've done the kitchen mostly, so I'll take this big room, ceiling an' walls first, then the winders, and the floor last."

"How's Mother today?"

"Looked as how she hadn't closed her eyes all night. Worried to death with you out here 'thout clothes or food. Packed yer things all morning. Said to tell you she'd git over but couldn't say when—the poor little thing!"

"And—Father?"

"Rippin' the town apart to find buyers. Can't shake the dust of

Eureka off his feet fast enough. Course it would have come anyhow, sooner or later."

"How did you know I'd be here?"

"Sent Faith down to Katie's. She said you'd be bound t' come here. Where's yer husband?"

"In town for supplies. Then Grossmutter will probably be buried today. He didn't say whether he'd be going to the funeral or not."

"H'm. That kind, eh? Does as he pleases. Gus had notions like that, too. Yuh wanta break 'em of that, quick. Course, though, you've married a foreigner. That'll make it harder. But no use cryin' over spilt milk, I allays say. That may've been Karl we saw on our way out—jest as we wuz leavin' town. I didn't get a good look."

As Michal carefully hung her dresses one by one in the wardrobe —the yellow-mink-trimmed, the pink chiffon, she asked slowly, "I wonder if I'll ever wear these clothes?"

The other snorted. "I'd like to know where!"

"But you know, Hetty, I don't care. Just think of the fun I'm going to have fixing this house up. I'm going to get Turkey-red cotton and blue denim and make pillows. And make my own rugs and quilts. Hang one or two good pictures. Have Karl make shelves for all my books. In that corner Karl will have his desk with his textbooks from college and a shelf for his farm and stock magazines. I'll raise chickens and have a big vegetable garden. And pick prairie flowers for the table. Karl is a good worker, strong and thrifty. We'll have children—" She stopped suddenly, blushing.

Sharp eyes softening, Hetty paused on her way to shake out the broom rag, touching Michal's cheek with her rough hand. "So it's like that, is it?"

"Yes. It's like that."

"And not with Lewis?"

"Not ever."

"Then all the pretty dresses in the world wouldn't make you happy like you'll be here. But it'll be no picnic. Lots o' hard work and heartbreak."

"I know." She lifted her head arrogantly. "But I can face anything."

"Yes, 'n' you'll have a plenty to face too, don't think you won't." She looked about cautiously and lowered her voice. "Don't ever tell yer maw this, but I was listening last night and got a peek at everything,

328

and yer Karl. And I don't blame yuh a bit. He's mighty fine lookin'. An' spunky! Lewis or no one else woulda stood up to John Ward the way he done."

"I was proud of him."

"But yuh gotta look out fer his kind. Don't let him walk on yuh."

"I won't."

"Now, let's git on with this woodwork."

When Gus came for Hetty, Michal walked out to the wagon. "Will you come back?" she asked anxiously as Hetty hoisted herself up onto the seat.

"Sure, we will," Gus said quickly. "Yer maw said to tell yuh she'd be out first chance she gits." Abstractedly he drew out his plug, paused a moment—then, politely—"Chaw, Miss Mike?"

"No, thank you, Gus; but"—she paused—"if you don't mind I'll take the star for my picture of heaven." As he handed it to her, for the first time in her memory she saw tears in his eyes as without another word he flicked the horses lightly with the whip and drove away. Michal watched them until they were out of sight; and the little tin star was clenched tight in her hand when she went into the house.

In the month that passed after their first day in the Switzer house, Michal and Karl had few visitors. Katie had come with a message from Mavis, but Katie's eyes were remembering and Michal knew she'd avoid this place for a while. And she didn't blame her.

Achsah had trudged up one day, so matter-of-fact about the whole situation, and so happy about it, that Michal lost all feeling of self-consciousness. Actually, Achsah's commonsense helped her through several difficult times, especially the afternoon a week later when Mavis stole an hour to visit with her daughter.

She came obviously without Father's knowledge or consent. While she stayed she tried hard to give of herself to her child in the way of a mother who knows she will soon be gone. As Gus drove up to get her, Mavis opened her bag and handed Michal a wrapped parcel, saying: "I'd always hoped to be with you when my first grandchild is born. But your father is bitter. When you want me in the years ahead, I won't be here. This is all I have to give you."

It was Mavis's book on tokology—so carefully guarded that Michal had never seen it; by its condition it had been well used and cherished.

"But, Mother, you'll need it."

"After all these years, I know it by heart."

"Maybe I'll never have a baby."

Mavis's brows lifted and a half-smile touched her lips. "You'll have a baby, all right. You've done what I did—married against all reason. Only, you've gone farther than I did—you've married a foreigner, a man whose blood and background are strange to you. Why, you don't even speak the same language, really. If it's been hard for me—married to a man like your father—what is it going to be for you with all that you have to face?"

"I love Karl," Michal said quietly.

"I know. I love your father. But soon I'll go once more into some new wilderness, at my age, and start again trying to find a new home, a new minister, new friends. And once more I remember the 'Lewis' in my life. I had a Lewis, and I haven't forgotten him."

"Do you regret him, Mother?"

Their eyes met and they both smiled. "No. I'd do it again, and so would you. But you'll have babies, my dear, and there'll be times—"

As they walked out to the buggy, Michal asked casually, "Has Father found a buyer?"

"Business buyers, yes. We are only waiting to sell the house. Of course, it's just a matter of time." Then Mavis embraced her daughter tenderly; and Michal knew by the set look on Mother's face that this was goodbye.

Remembering, Michal brushed away the tears that seemed to come so easily these days. She'd glanced curiously into the book that day and found tucked inside an envelope, containing a bank note, with the notation "For Michal and Karl from the Wards." The money had been nice, but she'd read the book avidly and then wondered why Mother had kept it a secret. After all, it was only like life on the prairie. It was comforting to know what a woman looked like inside and to know what a woman should eat to keep a baby small so that birth would be easy; but by the pictures it was no more complicated than the birth of a flower.

There was another gift on the back page which Michal had found only this morning when she'd finished the book. By the color of the ink and the change in handwriting it looked accidental. Through the years Mavis had jotted down a sort of summing up which touched Michal more than the book and the money. Already she knew the lines by heart, and as she busied herself finishing dinner for Karl, she said them over once again to herself:

Be courteous to God first—through prayer. Courtesy to husband, children, and friends will follow.

Ignore as much as possible. So many things pass.

Read the 13th Chapter of First Corinthians at least once a week.

When everything else fails, righteous indignation sometimes helps.

The last line had been added quite recently. Michal wondered if the sight of Karl had inspired that thought, although Mother had on occasion resorted to anger with Father—and effectively, too.

Rory's low growl interrupted her thoughts, and Michal whirled. Katrina Gross, a grim smile on her firm lips, stood in the door watching her. "Guten Tag."

"Why, good day, Mrs. Gross. Come in."

As the woman entered, despite her dignity Michal felt her uneasiness. "Please sit down. Karl should be here any minute."

As Michal set the table for three the other looked about her curiously. New curtains and the blue and red pillows all sewn by hand had brightened the rooms, and everything was clean though somewhat bare. "So much red looks hot at this season," apologized Michal, "but most of the year it is cool or cold in Dakota. I want to start my rugs and quilts soon."

"Karl is well?"

"Yes. You—have not seen him?"

A spasm of bitterness passed over her face. "Ven we buried Grossmutter."

"Oh." Michal fingered the thin old wedding band nervously. "I'm sorry for what happened—my father going out."

"It is done. You haf my son now."

"I want you to know that I love him very much. I'm going to make him a good wife." And involuntarily she glanced down at her work-reddened hands, then lifted her head. "Here he comes now."

Karl walked in swiftly—then, at sight of his mother, came to a full halt. Instantly Michal knew that he was surprised. The encounter at the Grosses' home on their wedding night must have been bad, then.

"Guten Tag."

Katrina rose. "You are surprised?" she asked in German.

331

"Ya."

She shrugged. "After all, you are my son."

He nodded and went over to the washstand. Pouring cold water from the pitcher into the basin, he sloshed it well on his face and hands. As they ate, Michal, waiting on the two, took little. Katrina and Karl took great helpings of food, washing it down with Arbuckle's coffee. Michal shuddered before their appetites, the smell of food, the heat, the tension. The room seemed to sway, and turn. And then, suddenly, she was running—out of the room, out of their sight—into the blinding sunlight toward the outhouse. Too late. She was sick in the yard—retching, bending—tears of self-pity and humiliation streaking her flushed cheeks. Then it was over, and wearily she returned to the house. Quietly Karl rose and, dipping a washcloth in cool water, wiped her face.

"She is with child." Katrina said calmly, scraping dishes.

"So?" His heavy brows rose.

"I'm with something." Michal went over and sat down weakly. "I've never been sick like this before."

"It will be a fine man-child." She looked up. He had forgotten her. Chest swelling, he strode across the room, then faced his mother. "A fine man-child. Part German. And part American. How will you like that, Mutter?" He spoke in English to his mother now.

Katrina pulled her black-fringed headshawl over her head, and turned. "Rest in the heat of the day," she said briefly, "or you may lose the child. Soon I will bring a gift of lace for your house." And, motioning Michal back as she started to rise, she added to Karl, "Bring her, when you are ready to come for your marriage portion."

"I'll take you home and go to town after. A clean shirt, Michal—" He followed her into the bedroom and spoke softly, almost to himself, but he was smiling. "Rest, little one."

XXIII

The house, smelling soapy, clean, and hot, was not yet cooled by the evening breeze. The sun dipped beyond the rim of the prairie; the sky paled into twilight; the earth darkened; but still Karl did not come. Impatiently Michal went to the door and listened for the sound of his team. There was nothing. Only a cricket shrilling and a dog barking far off.

The table looked gay with its red-and-white checked cloth and the fresh bread, a brown-gold mound of chicken and white frosted spice cake—her first. Something was missing. Flowers, of course. She heard Mother's voice through the years saying, "No meal is complete without flowers on the table."

Whistling for Rory she hurried out and off toward the place where the prairie roses grew. By the time she had found a clump and had gathered a small bunch, a few early stars were glinting faintly against the sky. Rory paced beside her in the dignified manner of an older dog. Michal's step quickened when she saw the lamp gleaming softly from the kitchen window.

But Karl, who was eating, looked up scowling. "Where haf you been?"

"Gathering flowers for the table."

"A man wants food on his table, not flowers."

Michal flushed. "A woman wants a husband on time for meals."

He took a large bite of cake. "Uncle Herman was there, and I stayed to talk."

Filling a heavy glass with water, she arranged the flowers carefully.

"Haf you eaten?" he asked mildly.

"No."

"Eat now. I'll take more coffee. It is goot."

He rolled a cigarette, lit it, then pushed back his chair. Rory rose, moved close to Michal. "Uncle Herman is come to find a house. I told him to see your father."

Michal stroked Rory's smooth head nervously. "That was kind of you."

He glanced at the dog. "We cannot haf two dogs. Wulf—"

Michal turned on him fiercely. "I'll never give up Rory!"

Karl took a long drag on his cigarette, inhaled deeply. "I say you will."

Michal picked up a plate and threw it violently to the floor, then whirled on her husband. "There! That for you and your orders! I'm sick and hot and worn out. Then you go calmly off with your mother to gossip with relatives while I work all through this sweltering afternoon so you'd have a clean house and good food to come home to and there's not a word of thanks. Just a scowl because I'd gone to pick flowers for the table. Now you tell me that we'll keep your old mongrel Wolf dog and let Rory go! If that's what marriage means to you, I'm through. I'll go to Montana and you can have your Frieda. Father was right." She stopped for breath. "We don't belong together."

Calmly Karl inhaled again, crushed out the cigarette with his fingers, shrugged. "So. The little Englisher quits so soon?"

"Yes! I've given up my family. But that's not enough. My dog too." She marched into the dark bedroom, opened the wardrobe door and—in a rage too deep for tears—began pulling out her clothes. Then Karl was behind her, his hands on her shoulders, turning her about, forcing her to stand quiet. "You are a woman now. Not a silly child." His calmness stilled her and she bent her head. "I talked with my people, ya, so I was late. When I came and you were gone—" He shrugged, and the pattern fell into place. He had been worried.

In a gush of remorse Michal said: "I'm sorry. I shouldn't have lost my temper. Tomorrow I'll take Rory back—"

"No. He means much to you. Keep him. I'll leave Wulf with Mutter. Listen now to me, Michal. Tomorrow, put on your best dress and we call on my people. Then we eat at the slough by the cool water—just you and me. Next day we work again—I outside, you in our house."

"Will this be a good year?"

"For most—no. Not enough rain. But I plow deep and cultivate often. So—my crop is better. When men of our people marry and leave home, they get from their parents a marriage portion, according to the help they have given and how much the old people are worth. I should have another quarter-section of land, a share of the farm machinery, two more horses, four cows, some pigs, geese, chickens. Today I looked over the stock and chose in my mind what I vish—the main reason I leave my wife so long alone." He smiled. "I begin soon now making pens and house for hogs; too, a small chicken house."

"I am sorry I have brought so little to our marriage."

"You have brought yourself." There was silence in the room, then, "Come, look," Karl said quietly.

Leading her to the window, he pushed it open and they stood looking out over the dark fields of sky and land. "On this prairie it is never still. Vinter storms bring water to the earth. But they help make good wheat for harvest. Hail or drought or crop failure cannot make us run away. Even so with you and me. A little storm"—he shrugged—

334

"and you vant to run away. I haf said this to you before. Do not forget again." Gripping her arms she felt his piercing black gaze even in the warm gloom, as he said softly, "Think you I vould ever gif you up?"

"No." Her voice was meek. Then she lifted her head proudly. "But I'll always fight for what I believe to be right."

"Even break a plate?" She could feel amusement deep under his question.

"Even that. When I get angry—"

"Then I do this." Slipping her dress down, he kissed her naked shoulder; then, lifting her easily he carried her to the bed. And as her flesh softened and warmed with desire and her lips parted for his, a breeze blowing from over their own acres—across pale prairie roses and rippling wheat—flowed unheeded through the room, bathing them gently with fragrance from the darkening earth.